Relational Economics and Organization Governance

This interdisciplinary book series examines recent developments concerning the "relational view" in economics. While the relational research perspective primarily has roots in philosophy, sociology and economic geography, this series offers contributions to the relational view from such diverse fields as institutional and organisational economics, management, organisational theory, and mathematics. Focusing on a relational approach to contracts and governance, leadership, rents, global cooperation, intersectoral cooperation and civil society, the series welcomes theoretical and empirical research on relational structures in market theory, institutional and organisational economics, the resource-based view of the firm, organisational studies, behavioural economics and economic sociology. Within this range of fields, researchers are invited to contribute to the further development of a relational view in economics.

Sabine Wiesmüller

The Relational Governance of Artificial Intelligence

Forms and Interactions

Springer

Sabine Wiesmüller
Zeppelin University
Friedrichshafen, Baden-Württemberg,
Germany

ISSN 2662-9852 ISSN 2662-9860 (electronic)
Relational Economics and Organization Governance
ISBN 978-3-031-25022-4 ISBN 978-3-031-25023-1 (eBook)
https://doi.org/10.1007/978-3-031-25023-1

This Springer imprint is published by the registered company Springer Nature Switzerland AG
The registered company address is: Gewerbestrasse 11, 6330 Cham, Switzerland

Dedicated to my parents,
Deike and Bernhard, with love and gratitude.

Foreword

The book "The Relational Governance of Artificial Intelligence—Forms and Interactions" by Sabine Wiesmüller deals both with the theoretical prerequisites and practical possibilities of the governance of "Artificial Intelligence" (AI) in the interplay of social, entrepreneurial, and ethical decision-making logics. In particular, Sabine Wiesmüller's book aims to contribute to the discussion of a theme that all societies are confronted with today and for which solutions are being sought, namely the complex interactions and network effects of the technological, economic and social aspects of AI.

The book focuses on a genuinely interdisciplinary analysis: The overlap and relationalisation between economic, system-theoretical, and ethical language games. Only through such a relationalisation—and this is one of the basic assumptions of the author—can the challenges of the rapidly developing technical and economic possibilities, risks, and challenges of artificial intelligence in the economy and society be understood and productively dealt with.

The aim of the analysis is therefore twofold: On the one hand, it provides a theoretical literature reconstruction of the polyvalent forms of governance of AI. On the other hand, it also addresses the practical possibilities for an intersectoral implementation of relational governance of AI. The latter means that the governance of AI must enable and promote the cooperation of the multiple stakeholders involved, especially their interests, resources and decision-making logics. It is therefore about the relational governance of economic and social transactions that relationalise technical logic, economic value creation and ethical demands such as self-interest, trust, integrity and stakeholder legitimacy. In this way, the adaptive approach to uncertainty and process dynamics becomes possible.

The book not only provides a knowledgeable review of the relevant theoretical literature of the aforementioned scientific disciplines, but also links this with a comparative and informative discussion about practical regulation and implementation of the AI ethics standards by the EU, OECD, and IEEE. The author has also developed a model that identifies both the preconditions for effective self-regulation by business enterprises with regard to AI and its ethical preconditions and consequences.

"The Relational Governance of Artificial Intelligence—Forms and Interactions" is therefore, at its core, a brilliant analysis and discussion of the possibilities and challenges of the relational governance of AI ethics in companies (and more generally organisations) and of the related appropriate social standards. It is an original and innovative academic and practice-oriented contribution to Relational Economics. On behalf of all editors, I am very pleased about its publication in the "Relational Economics & Organizational Governance (REOG) series".

Konstanz, Germany Josef Wieland

Contents

Abbreviations

AI	Artificial Intelligence
AIHLEG	High-level Expert Group on Artificial Intelligence
ANN	Artificial Neural Network
CSR	Corporate Social Responsibility
DMA	Digital Markets Act
DSA	Digital Services Act
E.U.	European Union
GDPR	General Data Protection Act
I	Individual in Relational Governance
MI	Machine Intelligence
O	Organisation in Relational Governance
OECD	Organisation for Economic Co-operation and Development
SFI	Societal Formal Institutions in Relational Governance
SII	Societal Informal Institutions in Relational Governance
U.K.	United Kingdom
U.S.	United States of America
UAE	United Arab Emirates
UN	United Nations
UNESCO	United Nations Educational, Scientific, and Cultural Organization
UNICRI	United Nations Interregional Crime & Justice Research Institute
WEF	World Economic Forum

List of Figures

List of Tables

Chapter 1
Introduction and Theoretical Foundations

> Liberalism always cherished political equality, and it gradually came to realise that economic equality is almost as important. For without a social safety net and a modicum of economic equality, liberty is meaningless. But just as Big Data algorithms might extinguish liberty, they might simultaneously create the most unequal societies that ever existed. All wealth and power might be concentrated in the hands of a tiny elite, while most people will suffer not from exploitation, but from something far worse – irrelevance (Harari, 2018, 3, p. 74).

More than ever, we find ourselves in an era of great change, happening at unknown pace (Harrington, 2018), and confronted with so-called exponential digital technologies (Moore, 2006). With these becoming accessible to the economy, their true disruptive potential (Leonhard & von Kospoth, 2017) unfolds and this is having a ripple effect on different sectors, industries, and entire business models (Parviainen et al., 2017; Schwab, 2016[1]; Stolterman & Fors, 2004). In particular, Artificial Intelligence (AI) is estimated to be the single most influential and disruptive factor for global economies and societies in the twenty-first century and the probable trigger for the next (industrial) revolution (Golić, 2019; Makridakis, 2017; Paschek et al., 2019; Pathak et al., 2019).

1.1 Introductory Remarks

In this book, I will define AI as an umbrella term for all technologies developed to analyse and interpret big sets of data or certain events, to assist human decision-making and thereby automating decision-making and actions performed by machines (Nilsson, 2009), particularly machine learning, as well as further advancements such as artificial neural networks (ANN) and deep learning.[2]

---

[1] Computational power is understood to be the main force for the third industrial revolution.

[2] The concepts mentioned will be further discussed in Chapter 2.

S. Wiesmüller, *The Relational Governance of Artificial Intelligence*,
Relational Economics and Organization Governance,
https://doi.org/10.1007/978-3-031-25023-1_1

Given the adaptable nature of AI, not being one specific technology or product but rather a tool, applicable to countless existing business models, processes, and products, it cannot be regulated based on one specific outcome or scenario, as there is a myriad of possible scenarios its application can lead to. Many authors voice the growing concerns in society accompanying these characteristics (Cath, 2018; Floridi, 2018; Floridi et al., 2018; Perc et al., 2019), particularly regarding the pace of AI development, leading to its global dynamics often being compared to an arms race (Cave & ÓhÉigeartaigh, 2019).

While, until the present, market power was defined by market share and pricing, it is now dependent on factors such as access to data and data ownership—which are necessary elements for implementing AI (Drexl, 2016, 2017) and pose a barrier for new companies wanting to enter the market (Drexl, 2016; Porter, 1980). Thereby, the bar for followers to enter the market constantly rises, while digital monopolies are on the rise—giving more power and data access to ever fewer people (Ciuriak, 2018; Watney, 2018). Therefore, the most powerful actors in AI research also happen to be some of the most prominent companies around the globe, such as IBM, Amazon, Google, and Facebook (Lee, 2018).

Thus, competition in AI research is fierce, as significant margins and business opportunities are attracting companies (PwC, 2019) and the effective implementation of AI has become crucial for companies to stay on top of their competitors and even stay in business (MIT, 2019; Rose, 2019). A recent study by PriceWaterhouseCoopers (PwC) predicted that by 2030, AI will contribute an expected 15.7 trillion dollars to the global economy, with an expected 45% of total economic gains originating in AI-enhanced products (PwC, 2019). Among other factors, the lack of regulation in the market puts companies in the position of either having to adapt to the race to secure their position in the market and continue to stay in business, or to let competitors get the better of them (Cave & ÓhÉigeartaigh, 2019).

In consequence, the market is prone to ethical dilemmas, especially since there are no official red flags in AI research and development (Pichai, 2020). While in many cases, such as the medical field, data usage and its implications are rather transparent (Llewellynn et al., 2017), this is not always the case (Faddoul et al., 2019). One well-known example of this dilemma happened with Cambridge Analytica, a company using Facebook profile data to analyse the political preferences of its users, and, as commissioned by a client, to actively influence the users' voting behaviour (Faddoul et al., 2019). This violation realised by corporate actors touched the core of the modern world's achievement of free will: democracy (Lomas, 2018).

While some companies have voluntarily agreed not to engage in critical research,[3] such as developing autonomous weapons, there is no legally binding document preventing their development (Future of Life, 2015; Pichai, 2020), and a growing number of initiatives call for not only robust AI but also a stronger common orientation to good (Future of Life, 2015).

---

[3] In this context, the term 'critical' refers to advancements which potentially pose a direct threat to society, such as the development of autonomous weapons (Cihon, 2019; Future of Life, 2015).

Still, so far, no regulatory institution exists to enforce global, continental, or regional governance standards of AI-based business models, processes, and products that are in accordance with societal concerns and moral expectations (Dafoe, 2018). Besides the per se reactive nature of regulatory bodies, this is because regulation and standard-setting have become increasingly difficult to implement, due to the complexity associated with these new dilemma structures (Dafoe, 2018). Further, corporations possess restricted access to the knowledge about the state of the art in technology (Ferraro et al., 2015), and current legislation and regulation lack the integration of data as a new market mechanism in law-making (Drexl, 2016; Wieland, 2018). Given the pace at which new technologies are entering the market and the fact that, by nature, regulation is developed reactively to the element it is designed to regulate. Current regulation is dealing poorly with the dilemmas coming with AI implementation (Askell et al., 2019; Dafoe, 2018), and does not consider data or a system based on data flow and is unable to integrate the logic of another system into legislation (Andriole, 2019; Wieland, 2018).

Thus, companies being the main driver of the change coming with new technologies are called on to take responsibility for their actions, mainly because of the rising visibility of the changes coming with AI adoption, but also due to the high information asymmetry between the public and private sector (Anderson et al., 2018; Askell et al., 2019). This also holds true for civil society, where research indicates the drastic barriers its representatives are facing in multi-stakeholder dialogues, due to particularly significant information asymmetry (Fassbender, 2020).

Over the course of this book, I will show how companies can engage in a collaborative approach, such as through self-regulatory approaches and multi-stakeholder dialogues, to minimise negative outcomes for society (Gruetzemacher, 2018; Rittel & Webber, 1973; Roberts, 2000). AI ethics play an essential role in the development of such governance measures, as they will help define 'red flags' and guiding principles for all actors involved (Dafoe, 2018). With this, I aim to contribute to the responsible adoption of AI, minimising the negative consequences associated with it, while still applying it to its best potential (Aliman & Kester, 2019; Gasser & Almeida, 2017).

In doing so, it aims to provide, particularly for economic actors, the necessary tools to shape the future of AI adoption.

1.2 Theoretical Foundations: Governing Artificial Intelligence

> The rise of powerful AI will be either the best or the worst thing ever to happen to humanity. We do not yet know which. (Hawking, 2016)[4]

As stated, the expression 'Artificial Intelligence' is an umbrella term for technologies and models that aim for machines to mimic human intelligence, which, when

[4] BBC News, 2016.

applied, can transform whole industries, economies, and society (Makridakis, 2017; Schwab & Davis, 2018). The development and rise of AI can be traced back to a few decisive factors that arose over recent decades. For one, computational power increased, which had an especially drastic influence on AI research. Moreover, the availability of big data grew dramatically over the last decades (Caulfield, 2009; Stolkel-Walker, 2018).

1.2.1 Artificial Intelligence

The progress made in research on Artificial Intelligence was enabled by and is part of a bigger phenomenon; namely, the digital transformation. According to Parviainen et al. (2017), the term 'digital transformation' is defined as "*changes in ways of working, roles, and business offering caused by adoption of digital technologies in an organization, or in the operation environment of the organization*" (2017, p. 16). Among others, Stolterman and Fors (2004) are convinced that "*digital transformation can be understood as the changes that the digital technology causes or influences in all aspects of human life*" (2004, p. 689).

A digital technology is defined as a machine or electronic device based on digital signals (Dyer & Harms, 1993), such as a computer, which is, again, defined as a machine that can be controlled and used efficiently by instructing it to follow a specific function. This instruction can come in the form of an algorithm, developed to solve the problem statement, and translated to a computer language to make it applicable to a machine (Bishop, 2006; Samuel, 1959). AI in its operationalised form, i.e., machine learning, is the software that can be applied to a digital machine, with the algorithm being its smallest entity (Awad & Khanna, 2015). However, AI is more than the mere application of a finite set of instructions to a machine (Brundage et al., 2018).

1.2.1.1 Scope of Artificial Intelligence

To gain a deeper understanding of AI and its governance, the main technology types—machine learning, artificial neural networks (ANNs), and deep learning[5]—and their interconnections, as depicted in Fig. 1.1, will be analysed in this book.

The modern phase of AI development started around 2010, with the ongoing commercialisation of the technologies and their application outside laboratories. The main technologies stemming from this era are advanced machine learning, natural language processing, and ANNs (Nilsson, 2009).

Machine learning is an umbrella term for a certain type of algorithm, namely learning algorithms, able to learn from experience or repetition. After going through

[5] Abbreviations will only be used within the main body of the book, not when first introducing the concepts.

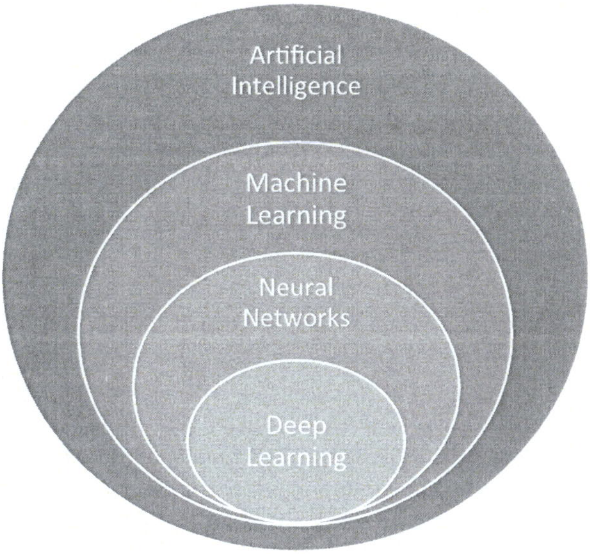

Fig. 1.1 Interrelatedness of critical concepts in AI research

this learning phase, the algorithm can be applied to actual cases (Nilsson, 2009). In machine learning, there are various subcategories: the most recognised are supervised and unsupervised machine learning (Awad & Khanna, 2015).

ANNs are developed based on the characteristics and structure of the neural networks of the human brain and learn by analysing examples without necessarily being programmed for a specific task (Sun, 2014). Neural networks work by approximation and not in an exact manner. This means that, as long as the neural network was not applied to a certain situation before, it cannot be predicted how it will react to a new pattern and the algorithm will decide stochastically (Grohs et al., 2019). Current fields of application are, among others, the recognition of patterns and symbols, natural language processing, prognostics, and trend prediction, as well as robotics, autonomous driving, and game development (Nilsson, 2009). One achievement of neural networks is their general ability to learn; another is that, once trained for a particular task, they can already solve it better and quicker than any human could by having all neurons work simultaneously, which can be of critical relevance, especially with time-sensitive and urgent tasks (Liang & Hu, 2015).

Deep learning is a method developed based on ANNs, part of machine learning, and functions by applying a representation-based learning approach. It allows various layers of complexity by including multiple hidden layers into its network (Wani et al., 2020). By adding more complexity, deep learning can depict the more complex processes of the mind and thereby help researchers get closer to the goal of recreating human thought processes, as it can understand and apply a causal chain to data. While, decades ago, neural networks had to be trained layer by layer, with advances in machine learning and computer power, layers can nowadays be trained jointly (Wani et al., 2020). While deep learning networks can operate with up to 10 billion computing operations per income date, the interpretation and explication of the results by a human controller is only partly possible and requires specific techniques. Moreover, deep learning is still at risk of being biased or even manipulated through the adaptation of input signals (Gilpin et al., 2019).

Nonetheless, deep learning is known as one of the most promising advancements in ANN research, since it is believed to be introducing a new era in AI research (Doshi-Velez et al., 2017). While, with previous technologies, such as machine learning, it was still possible to transparently monitor algorithmic decision-making, that is not the case anymore for deep learning, as the algorithm draws its own conclusions—which is why its decision-making is also referred to as opaque (Beaudouin et al., 2020; Doshi-Velez et al., 2017). This is because, in deep learning, the algorithm starts to draw conclusions that can hardly be retraced or explained by humans (Beaudouin et al., 2020; Preece, 2018). As for machine learning, researchers are working on options of how to make it more responsible, transparent, and explainable—mainly to ensure the execution of accountability and liability issues. However, these transparency measures will not be applicable to deep learning technologies (Beaudouin et al., 2020; Preece, 2018). Instead, deep learning will require a whole new form of governance, be it led by principles or ex-ante regulatory measures. Given its technological potential, it is probable that deep learning will become the mainstream AI technology in the soon-foreseeable future, necessitating new forms of holistic governance that exceed the presented, rather compliance-oriented, measures.

1.2.1.2 Outlook on a Potential Superintelligence and Resumée

Bostrom (2014) defines superintelligence as "*any intellect that greatly exceeds the cognitive performance of humans in virtually all domains of interest*" (2014, p. 22). Hence, an artificial superintelligence should be able to solve any kind of problem, understand all situations and be able to know and predict all options of decision-making, as it has access to expertise of any kind (Szocik et al., 2020). Further, it could develop entirely based on self-learning, and could work on problems it was not specifically designed to solve and for which it did not receive supervised training (Kaplan & Haenlein, 2019). It would be able to be creative, innovative, and think without limits. Thereby, it could solve all kinds of theoretical or practical challenges and would not be constrained theoretically or practically, unlike the human mind (Szocik et al., 2020).

As for the probability of this scenario becoming reality, AI experts agree that, at some point, AI will be able to rival human intelligence (Müller & Bostrom, 2016). 50% expect that by 2050, AI systems will have reached superhuman cognitive abilities and intelligence and that from there, within only a few decades, a superintelligence will be developed. 75% of experts stated this would take another 30 years. Hence by 2080, a superintelligence is expected to be fully developed (Müller & Bostrom, 2016). Thus, if research reached the point of creating software able to improve itself through recursive self-improvement, this could be a step towards the (self-) creation of a superintelligence (Yampolskiy, 2015). When asked about the implications of this expected trend, many researchers go as far as expecting a superintelligence to be a great danger to humankind. While Müller and Bostrom (2016) are cautious about this warning, they agree on demanding an investigation of the possible risks of a superintelligence. The ethical implications or apprehensions coming with the creation of a superintelligence are manifold, as, once created, its reactions and decisions cannot be predicted (Szocik et al., 2020).

To conclude, the aim of this book is to gain a deep understanding of the complex reality of AI governance and derive an in-depth analysis of its problem structure. Only with this foundation and risk assessment is it possible to state relevant implications for academia and practitioners, since the potency of any innovation always includes two sides of a coin: if it has the power to save a life, it most likely also has the power to take a life (Jonas, 1979). Translated to the immense transformational power AI possesses already in its current technological state and economic expansion, effective governance is necessary to steer and prevent possible negative outcomes from the development and adoption of AI to protect the rights of current societies and future generations.

1.2.2 Requirements for the Governance of Artificial Intelligence

As stated before, the research gap and the practical necessity on which this book is rooted arise from the explicit demand for effective AI governance—asked for by corporations and society (AlgorithmWatch, 2019; Crawford et al., 2019), as well as academia (Brundage et al., 2018; Bryson, 2018; Cihon et al., 2020). While some attempts have been made to develop the first technical standards and to apply normative ideas, such as human rights, to AI research (Latonero, 2018; Livingston & Risse, 2019; Mantelero, 2018; Raso et al., 2018; Risse, 2019), often the absence of a mandate to enforce these standards restricts their impact (Cihon et al., 2020).

However, scholars demand a more holistic approach to AI governance by including the perspectives of all stakeholders affected by AI (Bryson, 2018; Cihon et al., 2020; Greene et al., 2019; Schwab & Davis, 2018). Addressing this matter is also of great urgency, as AI is already affecting and influencing users and society as a whole on a daily basis and beyond. This is why a growing number of scholars and executives demand responsible technology design as well as proactive law-making and governance efforts by corporations (Brundage & Bryson, 2016; Bryson, 2018; Schwab & Davis, 2018; Brundage et al., 2018; Cihon et al., 2020). However, the focus in research should move towards their implementation via effective governance models (Hagendorff, 2020).

While there is no one definition of governance that mainstream literature agrees on, Stoker (1998) managed to provide a set of criteria stating that it consists of "*a complex set of institutions and actors that are drawn from but also beyond government*" (ibid, 1998, p. 18). Further, "*governance recognises the blurring boundaries and responsibilities for tackling social and economic issues"* (ibid, 1998, p. 18). Ideally, it "*identifies the power dependence involved in the relationships between institutions involved and collective action"* (ibid, 1998, p. 18) and is "*about the autonomous self-governing networks of actors*" (ibid, 1998, p. 18). Moreover, he states that governance does not mean relying on governmental power or authority to "*get things done"* (ibid, 1998, p. 18) but needs action to introduce new forms of collaboration and ways of governing others.

Thus, governance is the development of rules as a reference frame for decision-making, protecting the best interest of the collective, while taking into account the interest of each stakeholder. As governance measures are a product of consensus among all stakeholders involved, the institution organises itself through this shared purpose (Wieland, 2018, 2020). The constructs of the market, or even a network, can substitute the governmental functions existing in hierarchical forms of social coordination, and provide guidance and steering in collectively designed processes (Benz, 2004; Bevir, 2012).

For theoretical considerations, societies are often divided into spheres, commonly into the first sector (the state), the second sector (the economy), and a third sector, which is civil society (Murphy, 2001). Albeit there is criticism towards a coherent definition of civil society in systems theory (Luhmann, 2000), for reasons of simplification, this trichotomy will serve as a working definition for this book, with its focus being on the economy, the private sector, and its companies (Dasgupta, 2007). More specifically, it will deal with companies and their interrelatedness with state and civil society, as well as their responsibility towards these other sectors of society (Moon, 2014). Hence, the governance approach I present in this book will argue from a business perspective, stemming from the business sector, and can, in consequence, be referred to as private-sector governance.

Within the field of market governance, there are soft law alternatives, such as the development of standards, which aim at voluntarily changing the behaviour of corporations (Christensen & Tschirhart, 2011). However, the question is how to successfully convince corporations to engage in the process of jointly developing such standards, via networks, consisting of trust-based work in associations (Bevir, 2012; Jansen & Wald, 2007). Network governance is defined as an informal or organic mode of coordination between firms or organisations, which exists in a social system (Börzel & Panke, 2007). This form of governance differentiates itself by its pluralistic nature, compared to other, more centralised forms (Jones et al., 1997; Provan & Kenis, 2008). Thus, the creation of knowledge and social coordination takes place within the relationships of the actors involved. Through the development of collectively agreed-upon solutions, the self-regulatory power of these forms of governance seems higher than in other forms of governance (Brousseau et al., 2012). As AI affects almost all parts of society (Greene et al., 2019; Schwab & Davis, 2018), and despite the fierce dynamics of competition, a collective approach, be it in the form of multi-stakeholder processes or interfirm networks, seems to be highly relevant to the field of AI governance.

1.2.2.1 Analysis of the Underlying Problem Structure

When aiming to develop a problem-solving approach, design and social planning theory serve as a base for standard governance literature in all sectors, from public to private (Bevir, 2012).

A so-called 'tame' problem has a well-defined problem statement and a definite stopping point. The solution to the problem can be classified as either right or wrong, but the answer is definite in each case. Also, the solutions to tame problems can be replicated with similar problems, and in the process of reaching the ideal solution, trial-and-error principles can be used without any significant risk (Ritchey, 2011; Rittel & Webber, 1973). While a tame problem follows a strict pattern, 'wicked' problems require dialogue and good evaluation, arguing that there are neither true and false solutions nor easy, common-sense agreements (Rittel & Webber, 1973). Given the dynamic development of AI research and the involvement of stakeholders from all sectors of society and worldwide (Dafoe, 2018), the notion of a tame problem can be dismissed in the context of this book. Rittel and Webber developed a set of ten criteria for the definition of wicked problems; based on their description, I define solving the challenges for AI governance as a wicked problem.

Academia supports this statement insofar as AI governance has already been associated with the notion of wicked problems by a few scholars, namely Gurumurthy and Chami (2019) and Holtel (2016). Gruetzemacher (2018) even goes as far as to define AI governance as a so-called 'entangled superwicked problem'. As indicated by their name, superwicked problems represent the augmentation of the complexity coming with a specific problem, and its connection to AI governance further supports the need for a solid problem description of the governance process (Gruetzemacher, 2018).

Following Ackoff's (1974) line of thought, a messy problem is easiest defined by its outcome: the non-existence of one correct solution. Consequently, the concepts of entangled or messy environments describe the circumstance that a particular problem or issue cannot be understood, defined, or even analysed in an isolated manner. Thus, a messy problem will always be influenced by and integrated into its messy environment. As a result, when seeking holistic and sustainable solutions to a problem, it is essential to understand the complex dynamics of the situation and its interrelatedness to other situations and issues. Ackoff (1981) argues that a complex reality requires working with systems theory, as complexity occurs in systems. Furthermore, complexity rises in line with the number of interactions of the elements within the system.

Especially in the context of global AI governance, the technological advancements and the goal of eventually developing a superintelligence bear great uncertainty. The ethical implications, on the other hand, lead to growing complexity, as their multidimensionality marks most dilemma situations. The solving of wicked, or even superwicked problems (Gruetzemacher, 2018), now seems to require two aspects: first, solutions to a wicked problem need to be put into action to be evaluated; a purely theoretical consideration cannot give real insight (Rittel & Webber, 1973).

Thus, the theory of wicked problems serves to define a narrower problem statement and gives the justification for a new evaluation, where ethics have to be applied to the innovation process. Systems theory will ensure the effectiveness of the governance measures in alignment with dynamics affecting actors in AI governance—in this case, companies. Consequently, both elements need to be integrated into theory development, as they display the very nature of the phenomenon that requires new governance structures.

1.2.2.2 Collaboratively Solving Wicked Problems

When aiming to tackle wicked problems, known scholars such as Roberts (2000), describe the different approaches that can be taken (Treib et al., 2005): authoritative, competitive, or collaborative governance strategies. However, given the complexity of governing AI and the fact that there are no clear right and wrong, black and white solutions, the first option can seemingly be excluded from discussion (Gruetzemacher, 2018; Holtel, 2016). As competition in AI development intensifies and is characterised by the dynamics of global races for dominance in the market (Cave & ÓhÉigeartaigh, 2019; Dafoe, 2018), it is rather the collaborative approach that can do justice to the complexity of stakeholder interests involved (Holtel, 2016; Rittel & Webber, 1973) and lead to responsible AI adoption.

In detail, dissolving a wicked problem structure requires the interaction of many stakeholders, negotiation processes, and the suitability of a solution approach can only be tested by applying it to the situation (Elia & Margherita, 2018; Introne et al., 2013; Schoder et al., 2014). Thus, the first step is to identify actors and their interests, as well as constraints, and to address strategies for dealing with wicked problems (Van Bueren et al., 2003).

According to Roberts (2000), authoritative problem-solving strategies aim to lower the conflict levels among stakeholders by appointing or allowing only a few lead stakeholders to take on the matter. With this, it is up to this smaller group to define the problem and choose the preferred solution. Other affected stakeholders must accept this division of power and follow the decisions made by the leading stakeholders. While an authoritative approach decreases the levels of complexity by again reducing the number of actors involved in the decision-making process, it bears the risk of ending up with unfair or even wrong measures to solve the situation. Since it neglects the integration of all stakeholders involved, which is deemed crucial for its effective stakeholder management (Freeman, 1984; Freeman & McVea, 2001) and the success of the overall outcome and positive shareholder value (Berman et al., 1999; Hillmann & Keim, 2001), it does not seem suitable for ethically hazardous situations, such as wicked problem structures—and, thereby, AI governance.

Competitive strategies assume that a wicked problem situation can only be resolved in a win-/lose-constellation, meaning that there cannot be a positive, winning outcome for more than one stakeholder party. Thus, central to this approach is the pursuit of dominion and an exclusive power position in a particular field, or, in the case of technology development, in a market. An actor's goal in this context is to transform its position of power or dominion into a lasting authoritative position, allowing it to act and decide based on accepted leadership. The disadvantages of competitive approaches include extreme power struggles, resulting in, for example, warfare—a narrative already established in academia, known as the AI arms race (Cave & ÓhÉigeartaigh, 2019; Geist, 2016; Scharre, 2019; Tomasik, 2013). Consequently, the main risk of competitive approaches is a potential flip to an authoritative strategy by one or two powerful stakeholder parties (Roberts, 2000).

Finally, collaborative strategies assume that the individual gain can be raised collectively for all parties involved if a fair solution can be reached. As opposed to competitive approaches, where a finite set of shares is divided among all actors involved, these strategies follow the objective of providing every player involved with a just share (Elia & Margherita, 2018; Schoder et al., 2014). The advantages of engaging in such an approach are manifold: for one, the players involved in a joint project can share costs and benefits in the development process (Doz & Hamel, 1998). The same logic applies to the business context, where competitors for a specific product can raise the quality of their offering in the market by collaborating with other corporations (Doz & Hamel, 1998). Thus, synergies can be used efficiently by outsourcing activities and assigning each party its field of responsibility (Quinn et al., 1996). Especially with fair and effective collaboration, the individual outcome for all parties involved can be better and cost fewer resources than would be the case for the two options previously presented (Cave & ÓhÉigeartaigh, 2019; Geist, 2016; Scharre, 2019; Tomasik, 2013).

Since, in the case of AI governance, there is no global authority that could appoint a specific group of stakeholders to solve this wicked problem in an authoritative manner, the first option can likely only be reached by winning over the competition. However, as presented, inherent to the competitive approach is a constant race for market dominion regarding new technologies and products—a race which will possibly bring lasting, possibly irreversible, effects on society. Apart from risks arising from the mere pace of development that comes with this approach (Armstrong et al., 2016), other factors, such as possibly unformed cybersecurity measures, come into play (Nakashima, 2012).

Further, higher risks are involved in wicked problems: Since it is not possible to foresee whether dominion in the market would go hand in hand with a lasting and absolute power position for the dominant party (Cave & ÓhÉigeartaigh, 2019; Geist, 2016; Scharre, 2019; Tomasik, 2013) a highly competitive or no-win situation, which would eventually prioritise economic above societal interests (e.g., by fast research and market launches of new, unsupported products) should be prevented by a theory of AI governance. Instead, it should inherently foster collaboration among all actors involved in the governance process.

1.2.2.3 Multidimensional Economic Theory

Because the potential market volume for AI-based products is rising to unknown heights, incentives to gain long-term market dominion, meaning that one technology developed sets the standard for entire industries or product lines, are exceptionally high. One reason for this focus is the strong competitive forces, defined as the global race dynamics (Dafoe, 2018), influencing corporate decision-making in global AI research.

Regarding AI, due to high levels of information asymmetry (Fassbender, 2020), stakeholders depend on the services and engagement of private-sector organisations and networks. High levels of global competition are also one of the main driving forces for AI research (Cihon, 2019; Makridakis, 2017; PwC, 2019; Rowsell-Jones & Howard, 2019).

Besides mere financial incentives, organisations from all societal sectors and science alike recognise the opportunities coming with this new possibility of gaining valuable insights through new forms of big data analysis (Donnay, 2017). Thus, market or industry dominion through dominant AI technologies entails an economic power position and creates and further broadens information asymmetry, which allows the party in power—whichever societal sector it belongs to—to adapt and influence trends and dynamics for their own good. These trends confirm the role and relevance of economic actors in this phenomenon, which led to the economic perspective on AI governance being the focus of this book.

By being the primary owners and developers of new technologies, corporations largely retain competitive knowledge and power, strengthening their primacy in society (Mittelstadt, 2019). Moreover, (illiberal) public actors such as the government of the Republic of China are well-known for using this form of AI technology for criminal prosecution and social monitoring practices (Hoffman, 2017; Qiang, 2019). Hence, the risk of unknown levels of misuse cases is tremendous, due to the aforementioned information asymmetries among societal sectors (Dafoe, 2018; Fassbender, 2020).

For corporations, as the strongest drivers of change in AI research and consequently the implementation of AI-based products (Makridakis, 2017; Polyakova & Boyer, 2018; PwC, 2019), a collaborative approach to AI governance might seem counter-intuitive due to fierce global competition for market dominion. Thus, to react to and allow for opposition to possible competitive lock-in situations, a model for AI governance needs to integrate the logic of the economic system and observe these dynamics. Further, AI governance needs to enable a structured analysis of the environment within which companies find themselves when developing and implementing AI (Van Bueren et al., 2003).

To achieve this goal, there are additional requirements: competition in AI research and the effects of AI implementation take place on every economic and societal level. Thus, economic dynamics need to be analysed at the micro-, meso-, and macro-level, and therefore, an economic approach that applies to all levels is required for a holistic governance model. Transaction cost theory is such an approach, allowing for the analysis and definition of governance processes on every level—from small actions on the micro-level to strategies on the macro-level (Wieland, 2018, 2020). This is because, by focusing on the transaction as the unit of analysis, the insights and findings gathered by a transaction-cost-driven analysis can be scaled to other levels of economic and societal analysis. In contrast, other economic approaches often focus on one level of analysis or a particular aspect of the economy (Samuelson & Nordhaus, 2010). Furthermore, the claim made here is substantiated by the fact that transaction cost theory has already been associated with the technological and digital context by other scholars (Bahli & Rivard, 2017; Barandi et al., 2020; Benkler, 2002, 2006, 2017; Schmidt & Wagner, 2019). Hence, the economy must not be analysed and dealt with in an isolated manner as previously happened in academia, where the merely economic analysis of AI-based products ignores the effect they possibly have on society (Brundage & Bryson, 2016; Schwab & Davis, 2018; Mittelstadt, 2019).

1.2.2.4 Abstracting Complexity Through Systems Theory

While, as a technological solution, AI can help to reduce complexity in the context where it is applied, governing AI, on the other hand, is an undertaking with unprecedented levels of complexity. In the context of AI governance, the high connectivity of dimensions further enhances the complexity of the phenomenon. When combining Casti's (1994) and Ackoff's (1981) perspectives on complex problem structures, to solve a situation, it is necessary to grasp its structure by abstracting it. To do so, systems theory, which defines the prevalent systems and describes their interactions with each other, should be linked with contextual information, since Casti (1994) argues that complexity never arises within a single system but in the interactions among systems.

One of the mechanisms in systems theory that allow for the abstraction of systems is functional differentiation (Luhmann, 1998). The functionality of each system is described by using a binary code, e.g., political systems are characterised by the binary code of being in a position of power or not being in power (Luhmann, 1997, 1998), which is based on the understanding that these systems aim to make collectively binding decisions (Luhmann, 1997, 1998). Based on this binary code, actions can be analysed in an abstract manner, which again allows for the comparability of actions and a structured comprehension of patterns of behaviour. Thus, to even allow the capacity to act in AI governance, a mode of governance with an especially high level of abstraction is required—one that allows the development of decision-making strategies for each system and society as a whole, which is crucial for social coordination and hence, effective governance.

1.2.2.5 Non-Normative Governance

As AI governance deals with unprecedented uncertainty levels, no specific and well-grounded probability can be associated with any particular outcome (Dafoe, 2018; Makridakis, 2017). Without one ideal scenario, it falls within the scope of the governance process to ensure a just assessment of stakeholders and their fair participation (Van Bueren et al., 2003). It is the ethicality of the governance process and governance mechanisms that protects the rights of the stakeholders involved.

Given the diversity of ethical ideals and preferences apparent in the AI context, as well as known incidents of personal bias in the technology itself, it is all the more important for the process to be non-normative in nature. Hence, the theoretical foundation for AI governance needs to allow for the structural integration of the parameter ethics, without, however, prioritising one ethical approach or being ethically framed itself.

This is in line with statements made by scholars, such as Schwab and Davis (2018), saying that AI governance shall *"[…] promote the common good, enhance human dignity and protect the environment"* (2018, p. 16). The development of AI and AI-based technologies is at an early and therefore still manageable phase (Brundage & Bryson, 2016; Cihon et al., 2020; Schwab & Davis, 2018), as Cihon et al. (2020) confirm by saying: *"We are in the early days of global AI governance. Decisions taken early on will constrain and partially determine the future path"* (2020, p. 232). Thus, AI governance can still impose processual frames on the AI innovation cycle, which can inherently ensure fairness and general societal welfare (Cath et al., 2018; Morley et al., 2020; Wu et al., 2020).

Thus, its fundamental aim is to outbalance stakeholder legitimisation, ensure success in the market, and allow for the integration of an ethical dimension into the AI development process to create shared value.[6] By choosing a structural integration of ethics, the ethical dimension can be integrated into any stage of the process, diminishing threats such as manipulation in the form, for example, of biases, by applying principles such as fairness and inclusion (Cath et al., 2018; Morley et al., 2020; Wieland, 2018, 2020; Wu et al., 2020).

1.2.3 The Theoretical Foundation of Artificial Intelligence Governance

One theoretical approach that has been raising interest in the scientific community is the theorem of Relational Economics by Wieland (2018, 2020) and this seems the most suitable theory for AI governance, due to its ability to include and address all identified demands.

Wieland's approach draws from and combines transaction cost theory in Williamson's tradition (1979, 1986) with Luhmann's (1996, 1998) systems-theoretical approach (van Aaken & Schreck, 2015). Wieland (2014) defines a particular approach to stakeholder theory,[7] which stems from the theory of the firm (Wieland, 2008) as founded by Coase (1937). Corporations are defined as nexuses

[6] Shared Value Creation "can be seen in the size of the cooperation rent that can be achieved on the market, in the positive balance of an organisation's revenues and costs and in the creation of material and nonmaterial value for all organisations and persons involved in the cooperation process as stakeholders" (Wieland, 2020, p. 52).

[7] Stakeholder Theory is concerned with the identification, management and legitimization of all parties impacted by an organization's (firm's) decision-making, such as employees, suppliers, or certain groups of society (Freeman, 1984).

of stakeholders, a net consisting of various transactions and contracts that deeply intertwines an organisation with its stakeholders and, thereby, with society. With this definition goes the understanding that corporations inherently need to take on responsibility for the negative effects of their actions (Wieland, 2008, 2018). Thereby, Wieland derives and substantiates the inherent legitimisation of stakeholder demands towards an organisation. By defining ethics as a societal system, Wieland (2018, 2020) enables and allows for systematic integration of ethics into a specific transaction, and thereby, into governance structures. With this, the approach remains non-normative, as it does not impose one particular ethical concept but focuses on the structural inclusion of ethicality into decision-making processes.

In AI governance, its legislation, social acceptance, and ethical views that strongly defer and commonly correlate with geographical and regional preferences. According to Wieland (2020), it cannot be expected that these regional preferences vanish with the ongoing globalisation and digitalisation of the world. Therefore, the processes of negotiating desirable outcomes and scenarios for the stakeholders involved demand constant, dynamic governance. Wieland (2020) even states that rising levels of complexity are to be expected, and the aforementioned negotiation processes, indeed, require collaboration among all stakeholders, not least because of a need for the societal legitimisation of corporate decision-making.

The theoretical focus in this undertaking is on the entity of the firm and the processes revolving around it, rather than focusing on the specific role of any particular actor in society. Wieland's (2018, 2020) definition and application of the concept of the firm are closely related to Coase's definition (1937). For Wieland and Coase alike, the firm is the abstract form within which existing transactions and stakeholder demands are transformed into new transactions. While organisations follow one specific system logic, which serves as a base for their decision-making, they can integrate and add other logics to their decision-making process. It is often necessary to consider other factors to ensure a company's position in the market and to allow for cooperation while, at the same, the integration of other logics is exactly what is often asked for by society (Wieland, 2018). Thus, a company's ability to engage with other systems, communicate and negotiate in a system logic not inherent to it, is, according to Wieland (2018, 2020), crucial for its continued existence and success.

Thus, companies can choose to act and engage in a polylingual space. Whilst engaging in civil society and political spheres, they are still defined as an organisation of the economic sphere—but can temporarily become actors in, for example, civil society. In the AI context, where companies often engage with other systems, such as the political sphere, e.g., in standard-setting processes, it can explain the rise of these encounters and either redefine these a-priori attributions or provide governance measures to restrict actors from unleashing unintended consequences by AI adoption.

Wieland (2018, 2020) expands this concept by describing polylingual, polycontextual, and polycontextural spaces. By further developing Luhmann's (1998) notion of system logics and the languages inherent to these systems, Wieland (2018, 2020) allows for the analysis of interactions among systems and necessary abilities for actors that interact between systems. Table 1.1 demonstrates the characteristics of each concept to exemplify all possible levels of analysis.

Table 1.1 Own depiction according to Wieland (2018, 2020)

Polycontextuality	Polycontexturality	Polylinguality
Plural signification and interrelation of systems, influencing each other's environment, existence, and conditions to operate.	Existence of diverging systems and decision logics, which results in the necessity for organisations to adapt to these differences.	An actor's ability to engage and communicate according to different binary codes and in various systemic languages.

Thus, the inclusion of polylingualism into further considerations is necessary to define the dynamics within each system involved. The main focus of this book will, however, lie on the third concept, polycontexturality. It is polycontexturality, which is

> used [...] to refer to the interlinking and intertwining of a given system's various rationalities and decision logics. Polycontexturality plays an essential part in the analysis of structural coupling between different and potentially conflicting system logics [...]—an aspect that will prove extremely important with regard to the governance of polycontexturality (Wieland, 2020, p. 11).

Wieland (2020) defines structural coupling as the core of governance actions, the actual alignment of two or more decision-logics into one outbalanced action or decision. This integration and alignment of system logics is the main request posed of AI governance and the specific instrument that will enable the solution-finding process of AI governance in practice—exceeding currently existing guidelines by providing an implementation-oriented approach.

By applying Relational Economics to AI governance, my focus and contribution are twofold: for Relational Economics theory, the contribution consists of applying the theoretical model to the AI context. As presented, traditional system logics, such as politics, legislation and economy and ethics, have already been described and defined by Wieland (2018, 2020). In continuation of Wieland's theory, I will introduce AI to Relational Economics and develop a theoretical AI governance model allowing for the coordination of interrelated system demands and among actors to address this wicked problem (Elia & Margherita, 2018; Introne et al., 2013; Roberts, 2000; Schoder et al., 2014).

References

Ackoff, R. L. (1974). *Redesigning the future: A systems approach to societal problems*. Wiley.

Ackoff, R. L. (1981). *Creating the corporate future*. Wiley.

Algorithm Watch (2019). *Annual Report 2019*. https://algorithmwatch.org/en/wpcontent/uploads/2020/11/AW_annual_report_2019_final.pdf

Anderson, J., Rainie, L., Luchsinger, A. (2018). Artificial intelligence and the future of humans. In *Pew Research Center, Internet & Technology*. https://www.pewresearch.org/internet/wp-content/uploads/sites/9/2018/12/PI_2018.12.10_future-of-ai_FINAL1.pdf

Andriole, S. (2019). Technology, technologists, and technoligarchs. *Cutter Business Technology Journal, 32*(1). https://www.cutter.com/article/technology-technologists-and-technoligarchs-2019-502266

Armstrong, S., Bostrom, N., & Shulman, C. (2016). Racing to the precipice: A model of artificial intelligence development. *AI & Society, 31*, 201–206. https://doi.org/10.1007/s00146-015-0590-y

Askell, A., Brundage, M., & Hadfield, G. (2019). The role of cooperation in responsible AI development. *arXiv preprint* arXiv:1907.04534.

Awad, M., & Khanna, R. (2015). *Machine learning. Efficient learning machines*. Apress.

Bahli B., Rivard S. (2017). The information technology outsourcing risk: A transaction cost and agency theory-based perspective. In L. Willcocks, M. Lacity, & C. Sauer (Eds.), *Outsourcing and offshoring business services*. Palgrave Macmillan. https://doi.org/10.1007/978-3-319-52651-5_3

Barandi, Z., Lawson-Body, A., Lawson-Body, L. & Willoughby, L. (2020). Impact of Blockchain Technology on the continuous auditing: Mediating role of transaction cost theory. *Issues in Information Systems, 21*(2), 206–212. https://doi.org/10.48009/2_iis_2020_206-212

Beaudouin, V., Bloch, I., Bounie, D., Clémençon, S., d'Alché-Buc, F., Eagan, J., Maxwell, W., Mozharovskyi, P., and Parekh, J. (2020). *Flexible and context-specific AI explainability: A multidisciplinary approach*. https://arxiv.org/abs/2003.07703

Benkler, Y. (2002). Coase's penguin, or, Linux and the nature of the firm. *Yale Law Journal, 112*(3), 369–446. https://doi.org/10.2307/1562247

Benkler, Y. (2006). *The wealth of networks*. Yale University Press.

Benkler, Y. (2017). Peer production, the commons and the future of the firm. *Strategic Organization, 15*(2), 264–274. https://doi.org/10.1177/1476127016652606

Benz, A. (2004). *Governance—Regieren in komplexen Regelsystemen: Eine Einführung*. Springer.

Berman, S., Wicks, A., Kotha, S., & Jones, T. (1999). Does stakeholder orientation matter: The relationship between stakeholder management models and firm financial performance. *Academy of Management Journal, 42*(5), 488–506. https://doi.org/10.2307/256972

Bevir, M. (2012). *Governance: A very short introduction*. Oxford University Press.

Bishop, C. M. (2006). *Pattern recognition and machine learning*. Springer Link.

Börzel T.A., Panke D. (2007). Network governance: Effective and legitimate? In E. Sørensen, & J. Torfing (Eds.), *Theories of democratic network governance* (pp. 153–166). Palgrave Macmillan. https://doi.org/10.1057/9780230625006_9

Bostrom, N. (2014). *Superintelligence: Paths, dangers*. Oxford University Press.

Brousseau, E., Marzouki, M., & Méadel, C. (Eds.). (2012). *Governance, regulation and powers on the internet*. Cambridge University Press.

Brundage, M. & Bryson, J. J. (2016). Smart policies for artificial intelligence. Computing Research Repository. https://arxiv.org/abs/1608.08196

Brundage, M., Avin, S., Clark, J., Toner, H., Eckersley, P., Garfinkel, B., ... & Amodei, D. (2018). The malicious use of artificial intelligence: Forecasting, prevention, and mitigation. *arXiv preprint* arXiv:1802.07228

Bryson, J. J. (2018). Patiency is not a virtue: The design of intelligent systems and systems of ethics. *Ethics and Information Technology, 20*(1), 15–26. https://doi.org/10.1007/s10676-018-9448-6

Casti, J. L. (1994). *Complexification: Explaining a paradoxical world through the science of surprise*. Abacus Press.

Cath, C. (2018). Governing artificial intelligence: Ethical, legal and technical opportunities and challenges. *Philosophical Transactions of the Royal Society A, 376*(2133), 20180080. https://doi.org/10.1098/rsta.2018.0080

Cath, C., Wachter, S., Mittelstadt, B., Taddeo, M., & Floridi, L. (2018). Artificial intelligence and the 'good society': the US, EU, and UK approach. *Science and Engineering Ethics, 24*(2), 505–528. https://doi.org/10.1007/s11948-017-9901-7

Caulfield, B. (2009). What's the Difference Between a CPU and a GPU? GPUs have sparked an AI boom, become a key part of modern supercomputers and continued to drive advances in gaming and pro graphics. *Nvidia*. https://blogs.nvidia.com/blog/2009/12/16/whats-the-difference-between-a-cpu-and-a-gpu/

Cave, S., & ÓhÉigeartaigh, S. (2019). An AI Race for strategic advantage: Rhetoric and risks. *Conference Paper for: AI Ethics and Society, 2018*, 1. https://doi.org/10.1145/3278721.3278780

Cihon, P. (2019). Technical report. Standards for AI governance: International standards to enable global coordination in AI research and development. University of Oxford. https://www.fhi.ox.ac.uk/wp-content/uploads/Standards_-FHI-Technical-Report.pdf

Cihon, P., Maas, M. M., & Kemp, L. (2020). Should artificial intelligence governance be centralised? Design lessons from history. In *Proceedings of the AAAI/ACM conference on AI, ethics, and society* (pp. 228–234). https://doi.org/10.1145/3375627.3375857

Christensen, R., K., & Tschirhart, M. (2011). Organization theory. In M. Bevir (Ed.), *The SAGE handbook of governance theory* (pp. 65–75). SAGE Publications.

Ciuriak, D. (2018). The economics of data: Implications for the data-driven economy. In "Data governance in the digital age," Centre for International Governance Innovation. SSRN digital. https://doi.org/10.2139/ssrn.3118022

Coase, R. H. (1937). The nature of the firm. *Economica, 4*(16), 386–405. https://doi.org/10.2307/2626876

Crawford, K., Dobbe, R., Dryer, T., Fried, G., Green, B., Kaziunas, E., Kak, A., Mathur, V., McElroy, E., Nill Sánchez, A., Raji, D., Rankin Lisi, J., Richardson, R., Schultz, J., Myers West, S., & Whittaker, M. (2019). *AI now 2019 report*. AI Now Institute. https://ainowinstitute.org/AI_Now_2019_Report.html

Dafoe, A. (2018). AI governance: a research agenda. Governance of AI Program, Future of Humanity Institute, University of Oxford. https://www.fhi.ox.ac.uk/wp-content/uploads/GovAI-Agenda.pdf

Dasgupta, P. (2007). *Economics: A very short introduction*. OUP.

Donnay, K. (2017). Big Data for monitoring political instability. *International Development Policy, 8, Art. 1*. https://doi.org/10.4000/poldev.2468

Doshi-Velez, F., Kortz, M., Budish, R., Bavitz, C., Gershman, S., O'Brien, D., ... & Wood, A. (2017). Accountability of AI under the law: The role of explanation. *arXiv preprint* arXiv:1711.01134

Doz, Y. L., & Hamel, G. (1998). *Alliance advantage: The art of creating value through partnering*. Harvard Business School Press.

Drexl, J. (2016). Designing competitive markets for industrial data—Between propertisation and access. Max Planck Institute for Innovation & Competition Research, Paper No. 16-13. SSRN digital. https://doi.org/10.2139/ssrn.2862975

Drexl, J. (2017). Designing competitive markets for industrial data—Between propertisation and access, 8. JIPITEC 257 para 1. https://web.archive.org/web/20180421113504id_/http://www.jipitec.eu/issues/jipitec-8-4-2017/4636/JIPITEC_8_4_2017_257_Drexl

Dyer, S. A., & Harms, B. K. (1993). Digital signal processing. *Advances in Computers, 37*, 59–117. https://doi.org/10.1016/S0065-2458(08)60403-9

Elia, G-L. & Margherita, A. (2018). Can we solve wicked problems? A conceptual framework and a collective intelligence system to support problem analysis and solution design for complex social issues. *Technological Forecasting and Social Change, 133*, 279–286. https://doi.org/10.1016/j.techfore.2018.03.010

Faddoul, M., Kapuria, R., & Lin, L. (2019). *Sniper ad Targeting*. Final Report. UC Berkeley.

Fassbender, J., (2020). *Eine Untersuchung der Integration zivilgesellschaftlicher Akteure in Multistakeholder-Foren zum verantwortungsvollen Einsatz von Künstlicher Intelligenz*. [Master Thesis]. Zeppelin Universität.

Ferraro, F., Etzion, D., & Gehman, J. (2015). Tackling grand challenges pragmatically: Robust action revisited. *Organization Studies, 36*(3), 363–390. https://doi.org/10.1177/0170840614563742

Floridi, L. (2018). Soft ethics and the governance of the digital. *Philosophy & Technology, 31*(1), 1–8. https://doi.org/10.1007/s13347-018-0303-9

Floridi, L., Cowls, J., Beltrametti, M., Chatila, R., Chazerand, P., Dignum, V., Luetge, C., Madelin, R., Pagallo, U., Rossi, F., Schafer, B., Valcke, P., & Vayena, E. (2018). AI4People—An ethical framework for a good AI society: Opportunities, risks, principles, and recommendations. *Minds and Machines, 28*(4), 689–707. https://doi.org/10.1007/s11023-018-9482-5

Freeman, R. E. (1984). *Strategic management: A stakeholder approach.* Cambridge University Press.

Freeman, R. E. & McVea, J. (2001). A stakeholder approach to strategic management. In M. Hitt, R. E. Freeman, & J. Harrison (Eds.), *Handbook of strategic management* (pp. 189–207). Blackwell Publishing.

Future of Life (2015). Autonomous weapons: An open letter from AI & Robotics Researchers. At *IJCAI conference.* https://futureoflife.org/open-letter-autonomous-weapons/

Geist, E. M. (2016). It's already too late to stop the AI arms race—We must manage it instead. *Bulletin of the Atomic Scientists, 72*(5), 318–321. https://doi.org/10.1080/00963402.2016.1216672

Gilpin L., Bau, D., Yuan, B. Z., Bajwa, A., Specter, M. & Kagal, L. (2019). Explaining explanations: An overview of interpretability of machine learning. arXiv:1806.00069v3

Golić, Z. (2019). Finance and artificial intelligence: The fifth industrial revolution and its impact on the financial sector. *Proceedings of the Faculty of Economics in East Sarajevo, 19*, 67–81. https://doi.org/10.7251/ZREFIS1919067G

Greene, D., Hoffmann, A. L. & Stark, L. (2019). Better, nicer, clearer, fairer: A critical assessment of the movement for ethical artificial intelligence and machine learning. *Proceedings of the 52nd Hawaii International Conference on System Sciences*, 2122–2134. https://doi.org/10.24251/HICSS.2019.258

Grohs, P., Perekrestenko, D., Elbrachter, D., & Bölcskei, H. (2019). Deep neural network approximation theory. arXiv:1901.02220.

Gruetzemacher. (2018). Rethinking AI strategy and policy as entangled super wicked problems. *AIES '18: Proceedings of the 2018 AAAI/ACM conference on AI, ethics, and society.* https://doi.org/10.1145/3278721.3278746

Gurumurthy, A. & Chami, N. (2019). The wicked problem of AI governance. *Friedrich-Ebert-Stiftung India, Artificial intelligence in India* (Vol. 2). Electronic Edition. http://library.fes.de/pdf-files/bueros/indien/15763.pdf

Hagendorff, T. (2020). The ethics of AI ethics: An evaluation of guidelines. *Minds and Machines, 30*, 99–120. https://doi.org/10.1007/s11023-020-09517-8

Harari, Y. N. (2018). *21 Lessons for the 21st century.* Jonathan Cape.

Harrington, L. (2018). Exponential technology. *AACN Advanced Critical Care, 29*(1), 11–14. https://doi.org/10.4037/aacnacc2018728

Hawking, S. (2016). Stephen Hawking warns of dangerous AI. *BBC News.* https://www.bbc.com/news/av/technology-37713942/stephen-hawking-warns-of-dangerous-ai

Hillmann, A., & Keim, G. (2001). Shareholder value, stakeholder management, and social issues: what's the bottom line? *Strategic Management Journal, 22*, 125–139. https://doi.org/10.1002/1097-0266(200101)22:23.0.CO;2-H

Hoffman, S. (2017). Managing the state: Social credit, surveillance and the CCP's plan for China. *China Brief, 17*(11), 21–27. http://nsiteam.com/social/wp-content/uploads/2019/01/AI-China-Russia-Global-WP_FINAL_forcopying_Edited-EDITED.pdf#page=57

Holtel, S. (2016). Artificial Intelligence creates wicked problem for the enterprise. *Procedia Computer Science, 99*, 171–180. https://doi.org/10.1016/j.procs.2016.09.109

Introne, J., Laubacher, R., Olson, G., & Malone, T. (2013). Solving wicked social problems with socio-computational systems. *Künstliche Intelligenz, 27*, 45–52. https://doi.org/10.1007/s13218-012-0231-2

Jansen, D., & Wald, A. (2007). Netzwerktheorien. In A. Benz, S. Lütz, U. Schimank & G. Simonis (Eds.), *Handbuch governance. Theoretische Grundlagen und empirische Anwendungsfelder* (pp. 188–299). VS Verlag.

Jonas, H. (1979). *Das Prinzip Verantwortung: Versuch einer Ethik für die technologische Zivilisation* (2nd ed.). Suhrkamp Verlag.

Jones, C., Hesterly, W. S., & Borgatti, S. P. (1997). A general theory of network governance: Exchange conditions and social mechanisms. *Academy of Management Review, 22*(4), 911–945. https://doi.org/10.2307/259249

Kaplan, A., & Haenlein, M. (2019). Siri, siri, in my hand: Who's the fairest in the land? On the interpretations, illustrations, and implications of artificial intelligence. *Business Horizons, 62*(1), 15–25. https://doi.org/10.1016/j.bushor.2018.08.004

Latonero, M. (2018) Governing artificial intelligence: upholding human rights & dignity. *Data & Society*. https://datasociety.net/output/governing-artifcialintelligence/

Lee, K. F. (2018). *AI superpowers: China, Silicon Valley, and the new world order*. Houghton Mifflin.

Leonhard, G., & Von Kospoth, C.-A. (2017). Exponential technology versus linear humanity: Designing a sustainable future. In T. Osbourg & C. Lohrmann (Eds.), *Sustainability in a digital world: New opportunities through new technologies* (pp. 77–83). Springer.

Liang, M., & Hu, X. (2015). Recurrent convolutional neural network for object recognition. In *Proceedings of the IEEE conference on computer vision and pattern recognition* (pp. 3367–3375).

Livingston, S., & Risse, M. (2019). The future impact of artificial intelligence on humans and human rights. *Ethics and International Affairs, 33*(2), 141–158. https://doi.org/10.1017/S08926794190 0011X

Llewellynn, T., Fernández-Carrobles, M.M., Deniz, O., Fricker, S., Storkey, A., Pazos, N., Velikic, G., Leufgen, K.,Dahyot, R., Koller, S., Goumas, G., Leitner, P., Dasika, G., Wang, L., & Tutschku, K. (2017). BONSEYES: Platform for open development of systems of artificial intelligence. *In Proceedings of CF'17, 299–304*. https://doi.org/10.1145/3075564.3076259

Lomas, N. (2018). Facebook finally hands over leave campaign Brexit ads. *TechCrunch*. https://tec hcrunch.com/2018/07/26/facebook-finally-hands-over-leave-campaign-brexit-ads/

Luhmann, N. (1996). The sociology of the moral and ethics. *International Sociology, 11*(1), 27–36. https://doi.org/10.1177/026858096011001003

Luhmann, N. (1997). *Die Gesellschaft der Gesellschaft*. Suhrkamp Verlag.

Luhmann, N. (1998). *Die Gesellschaft der Gesellschaft* (2nd ed.). Suhrkamp Verlag.

Luhmann, N. (2000). *Organisation und Entscheidung*. VS Verlag für Sozialwissenschaften.

Makridakis, S. (2017). The forthcoming Artificial Intelligence (AI) revolution: Its impact on society and firms. *Futures, 100*(90), 46–60. https://doi.org/10.1016/j.futures.2017.03.006

Mantelero, A. (2018). AI and Big Data: A blueprint for a human rights, social and ethical impact assessment. *Computer Law and Security Review, 34*(4), 754–772. https://doi.org/10.1016/j.clsr. 2018.05.017

MIT Technology Review and Ernst & Young. (2019). Digital challenges: Overcoming barriers to AI adoption. *EY Digital*. https://www.technologyreview.com/2019/05/28/135184/digital-challe nges-overcoming-barriers-to-ai-adoption/

Mittelstadt, B. (2019). Ai ethics–too principled to fail?. *arXiv preprint* arXiv:1906.06668

Moon, J. (2014). *Corporate social responsibility: A very short introduction* (Vol. 414). Oxford University Press.

Moore, G. (2006). Moore's law at 40. In D. Brock (Ed.), *Understanding Moore's Law: Four decades of innovation* (pp. 67–84). Chemical Heritage Foundation.

Morley, J., Floridi, L., Kinsey, L., & Elhalal, A. (2020). From what to how: an initial review of publicly available AI ethics tools, methods and research to translate principles into practices. *Science and Engineering Ethics, 26*(4), 2141–2168. https://doi.org/10.1007/s11948-019-00165-5

Müller, V. C., & Bostrom, N. (2016). Future progress in artificial intelligence: A survey of expert opinion. In V. C. Müller (Ed.), *Fundamental issues of artificial intelligence*. Synthese Library (Studies in Epistemology, Logic, Methodology, and Philosophy of Science) (Vol. 376, pp. 555–572). Springer, Cham.

Murphy, M. (2001). The politics of adult education: State, economy and civil society. *International Journal of Lifelong Education, 20*(5), 345–360. https://doi.org/10.1080/02601370110059519

Nakashima, E. (2012). Stuxnet was work of U.S. and Israeli experts, officials say. *The Washington-Post*. https://www.washingtonpost.com/gdprconsent/?next_url=https%3a%2f%2fwww.washingtonpost.com%2fworld%2fnational-security%2fstuxnet-was-work-of-us-and-israeli-experts-officials-say%2f2012%2f06%2f01%2fgJQAlnEy6U_story.html

Nilsson, N. J. (2009). *The quest for artificial intelligence*. Cambridge University Press.

Parviainen, P., Tihinen, M., Kääriaäinen, J. & Teppola, S. (2017). Tackling the digitalization challenge: How to benefit from digitalization in practice. *International Journal of Information Systems and Project Management*, (5), 63–77. https://doi.org/10.12821/ijispm050104

Paschek, D., Mocan, A., & Draghici, A. (2019). Industry 5.0. the expected impact of the next industrial revolution. Management, Knowledge, Learning. *International Conference, Technology, Innovation and Industrial Management. TIIM, Piran, Slovenia.* http://www.toknowpress.net/ISBN/978-961-6914-25-3/papers/ML19-017.pdf

Pathak, P., Pal, P. R., Shrivastava, M., Ora, P. (2019). Fifth revolution: Applied AI & Human intelligence with cyber physical systems. *International Journal of Engineering and Advanced Technology (IJEAT), 8* (3). https://www.researchgate.net/profile/Parashu-Pal/publication/331966435_Fifth_revolution_Applied_AI_human_intelligence_with_cyber_physical_systems/links/5ca5efa2299bf118c4b0a484/Fifth-revolution-Applied-AI-human-intelligence-with-cyber-physical-systems.pdf

Perc, M., Ozer, M., & Hojnik, J. (2019). Social and juristic challenges of artificial intelligence. *Palgrave Communication, 5*(61). https://doi.org/10.1057/s41599-019-0278-x

Pichai, S. (2020). Why Google thinks we need to regulate AI. Companies cannot just build new technology and let market forces decide how it will be used. *Financial times*. https://www.ft.com/content/3467659a-386d-11ea-ac3c-f68c10993b04

Polyakova, A., & Boyer, S.P. (2018). The future of political warfare: Russia, the west and the coming age of global digital competition. *Brookings Institution*. https://www.brookings.edu/wp-content/uploads/2018/03/fp_20180316_future_political_warfare.pdf

Porter, M. E. (1980). *Competitive strategy*. Free Press.

Preece, A. (2018). Asking 'Why' in AI: Explainability of intelligent systems—Perspectives and challenges. *Intelligent Systems in Accounting, Finance and Management. An International Journal, 25*(2), 63–72.

Provan, K. G., & Kenis, P. (2008). Modes of Network Governance: Structure, Management, and Effectiveness. *Journal of Public Administration Research and Theory, 18*(2), 229–252. https://doi.org/10.1093/jopart/mum015

PriceWaterhouseCoopers. (2019). *Sizing the prize What's the real value of AI for your business and how can you capitalise*? PriceWaterhouseCoopers. https://www.pwc.com/gx/en/issues/analytics/assets/pwc-ai-analysis-sizing-the-prize-report.pdf

Qiang, X. (2019). The road to digital unfreedom: President Xi's surveillance state. *Journal of Democracy, 30*(1), 53–67. https://doi.org/10.1353/jod.2019.0004

Quinn, J.B., Anderson, P. & Finkelstein, S. (1996). Leveraging intellect. *Academy of Management Executive, 10*(3), 7–27. https://www.jstor.org/stable/4165335

Raso, F., Hilligoss, H., Krishnamurthy, V., Bavitz, C. & Kim, L. Y. (2018). Artificial Intelligence & Human Rights: Opportunities & Risks. *Berkman Klein Center Research, 2018-6*. https://cyber.harvard.edu/sites/default/files/2018-09/2018-09_AIHumanRightsSmall.pdf

Risse, M. (2019). Human rights and artificial intelligence: An urgently needed agenda. *Human Rights Quarterly, 41*(1), 1–16. https://doi.org/10.1353/hrq.2019.0000

Ritchey, T. (2011). Wicked problems—Social messes. Decision support modelling with morphological analysis. Springer.

Rittel, H. W. J., & Webber, M. M. (1973). Dilemmas in a general theory of planning. *Policy Sciences, 4*, 155–169. https://doi.org/10.1007/BF01405730

Roberts, N.C. (2000). Wicked problems and network approaches to resolution. *The International Public Management Review, 1*(1), 1–19. http://www.economy4humanity.org/commons/library/175-349-1-SM.pdf

Rose, C. (2019). Accelerating competitive advantage with AI. *Microsoft Digital.* https://info.microsoft.com/UK-DIGTRNS-CNTNT-FY20-10Oct-07-AcceleratingcompetitiveadvantagewithAI-AID-3001579-SRGCM3020_01Registration-FormInBody.html

Rowsell-Jones, A., & Howard, C. (2019). *2019 CIO survey: CIOs have awoken to the importance of AI. Gartner Research.* https://www.gartner.com/en/documents/3897266/2019-cio-survey-cios-have-awoken-to-the-importance-of-ai

Samuel, A. L. (1959). Some studies in machine learning using the game of checkers. *IBM Journal of Research and Development, 3*(3), 210–219. https://www.cs.virginia.edu/~evans/greatworks/samuel.pdf

Samuelson, P. A., & Nordhaus, W. D. (2010). *Economics* (19th ed.). McGraw-Hill Irwin.

Scharre, P. (2019). Killer apps: The real dangers of an AI arms race. *Foreign Affairs.* https://www.foreignaffairs.com/articles/2019-04-16/killer-apps

Schmidt, C. G. & Wagner, S. M. (2019). Blockchain and supply chain relations: A transaction cost theory perspective. *Journal of Purchasing and Supply Management, 25*(4), 100552.

Schoder, D., Putzke, J., Metaxas, P. T., Gloor, P., & Fischbach, K. (2014). Information systems for "Wicked Problems." *Business and Information Systems Engineering, 6*, 3–10. https://doi.org/10.1007/s12599-013-0303-3

Schwab, K. (2016). *Die vierte industrielle Revolution.* Pantheon.

Schwab, K., & Davis, N. (2018). *Shaping the fourth industrial revolution.* World Economic Forum.

Stoker, G. (1998). Governance as theory: Five propositions. *International Social Science Journal, 50*(155), 17–28. https://doi.org/10.1111/1468-2451.00106

Stolkel-Walker, C. (2018): Move over CPUs and GPUs, the Intelligence Processing Unit is the super-smart chip of the future. *Wired.* https://www.wired.co.uk/article/graphcore-ai-ipu-chip-nigel-toon

Stolterman, E., & Fors A. C. (2004). Information technology and the good life. In B. Kaplan, D. P. Truex, D. Wastell, A. T. Wood-Harper, J. I. DeGross (Eds.), *Information systems research. IFIP International Federation for Information Processing* (Vol. 143., pp. 687–692). Springer.

Sun, R. (2014). Connectionist models and neural networks. In K. Frankish & W. M. Ramsey (Eds.), *The cambridge handbook of artificial intelligence* (pp. 108–127). Cambridge University Press. https://doi.org/10.1017/CBO9781139046855.008

Szocik, K., Tkacz, B., & Gulczyński, P. (2020). The revelation of superintelligence. *AI and Society, 35*(3), 755–758. https://doi.org/10.1007/s00146-020-00947-7

Tomasik, B. (2013). International cooperation vs. AI arms race. *Foundational Research Institute, Center on Long-term Risk, 5.* https://longtermrisk.org/files/international-cooperation-ai-arms-race.pdf

Treib, O., Bahr, H., & Falkner, G. (2005). *Modes of governance: A note towards conceptual clarification* (European Governance Papers no.05-02). Eurogov.

Van Aaken & Schreck (Eds.). (2015). *Theorien der Wirtschafts- und Unternehmensethik.* Suhrkamp.

Van Bueren, E. M., Klijn, E.-H., & Koppenjan, J. F. M. (2003). Dealing with wicked problems in networks: Analyzing an environmental debate from a network perspective. *Journal of Public Administration Research and Theory, 13*(2), 193–212. https://doi.org/10.1093/jopart/mug017

Wani, M. A., Bhat, F. A., Afzal, S., & Khan, A. I. (2020). *Advances in deep learning.* Springer.

Watney, M. M. (2018, June). Evolution of illegal social media communication regulation. In *Proceedings of the 5th European conference on social media. Academic conferences and Publishing International Limited, UK* (pp. 345–352).

Wieland, J. (2008). Governanceökonomik: Die Firma als Nexus von Stakeholdern Eine Diskussionsanregung. In J Wieland (Ed.). *Die Stakeholder-Gesellschaft und ihre Governance, Studien zur Governanceethik* (6th ed., pp. 15–38). Metropolis.

Wieland, J. (2014). *Governance Ethics: Global value creation, economic organization and normativity.* Springer International Publishing.

Wieland, J. (2018). *Relational Economics. Ökonomische Theorie der Governance wirtschaftlicher Transaktionen.* Metropolis.

Wieland, J. (2020). *Relational economics: A political economy.* Springer.

Williamson, O. E. (1979). Transaction-cost economics: The governance of contractual relations. *Journal of Law and Economics, 22*(2), 233–261. https://doi.org/10.1086/466942

Williamson, O. (1986). Transaction-cost economics: The governance of contractual relations. In J. Barney & W. Ouchi (Eds.), *Organizational economics* (pp. 98–129). Jossey-Bass. http://www.jstor.org/stable/725118?origin=JSTOR-pdf

Wu, W., Huang, T., & Gong, K. (2020). Ethical principles and governance technology development of AI in China. *Engineering, 6*(3), 302–309. https://doi.org/10.1016/j.eng.2019.12.015

Yampolskiy, R. (2015). From Seed AI to technological singularity via recursively self-improving software. arXiv:1502.06512v1

Aliman, N. M., & Kester, L. (2019). Transformative AI governance and AI-empowered ethical enhancement through preemptive simulations. *Delphi – Interdisciplinary Review of Emerging Technologies, 2*(1), 23–29.

Gasser, U., & Almeida, V. A. (2017). A layered model for AI governance. *IEEE Internet Computing, 21*(6), 58–62. https://doi.org/10.1109/MIC.2017.4180835

Chapter 2
A Theoretical Approximation to Artificial Intelligence as an Autopoietic System

In the introductory chapter, AI development and adoption have been established as phenomena of trans-sectoral, global, and cross-industry relevance. This chapter presents the theoretical introduction of Artificial Intelligence to the Relational Economics as a foundation for the subsequent conceptualising of its Relational Governance in Chapter 3. Thus, my focus lies on developing a structural model for AI governance to address the correlation of ethical risks, the rising number of concerns about societal shifts, and consequential inequalities coming with its adoption. To achieve this objective, the model structurally integrates an ethical dimension, without, however, imposing one particular normative position.

At this stage of the book, the context of fierce competition in the private sector, on the one hand, and the demand for AI governance, on the other hand, seemingly oppose one another. Additionally, the negative externalities perceivable in practice, which affect society in an unchecked manner, seem to demand a collaborative approach to prevent these effects from happening. Hence, this chapter aims to move from a problem-oriented perspective of traditional AI ethics research to a rather solution-oriented approach in AI governance, as recommended by, for example, Berendt (2019), Mittelstadt (2019) and Hagendorff (2020).

To do so, AI governance is initially delineated from related research fields, such as internet governance and data governance. This brief review further allows first insights into relevant themes for AI governance and contributes to their structuring in the Relational AI Governance model which is developed later. Furthermore, research on AI is reviewed from both an economic and systems-theoretical perspective. This step substantiates the following categorisation of AI within Relational Economics, as this theory stems from the said disciplines. Consequently, the chapter concludes with the classification of AI as a system logic in its own right within Relational Economics.

S. Wiesmüller, *The Relational Governance of Artificial Intelligence*,
Relational Economics and Organization Governance,
https://doi.org/10.1007/978-3-031-25023-1_2

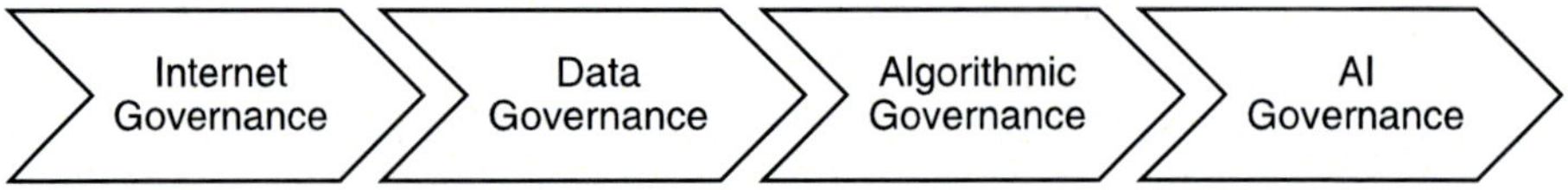

Fig. 2.1 Own depiction summarising results of literature synopsis[1]

2.1 Delimitation of Related Governance Disciplines

The delimitation of AI governance from governance concepts for related fields of application is presented in the following. Their presentation is structured chronologically in order of origination, which is important since their emergence correlates with the rise of technologies, particularly with the rise of AI. As presented in the introductory chapter, specific requirements were necessary to enable AI technologies to rise in to the level we see today: this includes a higher level of computational power, the internet, and the availability of large sets of data, as well as investments in the development of new forms and types of algorithms (Moore, 2006; Nilsson, 2009; Shin et al., 2020).

2.1.1 Related Governance Streams

Following this line of thought, connected governance approaches are presented in line with this sequential order—beginning with internet governance. The internet represents one of the basic requirements for digital technologies, and again, the availability of data is a fundamental element for the development and training of algorithms. While remaining aware that there is no sharp line between the particular approaches, the representation of related research scopes focuses on critical themes and differences—all while acknowledging the existence of potential overlaps. Thus, Fig. 2.1 depicts the sequential order in which the governance approaches are presented to the reader:

2.1.1.1 Internet Governance

The expression 'Internet Governance' arose in the mid-1990s, when the first challenges of using the internet became apparent to academia and society (Hofmann et al.,

[1] Given the scope of this work, additional governance approaches, with lesser overlaps, had to be excluded. Still, I am aware of the following research disciplines and recommends a close examination of possible synergies for further research. The disciplines identified include technology governance (Boesl & Bode, 2016), robotic governance (Boesl & Bode, 2017, 2019), information and IT governance (De Haes & Van Grembergen, 2004; Meyer et al., 2003), e-governance (Heeks, 2001; Meijer, 2015; Saxena, 2005), and digital governance (Almeida et al., 2020; Barbosa, 2017; Phillips et al., 2020).

2017). The discipline of internet governance defines, discusses, and elaborates shared rules and norms for the usage and further development of the internet (DeNardis, 2014; Dutton, 2013; Kurbalija, 2016). While, initially, the internet was perceived as just another device, scholars quickly realised that the internet was very different from other communication systems (Kurbalija, 2016). According to this approach, the internet separated social and political ties from physical nation-state borders by allowing the exchange of information and the formation of social connections across countries—requiring a new form of governance (Kurbalija, 2016). Especially since the almost parallel emergence of the internet and today's level of globalisation, organisations have been participating in business around the globe: a process that is further facilitated using the internet. These transnational transactions require organisations to follow international laws that are often not aligned with and contradict the sovereignty of national governments (Hathaway, 2014). This is a fact that can be interpreted as a threat to the security of a nation and its citizens (Perritt, 1998; Wu & Gereffi, 2018). Consequently, it is the tension between the relationship of the nation-state and national or global governance that is often at the centre of scholarly attention (Mueller, 2010). Mueller (2010) developed one possible depiction of this tension field in the form of the following graph and summarised the issue in an aggregated manner. He depicted (Fig. 2.2) the dualism of national and transnational interests, as well as hierarchic, protectionist tendencies which oppose the demand for collaboration, the need to solve transnational challenges:

Much as identified for AI governance, the field of internet governance confronts challenges on the meta-level, which involves various systems, such as politics, the law, and the economy. Further, topics within the field of internet governance range from normative questions regarding how and if the internet should be governed to

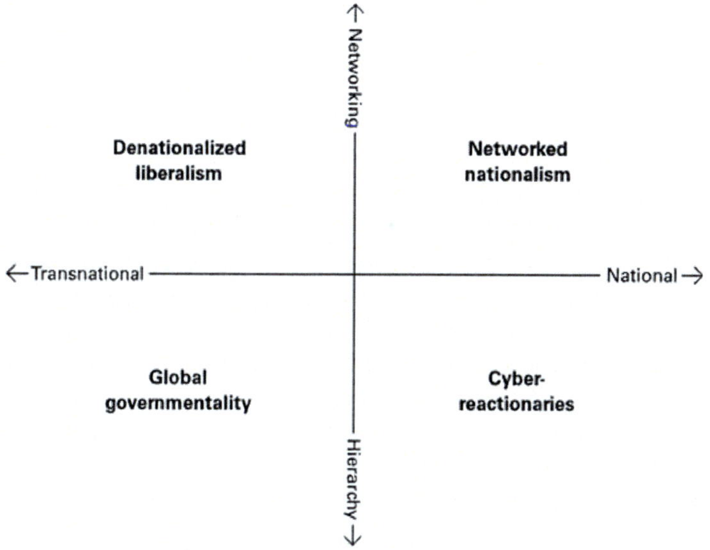

Fig. 2.2 Depiction of governance tension fields, as presented by Mueller (2010, p. 256)

the rights and duties of the various stakeholders involved and the history, present, and future of its governance (Dutton, 2013; Kurbalija, 2016; Mueller, 2010).

In detail, participation, transparency, and authority display themes of great interest in research on internet governance (DeNardis, 2010, 2014, 2020; Dutton, 2013; Kurbalija, 2016). As the internet is not one singular source, neither can its governance be attributed to one single organisation or government (DeNardis, 2014; Dutton, 2013; Kurbalija, 2016), and the complex interactions require more than mere command and control (Hofmann et al., 2017; Jessop, 2003; Mayntz, 2003). Therefore, research often focuses on pluricentric governance schemes and soft law (Feick & Werle, 2010; Mayntz, 2003).

Such a pluricentric approach is also necessary due to its definition as a global network, as the internet consists of a multitude of individual networks (Dutton, 2013; Kurbalija, 2016). In academia, more specific definitions of internet governance differ: Benkler (1999) defines internet governance as a three-layered model, consisting of the governance of physical infrastructure (hardware), the actual code (logical layer: software) and a content layer (fed-in information). Kurbalija (2016), on the other hand, considers research on more far-reaching consequences of legal, economic, or sociocultural nature of great importance. Again, DeNardis (2014) defines the scope of internet governance as "*policy and technical coordination issues related to the exchange of information over the Internet*" (DeNardis, 2014, abstract). Consequently, while research on internet governance is of relevance and serves as a base for further development and implementation of AI governance, the scope of research differs strongly. However, specific themes, research questions, and research findings—such as publications on participation, transparency, and challenges of authority in internet governance—may be transferrable to AI governance (DeNardis, 2010, 2014, 2020; Dutton, 2013; Kurbalija, 2016). This is because individual and societal participation are suspected to be of great relevance in AI governance in the near future (Dignum, 2017, 2019; Savaget et al., 2019), as "*machines mov[e] into the realm of making decisions concerning the political and legal organisation of our society*" (Kurbalija, 2016, p. 23).

2.1.1.2 Data Governance

Within the timeframe of only eight years, from 2013 to 2020, the overall number of data points rose by ten times, from 4.4 to 44 zettabytes (Abraham et al., 2019). As explained in the previous chapter, the availability and quality of data form the basis for AI research and development. Therefore, data becomes more valuable to organisations, which, first, leads to entire industries being more open to protecting their sets of data (Shin et al., 2020), and, second, requires companies to use their data as effectively as possible due to high levels of competition (Abraham et al., 2019). Given that data use and analysis have become critical for strategic decision-making in organisations (Tallon et al., 2013), so has its governance (Alhassan et al., 2018; Khatri & Brown, 2010). Thus, although specific research questions might differ, research on data governance is inherently connected to AI governance.

While the research discipline of data governance is divided into various research schools, they can mainly be grouped into research on micro-and macro-level implications for data governance (Aaronson, 2019; Abraham et al., 2019; Alhassan et al., 2018). Research on the macro-level is located at the intersection of global governance and international data governance (Aaronson, 2019; Aaronson & Leblond, 2018). In contrast, the former is instead to be located at an organisational level and addresses management issues arising from data usage within an organisation (Abraham et al., 2019; Alhassan et al., 2018; Morabito, 2015; Tallon et al., 2013). Research on the macro-level deals with data flows reaching across countries and, thereby, overarching mere national legislation and governance (Aaronson, 2019; Aaronson & Leblond, 2018). Data governance commits to a holistic analysis of norms and rules for all types of data—much like similar topics in internet governance.

Thereby, a similar categorisation of research topics might be advisable for AI governance to ensure the effective use of research synergies and a possible interlinkage of future findings. Furthermore, especially regarding data governance at the organisational level, existing research might serve as a foundation for governance measures in AI.

2.1.1.3 Algorithmic Governance and Governance of Algorithms

Given the above-mentioned rise in existing, available data and the resulting data saturation, algorithms have become almost irreplaceable for the analysis and consequential decision-making in increasingly complex environments (König, 2019). With the rise in the need for and application of algorithms, interest rose in the social and political role of applying algorithms. The trend of mechanising governance, e.g., through the application of algorithms, is not new and has always been based on data collected about and from the citizens whom the governance model was designed for. Thus, the mechanisation of analysing the data and the application of resulting findings have been realised since the computer's existence (Danaher et al., 2017; Hacking, 2006). The focus of this book lies on the private sector. Nevertheless, fields of research with possibly relevant content for AI governance cannot be collectively excluded, as, much like any other sector, the "*legal-bureaucratic organization of the state is subject to the same modernising trends*" (Danaher et al., 2017, p. 2).

For this reason, algorithms seem a suitable instrument for more effective public governance (Gillespie, 2014; Gritsenko & Wood, 2020). According to König (2019), there are two different streams in algorithmic governance research, which require mentioning: For one, algorithmic governance represents a discipline, which focuses on the realisation of governance or government tasks via the application of algorithms and AI technologies, where algorithms used by the public sector to enhance governing measures are the main focus of research (Dunleavy, 2016; König, 2019; Williamson, 2014). Thus, this research stream does not examine how to deal with a digital resource but the implementation of governance measures through digital technology and focuses on a modern, alternative form of social ordering.

In the second research stream, in algorithmic governance, the algorithms themselves and research focusing on how and if algorithm-based technologies should be implemented as instruments for political action are at the centre of scholarly attention (cf., König, 2019; Mittelstadt & Floridi, 2016; Pentland, 2013; Wachter et al., 2017). According to König (2019), independently of their application in the public sector, the use of algorithms for governance measures brings about rather general questions, as this combination allows for an entirely new level of social coordination. Therefore, Gritsenko and Wood (2020) demand academic interlinkages to concepts such as hierarchical governance or self- and co-governance concepts or even to internet governance to ensure a holistic analysis of the topic.

Those general questions mentioned above include a wide range of topics: Among others, König (2019) states that, in the legal sphere, algorithms are understood as new forms of institution, able to restructure and enforce behavioural rules (Hassan & De Filippi, 2017). In this context, scholars also refer to the rather static nature of algorithmic decision-making, and thus, algorithmic governance, which involves the risk of framing an otherwise dynamic development of society, culture, and social change—partially due to the susceptibility of algorithms to designer bias (Brundage & Bryson, 2016; Caliskan et al., 2017; König, 2019).

Further, Katzenbach and Ulbricht (2019) draw attention to a changed perspective in algorithmic governance: how is algorithmic governance different from human-led governance? Contrary to the mainstream perspective that algorithm-based governance becomes more powerful or even possesses invasive elements, the authors propose a different view highlighting a rather inclusive and responsible form of governance. Following this line of thought, Danaher et al. (2017) even go as far as denominating this circumstance as *algocracy*,[2] with reference to the possible control, manipulation, and constraints for human decision-making. While acknowledging the gains in efficiency, the authors draw attention to society's high risks (Danaher et al., 2017). Thus, they take a stand for algorithmic governance, stating that it "*is an effective means for achieving some policy goal, whilst remaining procedurally fair, open and unbiased*" (2017, p. 2).

Danaher et al. (2017) raise an important point, as the use of AI can, intentionally or unintentionally, open the doors for social or political manipulation on the micro- or even macro-level. To present an example: not only do cases of prioritisation and filtering of information exist, like the one involving Cambridge Analytica, but there are rising concerns regarding free political discourse in the case of applying algorithmic governance (Gamito & Ebers, 2021). Thus, Gamito and Ebers (2021) highlight that public governance, led and realised by algorithms, holds the risk of affecting

> fundamental values on which western societies are founded, leading to breaches of fundamental rights, including the rights to human dignity and self-determination, privacy and personal data protection. (2021, p. 3)

[2] Leading scholars define the tension field of 'algocracy' as the possible development of moral or political legitimacy problems in public decision-making, due to the adoption of AI in form of algorithmic governance (Danaher, 2016; Lorenz, 2019).

This statement describes a risk that is further maximised by the development of algorithmic governance no longer being exclusively applied by private but by governmental institutions, too (Gamito & Ebers, 2021; Hassan & De Filippi, 2017). Hence, the scholars conclude that, due to the disruptive nature of algorithmic governance and the use of algorithms in public governance, existing governance guidelines and research are not sufficient to cope with the societal effects and further unintended consequences (König, 2019).

Finally, Hassan and De Filippi (2017) shed light on yet another perspective on a trans-sectoral view of algorithmic governance. According to these authors, the digital environment every individual finds themselves in, ranging from communication channels to search engines to cloud solutions, fosters the constraint of individual freedom through software and algorithms—especially in combination with the internet (Lessig, 1999). This is, among other examples, due to the pre-sorting of search findings and almost oligarchic structures in the market. Additionally, the authors identify another new aspect of algorithmic governance: while classic jurisdiction determines what individuals shall and shall not do, codes—in the form of software—can already restrict the freedom of choice ex-ante by limiting user options (Hassan & de Filippi, 2017; Lessig, 1999; Rosenblatt et al., 2002). Algorithms change the traditional ex-post regulatory approach, as prevalent in Europe, to an ex-ante approach—as is often the case with AI—without public awareness. While this change might lead to greater effectiveness in governance measures, it also erases room for ambiguity and human error, which further reinforces the "*quest for the optimal performance*" (Kalpokas, 2019, p. 109), leaving no room for the right to human imperfection (Kalpokas, 2019).

To conclude, findings regarding public governance are disregarded, since I focus on private sector governance. However, the concepts of technological and social agency should not represent opposing positions (Gherardi, 2012; Kalpokas, 2019). Instead, a balance between both and a synergy of overlaps and potentials should be at the centre of attention—a line of thought that will be further pursued in this book.

2.1.2 Interim Conclusion

Regarding the field of internet governance, AI technologies share the characteristics of global availability and interconnectivity. Thus, legislation and governance need to be applicable across national borders. Due to the aforementioned global competition in the digital economy and industries, the coming of a new AI technology will inevitably lead to competitive products entering the global market, which again shows global interconnectivity and the need for a transnational approach. Therefore, drawing on (Mueller, 2010) synopsis, this would either lead to a denationalised liberalism or to global governmentality, with the latter confirming the need for this book.

Given that AI can only be as good as the data used to train it, and as the sets of data it is applied to, most topics in data governance inherently connect to AI governance.

For one, the general categorisation in data governance, namely the division of topics allocated on micro-and macro-level, will be applied to AI governance. Moreover, in data governance, the micro-level focus lies on questions of risk management and a rise in efficiency. Similar topics seem relevant on the organisational level for AI governance, especially when AI is used as a service and serves to enhance organisational processes or support strategic decision-making. As presented, on the macro-level of data governance, research that includes the governance of data flows across national borders or transnational legislation is of great relevance. Therefore, to enable interlinkages between the research discipline of data and AI governance, I will adopt the categorisation in the micro-and macro-level, as it is deemed practical for the topics thus far identified in AI.

In the discipline of algorithmic governance, questions of interest for AI governance mainly centre around humans being governed by algorithms and the consequences of that development, as well as the design and training these algorithms to receive. It is broadly acknowledged in research that the private sector already applies AI and uses it to analyse data and in strategic decision-making. Further, it is a fact that the public sector is moving in the same direction, which leads to a change from ex-ante to ex-post regulation—without public awareness or adapted legislation. While the consequences of implementing AI on the organisational level, as mentioned above, allow for clear differentiation, it is again on the macro-level that the themes torn out to be of a rather philosophical and ethical nature. Consequently, research in the discipline indicates that constant human involvement in the governance process will continue to be needed, in addition to supervising the initial training process (Brundage & Bryson, 2016; Caliskan et al., 2017; Johnson, 2017; König, 2019).

To conclude, the delimitation from other research streams allows a first structuring of themes for the conceptualisation of the relational governance of AI. First, the model needs to differentiate between topics allocated on the micro- as opposed to the macro-level. On the micro-level, short-term consequences include the psychological effects of AI implementation on employees or new job structures, risk management, and raising efficiency. Thus, research on a micro-level is likely to focus on the intra-firm challenges arising from AI implementation. In contrast, research on a macro-level is likely to focus on socio-economic and political questions, such as the economic arms race and hidden political agendas in AI research.

The second classification revolves around short-term and long-term implications and, correspondingly, individual as well as philosophical questions affecting society as a collective. An example of such questions on the meta-level is the redefinition of human rights in the context of AI and the normative goal of ensuring personal human autonomy and the individual's right to participate in civil society and be imperfect.

The third category is based on the technological level of advancement. As presented in the previous chapter, machine learning requires different forms of acceptance from deep learning regarding its responsible implementation. Thus, the level of AI application will determine further decisions for responsible AI implementation.

2.2 Conceptualisation of AI in the Relational Economics

Having decided to develop the governance model for Artificial Intelligence based on Wieland's (2018, 2020) Relational Economics theory, AI needs to be contextualised within the disciplines the theory draws on: transaction cost economics and systems theory. Therefore, AI is evaluated briefly from these two perspectives, before deciding on the form of its conceptual integration within Relational Economics.

2.2.1 Transaction Cost Economics Perspective on AI

Generally, in economics, interest in AI has risen, and its impact on economics has been examined from different perspectives. However, AI is often integrated into economic theory or dealt with as a means to an end, rather than analysing and interpreting the role and impact of AI from a theoretical point of view. Thus, to give a brief insight into current research connecting AI and economic theory, the following publications are allocated to this intersection.

To begin with, an increasing number of scholars often treat or denominate AI as a so-called 'general purpose technology' (Brynjolfsson & McAfee, 2017; Dafoe, 2018; Goldfarb et al., 2019; Klinger et al., 2018; Nepelski & Sobolewski, 2020; Razzkazov, 2020; Trajtenberg, 2018). Such technology is characterised by affecting entire economies, mostly even on a global level, and by permanently disrupting and changing previously existing economic and social structures (Goldfarb et al., 2019). While posing a few challenges to the consequently transforming economy, general-purpose technologies foster economic growth (Bresnahan & Trajtenberg, 1995; Klinger et al., 2018; Nepelski & Sobolewski, 2020; Petralia, 2020). Given the congruence of characteristics attributable to AI and the definition of this type of technology, this claim seems valid to me. Thus, this perspective confirms the high relevance of AI to the global economy, and the claim of AI leading to the next industrial revolution substantiated, as it was likewise general-purpose technologies that led to previous industrial revolutions (Brynjolfsson & Hitt, 1998; Klinger et al., 2018).

Apart from a first characterisation of AI from an economic perspective, the following brief review aims to present how the relation of AI with economic theory is currently examined from various perspectives:

On the one hand, Parkes and Wellman (2015) interpret development in AI as the pursuit of creating rational agents, a so-called *machina economicus*, and examine "*rules of interaction in multi-agent systems that come to represent an economy of AIs*" (2015, p. 267). Furthermore, they are convinced that the role of AI in economics will rise tremendously in the coming years. D'Hondt et al. (2019) shed light on the increase in efficiency due to AI application by presenting the example of financial decision-making. They further point to the possible advantages for society, as integrating AI into financial investment might allow risk-averse and low-income groups to engage in this field. Thus, again, the practical effect of AI on one aspect of the economy is analysed in this book.

Marwala and Hurwitz (2017), on the other hand, examine the impact of AI on economic theory and thus present more theoretical, in-depth findings. Still, by giving an overview of various economic theory disciplines, no specific interpretation is presented from a transaction cost economics perspective, and, again, AI is rather depicted as a means to an end. The theories examined include, among others, demand and supply analysis, where the authors conclude that

> AI through learning and evolution is able to ensure that the demand and supply curves are better modelled. The use of an AI machine reduces the degree of arbitrage in the market and therefore brings a certain degree of fairness into the market which is good for the efficiency of the economy. (Marwala & Hurwitz, 2017, p. 24)

For rational choice theory, AI can help "*make better rational expectations of the future, bringing decision-making closer to the theory of rational choice*" (2017, p. 36) and "*give higher probability of identifying a global optimum utility, and thereby bringing decision making closer to the theory of rational choice*" (2017, p. 36). Lastly, the authors conclude that "*advances in artificial intelligence result in making markets more efficient*" (2017, p. 109).

However, the connection to transaction cost economics was established as early as 2001 by Klos and Nooteboom, who focused on "*the use of agent-based computational economics' (ACE) for modelling the development of transactions between firms*" (2001, p. 503). Further, the authors state that "*transaction cost economics neglects learning and the development of trust, ignores the complexity of multiple agents, and assumes rather than investigates the efficiency of outcomes*" (2001, p. 503). Thus, in this book, AI is analysed as an instrument to gain better results for further analysis based on transaction cost economics, without however interpreting AI from the point of view of that discipline. Xu and Cheng (2017) follow the same path presented before when analysing the effect of AI on financial decision-making, where AI can "*help build the standardization, risk modelling, intelligent control system, and promote financial development*" (2017, p. 725). The authors state that "*development of financial technology will greatly reduce the transaction costs, [...] this is a trend which cannot be halted*" (2017, p. 725). Further, van de Gevel and Noussair (2013) present AI as a necessary prerequisite for the discipline of agent-based computational economics, a field that "*studies economic processes, including whole economies, as dynamic systems of autonomous interacting agents*" (2013, p. 5). While they examine transaction cost economies and the role of transaction networks, AI is again the instrument to reach that understanding, not part of the research question.

The same holds true for Agrawal et al. (2016), who focus on the effect of AI as a tool to raise the effectiveness of transactions and lower transaction cost and highlight AI's predictive power in this context. Once more, Jin (2019) reviews the role of AI for market efficiency and the factor of privacy, information asymmetry and highlights ethical dilemmas, such as the following:

> Since the benefits are more internalized to the owner of the data and AI than consumer risks, AI could encourage intrusive use of data despite higher risks to consumers. For the same

> reason, new benefits enabled by AI—say cost savings or better sales—could entice a firm to (secretly) abandon its promise in privacy or data security. (2019, p. 442)

While I will give essential insight into an ethical aspect of AI and transaction cost, it does not provide information on how to classify AI from a theoretical perspective. Still, it is possible to identify six publications which focus on the intersection of AI and transaction cost theory and attempt, to different extents, to theorise AI in this context. Thus, while no previous publication has covered this book's scope, partial elements of the following publications seem to be relevant.

First, more than three decades ago, Fai (1987) examined how AI could be implemented to categorise transactions and identify suitable governance structures that result. The author also stated that such an expert system could further be used for research in the overall discipline of transaction cost economics; hence, it is again portrayed as a service for promoting research, not as an element within the theory.

Second, Erdélyi and Goldsmith (2018) open the discussion by pointing to the "*growing legal vacuum in virtually every domain affected by technological advancement*" (2018, p. 95), especially by AI, and by highlighting the "*sustained economic competitiveness after the inevitable global transition to an AI-driven economy*" (2018, p. 95). According to the authors, this is because, in the context of AI, negative externalities transgress national borders, which is why transnational regulation is required. While stating that hard legalisation will reduce "*post-contracting transaction costs by restricting/constraining attempts to alter the status quo by way of frequent renegotiation*" (2018, p. 97), by lowering the risk of "*imperfect contracts*" (ibid., p. 97), the authors conclude that AI's true potential can best be exploited by initially lowering "*contracting costs with soft legalization and low institutional formalization*" (ibid., p. 100). Further, they suggest applying standardised processes at a later stage. Thus, for Erdélyi and Goldsmith (2018), AI plays an essential role in transaction cost economics, specifically regarding the concept of perfect and imperfect contracts.

Third, Aghion et al. (2017) analyse the relationship between AI and economic growth and, thereby, integrate AI as a theoretical element in economic theory: regarding transaction costs, the authors perceive AI as an instrument for automation, which requires high initial investments. Much like Erdélyi and Goldsmith (2018), Aghion et al. (2017) question whether AI can overcome contractual incompleteness. Hence, both publications focus on AI as an influential factor for contracting.

Cuypers et al. (2020) further develop this stream of research and aim to demonstrate how transaction cost theory can be connected to AI, again, with a focus on contracts. For one, they discuss applying AI to create contracts, which would minimise costs for contract enforcement and "*thereby making market-based transactions less costly*" (2020, p. 57). Moreover, the authors point to advantages for human resources regarding employees' monitoring options and further automation of strategic decision-making. Lastly, the authors point out that digital technologies have the potential to organise both hierarchies and market transactions more efficiently, which is why they highlight the importance of examining the cost of governing these technology-induced mechanisms (Cuypers et al., 2020).

Finally, Rindfleisch (2020) examines digital technologies and their connection to transaction cost economics from a theoretical point of view. While he does not explicitly focus on AI, his findings seem applicable, given that AI is subsumed under the umbrella term of digital technologies. According to Rindfleisch, it is not surprising that, as two of the founding fathers of transaction cost economics, neither Coase nor Williamson integrated digital technologies into their approaches to transaction cost economics. While the former did not witness this era, the latter deliberately decided not to include digital technologies in his more recent work (Rindfleisch, 2020; Williamson, 2016). However, Williamson (1985, 1993) commented on technology by stating that contracting was, indeed, influenced by technology, a fact confirmed by the aforementioned authors. Still, Williamson (1993) later stated that "*the choice between firm and market organization is neither given, nor largely determined, by technology*" (Williamson, 1993, p. 12).

Rindfleisch (2020) points to the more recent work of Benkler (2006) on transaction cost economics, who indeed integrates digital technologies and seeks to modernise transaction cost economics; Rindfleisch even goes as far as stating that "*Benkler's version of transaction cost theory revolves around technology*" (2020, p. 8). He further states that, by introducing a new economic element, as for the market, Benkler (2006) contributes to transaction cost economics. This is because Benkler describes this new form as the social production of goods, enabled through digital technologies and realised by new forms of economic cooperation (Benkler, 2006; Rindfleisch, 2020). By focusing on individuals, C2C-cooperation and the sharing economy as drivers of the economy, Benkler states that transaction cost economics could play an essential role in understanding and predicting the new, technology-driven economy. Thus, both Benkler and Rindfleisch stress the individual's importance as a partial substitute for former transactions inherent to firms. Further, Rindfleisch presents diverging views on whether or not digital technologies might foster opportunism, a question worth clarifying by further research in the context of transaction cost economics (Rindfleisch, 2020). Albeit Coase (1937) already confirmed that technology affects transaction costs (Vatiero, 2020), in this regard, Rindfleisch (2020) focuses on Benkler (2002, 2006, 2017) and his theoretical contribution.

To conclude, the existence of an intersection between AI and transaction cost economics in academia has been proven sufficiently by the aforementioned authors (Aghion et al., 2017; Agrawal et al., 2016; Cuypers et al., 2020; Erdélyi & Goldsmith, 2018; Fai, 1987; Jin, 2019; Klos & Nooteboom, 2001; van de Gevel & Noussair, 2013; Xu & Cheng, 2017). Therefore, while the importance of conducting research at this intersection is confirmed, none of the aforementioned scholars assessed and evaluated AI's meaning for the economy and society from a transaction cost economics perspective.

However, the suspected relevance of Rindfleisch's (2020) research for this book will be discussed briefly: Rindfleisch (2020) seems to agree with Benkler's view, as he agrees with his focus on individuals and their role in transaction cost economics in a technology-driven economy, rather than organisations or the market. Moreover, Benkler's (2006) work stems from both Coase (1937) and Williamson's (1985, 1993) theoretical foundations, which possibly makes them partially applicable to this book.

However, given that Wieland (2018, 2020) retains the firm as the unit of analysis, I will neither apply Benkler's (2006) nor Rindfleisch's (2020) impulses directly into the Relational AI Governance model, as integrating differing research streams into this book's contribution would go beyond the scope of this topic. Nevertheless, I support the presented works of Benkler (2006) and Rindfleisch (2020), in that the role and importance of individuals will increase, especially, for example, through the further rise of technologies of a decentralising nature, such as the blockchain, which will—in combination with AI—give additional influence and power to individuals in the market. Furthermore, the rise of the blockchain could strengthen and foster the concept of peer-to-peer governance (Vatiero, 2020).

2.2.2 Systems-Theoretical Perspective on AI

To further define and delimit AI and its classification from a systems-theoretical point of view, the following section will present a brief overview of systems-theoretical research streams to draw a first conclusion.

Beginning with the theoretical origin of one of the more prominent streams in systems theory, as early as 1996, when the development of AI was still rudimentary compared to today's advancements (Nilsson, 2009), Luhmann (1996) described complex technical machines as black boxes; that is, systems which are impossible to define and control from the outside. This definition appropriately describes the current view of AI, especially deep learning, in mainstream media and academia. Moreover, it highlights the difficulties of monitoring the machines' actions and indicates the controversy in academia regarding a consistent definition of the phenomenon (Floridi & Cowls, 2019; Schuett, 2019).

Before presenting the existing controversy among authors in the field, an in-depth description is required of relevant elements of this discussion within Luhmann's theory. This interim step is necessary to provide the context and give a reference point for the subsequent views on AI, which are almost entirely based on Luhmann's systems theory approach. Hence, an aggregated view of Luhmann's theory is presented here, referring to three of his older publications (Luhmann, 1995, 1996, 1997) and one posthumously published script (Luhmann & Kieserling, 2000).

2.2.2.1 Theoretical Introduction to Luhmann's Systems-Theoretical Approach

Generally, Luhmann does not evaluate and analyse societies' nature and functionality from the viewpoint of a single actor. Rather, he applies a very abstract level of analysis to depict the significant variables determining a society. Thus, in his view, logically, while social systems reproduce themselves through ongoing communicative actions by actors, it is the communicative operation, rather than the communicating actor, that is of interest to Luhmann (1995, 1996, 1997; Luhmann & Kieserling, 2000).

Hence, communication is perceived as an abstract operation and is the main layer of interest, while the operating agent portrays merely the means to an end.

Luhmann (1996, 1998) defines systems as entities that are separate or can separate themselves from their environment. Therefore, by definition, certain elements can be identified as existing inside or outside any given system. The differentiation between system and environment underlies all further conceptualisations made by Luhmann. Accordingly, a system is characterised by its ability to reproduce itself constantly, without external impulses or factors. While the notion of self-reproduction, also autopoiesis, originally stems from neurobiology, Luhmann integrates this concept into his theory and applies it to all his system forms. For Luhmann, each system reproduces itself by repeatedly conducting and creating its system-inherent, specific operations, which do not occur in its environment.

Thus, for the discussion evolving around AI, it is particularly the exact definition and explanation of psychic and social systems that is of relevance for the further development of this book. According to Luhmann (1996, 1998), three types of systems exist; namely, organic, psychic and social systems. For biological systems, such as human beings, organic processes represent such system-inherent operations. In contrast, for psychic systems, it is thoughts; and for social systems, it is communication. Consequently, as long as the respective last operation in a given system allows for the continuation of further operations of its kind, the system will continue to exist. For psychic systems, the existence of a consciousness is the essential requirement for autopoiesis. Based on this criterion, and as a general rule in Luhmann's theory (1996, 1998), social systems, which are 'merely' based on communication, cannot connect to psychic systems, and purely organic processes cannot be further reproduced by intertwining them with conscious thoughts. Consequently, according to Luhmann, system-specific operations cannot be integrated into another system with differing characteristics. Therefore, another one of Luhmann's theory's (1996, 1998) contributions is to explain how these separated systems can still interact and be connected to one another, despite their strict demarcation.

2.2.2.2 Luhmann's View on Communication Within and Among Systems

Nonetheless, Luhmann's (1996, 1998) primary focus is on defining the particular language of each system and its operational functioning on the operational level. For the scholar, communication inherently connects to the notion of systems being closed off from their environment: as such, communicative operations cannot leave their system of origin and become part of another system. A connection between systems is only possible through what Luhmann defines as structural coupling, which will be explained shortly. Consequently, Luhmann explicitly denies the commonly known sender-recipient model of communication and, instead, defines communicative operations as events. Thus, as mentioned before, communication exists as an entity in its own right and can be performed by entities in all systems of society. Accordingly, means of communication can include writing, physical presence, or even (results of) work.

Communicative operations become structurally visible and classifiable in theory by symbolism and a language-based dualism, which Luhmann defines as functional differentiation of a given system. This system-specific code makes the operations of functional systems within society more effective and fosters the reproduction process of communication in the system by guiding new operations and limiting the options for forming new communicative operations. Thus, each system has its specific binary code, which, in the political system, for example, is defined as having power versus not having power. By focusing on the particular communication logic within the system, its environment becomes everything that does not apply to this very logic. Luhmann does not focus on demarcating the respective environment itself, but states that everything outside a given system is classified as its environment.

Structural coupling allows for the bridging and connection between systems. While every system has its own binary coding, each system can raise its sensitivity towards other binary codes and system languages. In Luhmann's (1996, 1998) theory, structural coupling provides a solution for self-referential systems, otherwise unable to operate with(in) other systems or, generally speaking, within their entire environment. One example for a connection can be presented by looking at the medium 'money', which answers to the binary code of payment/non-payment and is, thus, part of the economic system. While the political system is based on the binary coding of 'government – opposition', translatable to the medium 'power', economic logic can be made tangible for the political system by developing aggregated data, such as tax ratios. Such information, albeit resuming economic logic, can affect the power position of either the government or opposition. Hence, this system-alienate information triggers a reaction within the receiving system by being translated to its inherent language (Luhmann, 1995, 1996, 1997; Luhmann & Kieserling, 2000).

Before presenting current research at the intersection of AI and system-theoretical research, one final remark shall be made: According to Luhmann, for successful communication, 'understanding' the true message carried by communicative operations is not the relevant part. Rather, the communicating agent or operator only needs to comprehend that another entity is communicating with them and acting accordingly. Thus, to reproduce communication, the operating actors involved do not necessarily need to understand the communicative action's true message. Given the discussion of consciousness in new AI technologies, this last aspect might be of importance when resuming other scholars' research position at this intersection and becomes crucial for the application and integration of AI into Relational Economics.

2.2.2.3 Review of Luhmann-Based Systems-Theoretical Research

The development of an effective AI Governance approach requires the conceptualisation of AI in Relational Economics. Based on this step, the Relational AI Governance model can derive governance mechanisms and correlating governance measures.

Hence, a review of research based on Luhmann's theory serves as a base for this conceptualisation.

According to Donick (2019), Luhmann's theoretical view remains of great importance, especially in an era characterised by the increase in technological black boxes. He specifically points to Luhmann's (2017) theoretical reflections on how to exert control in situations of high non-transparency and correctly highlights that such a form of control is never characterised by guaranteed success, as a degree of uncertainty always remains. Control resembles self-obliged monitoring of the system itself, that the machine obtained after the externally induced control impulse (Donick, 2019; Luhmann, 2017). Thus, Donick offers an interesting insight into the control aspect of implementing new technologies. However, he does not present a classification of AI within Luhmann's theory.

In contrast, Dickel (2019) presents a different view on AI: referring back to the rise of the internet, Dickel claims that existing available ascriptions based on Luhmann's theory are insufficient to describe and define either the internet or AI. Particularly for the internet, Dickel states that, in his view, the phenomenon could not merely be classified as part of the media. Instead, in his understanding, the internet manages to dissolve structural asymmetries among sender and recipient in an unknown manner, which further exemplifies its direct entanglement with the social sphere. Therefore, the internet should be understood as a part of the infrastructure of any given society. In Dickel's opinion, as a consequence of being an internet-based digital technology, this holds true for AI, too. While Dickel disagrees with the classification of weak and strong AI, he points out that even for the so-called weak AI, societal structures and infrastructures not only changed but were purposely adapted by society to make space for and integrate AI applications. Specifically, Dickel refers back to Floridi (2015) and uses the term of so-called 'AI agents', which in my view, underlines the importance Dickel ascribes to AI. Dickel explicitly confirms this view by stating that it seems a mistake to view AI in its current state as weak, merely because it is not acting like a human agent. With this, Dickel (2019) refers to a definition of AI first presented by Searle (1980), who stated:

> According to weak AI, the principal value of the computer in the study of the mind is that it gives us a very powerful tool. For example, it enables us to formulate and test hypotheses in a more rigorous and precise fashion. But according to strong AI, the computer is not merely a tool in the study of the mind: rather, the appropriately programmed computer really is a mind, in the sense that computers given the right programs can be literally said to understand and have other cognitive states. In strong AI, because the programmed computer has cognitive states, the programs are not mere tools that enable us to test psychological explanations; rather, the programs are themselves the explanations. (1980, p. 417)

Drawing on Searle's (1980) widely accepted definition, Dickel (2019) criticises the lack of recognition of AI technologies' current impact. Although the definition of so-called 'weak AI' includes all expert systems and supportive applications of AI, it diminishes its effect on society, which Dickel criticises strongly. In his perspective, in the present, societies are to be characterised as post-humanistic systems, where social and non-social agents interact and are linked to each other via communication interfaces. For Dickel, the symmetry between machines and humans already began with creating the computer, proceeding with the rise of the internet and might be completed by the development of current-day AI. Given the indispensability of debating this state of society, Dickel criticises the lack of engagement by the scholars from sociology—even though Luhmann (1997) already understood the inevitability of addressing this issue when questioning whether or not computers could endanger the special human status in the constant reproduction of society. Further, Dickel references the early work of Baecker (2001), who, in his view, is the leading scholar in sociology for addressing the societal challenges coming with AI development and adoption. Specifically, he concurs, Baecker's (2015) newer research, which considers digital machines and the involvement of intelligent machine actors in communication to be the main challenge for societies at present, seems highly relevant for academia. Dickel concludes that it is not about whether AI will ever reach levels of human consciousness but about the sociological meaning of AI and its function in society. Dickel currently only sees these issues addressed by Esposito (2001, 2017a, 2017b) and Baecker (2011, 2015). I agree that the AI phenomenon still requires a suitable depiction in sociological theory. Hence, a brief look at Baecker's (2015) research is required.

Baecker (2015) states that he understands this form of communication as the interconnection of subjectively acting, complex entities. Accordingly, the definition of machine intelligence (MI) rather stems from the impossibility and human inability to understand how the processing of information within these machines works. Baecker (2015) further specifies that communication should rather be defined as the connection of subjectively self-willed entities. Applied to the context of human-machine interaction and communication between the two, MI could, therefore, instead be interpreted as contributing information that is no longer retraceable to their human counterparts. More specifically, Baecker views intelligence as autonomous internal processes in the machine that can neither be controlled nor causally explained by an external observer (Baecker, 2015). Thus, seemingly in opposition to Luhmann (1995, 1996, 1997), Baecker connects the concept of consciousness into the communicative process. In contrast, Luhmann specifically excluded it from the equation when discussing the effectiveness of communicative reproduction.

Bammé (2017) critically discusses Baecker's (2014) claim that society finds itself in a so-called co-evolution of the human mind and technological and societal development and progress in the current situation. However, according to Bammé (2017), the true challenge is rooted in the fact that it is not clear whether or not the human mind can keep pace with the aforementioned technological advancements. Accordingly, there is an actual need for the creation of sound solutions for human and technological co-existence. Bammé states that it might only be possible for existing human deficiencies to be compensable by integrating formerly human mental abilities into artificially intelligent systems. Thereby, evolutionary malformation could be compensated to ensure the longevity of our societies. Thus, for Bammé, AI is no longer the dependent variable in human-machine-relations.

Esposito (2017a) offers a contrary position: accordingly, instead of mimicking the human mind and its abilities, algorithms, and thus, AI, should focus on the ability to communicate (Esposito, 2017a). In 2001, Esposito did, however, acknowledge that, since they create new, formerly non-existent content, computers need to be defined as authors in their own right, according to Luhmann's (1997) classifications. Esposito (2017b) further states that algorithms add complexity to existing communication in societies by introducing the aforementioned new information, which does not originate from human minds. Moreover, she criticises the development of algorithms without considering social or communicative elements in their design, as to her, it is the machinal output and its consequences for society that matter, not so much its internal machinal processes.

Regarding the classification of AI within Luhmann's systems theory, Esposito chooses a path which slightly differs from the original theoretical source: Luhmann (1995, 1996, 1997; Luhmann & Kieserling, 2000) states that it is not the understanding of information's true meaning that is necessary for the successful reproduction of communication. Rather, it is the understanding of the communicative pattern itself and the ability to constantly reproduce it that is of importance. Thus, from a present-day perspective, neither computers nor AI can be excluded from communication per se or declared irrelevant. However, Esposito (2001) declares that to integrate computers into the communicative structure and implement structural couplings, at a certain point, humans will need to comprehend and understand the true meaning of computational communication. In addition, in a later publication, Esposito (2017a) poses the claim that AI should not be viewed as an intelligent actor. Moreover, the focus should be on the communicative ability of AI, instead of its potential artificial consciousness or intelligence (2017a).

While Esposito states that, "even and especially if the algorithm is not an alter ego, [...], and does not understand its counterpart, in interaction with machines, human users can learn something that no one knew before" (2017a, p. 262), she further substantiates her claim by referring to Etzioni (2016). Accordingly, Etzoni states that an algorithm can only ever create knowledge or options that are somehow inherent in the data it is supplied with. Esposito concludes that an algorithm can never provide "contingency, but the contingency that the algorithm processes can [...] be the result of the interaction of human beings with the algorithm" (2017a, p. 262). Esposito's standpoint is that algorithms produce "informativity of communication. New forms of communication can combine the performances of algorithms with those of people, but not because algorithms are confused with people or because machines become intelligent" (2017a, p. 263). This quote represents Esposito's critical view of ongoing discussions regarding the existence of artificial consciousness or even intelligence in academia and places her on a rather traditionalist side of scholars dealing with AI. Consequently, Esposito states that by only analysing information without an in-depth understanding of its content, machines merely communicate but do not possess intelligence. In her view, reinforced learning algorithms, for example, are learning algorithms, which possess the ability to self-modify. Esposito (2017b) further discusses questions of liability, as, in her understanding, the consequence of the fact that algorithms merely process material without having a true understanding of the data creates unknown levels of ethical and legal challenges—a view many leading scholars concur with (Esposito, 2017b). While remaining with her position, she highlights her perception of Google's dealing with AI, namely that society

> must face algorithms directly as autonomous agents, with processes, procedures, and problems that cannot be traced back to our familiar forms of attribution and accountability. (2017b, p. 8)

In conclusion, society needs to learn to deal with AI as new communication operators that process information in a new manner, but not with new intelligent agents (Esposito, 2013).

While understanding the new role of AI, Esposito (2017a, 2017b) works closely with Luhmann's (1995, 1996, 1997) theory, and rather adds to the original theory than expanding it or even questioning its applicability to new circumstances, as by the disruption of society through AI. Thus, like Luhmann (1995, 1996, 1997; Luhmann & Kieserling, 2000), Esposito argues for an abstract analysis of AI-induced communication, without focusing on the operating agent, but by analysing and conceptualising the communicative operation itself. To conclude, according to Esposito (2001, 2017a, 2017b), AI in its current form can be attested to have the ability to contribute to communication or communicate, but not the characteristics of an agent in its own right. However, Luhmann, (1995, 1996, 1997), Esposito (2001, 2017a, 2017b) and (Baecker, 2007) agree that computers and, consequently, AI do engage in communication and can communicate, as AI not only reproduces information but processes data to present new information (Harth & Lorenz, 2017).

Baecker's and Esposito's views are discussed further by Harth and Lorenz (2017): the authors specifically focus on Baecker's (2011) concept of how to define and classify agents that show the potential for involvement in communication; namely consisting of "*independence, self-reference, and complexity*" (Baecker, 2011, p. 22). Formerly, those characteristics were merely ascribed to human communication partners. In contrast, in the present, machines could also be part of communication, as both Baecker (2016) and Harth and Lorenz agree. Baecker (2011) further states that any entity which is characterised by these ascriptions qualifies to be part of communication. Specifically, he describes independence as the existence of memory and the ability to reflect on the self and the environment. With this, he defines self-reference as the ability to differentiate between the self and the other, and complexity describes the multi-relational internal structure of the given entity, as well as memory, to reflect on the difference resulting from this multidimensional self.

Harth and Lorenz (2017) apply Baecker's (2011) conditions to the case of deep learning as one of the main advancements in AI. They proceed to produce evidence that, at least, this technological advancement can be identified as a new unit in communication systems. While the authors do not make a final decision about whether or not deep learning can be granted the status of human-like communication ability, they concur that deep learning seems to fulfil the requirements for this status, as developed by Baecker (2011). They do, however, raise the question of whether the algorithmic model itself or its human creator is the original source of the contributions made by the machine. Still, Harth and Lorenz confirm that societies will need to get used to machine agents as parts of communication and debate their potential role and positioning within society and theory. According to them, the question of whether society is willing and ready to engage with machines, as raised by Esposito (2001, 2017a, 2017b), can be dismissed, as ignoring machines as elements of societies and, thus, communication systems, does not seem an option.

The notion of AI as a general-purpose technology (cf., Dafoe, 2018) further backs this view, which shows its seemingly unstoppable but surely all-encompassing disruptive nature. For sociology, one question that remains, is how these new forms of interaction and communication will influence society. While this topic is also partially addressed by AI ethics (Dafoe, 2018; Harth & Lorenz, 2017; Mittelstadt, 2019), it is not within this book's scope.

Given these considerations, the question remains, how technology, and for this book, AI, should consequently be categorised within Luhmann's (1996, 1998) theoretical view: Reichel (2011) explicitly develops his understanding and conceptualisation of technology based on Luhmann's theory. Thus, due to a shared theoretical origin, his findings might be directly applicable here. Reichel defines technology

> as a self-making, self-referencing system, distinct from society and the human individual. Its basal operation is information in the medium of operativeness, processing along the binary code of work/fail. (2011, p. 105)

He further explains that by a close "*coupling with social systems as well as with human developers and users of technology, technological evolution is ensured as a co-evolutive network of technology and society*" (Reichel, 2011, p. 105). Thus, Reichel defines technology as a self-referential system in Luhmann's tradition, existing as a delimited, independent system within society that he further characterises as having a "*multitude of structural couplings with its environments*" (2011, p. 116). However, Reichel highlights the fact that technology is created in interrelation with society and human counterparts, as a software engineer, for example, inevitably incorporates his perceptions into the software he programs. Thus, Reichel concludes that humans create reality via technological advancements. He even goes as far as stating that "*there appears to be no way out of a technological trajectory for social evolution*" (2011, p. 117). Hence, Reichel ascribes substantial importance to technology, and thus, to digital technologies such as AI.

The broad findings of research on how to conceptualise AI based on Luhmann's theory are further discussed in the synthesis of this chapter. However, the insights prove that existing categories cease to grasp the complexity of the phenomenon. Consequently, the conceptualisation of a new category for AI in Relational Economics seems to be required.

2.2.2.4 Review Findings on AI Agents and AI Agency in Systems Theory

To further define the scope of the Relational AI Governance model, it is essential to sharpen my evaluation of whether or not AI is attributed agency in its decision-making. If this was the case, the AI application could directly be governed in its actions. In contrast, if agency is not given, it is the organisations which apply AI that are at the centre of attention, and need to establish governance measures.

A brief excursion shows that the view of AI as an agent in human-machine interaction is not uncommon in other streams of research in systems theory. Lom and Pribyl (2020) interpret systems theory and cyber-physical systems from a different angle: In contrast to Luhmann's (1996, 1998) understanding of systems theory, they base their work on Rousseau, who defines a system as

> a set of interacting or interdependent component parts forming a complex whole. Every system is delineated by its spatial and temporal boundaries, surrounded and influenced by its environment, described by its structure and purpose and expressed in its functioning. (Rousseau, 2015, as cited in Lom & Pribyl, 2020, p. 1)[3]

Thus, Lom and Pribyl connect systems theory and the theory of cyber-physical systems, with the latter being defined as consisting of interconnected physical and software elements. Thereby, data from the physical world is analysed by the virtual software element. Based on their definition of system theory, the authors conclude that "*Cyber-Physical systems can be treated like traditional systems, as the physical and virtual world are interconnected*" (2020, p. 3). Still, they highlight the importance of communication between the two systems via interfaces, representing the boundary between said systems. The authors apply their concept to smart cities and portray a smart city as an intelligent actor to demonstrate its dynamic nature. Accordingly,

> a smart city can be generally seen as an environment according to the Systems Theory, and particular systems (energy, buildings, transportation) within the smart city can be seen as systems. (Lom & Pribyl, 2020, p. 10)

In smart cities, systems are interconnected by energy or information relations. This concept might be applicable to AI systems, too, where information or data streams might also function as connectors. Additionally, by treating a hybrid system, such as a smart city, as a system in itself, a demarcated entity consists of diverging elements, such as physical and technical components. Thereby, Lom and Pribyl offer an impulse for the definition of AI in governance theory, although their understanding of systems theory diverges from the definition applied in Relational Economics, being based on models from natural sciences, not sociology.

Hossaini (2019) discusses agency in digital systems, and to this end, differentiates between mechanical and biological agency. He further claims that, in the development of AI, it seems more important to focus on agency than on intelligence itself, as with a rising level of machine autonomy, it is indispensable to have integrated an ethical element into AI before its full autonomy, e.g., in the form of a singularity. Nonetheless, he concludes that this is a matter of future relevance, which is why this notion does not require integration into the AI Governance model developed here.

Noble and Noble (2019) agree that machine agency requires regulation. However, they take a different stand on how this regulation should be designed: the authors do

---

[3] The source and, thereby, the reference used by the authors could not be verified, as this quote does not exist in the referenced paper. However, as this particular publication is not of direct relevance for this book and is merely included to highlight a contrasting view in system theoretical research, the paragraph is retained to demonstrate the overall perspective on AI as apparent in this research stream.

not share the belief that it is the machines themselves that need regulations but rather their creators who need to ensure liability. Further, Noble and Noble (2019) avoid the necessity of dealing with the ethicality of how to interact with such new agents by not granting machines the definition of agents. The authors define agents' action ability as: "*they can do so creatively, and not simply by following a predetermined algorithm*" (Noble & Noble, 2019, p. 130). By stating that technologies are currently not able to match this definition, Noble and Noble (2019) indicate that they argue on the machine learning level. This is because only recent advancements in deep learning can creatively develop solution approaches (Beaudouin et al., 2020; Doshi-Velez et al., 2017; Preece, 2018). They infer from their argumentation that machines would need to be able to interact with other systems and show an inherent form of iterative anticipation, which they are not willing to ascribe to algorithms. Thus, Noble and Noble (2019) do not view AI as a full-value agent and focus on questions of personal liability instead of governing the overall effects of AI.

Soto and Sonnenschein (2019) concur with the former Noble and Noble on the "need to regulate the design and use of AI, regardless of whether it or any other artefacts created by humans will ever be able to generate true agency" (Soto & Sonnenschein, 2019, p. 141). However, they share the view that AI is unlikely to develop a full, human-like agency. Much as in the current text, they instead highlight meta-level implications AI adoption can lead to:

> The pressing problem about AI is not the creation of minimal artificial agents or truly agentive intelligence, but rather the possibility that AI constructs might generate nefarious consequences totally attributable to human agency, human intelligence and the human ethical standards of their designers and users. (Soto & Sonnenschein, 2019, p. 141)

Hence, this concern is addressed here by presenting a governance model that, indeed, includes interfirm governance, and thereby, the governance of possibly connected AI applications.

Against the backdrop of rising concerns in society about autonomously acting machines, Balfanz (2017) questions and examines whether machines can truly reach autonomy from a Kantian perspective. At the core of this analysis is the relation between humans and machines and the further question, whether machines still merely serve humans or whether humans, at least partially, serve machines, too. Balfanz states that, generally, machines still serve humans. However, the personal experience of consumers and users might already differ strongly. Balfanz takes the stand that these systems should be denominated, in terms of their consequences, partially autonomous, highly automated systems to avoid and prevent wrongful ascriptions and expectations regarding their performance ability. Further, he points out the high knowledge requirements for anyone who wants to interact with these highly complex machines. To facilitate this interaction, Balfanz highlights two aspects: First, the machines' communication skills with their environment need to be enhanced, and second, instead of merely designing machines, human-machine-systems should directly be designed as integral cognitive systems. While he concludes that machines still serve humans, Balfanz explains that users might often feel a loss of autonomy, as machines usually serve their producer or operator instead of watching the user's interest. Due to these non-transparent, hidden agendas, users are likely to feel a certain sense of being at the machine's mercy (Balfanz, 2017). Lastly, Balfanz points out an urgent need for regulation and governance to design a legal frame that ensures greater transparency and a deeper understanding of the causal relations in this interaction and the protection of its limits.

To conclude, AI is established here as a phenomenon that does not possess agency and should not yet, therefore, be defined as an agent in its own right. Still, the option of conceptualising AI is revisited when relating the review findings to Relational Economics to ensure a solid research process. Nonetheless, in the governance model, AI will not be addressed as an agency-possessing agent but as part of an organisational operation. With this, the focus on the private sector and the analysis level of the firm remains adequate.

2.2.2.5 Review Findings on the Relation between Humans and AI

To establish a governance approach which realistically depicts the application of AI to organisations and society, I review research on the interaction and space around AI. The research presented next will support this aspect of AI's conceptualisation.

Henning (2019) focuses on the potential gain from the collaboration between humans and machines. He points out the hybrid character of human-machine systems and, therefore, a hybrid intelligence, where both human and artificial intelligence are combined for the best possible outcome. While Henning is not the only scholar highlighting this aspect, nor is it an entirely new thought, he sheds light on how the relationship between humans and machines and, consequently, this form of hybrid intelligence, changes once machines develop some form of consciousness and autonomous thought. He exemplifies his thinking by describing the partnership humans and animals form, where the partner is allowed free will and, at least partially, free decision-making. Thus, Henning characterises this form of hybrid intelligence as based on constant processes of negotiation and communication on equal terms (Henning, 2019). Although Henning's publication resembles a description of his view on this circumstance, rather than empirical research, his standpoint plays an important role, as similar thoughts have been discussed by Baecker (2016) and Harth and Lorenz (2017). This confirms the option of portraying AI as a crucial factor in the further development of society without, however, granting it full human-like agency. Nonetheless, it can be portrayed as a new element of equal importance and with great potential for collaboration.

Focusing on new forms of interaction, Neisig (2020) analyses a possible coupling of social, digital, and natural systems, which would lead to creating a network of "*complex intelligent systems*" (2020, p. 4). Further, such a human-technological collaboration may help build a structural coupling of polycentric social and technological networks. Such a development would be highly favourable, as "*collaboration of man-machine (and nature) may be one of the greatest promises*" (Neisig, 2020, p. 12), but presents major challenges regarding required knowledge about machine learning, transparency, and essential control mechanisms for polycentric systems. At this point, Neisig refers back to Luhmann's (1996) indication that complete control of polycentric systems will never be possible due to ever-existing blind spots in human-machine interaction. She describes polycentric systems as scenarios where AI supports humans, mainly by analysing the data and presenting first-level reasoning. Again, human collaborators remain in charge of meta-level reasoning (Jordan & Mitchell, 2015; Neisig, 2020). Nevertheless, Neisig (2020) perceives new systems of interacting machines, organisations, and biological systems as a likely scenario. Thereby, she again confirms an established requirement that AI imposes on a governance approach: namely, the ability to foster collaboration. This is not only necessary between corporations, as established when presenting the wicked problem structure of governing AI, but also between humans and AI.

Filk (2020) takes up a similar theme and poses the question of whether networks formed by social and non-social agents, e.g., by humans and intelligent machines, need to be classified as symmetric or asymmetric forms of interaction. He states that, in creating new knowledge, these networks have been known to work in a symmetrical form. Thus, AI in this context would be classified as an agent in its own right. Again, as an actor, AI can choose to act cooperatively or show counterproductive behaviour regarding the joint goal attainment of all actors involved (Filk, 2020). In consequence, he points to Rosa (2016), who described societies' current state as a postmodern phenomenon of rising growth, increasing speed, and constantly higher density in innovation. More specifically, Rosa raises concerns about the accelerated speed with which society changes due to tremendous levels of disruption. Filk (2020) continues this line of thought and defines his observations as a digital network society. This concept entails the evolution of society into a global, complex phenomenon emerging from the entanglement of economy and technologies. By doing so, he attributes to technologies the ability to shape society and thereby confirms their prominent role in societal development. Thus, he supports this book's position that AI Governance is a topic of vital societal interest.

Being neither interchangeable nor suited to be described by ascriptions of the respective other, Feustel (2020) highlights the necessity of understanding the connection and interaction of men and machines as co-existing systems. Moreover, he claims that it is crucial to focus on the fact that rotations from digital to societal worlds quickly seem to become more elaborate. He then concludes that, while being powerful, AI should be viewed as a new, different form of intelligence, rather than defining it by existing ascriptions developed for the human mind. This confirms the view of this book that existing categories will not be sufficient to cover AI.

Fuchs shares this view and states that artificial intelligence could be viewed based on a new understanding of time, a so-called "*différance*" (2020, pp. 225). It should be interpreted as a concession to AI being a completely new element, which cannot be described by applying existing categories. Further, he states that, even in the present, machinal processes cannot be viewed as happening in complete isolation. However, only with the creation of an organic computer, able to experience and act, a classification according to Luhmann (1996, 1998), could a machine be attributed a certain human-like form of consciousness (Fuchs, 2020). Much like research regarding AI agency, Fuchs substantiated the view taken here that AI cannot be regarded as a liable agent at present. Nonetheless, Fuchs also confirms this work's standpoint that AI requires a new theoretical conceptualisation.

In response, Vogd (2020a, 2020b) replies that, again, according to Luhmann (1997), conscious existence is, among other elements, based on learning to react to societal expectations—a trait AI could, in his opinion, learn very well: Following his argument, AI systems build correlations to a point where they become almost self-referential, not remembering the starting point that led to the first correlations, which in the end leads to self-referencing. Thereby, Vogd (2020a, 2020b) argues, machines could construct their own experiences and categorise them as their own, leading them to make decisions autonomously. To further substantiate his argument, he references Günther (1963), who claimed that the existence of consciousness was not defined as the ability to form experiences in a traditional sense. To be classified as a consciously acting unit, according to Günther, it is sufficient for a system to be able to reflectively assess its environment and view the net of correlations it is bound to from a meta-level. Being able to leave its original system, the machine proves the existence of a conscious element in the machine and can consequently address its former state of not knowing (2020a, 2020b). Given the newest developments in deep learning, such a form of consciousness might exist in the future. Therefore, Vogd's considerations should not be dismissed lightly when creating a future governance model but will not be considered in the Relational Governance approach this book presents, since its scope is limited to currently existing forms of AI.

2.2.2.6 Synthesis on Systems-Theoretical Review on AI

In conclusion, controversial views have been identified on AI's role and its classification within sociology, especially systems-theoretical research. On the one hand, AI is widely viewed as a new type of technological agent interacting with human agents. For some researchers, the main question lies in defining the true nature of AI. In contrast, for others, the focus lies on the emergence of a new space—a hybrid intelligence which can be developed between humans and machines. In addition to this great controversy, it was possible to identify four further specified research streams within this brief review:

1. AI as an agent in its own right (Dickel, 2019; Filk, 2020; Harth & Lorenz, 2017; Lom & Pribyl, 2020)
2. Debating AI agency and its possible autonomy (Balfanz, 2017; Hossaini, 2019; Noble & Noble, 2019; Soto & Sonnenschein, 2019; Vogt, 2020a, 2020b)
3. The potential of hybrid forms of artificial and human intelligence, co-creation and collaboration by humans and machines (Bammé, 2017; Feustel, 2020; Filk, 2020; Henning, 2019; Neisig, 2020)
4. Classification and allocation of AI within Luhmann's systems-theoretical construct (Baecker, 2011, 2014, 2015; Esposito, 2001, 2017a, 2017b; Fuchs, 2020; Reichel, 2011; Vogt, 2020a, 2020b).

In this book, specific questions regarding a possible autonomous-thinking machine, which acts in full consciousness, or scenarios of potential power shifts between humans and machines, are not at the centre of attention. However, I agree with the aforementioned publications that confirm the great importance and highly disruptive nature of the AI phenomenon. Further, I share the view that AI requires a classification within the theoretical model which grants AI sufficient space. By structurally including digital technologies and their inherent logic into a governance model, existing dilemma situations created by the all-encompassing, disruptive processes triggered by AI can be addressed and solved systematically.

2.2.3 *Interim Conclusion*

Based on the considerations from both transaction cost economics and systems theory, AI will subsequently be viewed and contextualised within Wieland's (2018, 2020) Relational Economics to understand better the functional logic required for the development of Relational AI Governance.

While the work of all authors mentioned is essential for the future of the discipline and to give a context for the said structural integration of AI, it is, in particular, the publications of Esposito (2001, 2017a, 2017b), Baecker (2011, 2014, 2015), and Reichel (2011) that can contribute to the proceedings of this book. This is because the contributions of these scholars, and of this book, share their root in Luhmann's (1996, 1998) systems-theoretical approach. Hence, their research is directly applicable here. Despite the fact these scholars neither share a common position nor suggest the same categorisation of AI, their contributions will help discuss AI within Relational Economics.

2.2.3.1 Applicability of Luhmann-based Research to the Relational Economics

To apply the research findings derived from the above review to Relational Economics, it is important to highlight which aspects of Luhmann's (1995, 1996, 1997; Luhmann & Kieserling, 2000) theory are applied to the Relational Economics theory and are, therefore, applicable. Wieland (2018, 2020) derives fundamental aspects of his theory from Luhmann's work and "*does [...] agree on the assumption that modern societies are functionally differentiated and ṇthat functional systems like the economy, law and politics are mutually autonomous*" (2020, p. 11). He also applies Luhmann's logic of binary codes and guiding differences, as explained briefly in the introductory chapter. Moreover, both authors agree that "*systems are also communicatively open and consequently capable of structural coupling and therefore being in relations with other systems*" (Wieland, 2020, p. 11). Further, Wieland applies a differentiation of systems, such as made by Luhmann (1995, 1996, 1997; Luhmann & Kieserling, 2000), and identifies functional, organisational, and psychic systems to be in no hierarchic relation with each other (Wieland, 2020). Defining the demarcation of system and environment by their difference, Wieland again agrees with Luhmann's original theory. Given the focus on economic actors in Relational Economics, he specifies the "*constitutive need for and ability of economic actors to connect and act in various social contexts*" (Wieland, 2020, p. 11) as polycontextuality.

Much like Luhmann (1995, 1996, 1997; Luhmann & Kieserling, 2000), Wieland (2020) defines social systems as consisting of constantly reproduced communication, which is why, accordingly, this book can directly apply system-specific languages and their coordination, as well as the modes of connection (Wieland, 2020). The connection between economics and sociology, for example, shows when Wieland presents the market's functional system, which is defined as monolingual, examining and assessing all events happening according to its binary code 'prices'. He also integrates Luhmann's notion of polylinguality, which addresses functioning entities, such as organisations and psychic systems. These entities can communicate or assess other system languages in addition to their own. Wieland (2020) adopts this differentiation made by Luhmann (1996, 1998) and specifically defines this trait as the

> communicative ability and means that a given system or actor can use different language games and decision logics to authentically (i.e., accurately) reconstruct, understand and communicate on an event or transaction. Moreover, polylingualism means that systems can compare such reconstructed events with their own guiding differences and integrate them in their decision-making processes [...]. (Wieland, 2020, p. 12)

Via their polylinguality, system-specific interests can be aligned sustainably by solving dilemma situations on the system level. Hence, it is crucial for Relational AI Governance to adopt this concept. Only by doing so can the application of the governance approach have a sustainable and lasting effect.

Having integrated Luhmann's (1995, 1996, 1997) sociological theory into an economic governance theory, Wieland (2018, 2020) adopted the majority of core concepts the former developed. Hence, it is possible to directly adopt the review findings presented above without theoretical restrictions. Furthermore, key concepts, such as the fundamental definition of systems, their environment, and their system-specific language, the binary coding, can be used as both original theories apply to them.

2.2.3.2 Applicability of Systems-Theoretical Findings to the Relational AI Governance

Despite the controversies that became apparent in the literature review, there are overlapping themes between economic and systems-theoretic publications. As presented, the majority of themes are not directly applicable to the classification of AI in Relational Economics, which is why the main research streams are contextualised briefly within the theory:

First, the possibility of including AI in the form of an agent will be discussed: Wieland (2018, 2020) does not apply a classical principal-agent scheme and ascribes various roles to agents. This circumstance makes it difficult to connect to the aforementioned publications focusing on AI as an agent. Furthermore, Wieland applies the definition of agent to different entities within his theory, such as the firm being a "*multi-stakeholder agent for the productive, value-creating proportioning*" (2020, p. 4). Thus, the notion of agents in Relational Economics does not match the definition applied in the aforementioned publications (Dickel, 2019; Harth & Lorenz, 2017; Noble & Noble, 2019), which is why—if the classification were chosen—no interconnection of research streams would be possible. Furthermore, in the focal theory, even person systems are presented as

> individuals as natural persons or as the agents within an organisation, defined by their roles, [which] form market and organisational systems and use them in order to pursue their own economic interests. (Wieland, 2020, p. 49)

While in this definition, individuals are grouped within one category and analysed from a meta-level perspective, the category's characteristics still cannot be applied to AI. These characteristics do not apply to AI, which is why person systems will also be dismissed.

Additionally, in the publications retrieved from the review process, there was considerable controversy as to whether AI systems could be classed as agents in their own right. In my opinion, at present, no finite evaluation is possible, either from an academic or a technological perspective, on whether AI can be viewed as an agent in its own right. This holds true especially when an agent is—among other characteristics—defined by holding an autonomous consciousness. Furthermore, by conceptualising AI as an agent, many current forms of AI adoption could not be depicted by the governance approach. One example of this is the application of 'AI as a service'[4]: while a few outstanding organisations develop and apply the most advanced AI technologies, such as deep learning, most companies currently apply machine learning to optimise processes and products. The development and mere existence of new technologies, such as deep learning, pose pressing and challenging AI governance tasks. However, so do machine learning applications, especially given the extent of their usage. Consequently, the Relational Governance approach will be developed in such a way that it covers both current and future development, as a governance approach directed too much towards the future and the newest technological advancements could not depict the factual economic reality.

Beyond that, it is not in my interest to develop a model which regulates singular AI-induced actions set off by an agent. Instead, a meta-level approach is pursued, in the form of a structural model for AI governance. To allow an analysis on the meta-level, e.g., examining the effects of AI on ex-ante and ex-post legislation mechanisms, from this point of view, a more general classification of AI is required. Hence, a systematic, holistic AI governance approach cannot conceptualise AI as an agent, which is why this classification approach will not be pursued further.

[4] When AI is applied as a service, it usually performs human-like tasks to support business processes and is implemented to raise efficiency in companies (Elger & Shanaghy, 2020).

2.2.3.3 Applicability of Luhmann-Based Findings to the Relational AI Governance

The research identified in the review that closely applies Luhmann's (1996, 1998) school of thought needs to be considered for the conceptualisation process. As established, this is because their specific contributions are relevant to this book. Moreover, the contributions are also applicable due to the shared theoretical root in Luhmann's system theory. Thus, this section contextualises the most promising publications. Particularly relevant in this regard are Esposito (2001, 2017a, 2017b), Baecker (2011, 2014, 2015), and Reichel (2011).

Baecker (2011, 2014, 2015) builds his argumentation with close reference to Luhmann's theory. However, he evolves the theoretical foundation he draws on and further develops Luhmann's categories for identifying and proving the nature of agents. As he focuses on conceptualising AI as an agent, an approach that is not pursued by this book, his research will not be integrated when categorising AI within Relational Economics. However, I will draw on Baecker's insights and his position on AI, and will refer back to his approach when critically discussing the self-developed governance approach. In this way, Baecker's research (2011, 2014, 2015) will serve as a reference point, which will help determine this book's truthfulness to reality and its applicability.

While Esposito (2001, 2017a, 2017b) focuses on the effect of AI on communication and the consequences of machinal communication for society, she delimits AI's role to that of a contributor, rather than a self-reliant agent in communication. She substantiates her position by stating that full-encompassing communication was only possible when possessing consciousness and the ability to comprehend the true meaning of the information that is communicatively shared. Esposito infers that AI is not able to communicate autonomously nor to reconstitute itself self-referentially. Thus, while her closeness to Luhmann's (1996, 1998) original theory positions her as a source for this work, I do not concur with her view: allocating a rather minor position to AI in the Relational AI Governance approach would prevent the model from becoming an instrument of proactive, future-oriented use in theory and practice. Therefore, Esposito's (2001, 2017a, 2017b) research will only be drawn on indirectly and will mainly be viewed as further confirmation of the existing research gap, which this work aims, partly also from a sociological perspective, to contribute to.

Reichel (2011) offers the unique conceptual proposition of integrating technology into Luhmann's theoretical construct in the form of a new system logic. While he did not specifically focus on AI, his attempt can serve as both reference and inspiration for AI's conceptualisation in Relational Economics. In his publication, he proposes three possible variations of conceptualising technology as a system:

First, Reichel discusses the option of introducing technology as a classical social system, which draws on communication as its mode of operation. Following this line of thought, no physical elements would be included in this definition, as he states that the social system "*would act as a social proxy for physical aspects of technology*" (Reichel, 2011, p. 109). Subsequently, he suggests 'work – fail' as the binary code and 'operativeness' as the medium for the system, which will help decide whether a particular technology is implemented; if it operates well, and thus, functions, it will be implemented, but if it does not, then another technology will be chosen. He further specifies that "*other social systems can emerge, most notably organisations of technology, e.g., standardisation organisations [...] or formalised innovation projects*" (2011, p. 109).

Second, the annexation of technology to another system, or, in other words, its integration, which makes it part of another system, such as science, is presented. This option applies the aforementioned binary code and medium for technology. However, no operating entities, such as organisations, emerge. Given the established existence of associations and interest groups in AI,[5] I dismiss this option. This is because active entities exist within the AI system, which proves its lack of suitability.

Third, in this publication the adoption is proposed of "*technology as an autopoietic system distinct from society and the human individual*" (Reichel, 2011, p. 109). Consequently, technology would be defined as a system different not only from its environment but from all existing social systems. Hence, in contrast to the other options, technology is not defined as a social system any longer; instead, it requires an entirely new definition. This sets a precedent case for this book, which considers conceptualising AI as a new system in Relational Economics. Apart from evidence from Luhmann's (1996, 1998) original theory, Reichel instances that "*society proceeds with its business only according to its rules, technology does by proceeding along technological rules*" (2011, p. 109). Therefore, it requires its own definition and cannot be developed based on existing definitions for another system. Nonetheless, both systems shape each other: technology is created by society, while society is shaped by its use of technology. Hence, they are deeply intertwined, even though they apply different system logics.

While Reichel does not discuss AI conceptually, he states that the continuity of an autopoietic system "clearly does not involve any form of artificial intelligence; intelligence is not a feature of autopoiesis and not necessary for it" (2011, p. 112). Thus, even if only focused on machine learning, instead of more advanced technologies, I could apply the approach chosen by Reichel. This is because intelligence is not a requirement for the reproduction of communication—which again is the basic requirement for an autopoietic system. Therefore, both options, classifying AI as a social system and as an entirely new system, will be evaluated in the next section when integrating these findings into Relational Economics.

To derive the extent to which the adoption of Reichel's (2011) approach can be realised, the level of integration of Luhmann's theoretical foundation within Relational Economics has to be delimited and examined. By doing so, I avoid construing errors in transferring the Luhmann-based review findings onto Relational Economics. Given Reichel's technology focus on research, the direct adoption or further development of his theory will not be possible, since I seek to develop a conceptualisation suitable for the depiction of AI. Thus, adaptation and sorting of transferable and

[5] The Association for the Advancement of Artificial Intelligence, or the European Association for Artificial Intelligence are examples of associations of this kind.

non-transferable elements are required. Consequently, Reichel's (2011) proposition will serve as a reference point to draw on.

In contrast, Esposito's and Baecker's positions will not be directly integrated into Relational AI Governance as they do not opt to develop AI in the form of a system. However, Baecker's criteria for defining AI do seem highly relevant to research in this field, as they substantiate the importance of the phenomenon and, more specifically, conceptualise the constantly more autonomous nature of technological advancements in AI. The same holds true for Esposito's research: while there are a few commonalities between her research and this book, such as that both views AI not as an agent with human-like intelligence but defined by its systematic relevance, Esposito's view on AI will not be applied here.

2.3 Classification and Conceptualisation of Artificial Intelligence as an Autopoietic System

Based on the outlined argumentation, AI is introduced here to Wieland's (2018, 2020) Relational Economics in the form of a new system logic. This decision not only stems from existing systems-theoretical literature but is confirmed by the following considerations:

First, the overarching and game-changing nature of AI is depicted and confirmed by its association with general-purpose technologies across disciplines (Brynjolfsson & McAfee, 2017; Dafoe, 2018; Goldfarb et al., 2019; Klinger et al., 2018; Nepelski & Sobolewski, 2020; Razzkazov, 2020; Trajtenberg, 2018). This is exemplified by Dafoe (2018), who shows that AI's classification as a general-purpose technology is already applied across disciplines and that scholars from various disciplines ascribe great societal and economic impact to it. Due to the all-encompassing nature of the effects of a general-purpose technology, a suitable classification is required within a theoretical conceptualisation of the current economic system, as attempted by Relational Economics.

Second, leading scholars in sociology, who apply Luhmann's theory (Luhmann, 1995, 1996, 1997; Luhmann & Kieserling, 2000), concur that AI is pushing the boundaries of Luhmann's theory and requires either an adaptation or expansion of the theory (Baecker, 2015; Donick, 2019; Reichel, 2011) or a new systems-theoretical approach altogether (Fuchs, 2020; Vogt, 2020a, 2020b). Hence, the undertaking of developing a new conceptualisation of AI is substantiated by several researchers and was potentially even foreseen by the original author, Luhmann, himself (1995, 1996, 1997), when wondering whether his theory would be sufficiently thought through to successfully accommodate complex new phenomena, such as computers were then, and AI is now.

Third, Wieland's (2018, 2020) Relational Economics inherently portray a progression and reinterpretation of Luhmann's theoretical foundation. Being rooted at the intersection of more than one discipline, the theory gives more interpretational room for adaptation in developing a new category for AI. This is because the theory is not subjected to the restricted views of monodisciplinary approaches and, in this way, allows an integral, interdisciplinary approach with references from both disciplines. Therefore, the further expansion of this modern and dynamic theoretical approach is sufficient and does not require the development of an entirely new sociological or economic concept—the two disciplines combined in Relational Economics.

Fourth, the idea of denominating and classifying technology as not just a singular element or side effect of another action but as an equally important separate system logic seems of great significance, as Reichel (2011) already made a case. Additionally, Reichel builds his argument on Luhmann (1995, 1996, 1997), making it applicable to Relational Economics and, thereby, to this book. Reichel claims that

> the argument taken here is that technology is neither physical nor social; it is above all technological. Its material artefacts are not technology itself just as the human bodies observable all around are not identical with the human beings they belong to. [...] Constructing a theory that observes technology as inherently technological [...], just as constructing a theory that observes society as inherently social, demands a precise definition of a non-physical, non-social basal operation of technology, of its non-physical, non-social medium of internal evolution, its general code, and the way it actually evolves and, connected to that issue, how it couples with its environment, especially with society and the human individual. (2011, p. 110)

Based on this argument, Reichel establishes technology as a new system within societies. Together with Scheiber and Roth, Reichel even contextualises AI as communication "*made by programmed computers (artificial intelligence, simulation, multi agents)*" (Scheiber et al., 2011, p. 102).

For this book, the close couplings between technology and social systems are—albeit aligned closely to Luhmann's (1995, 1997) traditional understanding of structural couplings—applicable to AI. However, not all aspects of Reichel's concept are applicable, such as his position as "*parting with the view of technology as being socially constructed. Quite on the contrary, technology as [a] system is constructing social reality*" (Reichel, 2011, p. 117). In this book, I view AI development as a reciprocal process between various systems, where technology shapes society but society also shapes technology. Nevertheless, the intended classification of technology as a system and the nature of its structural couplings with social systems are of great relevance.

Wieland (2020) describes the nature of systems by elaborating that "modern societies are functionally differentiated and that functional systems like the economy, law and politics are mutually autonomous" (2020, p. 18). Consequently, a system is defined as

> operatively closed and [performing] their functions by assessing events using binary codes and guiding differences. Further, they apply different decision logics, which are determined by these codes and differences. However, the systems are also communicatively open and, consequently, capable of structural coupling and therefore being in relations with other systems. At its core, this system theory is based on a distinction between the system and its environment, autonomy and relationality. (Wieland, 2020, p. 11)

Thus, for the sound conceptualisation of a new system logic in Relational Economics, the following elements need to be defined for Artificial Intelligence:

1. Title of the system
2. Categorisation of the system
3. Medium applied in the system
4. Binary coding of the system
5. Guiding difference of the system
6. Structural couplings with other systems.

2.3.1 *Title of the System*

The system aiming to depict AI can either remain titled 'technology', following Reichel's (2011) suggestions, or be further specified as 'Artificial Intelligence' or 'AI'. Given its integration into Relational Economics and the aggregatory level and detail of the other system denominations in the theory, the title 'Artificial Intelligence System' seems most suitable.

2.3.2 *Categorisation of the System*

For the categorisation of the system type applicable to AI, a brief reconstruction of the previously presented research positions is necessary to make an informed decision regarding its conceptualisation:

A. Luhmann (1995, 1996, 1997) stated that there are organic, psychic, and social systems. Based on the system definitions, as presented, only the form of social systems can be applied to AI. This is because I established that AI technologies neither have an organic element nor do they—in their current form—possess agency or consciousness. Further, Luhmann argued that for the successful reproduction of communication within a system, no understanding of the true meaning that is transmitted by the communicative operations is required. It is merely the ability to reproduce communication that is required.
B. According to Esposito (2001, 2017a, 2017b), AI should only be viewed as a form of communication; thus, neither as a communicating agent nor a system in its own right. For one, it lacks the necessary consciousness to be defined as an agent and, second, it does not fulfil the criteria to be defined as an autonomous system, as it cannot reproduce itself autonomously.
C. Reichel (2011) offers three positions: The first definition identifies technology as a social system, reproducing itself via communication. Therefore, the first definition does not involve the hard elements of a technology. The second definition presents technology as a possible subsystem of existing systems, such

as science. However, this option would only be suitable if there were no representations of technology in society, such as the formation of interest groups of associations—which can be denied for both technology in general and AI in particular. As a third definition, Reichel presents technology as an entirely new autopoietic system, which requires an additional definition to Luhmann's theoretical construct. Reichel, too, states that no form of technological or artificial intelligence is required for the reproduction of the technological system. Again, it is not understanding the message conveyed via the communicative chain but the mere ability to reproduce communicative operations that is required of a system.

Given the theoretical proximity of Luhmann's (1995, 1996, 1997) original theory and the previously presented research positions of Esposito and Reichel with Wieland's (2020) theory, all of the presented arguments are applicable and transferable to the context of Relational Economics. In particular, the previously presented system definition Wieland applies is identical to Luhmann's original definition, which further substantiated this claim. The same holds true for the definitions applied by Esposito (2001, 2017a, 2017b) and Reichel (2011). Consequently, I can base my conceptualisation of AI on established research without any theoretical adaptation being required.

2.3.2.1 Element 1: Artificial Consciousness and Intelligence

The first fundamental decision I make regards the positioning of technological advancements in AI. As for research focusing on the possible existence of artificial consciousness and AI's possession of agency, I specifically exclude these research streams from the scope of this book.

This is because my aim is to provide a practice-oriented approach, where machine and deep learning technologies currently predominate (Awad & Khanna, 2015; Beaudouin et al., 2020; Doshi-Velez et al., 2017). Further, these technologies represent the technological advancements with the highest level of current market penetration, and they share significant overlaps with regard to their particular governance requirements (Nilsson, 2009). Thus, the system logic developed is applicable to both and holds true for the governance of machine as well as deep learning. By applying the technologically lower standard of machine learning to its governance model, I ensure the broad applicability of my governance approach. At the same time, due to commonalities between the two technologies, this approach includes the deep learning logic and can be applied to create governance arrangements in both contexts.

By doing so, this approach is aligned with an objective of Wieland's (2018, 2020) Relational Economics, which is, among others, to develop a theory that truthfully depicts reality; more specifically, the current economy. To this end, it applies an inherent logic applied in Wieland's (2018, 2020) research, namely identifying the least common denominator that elements share, in this case the technological advancements, to allow for inclusive and holistic governance mechanisms. By depicting the common core of the chosen AI technologies, the applicability of the governance approach is accepted for machine learning, deep learning, and eventually for future advancements in the field.

According to Luhmann (1995, 1996, 1997) and Reichel (2011), consciousness and intelligence are neither required for successful communication nor are they known to hinder the successful reproduction of communication. This allows the conclusion that both more traditional and more advanced AI technologies can be depicted in the form of the 'Artificial Intelligence System', independently of the level of consciousness or intelligence they possess. To conclude, in this book both machine and deep learning are defined as autonomously learning and self-referential technologies (Alpaydin, 2020; Chen et al., 2020; Noh et al., 2018), but neither of them is attributed with the possession of an intelligence or consciousness of their own.

2.3.2.2 Element 2: Existence of Autopoiesis in the AI System

The epistemology of autopoietic systems originally stems from empirical biology (Maturana & Varela, 1984; Rodriguez & Torres, 2007). However, the theory of autopoietic systems constitutes a meta-theoretical theory, rather than a strictly biological view. Luhmann (1996, 1998) identified this concept to be of cross-disciplinary relevance and integrated the concept of autopoiesis, according to Maturana and Varela (1984), into the discipline of sociology. While, originally, the latter developed this concept to explain organisation among living beings, Luhmann recontextualised it in order to illustrate the functioning of societies (cf., Baraldi & Corsi, 2017; Koskinen & Breite, 2020; Maturana & Varela, 1984; Rodriguez & Torres, 2007).

Maturana and Varela discovered autopoiesis, the self-creation of a new element, by analysing molecular reaction chains. They discovered that, at a certain point, the emergence of a new, specific form of reaction chains led to the existence of autonomous, self-recreational systems. By reproducing themselves, these reaction chains self-organise in a way that allows them to differentiate between their own system structure and its environment. In detail, they defined autopoiesis by five characteristics: autonomy, emergence, operative closeness, and the independent development of structures that result in autopoietic reproduction itself (cf., Maturana & Varela, 1984; Rodriguez & Torres, 2007). While stemming directly from Maturana and Varela (1984), these characteristics are commonly agreed upon by scholars from systems-theoretical schools until today (Baraldi & Corsi, 2017; Hoche, 2020; Koskinen & Breite, 2020; Luhmann, 1995, 1996, 1997; Reichel, 2011; Wieland, 2020).

The first element, the 'autonomy' of an entity, is constituted as its unique existence, a combination of various elements. The new entity is worth more than the elements on their own, and its mere existence is proof of its ability to overcome its own environment. Thus, a growing distance to its environment is an integral part of forming a new autopoietic combination of elements—a new entity (cf., Baraldi &

Corsi, 2017; Hoche, 2020; Luhmann, 1997; Maturana & Varela, 1984; Rodriguez & Torres, 2007).

The second element, the 'emergence' of a new order, can only come into place and be defined when the new order has been successfully constituted. Only then can the cells—the entities Maturana and Varela used to explain this aspect—take up their activities. In doing so, they depend on the form they are organised in and the manner in this organisation was initiated with (cf., Hoche, 2020; Maturana & Varela, 1984; Rodriguez & Torres, 2007).

The third element, the characteristic of the 'operative closeness', is constituted as follows (Maturana & Varela, 1984): the closeness of the system is defined as the prerequisite for the interaction among systems. Only by having control over the operations happening within the respective system lines can it engage in cooperation with other systems in a controlled manner. The process of reproduction within a system is restricted to elements from within the system and follows certain system-specific patterns (cf., Baraldi & Corsi, 2017; Luhmann, 1997; Maturana & Varela, 1984; Rodriguez & Torres, 2007). Further, no elements alien to the system and no alien processes exist within a system's lines. Thereby, the "*interior of the system is a realm of reduced complexity*" (Hoche, 2020, p. 1).

The 'independent development' of system structures is the fourth element, which constitutes autopoiesis: given that reproductive processes happen within the smallest entity, no structure can be applied externally. Thus, the connection among entities needs to emerge due to the alignment of reproductive processes. The environment cannot interfere, as all reaction to the environment, be it adaptive or defensive, can only be initiated by the system itself (cf., Koskinen & Breite, 2020; Maturana & Varela, 1984; Rodriguez & Torres, 2007).

Maturana and Varela (1984) explain the organisation of all living beings by applying the four elements outlined above. These four characteristics contribute to the actual reproduction of the autopoiesis of a system. Luhmann adopts this view, by defining societies as close, self-referential nets (cf., Baraldi & Corsi, 2017; Luhmann, 1995, 1996, 1997; Maturana & Varela, 1984; Rodriguez & Torres, 2007). When confronted with the allegation of having presented a merely socio-biological theory, Luhmann stated that Maturana and Varela's theory should be viewed as a meta-theory describing the very concept of life. Thus, integrating it into the discipline of sociology should not be perceived as a diminishing of sociological research tradition but its progression to a meta-theoretical discipline (cf., Baraldi & Corsi, 2017; Koskinen & Breite, 2020; Maturana & Varela, 1984; Rodriguez & Torres, 2007).

Apart from a general theoretical introduction, in the context of AI, it is precisely the functioning of input and the connection of information in autopoietic epistemology that is of importance (Hall, 2005; Koskinen & Breite, 2020). Koskinen and Breite (2020) state that "*information does not equal knowledge, but it is a process that enables knowledge creation and sharing to take place*" (2020, p. 28). They further specify that

> the autopoietic system is self-referential rather than having an input-output relationship with the environment. This means that its knowledge structure is made up of closed components of interactions that make reference only to them; that is, in this sense, the autopoietic system

> is autonomous. However, although the autopoietic system is autonomous, it will be perturbed by changes in its environment. (Koskinen & Breite, 2020, p. 28)

Hoche argues that the information included in the reproductive process is filtered according to what "*is considered meaningful and what is not. If a system fails to maintain that identity, it ceases to exist as a system and dissolves back into the environment it emerged from*" (2020, p. 4). However, Hoche defines autopoiesis more freely and states that "*autopoiesis, the filtering and processing of information from the environment, enables logical distinctions*" (2020, p. 4). He further specifies that

> autopoietic systems continually construct themselves and their perspective of reality through processing the distinction between system and environment, and re-invent themselves as the product of their own elements. (Hoche, 2020, p. 4)

In conclusion, it is four elements that characterise autopoiesis; namely, autonomy, emergence, operative closeness, and independent development of structures (Baraldi & Corsi, 2017; Hoche, 2020; Koskinen & Breite, 2020; Maturana & Varela, 1984; Reichel, 2011; Rodriguez & Torres, 2007; Wieland, 2020). After this introduction to autopoiesis, the eventuation of these characteristics in the AI context should be discussed in the next section to determine whether the AI system can be defined as an autopoietic system.

2.3.2.3 Element 3: Definition of the System Type for 'Artificial Intelligence'

As for the third element, the system type of AI, there are three system type options as identified by Reichel (2011):

1. Subsystem to another system
2. Social system
3. Autoreferential new system form.

In Option 1, Reichel (2011) argues that technology cannot be defined as a subsystem of science, for example, as it entails active entities, such as representations or associations. The same holds true for AI, as many interest groups are known that represent the need for AI development and research in AI. Furthermore, psychic systems can categorically be excluded, as AI, as presented in this book, is not granted the existence of its own conscious, human-like intelligence or agency. Neither does it possess an organic entity, such as the human body, so it cannot, therefore, be categorised as an organic system, either. This leaves options 2 and 3 for the definition of a new system for AI. In Wieland's (2018, 2020) Relational Economics, social systems are the norm, and no precedent case exists for creating a new system that follows new autopoietic rules.

Option 2, the creation of a social system, is aligned with Wieland's definition of a social system, as both authors, Wieland (2020) and Reichel (2011), define this system type as being based on communication as its mode of operation and being operatively closed. Hence, this approach taken by Reichel could be applied to Relational Economics. Further, Reichel's notion that a social system could not entail the physical elements of AI technologies and "*would act as a social proxy for physical aspect of technology*" (Reichel, 2011, p. 109) does not seem to hinder its application to AI. However, it is the dualism of AI that comes as a challenge: On the one hand, AI is influenced by societal preferences, and it is the society that decides upon the adoption and implementation of certain AI technologies by granting or negating their legitimacy. On the other hand, the dilemma is established in this book of a certain power shift that comes with AI and leads to society being confronted with lower levels of freedom of choice. To present an example, by delimiting search results according to a user's search history, an algorithm can restrict access to information, and, thereby, the user's freedom of choice.

Option 3, the creation of an entirely new system logic, should define the given "*technology as an autopoietic system distinct from society and the human individual*" (Reichel, 2011, p. 109). Reichel further specifies that "*society proceeds with its business only according to its rules, technology does by proceeding along technological rules*" (2011, p. 109). Given the rising power coming with AI technologies, estimated to change societies and economies in an unknown manner (Golić, 2019; Makridakis, 2017; Paschek et al., 2019; Pathak et al., 2019), I agree with this statement. Additionally, the autopoiesis of the technology system "*clearly does not involve any form of artificial intelligence; intelligence is not a feature of autopoiesis and not necessary for it*" (Reichel, 2011, p. 112). Hence, even technology, a system that does not possess any form of intelligence, was defined as an autopoietic system. This is because it is not necessary for the system to understand the message it is conveying via the reproduction of its communicative patterns. With this, Reichel sets the precedent for a new autopoietic system in society.

2.3.2.4 Synthesis of the Autopoietic 'Artificial Intelligence System' in Relational Economics

The sweeping and highly disruptive nature of AI was established numerous times in the course of this book, as was its technological foundation and the base and logic of its decision-making processes. Given the significantly different nature of decision logics of AI and other social systems, its independent logic needs to be acknowledged by a new governance approach for it to be effective.

As for the question of whether the approach taken in this book grants AI the possession of human-like intelligence or an own consciousness, the answer is "No". However, this approach acknowledges that recent advances in the field of deep learning enable non-explainable actions taken by the technology, which account for its self-referentiality. Still, for the scope of this book, the aforementioned characteristics of consciousness, intelligence, and agency cannot be attested (Awad & Khanna, 2015; Gilpin et al., 2019; Nilsson, 2009; Wani et al., 2020). AI technologies have emerged as a new technological element, which can communicate distinctively from former system logics and deliver data-based information. However, AI cannot communicate directly with other technologies or other actors. To do so, communicative elements which are alien to the AI technology need to be translated into AI-understandable code or instructions. Since its emergence, AI has, therefore, developed into an independent set of structures, which communicates in a closed manner.

In this respect, it is essential to note that 'communication' in Luhmann's (1996, 1998) tradition does not mean direct communication between one AI agent and another. The objects of this definition are explicitly not cases of direct interaction, such as the talking heads experiment.[6] Rather, it is the theoretical interconnectivity, conformity, and shared, all-inherent system logic that all AI technologies share, which is the base for the system definition of AI.

Once developed and implemented, an AI technology makes decisions to support its own continued existence. Like an economic organisation, the initial phase of its existence requires external support by other actors and its development according to the respective underlying system logic. In AI, this applies to its training phase. After this phase, theoretically, the AI technology can run autonomously unless its supervisor or user wants to change its decision path or the specific task it was entrusted with. Hence, AI technologies follow their own logic and apply that logic to the tasks and processes where they are employed (Nilsson, 2009). Thereby, AI technologies act in operative closeness, as they neither communicate directly with other elements nor integrate external triggers automatically into their model, algorithm, or code.

From a technological perspective, AI in its current state has been granted the status of learning and advancing itself in an autonomous and self-referential manner (Chen et al., 2020; Davenport & Kirby, 2016; Faraj et al., 2018; Noh et al., 2018). From a sociological perspective, initially, Baecker (2011), as well as Harth and Lorenz (2017) and Vogd (2020a, 2020b), concur that deep learning fulfils the requirements to be denominated as a self-referential entity. Albeit only recent technologies fall under this definition, the overall group of AI technologies in their current state entails the ability for self-referential, communicative reproduction.

Derived from these findings, I acknowledge the self-referential ability of AI, which allows for the creation of an autonomously functioning system within Relational Economics. Therefore, out of the three system-types identified—sub-systems to existing systems, social systems, and autopoietic systems—that are based on Luhmann (1995, 1996, 1997) and Reichel (2011), the third option is chosen for this book. Thus, an entirely new system type will be developed, inspired by Reichel's conceptualisation, who also decided to theorise technology as an autopoietic system. Nonetheless, I apply the fundamentals of system functionality as presented by Wieland (2018, 2020), such as defining a binary coding, a medium, and guiding differences for the new system. By doing so, the AI system can be integrated into Relational Economics and can apply an existing governance mechanism as developed by Wieland (2018, 2020).

[6] The talking heads experiment entails AI technologies playing language games with each other (Steels, 2015).

This is because AI development and implementation are viewed as a dual process, where AI is shaped by society and shapes society—both directly and indirectly. These aspects are on the same eye level, as there is no direct dependency among the AI technologies system and other systems. Rather, high levels of interconnectivity and interrelatedness can be identified on various levels. Also, by defining AI as a new, independent system form, the existence, and nature of the hybrid space between AI and humans, a research focus identified in the system-theoretical review, can be examined.

It can be argued that this decision is in line with Luhmann's own assumption that the computer of the future might require an entirely new categorisation within systems theory (Dickel, 2019; Esposito, 2017a, 2017b; Luhmann, 1997). In a posthumous publication, Luhmann (Luhmann & Kieserling, 2000) reportedly describes the true merit of communication as the ability to synthesise information, message, and understanding. The communicative construction within the system gains this ability, that allows for binary 'yes – no' answers to all possibly insecure situations emerging in the respective system. Given the vigorous effect of AI in sorting and analysing valuable information, and its self-referential learning ability which allows for independent sorting of external irritations, AI can indeed be defined as an autonomously acting and autopoietic system.

Lastly, this depiction of AI allows for the structural analysis of the interaction between civil society, economy, and AI in the form of structural coupling. Further, by focusing on the private sector, possible gains for organisations in a knowledge-based economy can be structurally depicted by displaying how separate systems based on data and communication come together and create new information. Consequently, AI will be depicted as a new system form, functioning independently of other systems, communicating autonomously as well as self-referentially, and following its own rules—which will be presented in the following sections.

2.3.3 Medium of the System 'Artificial Intelligence'

To define the medium for this new system type, I draw on Luhmann's (1995, 1996, 1997) original definition, which was adopted as such by Wieland (2018, 2020), and combines it with functional requirements stemming from the nature of AI technologies. As the conceptualisation of the AI system was developed independently of the authors identified in the research process, those authors do not necessarily need to be considered at this stage of the conceptualisation process. Hence, the medium is defined based on AI's technological requirements and Wieland's theoretical foundation.

2.3.3.1 Luhmann's Definition of a Medium

Tracing back to Luhmann's (1995, 1996, 1997) original theory, the medium is defined as the abstract entity which the system-specific code is transmitted on. Thereby, the definition of the medium in a given system is the requirement for realising communication according to a system-specific binary code.

For Luhmann, the emergence and reproduction of communication is a process which is unlikely to happen in the first place; it is the system-specific media that enable communication by dissolving exceptionally high levels of complexity. With this, Luhmann differentiates between interaction media, such as speech, and symbolic communication media types, such as the truth in science or art. The definition further includes the notion that a medium which is inherent to a system only exists in connection to the respective system it stems from. Money, for example, is only a valid medium of symbolic importance as long as the economic system it originated in exists.

Regarding the nature of a system-specific medium, there are various types of media: a medium can be of either loosely or closely linked nature. Speech is a loosely linked medium, which can be transmitted into a specific form by displaying it, for example, as a body of text. This is important, as the medium itself cannot convey information. Only when brought into form can a message be passed on; for example, words only form meaning when presented as a phrase. Communication takes place in a combination of communicative media and a specific symbolism, presenting itself, for example, as money, power, or truth. However, it is the medium that allows for the connection between systems. To present an example: speech is the medium to transmit thoughts from psychic to social systems, and an order, for example, given to a subordinate, is the respective form for the medium of power. These representations show that it is the system-specific medium making a system connectable to other systems. After this view on the theoretical demands of the medium of choice, the following section is dedicated to deriving the technology-specific requirements which complement this section's findings.

2.3.3.2 AI-Specific Requirements for the Choice of Medium

To define the medium for AI, it is crucial to understand the 'currency' AI is based upon. Hence, in the following, I display and discuss various options.

AI is commonly understood to be a digital, data-based technology (Nilsson, 2009). Further, AI possesses certain abilities of the human mind, such as reasoning and learning (Rai et al., 2019). Machine learning, a sub-discipline of AI, which is one of the technologies this book focuses on (see Chapter 1), already includes such learning techniques (Alpaydin, 2020; Bishop, 2006). Machine learning applies the abilities mentioned above, e.g., to recognise recurring patterns as well as to develop and learn new rules (Awad & Khanna, 2015; Nilsson, 2009). To conclude, AI in its current state has the "*ability to interpret external data correctly, to learn from such data, and to use those learnings to achieve specific goals and tasks through flexible adaptation*"

(Kaplan & Haenlein, 2019, p. 3). By applying this definition to the development of the 'Artificial Intelligence System' in Relational Economics, AI is considered a self-learning technology that can autonomously generate learning processes and the resulting creation of information (Davenport & Faraj et al., 2018; Kirby, 2016). To determine the medium with which such a system operates, the elements included in the chosen concept require definition.

At this stage, the requirements for an autopoietic system that functions based on data, and the demand on AI technologies trained on data, coincide. However, the question remains whether AI runs on data or if it functions based on processed forms of data, such as information or even knowledge. Therefore, the concepts of data, information, knowledge, and their interrelation are delimited briefly to decide on the medium for AI.

According to Ackoff (1989), data is defined as symbols that "*represent the properties of objects and events*" (1989, p. 3) and have no further meaning (cf., Bellinger et al., 2004). Liew (2007) agrees with that definition. However, he adds that data can either exist in the form of symbols, and signals (cf., Haun, 2002), such as light and smell, or in the form of syntax (Rehäuser & Krcmar, 1996). Liew continues that, by being of representative nature, all data is, per se, a depiction of past events (cf., Haun, 2002). Numerous authors have shared this definition (Ackoff, 1989; Bellinger et al., 2004; Haun, 2002; Hislop, 2005; Hislop et al., 2018; Koskinen & Breite, 2020; Liew, 2007), which is why it is applied in this book.

Information is created by processing and contextualising this data. By providing higher informative content to the recipient, information is to be granted a higher order in relevance than data (Haun, 2002; Liew, 2007). Ackoff (1989) concludes that data is of structural nature. In contrast, information presents functional, comprised insight. Information contains a "*meaningful pattern*" (Hislop, 2005, p. 15), as additional elements were added to the raw data (Hislop, 2005). Thereby, information can explain questions, such as why, what, or how (Bellinger et al., 2004; Koskinen & Breite, 2020). Furthermore, according to Liew, information

> contains relevant meaning, implication, or input for decision and/or action. Information comes from both current (communication) and historical sources. In essence, the purpose of information is to aid in making decisions and/or solving problems or realizing an opportunity. (2007, p. 5)

Thus, only when data is processed into information can it become of future relevance; for example, by offering future prognostics (Haun, 2002; Liew, 2007).

In his conceptual paper, Reichel (2011) applies the following definition to the concept of 'information':

> Information shall be understood here as a pattern that influences the formation and transformation of other patterns. A pattern shall be understood as an order of any sort. The carrier of the pattern is of no importance, it "has an integrity independent of the medium by virtue of which you have received the information that it exists. (Fuller, 1982, 505.201)

At this point, the difference between Reichel's (2011) contribution and this book becomes fully apparent: Reichel focuses on technology, consisting of physical and non-physical elements, such as hardware and software. However, he does not focus on the content itself or the process with which the technology creates information. In contrast, AI—as the field of application in this book—is a fully digitalised entity whose main attribute is the creation of information and solving of content-related tasks. Contrary to Reichel's position, in AI, data, as the 'carrier of the pattern', is of great importance for identifying the pattern itself. While information is created when the medium serves as a connector between AI entities, or the 'Artificial Intelligence System' and other systems, the existence of information is strongly connected and intertwined with the medium as such. Therefore, the definition of information and the resulting identification of the medium, as Reichel deployed the terms, cannot serve this book for further reference.

Knowledge, the highest-order element in this triad, is traditionally defined as created by the processing of information through the human mind (Haun, 2002). At the same time, knowledge is understood to be the final outcome of the human mind's information-based learning process (Haun, 2002). Hislop (2005) offers a more general definition, stating that "*knowledge can be understood to emerge from the application, analysis, and productive use of data and/or information*" (2005, p. 15). Hislop argues that, by the interpretation of information and via its contextualisation within the reference system of the user, an additional "*layer of intellectual analysis*" (2005, p. 15), or simply put, a meaning, is added (Bellinger et al., 2004). Liew (2007) consequently summarises knowledge as a threefold process, consisting of the cognition of information, the ability to act on this insight, and understanding the message conveyed by the information. In the context of business, it is on the level of knowledge building that organisational value is created.

The relation among data, information, and knowledge is of triad-like nature. However, the fundamental interconnections of this triad can be summoned to function mainly in a unidirectional manner. Only after the basic connection is founded do those iterative processes of complementing the initial data take place: Fundamentally, data serves as a base to identify patterns which lead to insight and information, which again forms the foundation for knowledge creation. Nevertheless, knowledge can help identify and analyse new sets of data and new information, making the connection partly circular. Thus, the fundamental connection is the linear connection that begins with data, as depicted in Fig. 2.3:

When this connection is established, the knowledge gained is then applied to recontextualise the data and information analysed previously.

After having viewed said elements in a theoretical manner, in the context of AI, it is essential to contextualise them with digital technologies: Data and information have

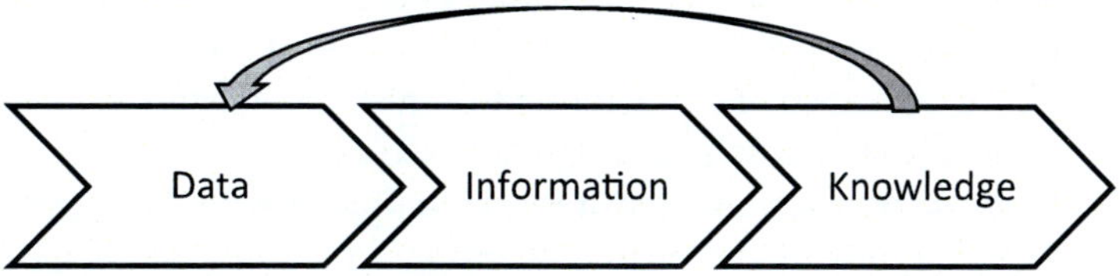

Fig. 2.3 Own depiction of interrelation among data, information, and knowledge

already become a part of connected systems through the development and implementation of the internet. The internet allows for a network of individual nets, all of which possess their own data. To present an example: Organisations that use telecommunication infrastructure and e-mail communication via the internet each represent a net—an effective measure due to the use of the internet and, often, cloud solutions (Haun, 2002; Singh et al., 2015). Thus, even without applying AI, dataflows exist across departments, organisations, and national borders (Aaronson, 2019; Abraham et al., 2019; Alhassan et al., 2018).

With the application of AI, these data flows, and company-specific data can be used to gain information relevant to the respective task, position, or organisation (Hartmann & Henkel, 2020; Tarafdar et al., 2019). As a result of this, the algorithms can substitute the role of the human mind and step in at the process of creating information. In this process, the human-like abilities recent AI technologies already possess are applied to solve tasks and create information (Alpaydin, 2020; Bishop, 2006; Hartmann & Henkel, 2020; Tarafdar et al., 2019).

Finally, the information created by the AI technologies based on dataflows can be formed into knowledge through human-AI interaction. It is in this hybrid space where the potential for new knowledge creation lies. According to Ackoff (1989) and Bellinger et al. (2004), wisdom is the highest form of knowledge creation, as it is "*an extrapolative and non-deterministic, non-probabilistic process*" (2004, p. 2). Furthermore, Bellinger et al. state that it "*beckons to give us understanding about which there has previously been no understanding, and in doing so, goes far beyond understanding itself. It is the essence of philosophical probing*" (Bellinger et al., 2004, p. 2). Thus, it can be concluded that AI runs on data and can create information, which in turn can be developed into knowledge in the form of human-machine interaction. Wisdom creation, however, will remain a human ability (Ackoff, 1989; Bellinger et al., 2004; Liew, 2013).

2.3.3.3 Choice of Medium

Regarding AI, the conceptualisation of the system-specific medium for the newly developed system has particularly far-reaching consequences. This is because AI, as a general-purpose technology, will influence each system in society (Brynjolfsson & McAfee, 2017; Dafoe, 2018; Goldfarb et al., 2019; Klinger et al., 2018; Nepelski & Sobolewski, 2020; Razzkazov, 2020; Trajtenberg, 2018). Due to the particular importance of this system and the expected interaction with all other systems, it is crucial that the medium for AI truly depicts the nature of the system. Only by doing so will it enable the visualisation of connections between all systems of society and allow their successful governance. Thus, data is not only the essential requirement and element of AI but also of modern economy and society:

Data can only be transformed into information patterns, and consequently, into knowledge by the informed and enabled consumer or user (Hartmann & Henkel, 2020; Liew, 2007; Tarafdar et al., 2019). Furthermore, differentiation and free choice among all existing options are only possible when the systems involved allow that choice and portray those options. To draw on an example presented by Wieland (2002): for a social revolution to begin, the dependent party needs to have access to data and to be able to convert the data into information, in order to be able to use this information in their favour. With this, the dependents can identify and understand their situation, and in consequence, use the information available to change their circumstances (Wieland, 2002). While this may seem to portray an extreme example, similar tendencies have been identified by research in the field of AI ethics. In this field, scientific and popular publications claim that the dense competition and concentration of power among very few companies leading in AI present the risk of high levels of resulting social dependency (Floridi et al., 2020; Whittaker et al., 2018).

Finally, Wieland (2002) states that information forms the base for knowledge, which, however, can only ever be reached through a process of human interaction and shared experience. According to Wieland (2002), in an information- and knowledge-based economy, which is no longer led by access to production sites and force of labour, access to information and knowledge creation become the decisive factor in competition. To build his argument, Wieland draws on Nonaka (1991), who describes the functioning of the knowledge-based economy as follows:

> In an economy where the only certainty is uncertainty, the one sure source of lasting competitive advantage is knowledge. Where markets shift, technologies proliferate, competitors multiply, and products become obsolete almost overnight, successful companies are those that consistently create a new knowledge. (1991, p. 22)

Thus, in a knowledge economy, the demand rises for collaboration to create knowledge among actors of all kinds, especially of economic actors. Again, this hints at the need for effective trans-sectoral governance in the pursuit of lasting competitive advantages.

In conclusion, data is identified as the medium the 'Artificial Intelligence System' is set upon. Following the above definitions of data, information, and knowledge creation, data is the basic requirement for the successful training of an algorithm and lasting gains in information. Thus, it is through the combination of data and the trained algorithm that data becomes information. Proceeding from this base, the structural interaction of the AI system with society and economy then allows for the creation of knowledge, enabling the parties involved to gain lasting advantages.

2.3.4 Binary Coding of the System 'Artificial Intelligence'

Having identified 'data' as the communicative foundation for the binary coding of AI, the next requirement is to define the binary code itself. According to Wieland, "*systems are operatively closed and perform their functions by assessing events using binary codes and guiding differences. Further, they apply different decision logics, which are determined by these codes and differences*" (2020, p. 11). Following this line of thought, the new system's binary coding will determine all the following elements; namely, the guiding difference, structural coupling, and the governance process among the various systems themselves. Thus, the binary code needs to depict the system's true nature, as it is the one element whose reproduction will ensure the continuity of the system.

The following Table 2.1 by Wieland (2020) portrays standardised systems, which occur in any given society. Further, it summarises the system-specific binary codes as well as respective guiding differences. Therefore, as depicted in Table 2.1, it will serve as a base for the definition of this binary code:

If AI was viewed in terms of the code-based nature of the technologies, all events would be assessed on whether or not their interaction with other technological elements functions or whether the technology itself is able to process the

Table 2.1 Overview of binary codes and guiding differences, as presented by Wieland (2020, p. 58)

	Binary Codes		Guiding Difference
	Market Payment – Non-payment	↔	Firm Earnings – Costs
	Politics Power – Non-power	↔	Political Parties Govern – Oppose
	Law Legal – Illegal	↔	Courts of Law Guilty – Non-guilty
RT=	Civil Society The Common Good – Private Interests	↔	NGO Engagement – Non-Engagement
	Ethics Right – Wrong	↔	Moral Agency Conformity – Non-conformity
	Religion Transcendence – Immanence	↔	Religious Communities Belief – Non-belief
	Science True – False	↔	Universities Academic – Not-academic

task in question. Following Reichel's (2011) proposition, the binary coding for such a technological system should be defined as 'work – fail'. Thus, if technological interaction and application functions, it is ascribed the term 'work', whereas in the opposite case, it has failed.

In this book I view AI as a code-based model, which belongs to the software, rather than hardware, category. For Reichel (2011), the technology system explicitly includes both. However, the binary code is inherent to the code-level of the 'Artificial Intelligence System': For one thing, code languages apply the very nature of binary coding. Thereby, code-based technologies, such as AI, can be contextualised within Luhmann's (1995, 1996, 1997) and Wieland's (2020) conceptual model without any adaptation. Furthermore, due to more recent advancements in AI, specifically in deep learning, newer technologies learn by and are based on their own algorithmic experience (Harth & Lorenz, 2017; Vogt, 2020a, 2020b). Thus, AI realises new forms of self-referencing and learning that result from iterative learning processes. In these processes, the binary code 'work – fail', as presented by Reichel (2011) for the system technology, is applied by the algorithm as part of the learning process (Awad & Khanna, 2015; Beaudouin et al., 2020; Doshi-Velez et al., 2017; Nilsson, 2009). The following statement from Reichel partially holds true for the learning process of the algorithm and any AI technology:

> The evolution of technology as system is then driven by information about the working or failing of technology, with working as the preferred side and with failing as useful information into which directions not to go. (2011, p. 111)

Nonetheless, the binary code 'work – fail' does not entail the information-based operations of an AI technology. Again, Reichel's focus is on the operational functionality of a technology. In contrast, I take on the perspective of the respective, active entity: like the firm, the 'Artificial Intelligence System' observes its environment from the perspective of its own operations. The market structures transactions according to 'payment – non-payment'. Likewise, the 'Artificial Intelligence System' analyses the content it is applied to and its environment according to system-specific preferences, which are presented in the following. Hence, for this system level, in this book, I suggest the following binary code (Table 2.2):

Based on the collected information, the binary coding of the system 'Artificial Intelligence' as 'matching – non-matching' seems most suitable. This code describes the AI system's active decision when confronted with new information for the solution of its task. Compared to the binary code 'work – fail', which rather describes the learning process of AI, this code entails and describes both its decision-making and filtering process. Further, it entails the operative decision logic of the system, which ensures its continued existence. This is since, to solve its task, the AI needs to filter relevant data and information, as is presented in detail in the following.

A fitting example to describe this binary code stems from the field of AI ethics. Frequently, the concern is raised that AI serves as a channel or filter, which pre-sorts search findings and aggregates as well as filtering information before offering it to the consumer (Danaher, 2018; Floridi et al., 2018; Hagendorff, 2020; Milano et al.,

Table 2.2 Own depiction of binary code for 'artificial intelligence, based on Wieland (2020)

Binary Code
AI Technologies System
Matching – Non-Matching

2020). The general idea of technologies shaping social interaction and decision-making was also raised by Reichel (2011), who stated that "*technology as [a] system is constructing social reality*" (2011, p. 117). While I understand this evaluation to be correct, the ethical concern is mainly about the lack of transparency regarding this algorithm-controlled sorting of information.

On a technological level, the algorithm's actual operation does indeed classify information as relevant or irrelevant to the algorithmic objective. More specifically, the algorithm analyses the encountered information regarding its value for the task or question that it was given. With this, the algorithm categorises information as 'matching – non-matching' to achieve the respective task. At this stage, it is important to note that biases within the AI system often happen due to biassed data sets or systems, but not necessarily because of externally biassed evaluation of data (Dastin, 2018; Roselli et al., 2019; Silberg & Manyika, 2019). Consequently, the binary code as suggested in this book truly depicts the operative action conducted by an AI technology, rather than depicting its internal decision-making process. This binary code further inheres to two aspects of AI operations: for one, it represents the algorithm-led or algorithm-controlled filtering process. Moreover, it illustrates the algorithmic mode of action, that is, the lenses with which the algorithm operates, when fed new data (Awad & Khanna, 2015; Beaudouin et al., 2020; Doshi-Velez et al., 2017; Nilsson, 2009).

Furthermore, via the medium of data, a given algorithm, and ultimately the 'Artificial Intelligence System', is provided with the necessary base for its operations. To draw a comparison, in the economic system, money is the medium for economic actors, and they filter information conveyed via this medium according to 'payment – non-payment'. The same holds true for AI technologies, and, consequently, the 'Artificial Intelligence System': as organisations operate based on the medium of money, data is the currency AI technologies are run on. If the data received by the AI technology fits its task and scope, it will be tagged as 'matching'. Thus, it leads to a positive, because desired, reaction chain. If the data does not match the scope of the AI technology, it is denominated as 'non-matching'—much as withholding money leads to the economically undesired reaction, 'non-payment' (Wieland, 2018, 2020).

To conclude, the 'Artificial Intelligence System' is operatively closed and carries out its operations by assessing upcoming events, as well as applying its binary code (Luhmann, 1995, 1996; Wieland, 2018, 2020). It functions as a never-ending chain of events within the algorithm, which leads to constant decision-making processes. The outcome of this decision-making process becomes tangible in the form of information presented to the AI technology's environment, e.g., the consumer, or another machine, which works based on those findings.

2.3.5 Guiding Difference of the 'Artificial Intelligence System'

Guiding differences serve as the "*operationalisation of the system's binary coding*" (Wieland, 2020, p. 62). To draw on Wieland's example of the market,

> the binary market code 'payment – non-payment' and the firm's guiding code 'earnings – costs' are in a relationship of mutual causality. Successfully combining the two is the life's blood of the economy. (2020, p. 24)

Hence, he further states that system-native actors operate

> based on the positive, value-creating aspects of this guiding difference. In a given timeframe, for every rational actor, the earnings or revenues from his or her resources must be greater than the costs associated with them. (2020, p. 22)

To conclude: while a system is based on binary coding, it reveals itself to other actors via its guiding difference, which determines the system-native actors' decision-making.

Within the system 'Artificial Intelligence', the individual AI technologies (consisting of data, algorithms, and a model, such as a neural network) form a separate entity, as organisations do within the economy. Thus, the overarching system 'Artificial Intelligence' comprises numerous separate operating entities of 'AI Technology',[7] which all apply the same basic decision logic. Consequently, the individual entity applies a guiding difference, such as the organisation and AI technologies. In the case of AI, internal processes, especially regarding deep learning technologies, remain non-transparent to the environment. Thereby, it is merely the output of the 'AI Technology' that can be evaluated by applying the guiding difference. The guiding difference applied by an 'AI Technology' will not display why an 'AI Technology' chose specific options but focus on the value created for and within the model. Thus, as Wieland presents for the economic actor, the focus will be on the "*value-creating aspects of this guiding difference*" (2020, p. 22).

---

[7] AI Technology is spelled in upper-case letters when referring to the theoretical concept. If AI is referred to as a practical example, the spelling will remain in lower-case letters.

Three possible variations for such a guiding difference in the 'Artificial Intelligence System' seem to depict the nature of an AI technology, as all three options portray a critical facet of the operating mode of AI technologies. However, it is essential to choose the one option which continues the line of thought applied to system logics, as established by Maturana and Varela (1984), continued by Luhmann (1995, 1996, 1997), and further developed by Wieland (2020).

Option 1 focuses on whether or not the data received by the AI technology is informative for the completion of the task it was entrusted with (Table 2.3). Thereby, this first approach focuses on the outcome of the algorithmic decision and the question if the data carries information within the scope of the task.

Option 2 shifts the perspective towards the algorithm and the quality of the technological model itself (Table 2.4). By asking whether the quality of the data received will allow for the enhancement of the algorithmic model, the AI technology categorises encountered information according to AI- 'enhancing – non-enhancing'. Consequently, this option's focus lies on the learning processes performed by the algorithm. With this, the question posed in this scenario is whether the data quality encountered is sufficient to allow for the further development of the AI technology applying the algorithm.

Option 3 offers a slightly different view on the algorithmic model, as it focuses on whether the data set received by the model will enrich the existing data set (Table 2.5).

Table 2.2 Own depiction for AI guiding difference, option 1—focus on scope of AI technology

Binary Code		Guiding Difference
Artificial Intelligence System		AI Technology
Matching – Non-Matching	⇔	Informative – Non-Informative

Table 2.4 Own depiction for AI guiding difference, option 2—focus on technological enhancement of AI Technology

Binary Code		Guiding Difference
Artificial Intelligence System		AI Technology
Matching – Non-Matching	⇔	Enhancing – Non-Enhancing

Table 2.5 Own depiction for AI guiding difference, option 3—focus on data enrichment of AI technology

Binary Code	Guiding Difference
Artificial Intelligence System	AI Technology
Matching – Non-Matching	Enriching – Non-Enriching

More concretely, it centres around the question of whether the new data can enrich the information already received by the AI technology during its training phase. Here, the focus is on the further development of the algorithm's decision ability.

All three options presented have advantages regarding their conceptualisation within Relational Economics. The first option allows for a stronger outcome orientation. In contrast, the second and third facilitate a process-focused inspection of the AI technology. However, Option 2, 'enhancing – non-enhancing', and Option 3, 'enriching – non-enriching', could be synthesised under Option 2, given their shared focus on the betterment of the respective AI technology. As the data serves as a base for enhancing algorithmic elements within the model, I argue that Option 2, 'enhancing – non-enhancing', is the more practical variation of the two aligning options. Furthermore, much as for the entity of the 'firm', 'enhancing – non-enhancing' focuses on the continued existence of the technology, which is in line with existing system logics in Relational Economics. Hence, it is the more suitable option.

Consequently, the decision regarding the guiding difference of the system remains between Option 1 and Option 2. For the final step of the conceptualisation of this system element, two factors need to be taken into account: For one, the continuity of the system logic, as set with the binary coding of the system, needs to be factored into the choice of a fitting guiding difference. Second, the self-interested element of the actor applying the algorithm needs to be part of the decision process, too. To present an example: within the system of the 'Market', the organisation, as an active entity, decides in its own best interest, which in turn ensures its continued existence. In detail, the organisation evaluates events according to cost and earnings, with earnings being the economically preferred decision outcome (Wieland, 2020). In the guiding difference for AI, the same striving for continuity in system logic and operative success needs to be reflected.

The 'Artificial Intelligence System' works based on the binary decision code of 'matching – non-matching'. Thereby, the decision process regarding information that an AI system encounters is depicted in a general manner. For the guiding difference to continue this line of thought, the AI's successful reproduction and continuity, that is, the algorithms own enhancement, need to be constantly fostered. The informative aspect of data encountered by an AI technology is an important factor regarding an ethical evaluation of AI adoption and implementation. However, for the success of the AI technology, the quality of its technological 'foundation', namely of the algorithm and model, is most relevant. Thus, within the system logic of 'Artificial Intelligence', Option 2 seems the most suitable alternative for the guiding difference.

2.3.6 Outlook on Structural Couplings with 'Artificial Intelligence System'

As the final step of introducing AI to Relational Economics (Wieland, 2018, 2020), I subsume its interconnection with other systems.

2.3.6.1 Theoretical Background on the Structural Coupling among Systems

The potential for structural couplings among systems is given due to their respective communicative openness (Luhmann, 1995, 1996; Wieland, 2018, 2020). Specifically, Wieland states that "*systems are also communicatively open and, consequently, capable of structural coupling and therefore being in relations with other systems*" (2020, p. 11). Further, Wieland (2020) defines contexts, decision logics, and system-specific languages as being interconnected. Consequently, he presents a three-levelled concept to define points of interconnection.

First, polycontextuality depicts the difference between the system and environment and is distinguished by higher levels of complexity outside than inside the system. This level directly stems from Maturana and Varela's (1984), as well as Luhmann's (1995, 1996, 1997) definition of autopoietic systems but adds the notion of a system being embedded in various contexts. Thereby, Wieland (2020) hints at the diversity of environmental contexts, instead of merely differentiating between system and environment. According to Wieland,

> polycontextuality [...] describe[s] the fact that modern societies consist of multiple systems that serve as environments, existential and operational conditions for one another [...]; however, there is no relation of 'embeddedness' or hierarchy. (2020, p. 11)

As Wieland negates the firm's traditional economic view as a monolingual economic actor, polycontextuality depicts the interconnectedness of a firm by confirming the "*constitutive need for and ability of economic actors to connect and act in various social contexts*" (2020, p. 11). Hence, polycontextualism allows the definition of the functionality of a given system as well as the operational implementation and actual management of the demand directed towards a company by its stakeholders.

Second, successful interaction with other systems requires a reduction of both system-internal levels of complexity and the complexity of the environment. This constitutes the second level of Wieland's (2018, 2020) concept: polycontexturality focuses on the structural coupling of different decision logics as "*the unity of difference of system and environment*" (Wieland, 2020, p. 12). In the process of this alignment, not only the decision logic and the binary code but also the system-specific languages are aligned, the latter being defined as polylingualism. Hence, polylingualism is the third and final level of Wieland's concept.

Achieving a reduction in complexity associated with these interconnections requires structural couplings – an alignment of system logics. The process of coupling is at the core of polycontextural governance and "*involves the categorical relationalisation of various logics (binary codes, guiding differences) and their corresponding language modes (polylingualism)*" (Wieland, 2020, p. 12). This quote depicts how the three levels of governing interconnections in a complex, multi-system environment are interdependent elements within the Relational Governance approach. Thus, before developing this governance approach for AI on a polycontextural level, possible couplings need to be understood from a polycontextual perspective.

The actual governance action is based on the smallest entity of structural couplings, which is the event itself. The diverse resources needed to perform a given task lead to events inherently consisting of relations between various other events. Through a Relational Governance approach, the relations between said events are activated (Wieland, 2018, 2020). Drawing on Luhmann's differentiation (1995, 1996, 1997), these particular relations among events depict the actual structural coupling. More specifically, the realisation of structural couplings happens on the micro-level of events, rather than on the macro-level of systems.

To present an example: consumers purchasing socially responsibly produced goods combine various system logics, which in return present a multidimensional, hence, relational value (Wieland, 2020). By aligning the system demand through its governance structure, the firm creates a formerly non-existent relational value in the form of a socially and ethically responsible, yet economically profitable product. Purchasing such a good allows consumers to raise and produce economic value, but also social and ethical value, as the price is no longer the only decision criterion. Wieland connects this view to research on collaborative forms of value creation (Arnould & Thompson, 2005; Grönroos & Voima, 2013; Wieland, 2020), a decision which is in line with the inherent aim of this book: presenting a Relational Governance approach that allows for collaborative value creation through AI and turns negative externalities into relational value. Traditionally,

> events are portrayed as negative external effects because they cannot be quantified or reflected in the pricing language used by the market. Accordingly, each must be transformed into a polycontextually compatible term, which in turn shapes the course of development for the process of internalising externalities. (Wieland, 2020, p. 91)

Wieland even outlines a precedent case for this objective by stating that, regarding social systems:

> the societal discourse must first of all succeed in translating the negative external effects of economic transactions (human rights violations, failing to comply with social standards,

lack of sustainability) into a variety of language games, which are compatible with multiple systems. (2020, p. 91)

According to Wieland (2020), the title "*permits this structural coupling, as it holds economic, organisational, legal and societal connotations that allow the subject matter involved to be cooperatively addressed*" (2020, p. 91). The realisation and success of such a relational form of value creation be enabled through the governance structure of the firm and can include every system in society. Thus, consumer awareness and demand can serve as a push factor as well as, for example, the introduction of new laws,[8] be it hard or soft law[9] (Wieland, 2020). Hence, for a company, one widespread form of relational value creation happens via the introduction of "*innovative products or policies with a societal welfare component*" (Wieland, 2020, p. 91). As for AI, to achieve this inclusion, all systems involved, as well as their interdependencies, need to be analysed and aligned.

2.3.6.2 Scope of Structural Couplings with the 'Artificial Intelligence System'

As initially suggested by Baecker (2016), from a sociological perspective, the interaction and interrelation of systems are best analysed in the context of structural couplings, which allow for the inclusion of non-human communicators (Harth & Lorenz, 2017).

Due to the all-encompassing nature of the AI phenomenon, which is best resumed with being a 'general-purpose technology' (Brynjolfsson & McAfee, 2017; Dafoe, 2018; Goldfarb et al., 2019; Klinger et al., 2018; Nepelski & Sobolewski, 2020; Razzkazov, 2020; Trajtenberg, 2018), structural couplings are to be expected with all other social systems –sooner rather than later. Figure 2.4 gives an overview of the societal systems identified by Wieland (2020) and the new system, 'Artificial Intelligence':

As marked in Fig. 2.4, the focus of Relational AI Governance is on two structural couplings of the 'Artificial Intelligence System', namely with the 'Market' and with 'Ethics' (Wieland, 2020).

I choose to focus on the 'Market' and its coupling with the 'Artificial Intelligence System' due to their many interconnections. For one, I apply a private sector perspective to AI governance. Again, this is since the consequences of economic competition make this sector one of the main drivers for AI development and adoption (Dafoe, 2018; Makridakis, 2017; Polyakova & Boyer, 2018; PwC, 2019). Thereby, the effect of AI on society is accelerated through the economy. Furthermore, AI has a direct

[8] An example for this is the German supply chain law against exploitation in global supply chains, passed in spring 2021 (cf., von Westphalen, 2020).

[9] Hard law is defined as legally binding, whereas soft law is not legally binding (Abbott & Snidal, 2000), e.g., the IEEE Global Initiative on Ethics of Autonomous and Intelligent System (Marchant, 2019).

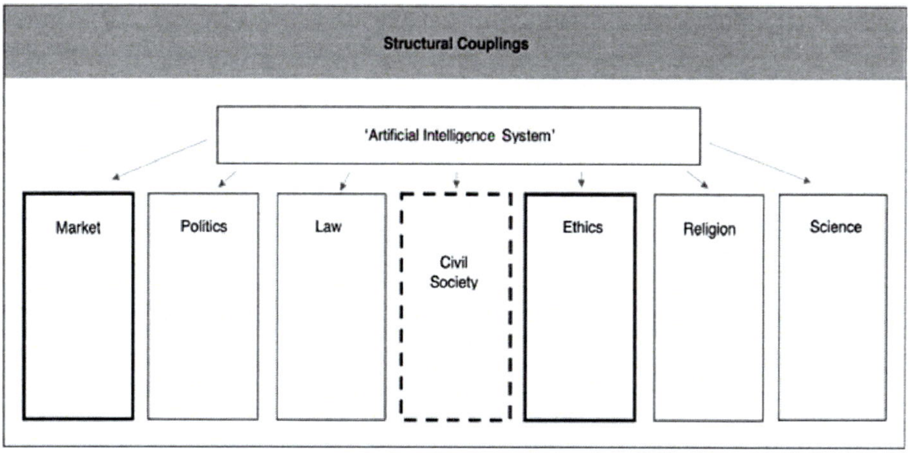

Fig. 2.4 Own depiction of expected structural couplings with 'artificial intelligence system'

effect on the economy, e.g., on its growth (Bresnahan & Trajtenberg, 1995; Klinger et al., 2018; Nepelski & Sobolewski, 2020; Petralia, 2020).

Further, management practices, such as CSR, show that it is indeed possible to create relational value through a governance process including various system logics. To do so, system logics are aligned via the Relational Governance approach, which ensures the continuity of a firm in the market, as well as the simultaneous creation of societal welfare (Wieland, 2018, 2020). It is through the governance form of the firm, that the relations among systems are materialised, that the resources are combined, and relational value is created. Hence, by applying this governance approach, firms can secure sustainable competitive advantages, e.g., in the form of reputational gains for ethically responsible AI development. With this, they avoid negative costs like reputational losses for not having implemented a suitable AI ethics strategy (Hagendorff, 2020; Mittelstadt, 2019). Thereby, the private sector is able to implement AI governance and ensure its social compatibility (Brundage et al., 2018; Bryson, 2018; Cihon, 2019; Schwab & Davis, 2018).

Due to the chosen definition of the firm as a nexus of stakeholders, the economic system is inherently connected to other systems in society (Wieland, 2018, 2020). Therefore, the second structural coupling this book focuses on is that of 'Artificial Intelligence' and 'Ethics'. Structurally, this coupling follows the same logic as the coupling of the 'Market', in the form of 'Business' and, again, 'Ethics', as presented by Wieland (2018, 2020). While the latter systematically addresses "*moral-economic events*" (Wieland, 2020, p. 12), AI ethics subsumes moral-technological events, which originate in the Artificial Intelligence and Ethics systems. Hence, academic advancements in the field of AI ethics are systematically depicted within the model through a structural coupling.

As the ethical evaluation of AI mostly stems from its effect on societies, a societal perspective is inherent to the ethical evaluation of AI. Hence, the system 'Civil

Society' is marked with a dashed line—depicting its indirect integration into Relational AI Governance. Furthermore, I adopt Reichel's (2011) hypothesis that an autopoietic, technological system, in this case, the 'Artificial Intelligence System', shapes society and vice versa. Therefore, there is another indirect connection between AI and society: not only does AI have an effect on society and shape its development, but society also shapes the development and training of an AI technology. Regarding the impact and role of the technology system, Reichel (2011) concludes:

> Technology has progressed through establishing multiple couplings with its environment: with the human designers and users of technology, but even more with society and its function systems. Clearly this progress is co-evolutionary and technology appears to have managed to infuse its code and internal conduct into society as well as the mind of the engineer. [...] Through this coupling society constructs reality through the lens of technology and there appears to be no way out of a technological trajectory for social evolution. This clearly is parting with the view of technology as being socially constructed. Quite on the contrary, technology as system is constructing social reality. Not only is the future of technology solely decided within and through technology, but the future of society is also decided technologically. (2011, pp. 116–117)

I agree that the connection between AI and society is reciprocal in nature.

In conclusion, this book addresses the aforementioned structural couplings of the 'Artificial Intelligence System' with the 'Market' and 'Ethics'. Nonetheless, other structural couplings are of great relevance for the successful adoption of AI by society, such as couplings with 'Law' and 'Politics', but are outside its scope.

2.3.7 Contributions and Critical Reflection

The conceptualisation presented in this chapter makes two academic contributions:

For one, there is a research gap in sociology, particularly for research originating in Luhmann's theory. Until today, no scholar has examined the option of conceptualising AI as a new, autopoietic system in society. Leading researchers mostly refer to AI as a form of communication (Esposito, 2017a, 2017b) or discuss its characterisation as an agent (Baecker, 2011, 2015). Despite recognising the growing importance of AI for sociology (Bammé, 2017; Dickel, 2017; Donick, 2019; Harth & Lorenz, 2017) and the call for new sociological concepts to define AI (Dickel, 2019; Fuchs, 2020; Vogt, 2020a, 2020b), no other paths have been explored. However, one publication entertains the idea of conceptualising the broader definition of 'technology' as an autopoietic system in society (Reichel, 2011). In this book, I have combined this impulse with the theoretical foundation of Luhmann's theory, as adopted by Wieland (2014, 2018, 2020), and developed a new definition of AI as an autopoietic system in Luhmann's tradition for Relational Economics.

Moreover, this book connects Relational Economics to the general-purpose technology, AI, which has and will continue to have a tremendous effect on the global economy. Therefore, any modern economic theory should be able to address this phenomenon theoretically. Since no precedent case exists for the conceptualisation of AI as an autopoietic system, it was established entirely conceptually, and I acknowledge that extensive research and empirical testing are required to formalise her conceptual proposition.

References

Aaronson, S. A. (2019). Data is different, and that's why the world needs a new approach to governing cross-border data flows. *Digital Policy, Regulation and Governance* (CIGI Papers, 197). Centre for International Governance Innovation. https://www.cigionline.org/sites/default/files/documents/paper%20no.197_0.pdf

Aaronson, S. A., & Leblond, P. (2018). Another digital divide: The rise of data realms and its implications for the WTO. *Journal of International Economic Law, 21*(2), 245–272. https://doi.org/10.1093/jiel/jgy019

Abbott, K. W., & Snidal, D. (2000). Hard and soft law in international governance. *International Organization, 54*(3), 421–456. https://doi.org/10.1162/002081800551280

Abraham, R., Schneider, J., & vom Brocke, J. (2019). Data governance: A conceptual framework, structured review, and research agenda. *International Journal of Information Management, 49*, 424–438. https://doi.org/10.1016/j.ijinfomgt.2019.07.008

Ackoff, R. L. (1989). From data to wisdom. *Journal of Applied Systems Analysis, 16*(1), 3–9. http://www-public.imtbs-tsp.eu/~gibson/Teaching/Teaching-ReadingMaterial/Ackoff89.pdf

Aghion, P., Jones, B. F., & Jones, C. I. (2017). *Artificial intelligence and economic growth* (No. w23928). National Bureau of Economic Research. https://web.stanford.edu/~chadj/AJJ-AIandGrowth.pdf

Agrawal, A., Gans, J., & Goldfarb, A. (2016). The simple economics of machine intelligence. *Harvard Business Review, 17*, 2–5. https://hbr.org/2016/11/the-simple-economics-of-machine-intelligence

Alhassan, I., Sammon, D., & Daly, M. (2018). Data governance activities: A comparison between scientific and practice-oriented literature. *Journal of Enterprise Information Management, 31*(2), 300–316. https://doi.org/10.1108/JEIM-01-2017-0007

Almeida, V., Filgueiras, F., & Gaetani, F. (2020). Digital governance and the tragedy of the commons. *IEEE Internet Computing, 24*(4), 41–46. https://doi.org/10.1109/MIC.2020.2979639

Alpaydin, E. (2020). *Introduction to machine learning* (4th ed.). MIT Press.

Arnould, E. J., & Thompson, C. J. (2005). Consumer culture theory (CCT): Twenty years of research. *Journal of Consumer Research, 31*(4), 868–882. https://doi.org/10.1086/426626

Awad, M., & Khanna, R. (2015). *Machine learning: Efficient learning machines*. Apress.

Baecker, D. (2001). Niklas Luhmann in der Gesellschaft der Computer. *Merkur, 627*, 597–609. https://volltext.merkur-zeitschrift.de/article/99.120210/mr-55-7-597

Baecker, D. (2011). Who qualifies for communication? A systems perspective on human and other possibly intelligent beings taking part in the next society. *Technikfolgenabschätzung—Theorie und Praxis, 20*(1), 17–26. https://doi.org/10.14512/tatup.20.1.17

Baecker, D. (2014). *Neurosoziologie. Ein Versuch*. Suhrkamp.

Baecker, D. (2015). Ausgangspunkte einer Theorie der Digitalisierung. In B. Leukert, R. Gläß, & R. Schütte (Eds.), *Digitale Transformation des Handels* (pp. 1–26). Springer Verlag.

Baecker, D. (2016). Systemtheorie als Kommunikationstheorie. In D. Baecker (Ed.), *Wozu Theorie?* (pp. 134–145). Suhrkamp Verlag.

Balfanz, D. (2017). Autonome Systeme. Wer dient wem? In W. Schröter (Ed.), *Autonomie des Menschen–Autonomie der Systeme* (pp. 137–150). Talheimer Verlag.

Bammé, A. (2017). Transhumane Kommunikation. *Soziologie-Forum der Deutschen Gesellschaft für Soziologie, 3*(46), 251–295. https://publikationen.soziologie.de/index.php/soziologie/article/view/933/1164

Baraldi, C., & Corsi, G. (2017). Social systems theory. In C. Baraldi & G. Corsi (Eds.), *Niklas Luhmann education as a social system* (1st ed., pp. 11–36). Springer. https://doi.org/10.1007/978-3-319-49975-8

Barbosa, L. S. (2017). Digital governance for sustainable development. In *Conference on e-Business, e-Services and e-Society,* (85–93). Springer. https://doi.org/10.1007/978-3-319-68557-1_9

Beaudouin, V., Bloch, I., Bounie, D., Clémençon, S., d'Alché-Buc, F., Eagan, J., Maxwell, W., Mozharovskyi, P., & Parekh, J. (2020). *Flexible and context-specific AI explainability: A multidisciplinary approach.* https://arxiv.org/abs/2003.07703

Bellinger, G., Castro, D., & Mills, A. (2004). *Data, information, knowledge, and wisdom.* Gene Bellinger Online. https://www.systems-thinking.org/dikw/dikw.htm

Benkler, Y. (1999). From consumers to users: Shifting the deeper structures of regulation toward sustainable commons and user access. *Federal Communications Law Journal, 52*(3), Art. 9. https://www.repository.law.indiana.edu/fclj/vol52/iss3/9

Benkler, Y. (2002). Coase's penguin, or, Linux and the nature of the firm. *Yale Law Journal, 112*(3), 369–446. https://doi.org/10.2307/1562247

Benkler, Y. (2006). *The wealth of networks.* Yale University Press.

Benkler, Y. (2017). Peer production, the commons and the future of the firm. *Strategic Organization, 15*(2), 264–274. https://doi.org/10.1177%2F1476127016652606

Berendt, B. (2019). AI for the common good? Pitfalls, challenges, and ethics pen-testing. *Paladyn, Journal of Behavioral Robotics, 10*(1), 44–65. https://doi.org/10.1515/pjbr-2019-0004

Bishop, C. M. (2006). *Pattern recognition and machine learning.* Springer.

Boesl, D. B., & Bode, B. M. (2016). Technology governance. In *IEEE International Conference on Emerging Technologies and Innovative Business Practices for the Transformation of Societies (EmergiTech)* (pp. 421–425). https://doi.org/10.1109/EmergiTech.2016.7737378

Boesl, D. B., & Bode, M. (2017). Roboethics and robotic governance—A literature review and research agenda. In A. Ollero, A. Sanfeliu, L. Montano, N. Lau, & C. Cardeira (Eds.), *Iberian robotics conference* (pp. 140–146). Springer Publishing.

Boesl, D. B., & Bode, M. (2019). Signaling sustainable robotics—A concept to implement the idea of robotic governance. In *IEEE 23rd International Conference on Intelligent Engineering Systems (INES)* (pp. 000143–000146).https://doi.org/10.1109/INES46365.2019.9109458

Bresnahan, T. F., & Trajtenberg, M. (1995). General purpose technologies 'engines of growth'? *Journal of Econometrics, 65*(1), 83–108. https://econpapers.repec.org/RePEc:eee:econom:v:65:y:1995:i:1:p:83-108

Brundage, M., Avin, S., Clark, J., Toner, H., Eckersley, P., Garfinkel, B., Dafoe, A., Scharre, P., Zeitzoff, T., Filar, B., Anderson, H., Roff, H., Allen, G. C., Steinhardt, J., Flynn, C., hÉigeartaigh, S. O., Beard, S., Belfield, H., Farquhar, S., … Amodei, D. (2018). *The malicious use of artificial intelligence: Forecasting, prevention, and mitigation.* arXiv:1802.07228

Brundage, M., & Bryson, J. J. (2016). Smart policies for artificial intelligence. *Computing Research Repository.* https://arxiv.org/abs/1608.08196

Brynjolfsson, E., & Hitt, L. M. (1998). Beyond the productivity paradox. *Communications of the ACM, 41*(8), 49–55.

Brynjolfsson, E., & McAfee, A. (2017). The business of artificial intelligence: What it can and cannot do for your organization. *Harvard Business Review,* 1–20. https://hbr.org/2017/07/the-business-of-artificial-intelligence

Bryson, J. J. (2018). Patiency is not a virtue: The design of intelligent systems and systems of ethics. *Ethics and Information Technology, 20*(1), 15–26. https://doi.org/10.1007/s10676-018-9448-6

Caliskan, A., Bryson, J. J., & Narayanan, A. (2017). Semantics derived automatically from language corpora contain human-like biases. *Science, 356*(6334), 183–186. https://doi.org/1010.1126/science.aal4230

Chen, P. Y., Chang, H. J., Liu, Y. C., & Chiang, Y. T. (2020). Effect of self-referential linear processing on deep-learning-based image classification. In *Conference Paper for: The 34th Annual Conference of the Japanese Society for Artificial Intelligence*. https://doi.org/10.11517/pjsai.JSAI2020.0_2K1ES201

Cihon, P. (2019). *Technical report: Standards for AI governance—International standards to enable global coordination in AI research & development*. University of Oxford. https://www.fhi.ox.ac.uk/wp-content/uploads/Standards_-FHI-Technical-Report.pdf

Coase, R. H. (1937). The nature of the firm. *Economica, 4*(16), 386–405. https://doi.org/10.2307/2626876

Cuypers, I., Hennart, J. F., Silverman, B., & Ertug, G. (2020). Transaction cost theory: Past progress, current challenges, and suggestions for the future. *Academy of Management Annals, 15*(1), 111–150. https://doi.org/10.5465/annals.2019.0051

D'Hondt, C., De Winne, R., Ghysels, E., & Raymond, S. (2019). Artificial intelligence alter egos: Who benefits from robo-investing? arXiv:1907.03370

Dafoe, A. (2018). *AI governance: A research agenda*. Governance of AI Program, Future of Humanity Institute, University of Oxford, Oxford, UK. https://www.fhi.ox.ac.uk/wp-content/uploads/GovAI-Agenda.pdf

Danaher, J. (2016). The threat of algocracy: Reality, resistance and accommodation. *Philosophy & Technology, 29*(3), 245–268. https://doi.org/10.1007/s13347-015-0211-1

Danaher, J. (2018). Toward an ethics of AI assistants: An initial framework. *Philosophy* https://doi.org/10.1007/s13347-018-0317-3

Danaher, J., Hogan, M. J., Noone, C., Kennedy, R., Behan, A., De Paor, A., Flezmann, H., Haklay, M., Khoo, S-M., Morison, J., Murphy, M. H., O'Brolchain, N., Schafer, B., & Shankar, K. (2017). Algorithmic governance: Developing a research agenda through the power of collective intelligence. *Big Data & Society, 4*(2). https://doi.org/10.1177%2F2053951717726554

Dastin, J. (2018). Amazon scraps secret AI recruiting tool that showed bias against women. *Reuters Technology News*. https://www.reuters.com/article/us-amazon-com-jobs-automation-insight-idUSKCN1MK08G

Davenport, T. H., & Kirby, J. (2016). *Only humans need apply: Winners and losers in the age of smart machines*. Harper Business.

De Haes, S., & Van Grembergen, W. (2004). IT governance and its mechanisms. *Information Systems Control Journal, 1*, 27–33. http://www.gti4u.es/curso/material/complementario/de_haes_y_van_grembergen_2004.pdf

DeNardis, L. (2010). *The emerging field of internet governance* (Yale Information Society Project Working Paper Series). SSRN digital. https://doi.org/10.2139/ssrn.1678343

DeNardis, L. (2014). *The global war for internet governance*. Yale University Press.

DeNardis, L., Cogburn, D., Levinson, N. S., & Musiani, F. (Eds.). (2020). *Researching internet governance: Methods, frameworks, futures*. MIT Press.

Dickel, S. (2019). Infrastruktur, interface, intelligenz. In B. N. Heyen, S. Dickel, & A. Brüninghaus (Eds.), *Personal health science* (pp. 219–239). Springer Verlag.

Dignum, V. (2017). Responsible artificial intelligence: Designing AI for human values. *ITU Journal: ICT Discoveries, 1*, 1–8. https://www.itu.int/en/journal/001/Documents/itu2017-1.pdf

Dignum, V. (2019). *Responsible artificial intelligence: How to develop and use AI in a responsible way*. Springer Nature.

Donick, M. (2019). *Die Unschuld der Maschinen*. Springer Fachmedien.

Doshi-Velez, F., Kortz, M., Budish, R., Bavitz, C., Gershman, S., O'Brien, D., Schieber, S., Waldo, J., Weinberger, D., & Wood, A. (2017). *Accountability of AI under the law: The role of explanation*. arXiv:1711.01134

Dunleavy, P. (2016). "Big data" and policy learning. In G. Stoker & M. Evans (Eds.), *Evidence-based policy making in the social sciences: Methods that matter* (pp. 143–157). Policy Press.

Dutton, W. H. (Ed.). (2013). *The Oxford handbook of internet studies*. Oxford University Press.

Elger, P., & Shanaghy, E. (2020). *AI as a service: Serverless machine learning with AWS*. Manning Publications.

Erdélyi, O. J., & Goldsmith, J. (2018). Regulating artificial intelligence: Proposal for a global solution. *Proceedings of the 2018 AAAI/ACM Conference on AI, Ethics, and Society* (pp. 95–101). https://arxiv.org/abs/2005.11072

Esposito, E. (2001). Strukturelle Kopplung mit unsichtbaren Maschinen. *Soziale Systeme, 7*(2), 241–252. https://doi.org/10.1515/sosys-2001-0204

Esposito, E. (2013). Digital prophecies and web intelligence. In M. Hildebrandt & K. de Vries (Eds.), *Privacy, due process and the computational turn: The philosophy of law meets the philosophy of technology* (pp. 121–142). Routledge.

Esposito, E. (2017a). Artificial communication? The production of contingency by algorithms. *Zeitschrift Für Soziologie, 46*(4), 249–265. https://doi.org/10.1515/zfsoz-2017-1014

Esposito, E. (2017b). Algorithmic memory and the right to be forgotten on the web. *Big Data & Society, 4*(1), 2053951717703996. https://doi.org/10.1177%2F2053951717703996

Etzioni, O. (2016). *Deep learning isn't a dangerous magic genie: It's just math.* wired.com. https://www.wired.com/2016/06/deep-learning-isnt-dangerous-magic-genie-just-math/

Fai, L. M. (1987, September 2–4). Artificial intelligence for transaction cost economizing. *Economics and Artificial Intelligence, Proceedings of the Ifac/ifors/ifip/iasc/afcet Conference, Aix-En-provence, France* (pp. 115–119). https://doi.org/10.1016/B978-0-08-034350-1.50028-0

Faraj, S., Pachidi, S., & Sayegh, K. (2018). Working and organizing in the age of the learning algorithm. *Information and Organization, 28*(1), 62–70. https://doi.org/10.1016/j.infoandorg.2018.02.005

Feick, J., & Werle, R. (2010). Regulation of cyberspace. In R. Baldwin, M. Cave, & M. Loge (Eds.), *The Oxford handbook of regulation* (pp. 523–547). Oxford University Press.

Feustel, R. (2020). Homo digitalis. *Berliner Debatte Initial, 31*(1), 85–96. www.hsozkult.de/journal/id/z6ann-111152

Filk, C. (2020). „Die Maschinen werden zu einer einzigen Maschine: Eine technikphilosophische Reflexion auf ‚Computational Thinking', Künstliche Intelligenz und Medienbildung. *Medienimpulse, 58*(1), 1–53. https://doi.org/10.21243/mi-01-20-18

Floridi, L. (2015). *Die 4. Revolution. Wie die Infosphäre unser Leben verändert*. Suhrkamp.

Floridi, L., & Cowls, J. (2019). A unified framework of five principles for AI in society. *Harvard Data Science Review, 1*(1). https://doi.org/10.1162/99608f92.8cd550d1

Floridi, L., Cowls, J., Beltrametti, M., Chatila, R., Chazerand, P., Dignum, V., Luetge, C., Madelin, R., Pagallo, U., Rossi, F., Schafer, B., Valcke, P., & Vayena, E. (2018). AI4 people—An ethical framework for a good AI society: Opportunities, risks, principles, and recommendations. *Minds and Machines, 28*(4), 689–707. https://doi.org/10.1007/s11023-018-9482-5

Floridi, L., Cowls, J., King, T. C., & Taddeo, M. (2020). How to design AI for social good: Seven essential factors. *Science and Engineering Ethics, 26*(3), 1771–1796. https://doi.org/10.1007/s11948-020-00213-5

Fuchs, P. (2020). Redebeitrag in Vogt, W. (2020). Verschränkung in der soziologischen Systemtheorie. In W. Vogt (Ed.), *Quantenphysik und Soziologie im Dialog* (pp. 199–1244). Springer Spektrum.

Fuller, R. B. (1982). *Synergetics: explorations in the geometry of thinking*. Estate of R. Buckminster Fuller.

Gamito, M. C., & Ebers, M. (2021). Algorithmic governance and governance of algorithms: An introduction. In M. Ebers & M. C. Gamito (Eds.), *Algorithmic governance and governance of algorithms* (pp. 1–22). Springer.

Gherardi, S. (2012). *How to conduct a practice-based study: Problems and methods*. Edward Elgar.

Gillespie, T. (2014). The relevance of algorithms. In T. Gillespie, P. J. Boczkowski, & K. A. Foot (Eds.), *Media technologies: Essays on communication, materiality, and society* (pp. 167–194). The MIT Press.

Gilpin, L., Bau, D., Yuan, B. Z., Bajwa, A., Specter, M., & Kagal, L. (2019). Explaining explanations: An overview of interpretability of machine learning. In *IEEE 5th International Conference on data science and advanced analytics (DSAA)*. IEEE. arXiv:1806.00069v3

Goldfarb, A., Taska, B., & Teodoridis, F. (2019). *Could machine learning be a general-purpose technology? Evidence from online job postings*. SSRN digital. https://doi.org/10.2139/ssrn.3468822

Golić, Z. (2019). Finance and artificial intelligence: The fifth industrial revolution and its impact on the financial sector. *Proceedings of the Faculty of Economics in East Sarajevo, 19*, 67–81. https://doi.org/10.7251/ZREFIS1919067G

Gritsenko, D., & Wood, M. (2020). Algorithmic governance: A modes of governance approach. *Regulation & Governance*. https://doi.org/10.1111/rego.12367

Grönroos, C., & Voima, P. (2013). Critical service logic: Making sense of value creation and co-creation. *Journal of the Academy of Marketing Science, 41*(2), 133–150. https://doi.org/10.1007/s11747-012-0308-3

Günther, G. (1963). Das Bewußtsein der Maschinen. Baden-Baden: Agis Verlag.

Hacking, I. (2006). *The emergence of probability* (2nd ed.). Cambridge University Press.

Haenlein, M., & Kaplan, A. (2019). A brief history of artificial intelligence: On the past, present, and future of artificial intelligence. *California Management Review, 61*(4), 5–14. https://doi.org/10.1177/0008125619864925

Hagendorff, T. (2020). The ethics of AI ethics: An evaluation of guidelines. *Minds and Machines, 30*, 99–120. https://doi.org/10.1007/s11023-020-09517-8

Hall, W. P. (2005). Biological nature of knowledge in the learning organisation. *The Learning Organization: An International Journal, 12*(2), 169–188.

Harth, J., & Lorenz, C.-F. (2017). "Hello World"—Systemtheoretische Überlegungen zu einer Soziologie des Algorithmus. *kommunikation @ gesellschaft, 18*, 1–18. https://nbn-resolving.org/urn:nbn:de:0168-ssoar-51502-9

Hartmann, P., & Henkel, J. (2020). The rise of corporate science in AI: Data as a strategic resource. *Academy of Management Discoveries, 6*(3), 359–381. https://doi.org/10.5465/amd.2019.0043

Hassan, S., & De Filippi, P. (2017). The expansion of algorithmic governance: From code is law to law is code. *Field Actions Science Reports* (Special Issue 17), 88–90. http://journals.openedition.org/factsreports/4518

Hathaway, M. (2014). Connected choices: How the internet is challenging sovereign decisions. *American Foreign Policy Interests, 36*(5), 300–313. https://doi.org/10.1080/10803920.2014.969178

Haun, M. (2002). *Handbuch Wissensmanagement: Grundlagen und Umsetzung*. Springer Verlag.

Heeks, R. (2001). Understanding e-governance for development. *Institute for Development Policy and Management, 11*(3). https://doi.org/10.13140/RG.2.2.14715.46882

Henning, K. (2019). *Smart und digital: Wie künstliche Intelligenz unser Leben verändert*. Springer Verlag.

Hislop, D. (2005). *Knowledge management in organizations: A critical introduction*. Oxford University Press.

Hislop, D., Bosua, R., & Helms, R. (2018). *Knowledge management in organizations: A critical introduction*. Oxford University Press.

Hoche, M. (2020). *Social theory* (Technical report Stanford). https://doi.org/10.13140/RG.2.2.26009.36965

Hofmann, J., Katzenbach, C., & Gollatz, K. (2017). Between coordination and regulation: Finding the governance in internet governance. *New Media & Society, 19*(9), 1406–1423. https://doi.org/10.1177%2F1461444816639975

Hossaini, A. (2019). Modelling the threat from AI: Putting agency on the agenda. In E. De Angelis, A. Hossaini, R. Noble, D. Noble, A. M. Soto, C. Sonnenschein, & K. Payne (Eds.), Forum: Artificial intelligence, artificial agency and artificial life. *The RUSI Journal, 164*(5–6), 120–144. https://doi.org/10.1080/03071847.2019.1694264

Jessop, B. (2003). Governance and meta-governance: On reflexivity, requisite variety and requisite irony. In H. P. Bang (Ed.), *Governance as social and political communication* (pp. 101–116). Manchester University Press. http://www.comp.lancs.ac.uk/sociology/papers/Jessop-Governance-and-Metagovernance.pdf

Jin, G. Z. (2019). Artificial intelligence and consumer privacy: National Bureau of Economic Research. In A. Agrawal, J. Gans, & A. Goldfarb (Eds.), *The economics of artificial intelligence: An agenda* (pp. 439–462). University of Chicago Press.

Johnson, D. G. (2017). Can engineering ethics be taught? *The Bridge, 47*(1), 59–64. https://www.nae.edu/168649/Can-Engineering-Ethics-Be-Taught

Jordan, M. I., & Mitchell, T. M. (2015). Machine learning: Trends, perspectives, and prospects. *Science, 349*(6245), 255–260. https://doi.org/10.1126/science.aaa8415

Kalpokas, I. (2019). *Algorithmic governance: Politics and law in the post-human era.* Springer Nature.

Katzenbach, C., & Ulbricht, L. (2019). Algorithmic governance. *Internet Policy Review, 8*(4), 1–18. https://doi.org/10.14763/2019.4.1424

Khatri, V. & Brown, C.V. (2010). Designing data governance. *Communications of the ACM, 53*(1), 148–152. https://doi.org/10.1145/1629175.1629210

Klinger, J., Mateos-Garcia, J. C., & Stathoulopoulos, K. (2018). *Deep learning, deep change? Mapping the development of the artificial intelligence general purpose technology.* Mapping the Development of the Artificial Intelligence General Purpose Technology. https://arxiv.org/abs/1808.06355

Klos, T. B., & Nooteboom, B. (2001). Agent-based computational transaction cost economics. *Journal of Economic Dynamics and Control, 25*(3–4), 503–526. https://econpapers.repec.org/RePEc:eee:dyncon:v:25:y:2001:i:3-4:p:503-526

König, P. D. (2019). Dissecting the algorithmic leviathan: On the socio-political anatomy of algorithmic governance. *Philosophy & Technology*, 1–19. https://doi.org/10.1007/s13347-019-00363-w

Koskinen, K. U., & Breite, R. (2020). Social autopoietic systems. In K. U. Koskinen & R. Breite (Eds.), *Uninterrupted knowledge creation: Process philosophy and autopoietic perspectives* (pp. 63–84). Springer.

Kurbalija, J. (2016). *An introduction to internet governance* (7th ed.). Diplo Foundation.

Lessig, L. (1999). *Code and other laws of cyberspace.* Basic Books.

Liew, A. (2007). Understanding data, information, knowledge and their inter-relationships. *Journal of Knowledge Management Practice, 8*(2), 1–16. http://www.tlainc.com/articl134.htm

Liew, A. (2013). DIKIW: Data, information, knowledge, intelligence, wisdom and their interrelationships. *Business Management Dynamics, 2*(10), 49–62. http://bmdynamics.com/issue_pdf/bmd110349-%2049-62.pdf

Lom, M., & Pribyl, O. (2020). Smart city model based on systems theory. *International Journal of Information Management*, 102092. http://dx.doi.org/10.1016/j.ijinfomgt.2020.102092

Lorenz, L. C. (2019). *The algocracy: Understanding and explaining how public organizations are shaped by algorithmic systems* (Master's thesis). University of Utrecht. http://dspace.library.uu.nl/bitstream/handle/1874/388696/Master%20thesis%20Lukas%20Lorenz.pdf?sequence=2&isAllowed=y

Luhmann, N. (1995). *Social systems.* Stanford University Press.

Luhmann, N. (1996). The sociology of the moral and ethics. *International Sociology, 11*(1), 27–36. https://doi.org/10.1177%2F026858096011001003

Luhmann, N. (1997). *Die Gesellschaft der Gesellschaft*. Suhrkamp Verlag.

Luhmann, N. (1998). *Die Gesellschaft der Gesellschaft* (2nd ed.). Suhrkamp Verlag.

Luhmann, N. (2017). *Die Kontrolle von Intransparenz.* Suhrkamp.

Luhmann, N., & Kieserling, A. (2000). *Die Politik der Gesellschaft* (Vol. 220). Suhrkamp.

Makridakis, S. (2017). The forthcoming artificial intelligence (AI) revolution: Its impact on society and firms. *Futures, 100*(90), 46–60. https://doi.org/10.1016/j.futures.2017.03.006

Marchant, G. (2019). "Soft law" governance of artificial intelligence. *UCLA: The Program on Understanding Law, Science, and Evidence (PULSE).* https://aipulse.org/soft-law-governance-of-artificial-intelligence/

Marwala, T., & Hurwitz, E. (2017). *Artificial intelligence and economic theory: Skynet in the market* (1st ed.). Springer Publishing.

Maturana, H., & Varela, F. (1984). *Der Baum der Erkenntnis. Die biologischen Wurzeln menschlichen Erkennens*. Goldmann.

Mayntz, R. (2003). New challenges to governance theory. In H. P. Bang (Ed.), *Governance as social and political communication* (pp. 27–40). Manchester University Press. http://hdl.handle.net/21.11116/0000-0003-4F0B-A

Meijer, A. (2015). E-governance innovation: Barriers and strategies. *Government Information Quarterly, 32*(2), 198–206. https://doi.org/10.1016/j.giq.2015.01.001

Meyer, M., Zarnekow, R., & Kolbe, L. M. (2003). IT-Governance. *Wirtschaftsinformatik, 45*(4), 445–448. https://doi.org/10.1007/BF03250909

Milano, S., Taddeo, M., & Floridi, L. (2020). Recommender systems and their ethical challenges. *AI & Society, 35*(4), 957–967. https://doi.org/10.1007/s00146-020-00950-y

Mittelstadt, B. (2019). *AI ethics—Too principled to fail?* arXiv:1906.06668

Mittelstadt, B. D., & Floridi, L. (2016). The ethics of big data: Current and foreseeable issues in biomedical contexts. *Science and Engineering Ethics, 22*(2), 303–341. https://doi.org/10.1007/s11948-015-9652-2

Moore, G. (2006). Moore's law at 40. In D. Brock (Ed.), *Understanding Moore's Law: Four decades of innovation* (pp. 67–84). Chemical Heritage Foundation.

Morabito, V. (2015). *Big data and analytics: Strategic and organizational impacts*. Springer International Publishing.

Mueller, M. L. (2010). *Networks and states: The global politics of internet governance*. MIT press.

Neisig, M. (2020). Moral or ethical heuristics, higher order autopoiesis and sophisticated digital tools. The fragile system-environment relation, blind spots, paradoxes and deparadoxication. In *The Luhmann Conference 2020 on "Moral communication. Observed with social systems theory"*. https://iuc.hr/file/1095

Nepelski, D., & Sobolewski, M. (2020). *Estimating investments in general purpose technologies*. The case of AI investments in Europe. Publications Office of the European Union, Luxembourg. https://doi.org/10.2760/506947

Nilsson, N. J. (2009). *The quest for artificial intelligence*. Cambridge University Press.

Noble, R., & Noble, D. (2019). Could artificial intelligence (AI) become a responsible agent: Artificial agency (AA)? In E. De Angelis, A. Hossaini, R. Noble, D. Noble, A. M. Soto, C. Sonnenschein, & K. Payne (2019). Forum: Artificial intelligence, artificial agency and artificial Life. *The RUSI Journal, 164*(5–6), 120–144. https://doi.org/10.1080/03071847.2019.1694264

Noh, K., Chung, S., Lim, J., Kim, G., & Jeong, H. (2018). Speech emotion recognition framework based on user self-referential speech features. In *IEEE 7th Global Conference on Consumer Electronics (GCCE)*, Nara, Japan (pp. 341–342). https://doi.org/10.1109/GCCE.2018.8574676

Nonaka, I. (1991). The knowledge-creoting compony. *Harvard Business Review*.

Parkes, D. C., & Wellman, M. P. (2015). Economic reasoning and artificial intelligence. *Science, 349*(6245), 267–272. https://doi.org/10.1126/science.aaa8403

Paschek, D., Mocan, A., & Draghici, A. (2019). Industry 5.0. The expected impact of the next industrial revolution. Management, knowledge, learning. *International Conference, Technology, Innovation and Industrial Management*, TIIM, Piran, Slovenia. http://www.toknowpress.net/ISBN/978-961-6914-25-3/papers/ML19-017.pdf

Pathak, P., Pal, P. R., Shrivastava, M., & Ora, P. (2019). Fifth revolution: Applied AI & human intelligence with cyber physical systems. *International Journal of Engineering and Advanced Technology (IJEAT), 8*(3). https://www.researchgate.net/profile/Parashu-Pal/publication/331966435_Fifth_revolution_Applied_AI_human_intelligence_with_cyber_physical_systems/links/5ca5efa2299bf118c4b0a484/Fifth-revolution-Applied-AI-human-intelligence-with-cyber-physical-systems.pdf

Pentland, A. (2013). The data-driven society. *Scientific American, 309*(4), 78–83. https://doi.org/10.1038/scientificamerican1013-78

Perritt, H. (1998). The internet as a threat to sovereignty? Thoughts on the internet's role in strengthening national and global governance. *Indiana Journal of Global Legal Studies, 5*(2), 423–442. https://www.repository.law.indiana.edu/ijgls/vol5/iss2/4

Petralia, S. (2020). Mapping general purpose technologies with patent data. *Research Policy, 49*(7), 104013. https://doi.org/10.1016/j.respol.2020.104013

Phillips, T., Kira, B., Tartakowsky, A., Dolan, J., & Natih, P. (2020). *Digital technology governance: Developing countries' priorities and concerns* (Digital Pathways at Oxford Paper Series, 3). Oxford, UK. https://pathwayscommission.bsg.ox.ac.uk/sites/default/files/2020-05/final_digital-tech-gov-21may20_0.pdf

Polyakova, A., & Boyer, S. P. (2018). *The future of political warfare: Russia, the west and the coming age of global digital competition.* Brookings Institution. https://www.brookings.edu/wp-content/uploads/2018/03/fp_20180316_future_political_warfare.pdf

Preece, A. (2018). Asking 'why' in AI: Explainability of intelligent systems—Perspectives and challenges. *Intelligent Systems in Accounting, Finance and Management. An International Journal, 25*(2), 63–72.

PriceWaterhouseCoopers. (2019). *Sizing the prize what's the real value of AI for your business and how can you capitalise?* PriceWaterhouseCoopers. https://www.pwc.com/gx/en/issues/analytics/assets/pwc-ai-analysis-sizing-the-prize-report.pdf

Rai, A., Constantinides, P., & Sarker, S. (2019). Next-generation digital platforms: Toward human–AI hybrids. *MIS Quarterly, 43*(1), iii–x. https://www.researchgate.net/profile/Panos-Constantinides/publication/330909988_NextGeneration_Digital_Platforms_Toward_Human-AI_Hybrids/links/5c5d7a41299bf1d14cb3c8bc/Next-Generation-Digital-Platforms-Toward-Human-AI-Hybrids.pdf

Razzkazov, V. E. (2020). Financial and economic consequences of distribution of artificial intelligence as a general-purpose technology. *Finance: Theory and Practice, Scientific and Practical Journal, 24*(2), 120–132. https://doi.org/10.26794/2587-5671-2020-24-2-120-132

Rehäuser, J., & Krcmar, H. (1996). *Wissensmanagement in Unternehmen.* Lehrstuhl für Wirtschaftsinformatik.

Reichel, A. (2011). Technology as system: Towards an autopoietic theory of technology. *International Journal of Innovation and Sustainable Development, 5*(2–3), 105–118. https://doi.org/10.1504/IJISD.2011.043070

Rindfleisch, A. (2020). Transaction cost theory: Past, present and future. *AMS Review, 10*(1), 85–97. https://doi.org/10.1007/s13162-019-00151-x

Rodriguez Mansilla, D., & Torres Nafarrate, J. (2007). Autopoiesis, die Einheit einer Differenz: Luhmann und Maturana. In P. Birle & F. Schmidt-Welle (Eds.), *Wechselseitige Perzeptionen: Deutschland - Lateinamerika im 20. Jahrhundert* (pp. 79–108). Vervuert Verlag.

Rosa, H. (2016). *Resonanz. Eine Soziologie der Weltbeziehung.* Suhrkamp.

Roselli, D., Matthews, J., & Talagala, N. (2019). Managing bias in AI. *In Companion Proceedings of the 2019 World Wide Web Conference* (pp. 539–544). https://doi.org/10.1145/3308560.3317590

Rosenblatt, B., Trippe, B., & Mooney, S. (2002). *Digital rights management business and technology.* M&T Books.

Savaget, P., Chiarini, T., & Evans, S. (2019). Empowering political participation through artificial intelligence. *Science and Public Policy, 46*(3), 369–380. https://doi.org/10.1093/scipol/scy064

Saxena, K. B. C. (2005). Towards excellence in e-governance. *International Journal of Public Sector Management, 18*(6), 498–513. https://doi.org/10.1108/09513550510616733

Scheiber, L., Roth, S., & Reichel, A. (2011). The technology of innovation. *International Journal of Innovation and Sustainable Development, 5*(2–3), 100–104. http://andrereichel.de/resources/Technology-as-System.pdf

Schuett, J. (2019). A legal definition of AI. *SSRN Electronic Journal.* https://doi.org/10.2139/ssrn.3453632

Schwab, K., & Davis, N. (2018). *Shaping the fourth industrial revolution.* World Economic Forum.

Searle, J. R. (1980). Minds, brains, and programs. *Behavioral and Brain Sciences, 3*(3), 417–424. https://doi.org/10.1017/S0140525X00005756

Shin, P. W., Lee, J., & Hwang, S. H. (2020). Data governance on business/data dictionary using machine learning and statistics. In *2020 International Conference on Artificial Intelligence in*

Information and Communication (ICAIIC) (pp. 547–552). https://doi.org/10.1109/ICAIIC48513.2020.9065194

Silberg, J., & Manyika, J. (2019). *Notes from the AI frontier: Tackling bias in AI (and in humans)*. McKinsey Global Institute. https://www.mckinsey.com/~/media/mckinsey/featured%20insights/artificial%20intelligence/tackling%20bias%20in%20artificial%20intelligence%20and%20in%20humans/mgi-tackling-bias-in-ai-june-2019.pdf

Singh, J., Powles, J., Pasquier, T., & Bacon, J. (2015). Data flow management and compliance in cloud computing. *IEEE Cloud Computing, 2*(4), 24–32. https://doi.org/10.1109/MCC.2015.69

Soto, A. M., & Sonnenschein, C. (2019). Could machines develop autonomous agency? In E. De Angelis, A. Hossaini, R. Noble, D. Noble, A. M. Soto, C. Sonnenschein, & K. Payne (2019). Forum: Artificial intelligence, artificial agency and artificial life. *The RUSI Journal, 164*(5–6), 120–144. https://doi.org/10.1080/03071847.2019.1694264

Steels, L. (2015). *The talking heads experiment: Origins of words and meanings* (Vol. 1). Language Science Press.

Tallon, P. P., Ramirez, R. V., & Short, J. E. (2013). The information artifact in IT governance: Toward a theory of information governance. *Journal of Management Information Systems, 30*(3), 141–178. https://doi.org/10.2753/MIS0742-1222300306

Tarafdar, M., Beath, C. M., & Ross, J. W. (2019). Using AI to enhance business operations. *MIT Sloan Management Review, 60*(4), 37–44. https://sloanreview.mit.edu/article/using-ai-to-enhance-business-operations/

Trajtenberg, M. (2018). *AI as the next GPT: A political-economy perspective* (No. w24245). National Bureau of Economic Research. https://doi.org/10.3386/w24245

Van de Gevel, A. J., & Noussair, C. N. (2013). The nexus between artificial intelligence and economics. In A. J. W. van de Gevel & C. N., Noussair (Eds.), *The nexus between artificial intelligence and economics* (pp. 1–110). Springer.

Vatiero, M. (2020). *The theory of transaction in institutional economics: A history*. Routledge.

Vogd, W. (2020a). Die Verschränkung in der Quantentheorie. In W. Vogt (Ed.), *Quantenphysik und Soziologie im Dialog* (pp. 179–197). Springer Spektrum.

Vogd, W. (2020b). Supertheorien im Dialog–und jetzt? In W. Vogt (Ed.), *Quantenphysik und Soziologie im Dialog* (pp. 245–271). Springer Spektrum.

von Westphalen, F. G. (2020). Einige Vorüberlegungen zum bevorstehenden Lieferkettengesetz. ZIP 2020: *Zeitschrift für Wirtschaftsrecht, 41*(49), 2421–2431. https://www.zip-online.de/65567_MTM2MQ.htm

Wachter, S., Mittelstadt, B., & Floridi, L. (2017). Why a right to explanation of automated decision-making does not exist in the general data protection regulation. *International Data Privacy Law, 7*(2), 76–99. https://doi.org/10.1093/idpl/ipx005

Wani, M. A., Bhat, F. A., Afzal, S., & Khan, A. I. (2020). *Advances in deep learning*. Springer.

Wieland, J. (2002). *Wissen als kooperative und moralische Ressource* (No. 02/2002) (KIeM Working Paper).

Wieland, J. (2014). *Governance Ethics: Global value creation, economic organization and normativity*. Cham: Springer International Publishing.

Wieland, J. (2018). *Relational economics. Ökonomische Theorie der Governance wirtschaftlicher Transaktionen*. Metropolis.

Wieland, J. (2020). *Relational economics: A political economy*. Springer.

Williamson, B. (2014). Knowing public services: Cross-sector intermediaries and algorithmic governance in public sector reform. *Public Policy and Administration, 29*(4), 292–312. https://doi.org/10.1177/0952076714529139

Williamson, O. E. (1985). *The economic institutions of capitalism*. Free Press.

Williamson, O. E. (1993). Opportunism and its critics. *Managerial and Decision Economics, 14*(2), 97–107. https://doi.org/10.1002/MDE.4090140203

Williamson, O. E. (2016). The transaction cost economics project: Origins, evolution, utilization. In C. Menard & E. Bertrand (Eds.), *The Elgar companion to Ronald H. Coase* (pp. 34–42). Edward Elgar.

Whittaker, M., Crawford, K., Dobbe, R., Fried, G., Kaziunas, E., Mathur, V., West, S. M., Richardson, R., Schultz, J., & Schwartz, O. (2018). *AI now report 2018* (pp. 1–62). AI Now Institute at New York University.

Wu, X., & Gereffi, G. (2018). Amazon and Alibaba: Internet governance, business models, and internationalization strategies. In R. van Tulder, A. Verbeke, & L. Piscitello (Eds.), *International business in the information and digital age* (Vol. 13, pp. 327–356). Emerald Publishing Limited. https://doi.org/10.1108/S1745-886220180000013014

Xu, Z., & Cheng, X. (2017). The impact of financial intelligence on commercial banking from the perspective of transaction cost. In *3rd International Conference on Economics, Social Science, Arts, Education and Management Engineering (ESSAEME 2017)*. Atlantis Press. https://doi.org/10.2991/essaeme-17.2017.147

Chapter 3
Conceptualisation of the Relational Governance of Artificial Intelligence

Having established AI as an element of Relational Economics, this chapter proceeds to conceptualise the Relational Governance of AI. To this end, it is divided into three sections:

First, it delimits Wieland's (2018, 2020) concept of Relational Governance from existing research about 'Relational Governance'. Thereafter, critical elements of Wieland's (2018, 2020) theory of Relational Governance are summarised and interpreted for the AI context.
Second, it addresses the identified theoretical need for additions and adaptations of Wieland's (2018, 2020) governance approach for the AI context. Hence, it begins with a depiction of the relational transaction underlying AI governance by presenting each element of the transaction and the interlinkages among them.
Third, it proceeds to present its conceptualisation of Relational AI Governance by introducing the governance formula depicting this underlying transaction for AI governance.[1] The formula depicts the overall governance structure and the governance parameters existing in the AI context. The governance parameters, in particular, subsume important content-related themes, e.g., AI ethics, providing the base for the operationalisation of Relational AI Governance in organisations.

Based on the conceptualisation of the individual parameters, the third section presents suitable governance mechanisms for the governance parameters and discusses their adaptivity. The adaptivity of both the formula and the governance parameters is exemplified in two scenarios. Scenario one addresses the current status quo of AI governance, with no official regulation for AI research and adoption being

[1] The book does not claim to present a complete function at this stage. It was developed to the author's best knowledge and according to the current state of knowledge in academia and practice.

S. Wiesmüller, *The Relational Governance of Artificial Intelligence*,
Relational Economics and Organization Governance,
https://doi.org/10.1007/978-3-031-25023-1_3

passed anywhere around the globe. However, since the E.U. has presented a proposition for possible regulation of AI, scenario two briefly discusses the implications of a partially regulated market—with the E.U. being the only regulated region in the global economy. The chapter closes with a critical discussion of the model and its relation-building mechanisms.

3.1 Theoretical Foundation for Relational AI Governance

According to Wieland (2018, 2020), the failure of public-sector regulation "*is the systematic point of departure for governance economics, which links it to [...] private ordering on the part of NGOs like civil society organisations or by firms, based on contracts*" (2020, p. 39).

While Wieland directed this quote to the lack of regulation in the globalised economy, the same holds true for the current lack of regulation regarding AI development and AI adoption as faced by companies (Balfanz, 2017; Cave & ÓhÉigeartaigh, 2019). This is because corporations are the main driver for the AI revolution (Mittelstadt, 2019a), and public-sector regulation currently fails to address issues of AI governance (Cave & ÓhÉigeartaigh, 2019; Geist, 2016; Scharre, 2019; Tomasik, 2013). Furthermore, numerous scholars point to the unsuitability of mere hard laws and standardised regulatory measures to address AI issues (Dafoe, 2018; Gasser & Almeida, 2017; Weng & Izumo, 2019). Thus, it is the lack of public-sector regulation that is the precise reason for the need to connect economic and system-theoretical theory, as their linkage allows us to explain the phenomenon of private ordering holistically and depict possible challenges or dilemma structures in-depth. On the operational level, this book applies Wieland's (2018, 2020) definition of the firm as a nexus of stakeholders, an entity woven into society, and an instrument of private sector governance. Thereby, it aims to facilitate companies with a suitable governance approach, able to address the complexity coming with this endeavour.

3.1.1 Delimitation of Wieland's Relational Governance

From a theoretical viewpoint, Wieland's (2018, 2020) governance concept is closely linked to contract theory. This makes Relational AI Governance a part of contract theory, too, which is why it is crucial to understand how it is to be positioned in existing research.

Stemming from Williamson's (1979) tradition of transaction cost economics, Wieland (2014, 2018, 2020) also applies its continuation in the form of governing transactions via contracts in Relational Economics. Williamson (1979) specified his transaction cost economics approach as the governance of contractual relations and as "*an interdisciplinary undertaking that joins economics with aspects of organization theory and overlaps extensively with contract law*" (1979, p. 261). Hence, an analysis on the meta-level helps understand the system-specific characteristics of each societal system and indicates dilemma situations arising due to the collision of system logic. Based on an extensive examination, the governance challenge is subsequently solved on the transaction level. This allows dilemma situations to be solved structurally, which is highly relevant to the AI context since wicked problems continue to exist from a societal meta-level to the micro-level.

To realise the identified dilemma solution, the governance structure within the firm is operationalised in the form of formal and informal social contracts among its stakeholders (Wieland, 2020). Wieland specifies Relational Governance as an informal governance structure, acting as an informal contract, which is based on shared values and trust among the parties involved. In detail, informal and formal contracts can interact, complement, or substitute each other or be eligible for combination (Wieland, 2018, 2020). Thus, a governance structure consists of formal and informal contracts, as well as enforcement mechanisms. With this approach, Wieland's theory shows significant interrelations with existing research, as will be highlighted in the following.

The first identified research stream focuses on the objectives and foundations of relational governance, such as shared values. Colombelli et al. (2017) describe relational governance as being "*rooted in implicit understandings, shared cooperative norms, and informal routines that are mutually defined and adjusted by the parties*" (2017, p. 4), whereas Wacker et al. (2016) and Abraham et al. (2019) view it as fostering and enabling collaboration among all stakeholders in a given situation.

This second research stream focuses on the interplay of contractual and relational governance (Benítez-Ávila et al., 2019; Cao & Lumineau, 2015; Claro et al., 2003; Ferguson et al., 2005a; Wacker et al., 2016), and is extensively mentioned by Wieland in his publications. In detail, Poppo and Zenger (2002) examined whether formal contracts and relational governance function as complements. Uhlaner et al. (2007) add that relational governance seems complementary to formal contracts. Poppo et al. (2008) found that as "*relational governance safeguards parties from the risk inherent in many market transactions [...], it can complement the use of formal contracts*" (2008, p. 1195). Ferguson et al. (2005a) show that informal structures need to complement formal ones for relational governance to be put in place successfully. As stated, Wieland (2018, 2020) subsumes all these findings by defining formal and informal contracts to interact in four forms: substitution, combination, complementation, and interaction, and focusing on their theoretical derivation, as well as their operationalisation.

Third, Grandori (2006) and Ndubisi et al. (2016) focus on the favourable environment needed to complement incomplete contracts. Ndubisi et al. specifically define "*contracts as elements of relationships, and instruments of collaborating parties to take on opportunities through collaboration*" (2016, p. 127).

The fourth research stream examines relational governance from a relationship management view (Chu et al., 2020; Ju & Gao, 2017; Sjödin et al., 2019; Zheng et al., 2008) and specifically intra- (Liu et al., 2017) as well as interfirm relations (Chatterji et al., 2019; Zaheer & Venkatraman, 1995).

Albeit Relationship Governance is a known term in academia, this book does not represent any of the presented schools of thought. Instead, the relational character of this book's approach is displayed in the relationing mechanisms serving to connect the different system logics apparent in AI governance. Although various publications stem from Williamson's (1979) transaction theory or integrate the concept of relational contracts, like Wieland (2018, 2020), existing research mainly focuses on the connection between relational and contractual governance (Benítez-Ávila et al., 2019; Cao & Lumineau, 2015; Claro et al., 2003; Ferguson et al., 2005a; Poppo & Zenger, 2002; Poppo et al., 2008; Uhlaner et al., 2007; Wacker et al., 2016). While there is an overlap in the theoretical origins of these publications and this book, the research foci of both Wieland's Relational Economics and this book differ strongly from the identified publications. Despite agreeing with the mentioned researchers and their findings, Wieland's (2018, 2020) definition exceeds their positions and goes one step further, namely towards applying formal and informal governance structures to practise in order to successfully align differing system logics.

3.1.2 Essential Concepts of Wieland's Relational Governance

According to Wieland (2014, 2018, 2020), the economy is defined as a global network, consisting of transactions through which individual and collective actors interact. With this, he differentiates between a global economy and national political or administrative spaces, such as national economies. Globalisation in this context is not defined as homogenous; rather, it is understood as a tension field between globalised economic value creation and consumer preferences, while at the same time being bound to national political legislation and nationally oriented cultural belief systems (Wieland, 2020).

The key challenge for such a global network consists in the effective governance of interaction dynamics among regional, national, transnational, and international transactions of all stakeholders involved. Further, the actors involved can include both individual and collective actors from all systems presented in the previous chapter, but "*especially from the economy, politics, and civil society. Though these actors are in competition with one another, they are nonetheless potentially also cooperating economic, political and civil-society actors*" (Wieland, 2020, p. 2). Following Wieland's (2018, 2020) logic, economic transactions consequently attract societal interaction, such as from the system 'Politics' or 'Civil Society'. Therefore, the required governance structure will organise these interactions to generate reciprocal value creation. It is the continuity of these cooperative relations that determines the performance level of a relational economy and its actors.

Consequently, the basic unit of analysis in Relational Economics, specifically in Relational Governance, is the relational transaction (Wieland, 2018, 2020). The single transaction attracts various decision logics and sources of value creation, thereby serving as "*the focal point in a complex system*" (Wieland, 2020, p. 21). Given the complexity of such networks, Wieland decided to substitute the traditional economic exchange transaction with a relational transaction, which can genuinely depict the complexity of modern realities—instead of the merely binary mechanism an exchange transaction functions on. In the light of relational transactions, the global economy no longer consists of the simple addition of exchange transactions but the identification and shaping of transactional relations (Wieland, 2020). Consequently, the performance of such a network is built on the foundation of its transactions' functionality and connections.

The term 'relation' is defined as *"the successful integration of multiple rationalities in an adaptive governance structure for the dynamic processing and development of specific economic transactions"* (Wieland, 2020, p. 9). Hence, transforming a potential relation into an actual one requires the existence of a governance structure (Wieland, 2018, 2020). Operatively, the chosen governance structure needs to function in a closed manner, at least temporarily, to allow for the realisation of a particular transaction. Nonetheless, it always remains communicatively open to its environment (Wieland, 2018).

The context for the firm as a governance structure is the system 'Market'. This system is binarily coded and cannot integrate other decision logic within itself, despite being communicatively open to other systems. This is because *"the polyvalent processing of economic transactions, can work efficiently and effectively at the organisational level, but not at the level of the market"* (Wieland, 2020, p. 9). In consequence, the governance of relational transactions requires the firm to be the governance form and process for relational transactions. This is because, compared to the 'Market', the firm exists independently of its stakeholders with the infinite aim of ensuring the continued existence of its own collective action form (Wieland, 2018, 2020). In short, the firm is *"a form of governance for stakeholder relations and [...] a process of relationalising stakeholder resources"* (Wieland, 2020, p. 71). The cooperation rent measures the outcome of such a process, specifically the outcome of a relational transaction in Relational Economics, by what rent it achieves on the market. Again, this value can only be created through the governance forms integrated into the relational transaction. The outcome portrays the value achieved for all actors involved; hence, a shared value (Wieland, 2020).

3.1.2.1 The Operationalisation of Shared Value Creation Through Relational Governance

When it comes to the application of Relation Governance in practice, it is not only the identification of the firm as a governance form that is of relevance: Williamson (2002) originally stated that *"contract/private ordering/governance leads naturally into the reconceptualization of the firm not as a production function in the science of choice tradition, but instead as a governance structure"* (2002, p. 191). This indicates that by opting for private sector ordering, corporations move from the economic system and engage as actors of civil society or politics. Thereby, the firm becomes a multi-stakeholder entity, responsible for aligning all its stakeholders' interests and the effective collaborative management of their invested resources (Wieland, 2014,

2018, 2020). In doing so, managing the interests directed towards a company ensures its continued existence and provides shared value to society (Wieland, 2008, 2014, 2018, 2020).

To give an example that substantiates this theoretical derivation: An economic actor, an organisation whose original affiliation is in the economic system, needs to account for the binary code of the economy, which is 'payment - non-payment'. Within the organisation, this translates into the specific guiding difference of 'earnings - costs' (Wieland, 2018). Thus, when an organisation moves into the realm of ethics, for example, it is confronted with the binary code of 'right - wrong' and the guiding difference 'conformity - non-conformity'. This requires a governance form to align these diverging system logics and create a 'win–win' situation; a higher cooperation rent for actors from both societal systems. Such an alignment can be acquired through a structural coupling in the form of polycontextual management, with which relational value is created.

The value of a new transaction exceeds the mere connection and integration of two systems' logics, as, by adapting morality and creating new relational transactions, the firm creates a new value for both parameters—a new moral element and new economic value. In the case of human rights protection in a corporate environment, a new relational transaction can change the daily routine and actual level of personal safety for a worker, who formerly might have been employed under inadequate conditions that involved risk. For the corporation, economic gains can be traced to a positive reputation due to these actions and, therefore, approval by consumers, which can again translate into higher sales figures. Thus, the relational value of the transaction exceeds abstract morality and direct cost or earnings. It may not only have a ripple effect on other stakeholders but also create indirect benefits for, as suggested, the workers who benefit from new measures, their families, and even their community (Wieland, 2020).

Consequently, a governance task, as defined in relational economics,

> consists in interlinking economic competitiveness [...] and societal normativity (law, ethical standards) in such a way as to create a new business model [...]. In other words, business ethics is not business plus ethics, but rather a new entity of its own, a new relational transaction in which the previous transactions continue to exist but are modified by new events that become coupled with them. (Wieland, 2020, p. 59)

The company does not change its original affiliation to its economic system but integrates the guiding difference of other systems into specific processes by creating relational transactions. Still, by focusing on the 'earnings – costs' guiding difference, the economic actor ensures its own competitiveness and continued existence in its original system, namely the market. While no system logic is privileged or handled advantageously, the focus on the corporation's guiding difference does justice to the formerly mentioned overall objective inherent to all governance measures: ensuring the continuity of existence for the entity realising them. Through the governance process, the firm fosters and facilitates cooperation among its stakeholders and, thereby, plays an important role in its own social legitimisation (Wieland, 2020). If confronting and integrating stakeholder demand is not deemed desirable, the only alternative for the company is to leave this particular market and enter a less demanding one with a different set of stakeholders (Wieland, 2020).

Consequently, governance structures are necessary to create a new unity from these differences, and a new value, which allows for value creation amidst the two systems and across sectors (Wieland, 2020). To achieve this goal, companies need to be able to translate this external demand into processes and measures that are compatible with their original guiding difference. In the case of coupling the market and ethics—translating to business logic and morality on the company level—measures of corporate ethical behaviour need to be translated into the costs and the possible contributions they can bring to the corporation (Wieland, 2014, 2020). Given the firm's embeddedness into society, any given company's strategic management and governance need to address the demand arising from its stakeholders' needs and rights if it aims to ensure the continuity of its business. However, a company does not have to use these measures and engage in polycontextual management processes because it prioritises societal welfare (Wieland, 2018, 2020). Rather, the arguments for such decisions can be grounded in a cost analysis of all options available or an evaluation of potential economic gains stemming from applying more ethical procedures, such as economic gains due to a rise in reputational value. Hence,

> managing normativity is a form of risk management and can only succeed if a given firm is truly capable of accurately interpreting society's preferences, both for the present and for the foreseeable future. (Wieland, 2020, p. 90)

This includes the "*ability to create governance structures for relational [...] transactions, which require adaptive structures in order to efficiently and effectively cope with the diversity of contexts*" (Wieland, 2020, p. 90).

3.1.2.2 The Governance Mechanisms of Wieland's Relational Governance

In economic theory, a governance structure for transactions can include their coordination as well as the fostering of cooperation among them. Its effectiveness in doing so determines its performance.

However, Relational Economics differentiates between the two concepts. Wieland (2018, 2020) defines coordination as a thing-to-thing relation that requires the ex-post securing of existing rules. By contrast, cooperation fosters the ex-ante agreement of a particular number of parties and, thereby, is constituted as an actor-to-actor relation. Unlike in other governance forms, Wieland (2020) points out that, for the firm, individual characteristics of actors and parties involved play an important role in the governance structure's effectiveness. Hence, within a firm, formal modes of coordination, such as monitoring, need to be combined with information modes of cooperation in the form of values—such as "*moral or cultural standards*" (2020, p. 28).

Further, given that no relational transaction is the same, each one requires a tailored governance structure—developed according to the specific situational context. Therefore,

> relational governance is understood as an informal governance structure, as an implicit contract based on shared norms and, as such, on mutual trust, on interpersonal relationships and on the actors' respective reputations. (2020, p. 43)

Wieland (2018, 2020) adds that, within the firm, social norms do not exist in a self-enforced manner but are enforced by control mechanisms and negative incentives, such as social criticism. He specifies the relation between formal and informal governance structures in a fourfold manner: they can complement or substitute each other, interact with each other, or be combined. However, the complementarity and combinability of both formal and informal governance measures is viewed as the dominant mode of interaction. Wieland (2020) displays this shared view with other scholars, such as Cao and Lumineau (2015), in the following function that depicts the co-existence of formal and informal measures for any given relational transaction:

$$RT = f\{I,\ O,\ SII,\ SFI\}$$

This formula summons the Individual (I), the Organisation (O), and the informal (SII) and formal institutions of society (SFI). Actual interaction and equivalence between these four parameters can only exist when they are equally accessible within a governance structure.

Thus, within the governance form, the implementation of formal contracts can be a sign of investment and commitment, rather than control, and can even increase trust within the network or organisation they are applied to (Wieland, 2020). To further clarify the relations among the specific parameters, Fig. 3.1 displays an overview of their interconnections within a given governance structure.

As Fig. 3.1 portrays, there are two forms each for informal and formal governance measures. Further, there are interrelations between 'O' and 'SII' as well as 'SFI' and 'I'. The parameters 'O' and 'SII' can either complement each other or be combined. The relation between 'SFI' and 'I' can either be of substitutive or interactive nature. However, in ideal form, all parameters are activated and managed within the governance structure (Wieland, 2018, 2020).

To exemplify this rather abstract depiction, a practical example is taken. In a firm, the mere enforcement of compliance management measures via formal contracts is often ineffective. It is in combination with

> the parameters I (leadership integrity) and O (the compliance system) with informal SIIs (societal informal institutions/the corporate culture) and formal SFIs (societal formal institutions/organisational liability, due diligence specifications) (Wieland, 2020, p. 44)

that they become most successful. Consequently, the underlying aim of relational governance and the realisation of relational transactions lies in the joint problem-solving of the parties involved by developing trust and shared values—and complementing them with formal governance measures.

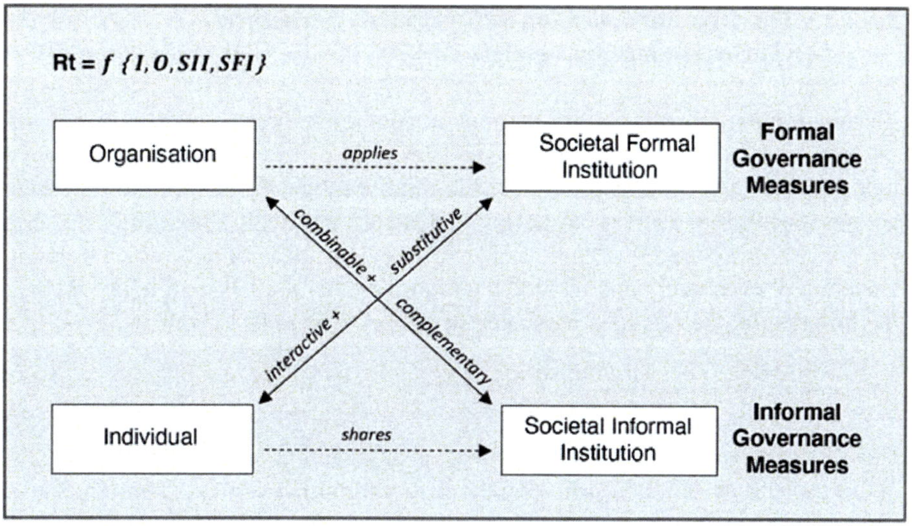

Fig. 3.1 Own depiction of governance parameters, according to Wieland (2020)

The quality of a relational transaction within the governance form of the firm is ensured through its informal structure, which is mostly determined by implicit contracts and the pro-social behaviour of its actors in their relations (Wieland, 2018, 2020). In this context, the task of governance is the appropriate proportioning of multiple governance forms and mechanisms for the particular transaction. Thereby, it realises the continuity of cooperative relations, allowing for the relationalisation process to create value (Wieland, 2018). The result of this governance process becomes tangible in the form of cooperation rents, as well as material and immaterial value for all stakeholders involved in the cooperation process (Wieland, 2018, 2020).

The actual process of relationalisation of resources within a governance form is marked by three main characteristics: recursivity, simultaneity, and productivity (Wieland, 2020). These characteristics determine the level of private and social value creation realised through a particular relational transaction:

Recursivity determines how the outcome of a relational transaction affects the events involved and their relations with one another.
Simultaneity describes all processes and parameters in the relational transaction functioning simultaneously and being of equal validity. Neither one can be eliminated through governance; they can, however, be combined, compensated for, or substituted each other if they are functionally equivalent.
Productivity of a relational transaction is based on the constraining or enabling effects the parameters involved have on one another, as they can either block or foster each other's productivity.

These three characteristics can serve as indicators for the quality and applicability of a given governance structure to a practical case.

3.1.2.3 The Operationalisation of Governance Structures via Governance Parameters

The requirements, in other words the content, for the previously presented governance measures, are polycontextural in nature. Thus, they can stem, for example, from the fields of law, the economy, or ethics, and require a transformation into polylingual actions, such as incentives, to be implementable and realisable within the firm's governance structure (Wieland, 2020). To integrate these objectives of Relational Governance effectively and include the requirements of all system logics involved, the firm operationalises its governance structure on two main levels:

- **First Level**: *The Internalisation and Governance of Social Normativity in Companies*

This phase portrays the overall process of aggregating social normativity in the entire societal system and positions the firm within this context. Through societal discourse, the expectations regarding a current dilemma situation need to be declared (Wieland, 2018, 2020). Such dilemmas, in the context of companies, are also defined as negative externalities—events outside the economic logic, needing to be integrated through a governance form as "*they cannot be quantified or reflected in the pricing language used by the market*" (Wieland, 2020, p. 91). Based on such a formulation, regarding, for example, society's viewpoint on corporate decision-making and its negative externalities, the firm can engage in polycontextual management and begin the process of aligning diverging demands. Therefore, society's demand "*must be transformed into a polycontextually compatible term, which in turn shapes the course of development for the process of internalizing externalities*" (Wieland, 2020, p. 91). The translation of system-specific demands into a corporate structure is portrayed in Fig. 3.2.

While the 'Market' remains a binary-coded system, which only allows for exchange transactions based on prices, the firm and the government can engage in relational transactions and combine various system logics. Within the firm, certain governance parameters come into play to realise the governance objectives identified via the social formulation. Thus, a company can contribute, for example, to the goal of corporate social responsibility, which portrays society's demand for companies to internalise the negative externalities of their actions. The company can do so, as depicted in Fig. 3.2, through, for example, management corrections, the development of new, socially desirable innovations and, most importantly, the creation of shared value.

- **Second Level**: *Translating System Requirements into Corporate Governance Measures*

After having identified the requirements stemming from each system involved in the relational transaction on a meta-level, the internalisation process within the firm is initiated. As depicted in Fig. 3.3, each societal system involved in the transaction leads to system-specific requirements for the internalisation process.

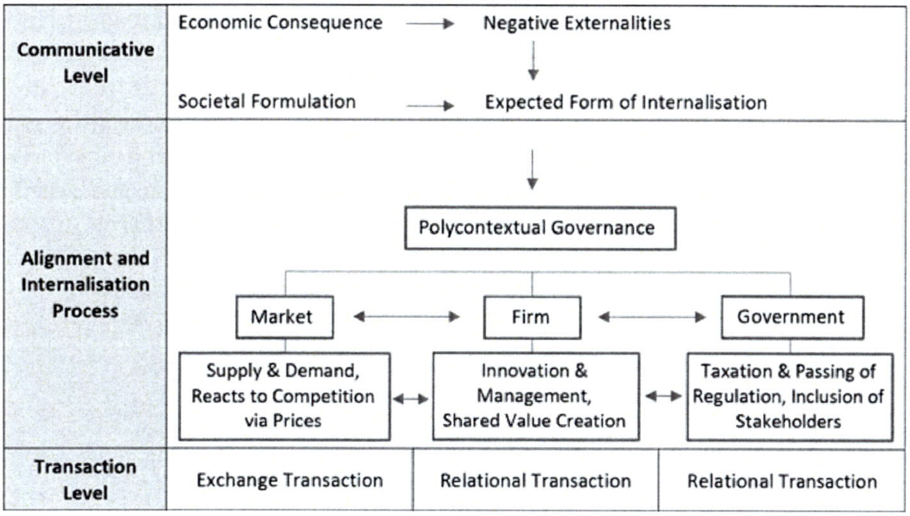

Fig. 3.2 Own depiction of polycontextural governance, according to Wieland (2020)

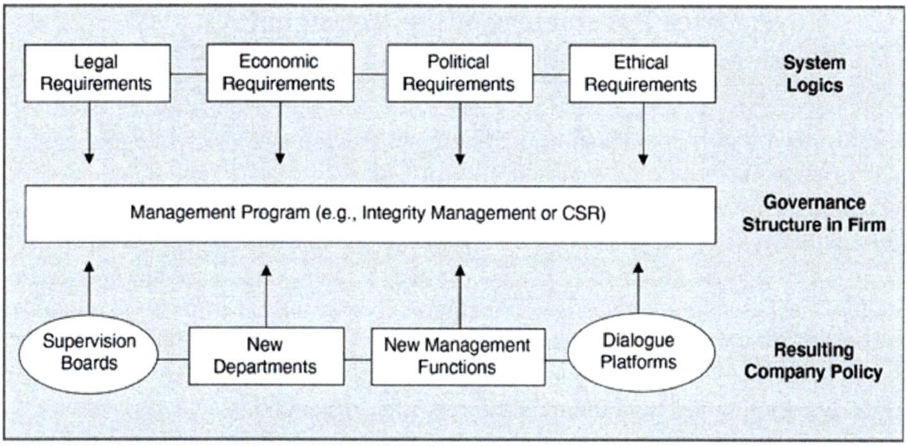

Fig. 3.3 Own depiction of company-internal governance measures, according to Wieland (2020)

This process is operationalised through an individualised governance structure in the form of a management program within the firm. In reaching the society's expected form of internalisation, the firm can benefit, for example, from suitable regulations. This is because the firm can combine them with appropriate corporate measures that serve its internalisation strategy, depending on which combination "*yields optimal efficiency and effectiveness*" (Wieland, 2020, p. 91). Further, Fig. 3.3 presents exemplary corporate policies resulting from the management program, which will help solidify the governance of transactions and the alignment of objectives the firm realises as a governance form. To achieve the realisation of such a governance structure through correlating governance processes, the firm can apply formal and informal contracts, which in turn are reinforced through, for example, legislation, shared values, and trust.

In conclusion, the overarching aim of Relational Governance is to provide a structure within which to pursue the relationalisation of events. Thereby, unity in diversity, and an alignment is created of differing decision logics coming with the realisation process. In this way, the efficiency and effectiveness of the governance structure determine its success. Apart from diverse decision logics, the governance structure needs to adapt flexibly to the social norms it encounters, which, as presented, can diverge across cultures, nations, and even regions. This is because values

> aren't stable entities that actors can use as ultimate points of orientation for their decisions; rather, they are dynamic events [...] which must be made more concrete [through] adaptive micro-mechanisms of governance. (Wieland, 2020, p. 10)

Particularly for unregulated dilemma situations, such as AI governance, the integration of social norms and values through a governance parameter becomes particularly important, as no hard law regulation is in place to govern economic decision-making.

3.2 Governance Parameters of the Relational AI Governance

The following conceptualisation of Relational Governance for AI begins with the definition of the relational transaction of private sector-led AI development, since, according to Wieland (2020), "*adopting the category of transaction as an attractor for multiple actors and polyvalent events is intended to restore access to the analysis of economic interactions*" (2020, p. 9). Further, he adds that "*these relational transactions necessarily take the form of relational contracts and the respective forms of governance used for them must be tailored accordingly*" (2020, p. 9). Thus, to be able to develop such a tailor-made governance approach for AI, a focus on the underlying relational transaction is the necessary requirement.

While systems theory proved to be suitable on the meta-level, for the actual governance of the demand stemming from these societal systems, transaction cost economics comes into play. This is because neither Luhmann's original theory (1995, 1996, 1997) nor Wieland's Relational Economics (2018, 2020) establishes societal systems as relational elements. Instead, the operationalisation process of developing governance measures requires a move from system-level to transactional level.

This step is required to make "*complexity manageable*" (Wieland, 2018, p. 23) via relational governance challenges, as only a governance form on operational level is able to the realise the "*integration of various rationalities*" (Wieland, 2018, p. 86). Hence, the single transaction, more specifically the "*relational transaction*" (Wieland, 2020, p. 46), serves as a basic unit for analysis.

3.2.1 *The Relational Transaction of Corporate AI Development & Adoption*

Essentially, one transaction always connects one element or actor to another. In the case of the economy, it connects the necessary resources for economic exchange. Wieland (2018, 2020) differentiates between the traditional economic exchange transaction, which aims to maximise the respective advantage of each party involved, and the objectives of a relational transaction, which are to plan and solve problems cooperatively (Wieland, 2020).

As soon as resources are connected to others through a specific transaction, their characteristics and their mode of action change (Wieland, 2018). Thus, the resources forming part of a transaction are transformed through the productivity-generating net of relations they share. It is important to note that it is only through their inter-linkage—their relation—that they can gain their specific productivity. This makes the relationship a productive resource in its own right, as it creates a transaction from the resources available and, thereby, a new union and shared value. In doing so, it sets the foundation for any collaborative governance forms (Roberts, 2000; Wieland, 2020).

Within each system and across systems, a multitude of transactions are taking place. Apart from monolingual transactions, such as the economic exchange transaction, there are also relational transactions—hubs consisting of interlinked system logics. As depicted in Fig. 3.4, within the form of the 'Market', numerous exchange transactions take place (Wieland, 2018, 2020). To build a suitable governance structure and address all logic included in the relational transactions underlying AI governance, an analysis of all relevant systems is necessary. Therefore, the relational transaction 'Rt' is marked with dashed lines.

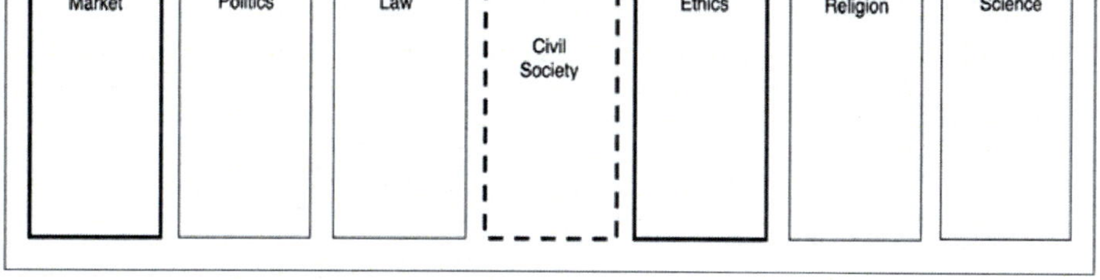

Fig. 3.4 Own depiction the relational transaction of AI adoption

Figure 3.4 exemplifies the emergence of a relational transaction for the AI context: as soon as a transaction attracts more than one other system logic, and thus consists of various interlinked dimensions, it is defined as a relational transaction (Wieland, 2018, 2020). As established in the previous chapter, the connection between the systems of 'Artificial Intelligence', the 'Market', 'Civil Society', and 'Ethics' must be analysed on the transactional level. After having understood the connection among those systems, the applicability of Wieland's Relational Governance for the AI context can be tested.

As for the system 'Artificial Intelligence', the higher availability of big data and computational power allowed new technologies to emerge, especially in machine learning and deep learning (Moore, 2006; Nilsson, 2009). Further, its all-encompassing disruptive power led to AI mostly being portrayed as a general-purpose technology (Brynjolfsson & McAfee, 2017; Dafoe, 2018; Goldfarb et al., 2019; Klinger et al., 2018; Nepelski & Sobolewski, 2020; Razzkazov, 2020; Trajtenberg, 2018).

When the broad opportunities for the application of AI became apparent to the economy, companies began to invest heavily into its development—a process continuing to this day (Bughin & Hazan, 2017; Bughin et al., 2017; Nilsson, 2009). From the transactional lenses of Relational Economics, this means that 'Artificial Intelligence'—to be precise, the monolingual AI transaction—attracted another system logic, namely, the 'Market'. Hence, the market logic and AI formed a structural coupling. This results in the linking of the formerly singular AI transaction to an economic transaction, spawning a relational AI-economic transaction. The relationship between 'Artificial Intelligence' and the 'Market' is reciprocal in nature, as AI transforms and elevates the economy (Bresnahan & Traijtenberg, 1995; Klinger et al., 2018; Nepelski & Sobolewski, 2020; Petralia, 2020). In turn, the economy—by investing heavily—promotes the progress made in AI research and broadens the impact of AI through rapid corporate adoption of AI (Bughin & Hazan, 2017; Bughin et al., 2017; Nilsson, 2009) (Fig. 3.5).

In detail, the private sector is affected by AI in two possible ways: for one, AI has a direct effect on economic growth (Bresnahan & Traijtenberg, 1995; Klinger et al., 2018; Nepelski & Sobolewski, 2020; Petralia, 2020), and, by adopting AI in its products and processes, the identity of an organisation changes, as it is exposed to the transformational power of AI (Bryson, 2018; Cihon, 2019; Cihon et al., 2020; Kaplan & Haenlein, 2019; Makridakis, 2017).

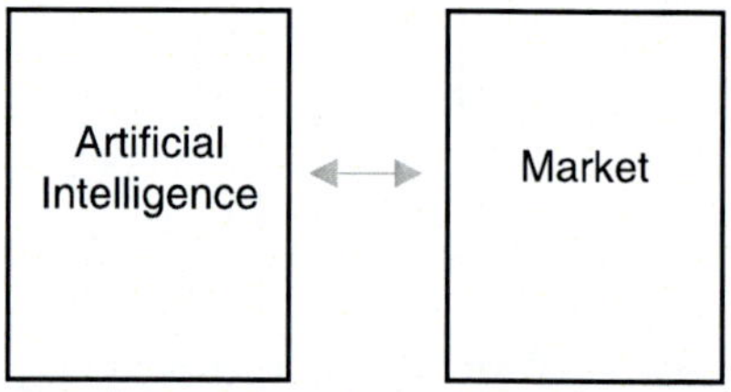

Fig. 3.5 Own depiction of reciprocal relation between systems 'AI' and 'Market'

Additionally, all companies, whether they apply AI or not, are affected by the rising competitive pressure in the market. This is because the effectiveness of companies applying AI rises, bringing them ahead of a competitor's cost structure. Moreover, oligarchic structures have already been established in the market for AI development, a development putting further pressure on companies to develop AI solutions quickly to gain market shares (Cave & ÓhÉigeartaigh, 2019; Dafoe, 2018; Horowitz, 2018). In particular, competition to access sufficiently big, high-quality data sets, which are the foundation for the development of new AI solutions, and the overall pressure to cover niches in the market, are often compared to an 'arms race' in AI (Cave & ÓhÉigeartaigh, 2019; Horowitz, 2018; Taddeo & Floridi, 2018b; Tomasik, 2013). This pace of development comes at a price, since corporate decision-making on AI adoption has direct effects on civil society, as previously established (Dafoe, 2018; Makridakis, 2017; Polyakova & Boyer, 2018; PwC, 2019).

Therefore, while being chased by competition and faced with time pressure, a firm needs to integrate various dimensions into its corporate decision-making. This is because, with the interlinkage of AI and the market, another indirect relation is created: the disruptive processes unleashed by AI are carried forward to another system via the close link between the economy and civil society. From a Relational Economics viewpoint, the progression of AI's impact on civil society can be explained as follows: Wieland (2014) defines the firm as a "*nexus of stakeholders*" (2014, p. 106). In detail, the firm entails "*a cooperative process between stakeholders [...] [aiming] to achieve success and growth for all of the stakeholders involved and to satisfy them by creating added value*" (Wieland, 2014, p. 110). Consequently, a firm—the operational entity of the system 'Market'—is inherently intertwined with civil society, as portrayed in the following Fig. 3.6.

Since the broadening impact of AI on civil society is mainly due to AI development performed by the private sector (Mittelstadt, 2019a) and the adoption of AI in firms, the system 'Market' acts as a channel for the transformative power of AI. Thus, in AI also, the firm is confronted with the negative externalities of its actions. As with CSR, the firm needs to become "*an actor in the world of politics and civil society, without becoming an organisation in political or civil society*" (Wieland, 2020, p. 60). With the private sector being the driver of this progress and the beneficiary of integrating AI into its processes, it is also confronted with the expectations of society. This is because, with the implementation of AI into the processes of companies and their integration into products, AI is introduced to civil society, in the form of users and

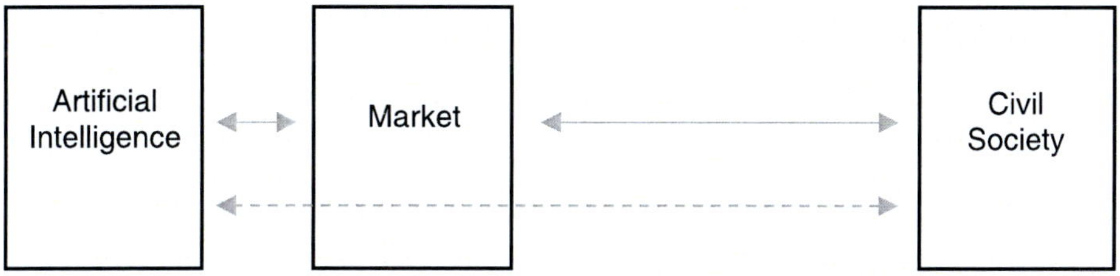

Fig. 3.6 Own depiction of reciprocal relation between systems 'AI' and 'Market'

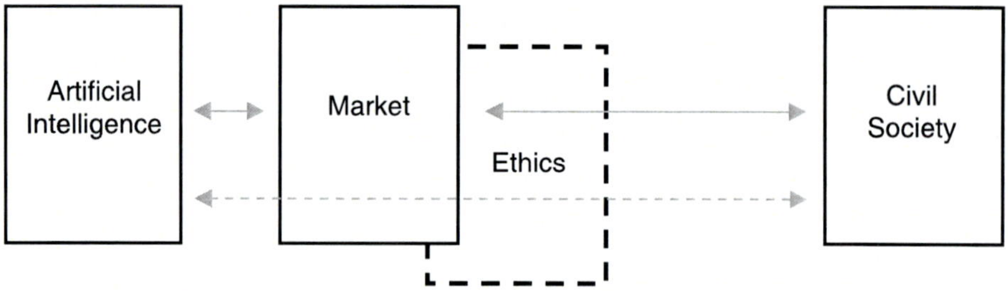

Fig. 3.7 Own depiction of relations between systems 'AI', 'Market', 'Ethics', and 'Civil Society'

consumers, at a rapid pace (Dafoe, 2018; Makridakis, 2017; Polyakova & Boyer, 2018; PwC, 2019).

Due to AI's disruptive and overarching nature, the effect of AI on society encompasses operational and philosophical challenges, as well as dilemma situations (Dafoe, 2018; Daly et al., 2019; Hagendorff, 2020; Jobin et al., 2019). Hence, as with CSR and business ethics, the system 'Ethics' adds to the initial attractor 'Artificial Intelligence'. Since it is the firm that instrumentalises AI for its particular interest, the need for ethical evaluation is again linked tightly to the system of the 'Market' (Fig. 3.7).

However, as for the characteristics of the systems 'Ethics' and 'Artificial Intelligence', two specifications need mentioning:

> First, both systems function self-referentially and do not require linkage with other systems to ensure their existence. For 'Artificial Intelligence', as apparent in the first decades since its invention, AI was a phenomenon of merely informatic interest (Kaplan & Haenlein, 2019; Makridakis, 2017; Nilsson, 2009). It was only when its use for the fulfilment of corporate objectives became apparent that it attracted the 'Market' system. Thus, while it existed before in a self-referential manner, it is particularly when linked to other system logics that its transformative power is maximised, and its impact broadens. The same holds for 'Ethics': while it exists as an individual system, its impact is, again, maximised by linking it to a field of application; in this case to the 'Market' and 'Artificial Intelligence'.
>
> Second, coming back to the notion of AI being a general-purpose technology: while the scope of this book focuses on the private sector, the system 'Artificial Intelligence' not only attracted the 'Market'. Instead, it has already and will eventually attract (all) other systems in a given society that apply AI to improve their performance or interact with it. Nowadays, the public sector is already engaging in AI adoption, as partly portrayed when discussing algorithmic governance in the previous chapter (Dunleavy, 2016; Gillespie, 2014; Gritsenko & Wood, 2020; König, 2019; Williamson, 2014). From this book's perspective, the public sector is in a similar role to the private sector, as it channels AI's transformative power and fosters its interaction with users and consumers. Hence, much like the private sector, the public sector is, and will be more so, confronted with consumer pressure

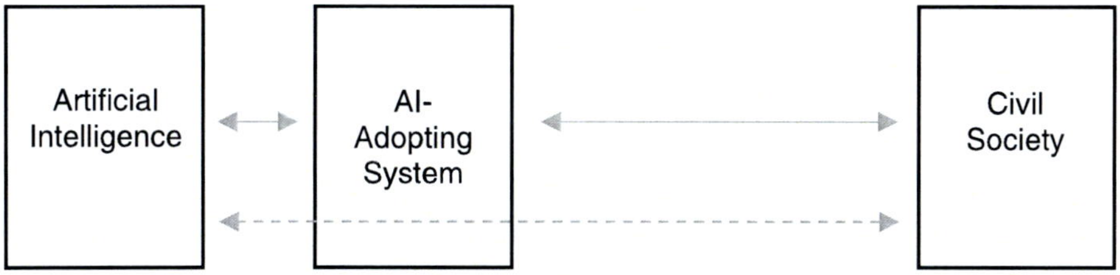

Fig. 3.8 Own depiction of relations between system 'AI', an exemplary system, and 'Civil Society'

regarding the responsible adoption of AI. Specifically, the demand for responsible AI implementation will rise with a constantly growing number of use cases (Danaher et al., 2017; Gamito & Ebers, 2021; Hassan & De Filippi, 2017; König, 2019) and, thus, greater exposure to civil society.

Hence, as portrayed in Fig. 3.8, a similar dynamic to that identified for the private sector is suspected to hold true for other societal systems interacting with AI. To take an example: the ethical concerns linked to algorithmic governance—the application of algorithmic control and regulation mechanisms by and to the public sector (Dunleavy, 2016; Gillespie, 2014; Gritsenko & Wood, 2020; König, 2019; Williamson, 2014)—show similarities with those in the context of private-sector AI adoption and the reaction of civil society to it. Therefore, this book's analysis encourages further research to focus on this intersection, since the conceptualisation of trans-sectoral AI governance is outside its current scope.

To conclude, from a private-sector perspective, AI adoption, and more so its governance, is based on a relational transaction including various system logics. Specifically, companies partially employ the binary coding of 'Artificial Intelligence' to enhance the effectiveness of company-internal processes (Wieland, 2020). Hence, the challenge for companies adopting AI

> consists in programming the changed contexts and logics that now apply to its transactions in a way that allows it to continue to conduct its former Exchange Transactions on the market, now in the form of Relational Transactions. (Wieland, 2020, p. 60)

However, due to the newness of the phenomenon, its competitive dynamics, and the market being currently unregulated, strategies in AI governance differ from the governance of previously existing issues, such as CSR.

3.2.1.1 The Role of the Firm in the Polycontextual Governance of Artificial Intelligence

The polycontextual governance of AI is developed based on its relational transaction and aims to address and integrate the social normativity coming with the phenomenon. Consequently, Fig. 3.9 depicts the societal context of AI governance and serves as a structure for this section.

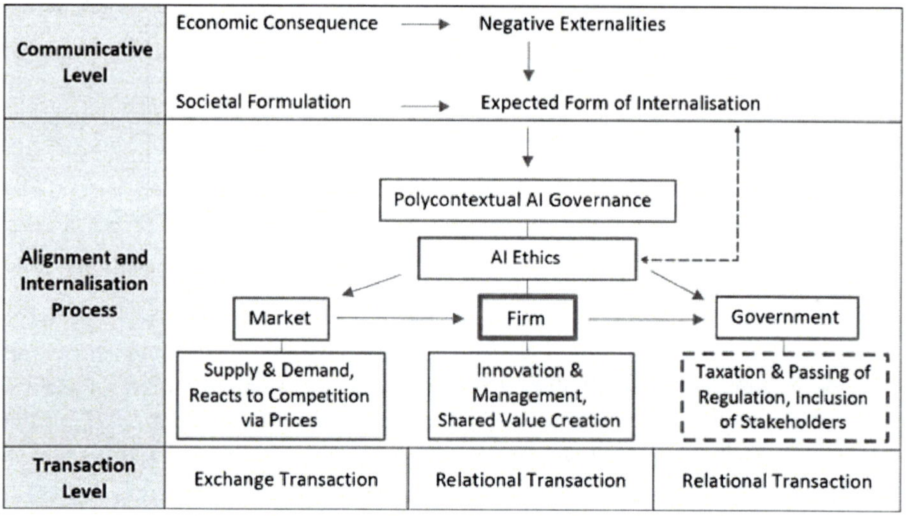

Fig. 3.9 Own depiction of polycontextural AI governance, according to Wieland (2020)

Negative Externalities

Beginning with the communicative level, this book has extensively established the economic consequences and negative externalities of AI development and AI adoption by the private sector in previous chapters (Cihon et al., 2020; Dafoe, 2018; Mittelstadt, 2019a; Polyakova & Boyer, 2018; Polyakova & Meserole, 2019).

Societal Formulation

Society has already formulated its expectation (Wieland, 2018) towards companies to internalise these negative externalities by expressing rising concerns (Cath, 2018; Floridi, 2016, 2018; Harari, 2018; Perc et al., 2019; Rosa, 2016), also referred to as the AI control problem (Bostrom, 2014; Yampolskiy, 2015). This entails worries about the mid-to-long-term consequences of AI adoption, e.g., loss of jobs, or rather overarching challenges, such as a possible power shift in society and the restriction of freedom of choice (Balfanz, 2017; Dafoe, 2018; Hassan & de Filippi, 2017; Helbing et al., 2019; Lessig, 1999; Rosenblatt et al., 2002). Further, the expectation for private-sector regulation to be implemented is reflected in the growing number of scholars dealing with the topic, and the significant emergence in academic publications subsuming the types of externalities coming with AI adoption and possible approaches to solutions (Balfanz, 2017; Berendt, 2019; Cath, 2018; Cihon, 2019; Cihon et al., 2020; Dafoe, 2018; Floridi, 2018; Future of Life, 2015; Hagendorff, 2020; Mittelstadt, 2019a; Perc et al., 2019).

AI Ethics

Research disciplines such as AI ethics play a big part in verbalising, systematising, and visualising societal concerns and society's expectations towards companies. They do so by focusing on the development of a shared understanding of protection-worthy values regarding AI, such as transparency or privacy. This is of high importance, as Wieland (2020) points out that "*social norms and relational governance are not self-enforced; rather, they are enforced by means of other punitive mechanisms like social criticism and loss of status or reputation*" (2020, p. 43). Thus, the aggregation and systematisation of such criticisms help point out cases of misconduct on the part of the companies, which in turn threatens their reputation, and gives bargaining power to society (Dafoe, 2018; Wieland, 2018, 2020).

Government

Compared to other phenomena, polycontextual management in AI Governance is confronted with a specific challenge: while various nations and companies do support the development of regulations for AI research, the development of AI-based production, and specific regulations for its implementation, so far, according to the United Nations Interregional Crime and Justice Research Institute (UNICRI), no all-encompassing law, regulation or bill has been passed to regulate AI, anywhere around the globe (UNICRI, 2021).

However, various countries, e.g., China and the U.S., passed national strategies and policy plans, as early as 2016 (UNICRI, 2021), which the U.S. renewed in 2019 under the title 'Guidance for Regulation of Artificial Intelligence Applications' (Vought, 2020). Also in 2019, the United Nations Educational, Scientific and Cultural Organization (UNESCO) communicated its intention to develop a global standard-setting instrument for AI by the end of 2021 (UNESCO, 2019). In the European Union (E.U.), the member states mostly follow national AI strategies, but these national plans are mostly convergent and are further guided by the E.U.'s Strategy on AI, which a high-level expert group leads. In 2019, this European Commission presented its guidelines for Trustworthy AI, aiming for European AI to be lawful, ethical, and robust (AIHLEG, 2019). In 2020, it published a White Paper on the European Approach to Excellence and Trust in AI (European Commission, 2020a), which presents its suggestions for an ecosystem of excellence and an ecosystem of trust. As part of the second aspect, trust, the White Paper differentiates applications in AI according to their risk level for society and introduces the categories 'high-risk' and 'non-high-risk'. The category 'high-risk' is again determined by two factors; namely the criticality of its use and its application sector (European Commission, 2020a). In April 2021, the European Commission presented the first global proposal for an AI regulatory framework (European Commission, 2021a). With this risk-based framework, the E.U. presents a first effort to level the ground for companies to engage in regulatory action in AI development as, depending on the risk level of the application, it demands adaptation in data training, data keeping, and high levels of robustness, as well as human oversight in development.

Market

Translated to the Relational Governance of Artificial Intelligence, this means that, for now, the (global) system 'Market'—even with European regulation on AI safety in preparation—remains vastly unregulated. Consequently, it is probable that advantages will be gained over competitors at the expense of ethical considerations and societal concerns such as AI safety, because the actors involved face the pressure to prioritise pace over caution (Dafoe, 2018). This is because a regulatory gap opens the door for strong competition in innovation-driven markets: as with all types of innovation, the market is influenced by the advancements and state of the art in corresponding research (Rothwell, 1994). With AI, it is precisely the pace of its development and advancements that pushes its adoption in organisations. The risks can range from a high concentration of power in society to an accelerated pace of development due to possible economic or military benefits stemming from a first-mover advantage. Technological arms races are particularly characterised by high economic gains from such advantages, which is why reaching market dominance serves as a strong incentive for companies (Dafoe, 2018). This development would come with so-called 'collateral damage', meaning that the prioritisation of pace over caution will lead to acquiescence to negative consequences, which can then only be dealt with ex-post—possibly after damage has been done or irreversible consequences have taken place (Allen & Chan, 2017; Armstrong et al., 2016; Nakashima, 2012; Polyakova & Boyer, 2018; Scharre, 2019).

Firm

Since no definite internalisation or alignment process of societal interest has been established as the governance form for AI, alignment efforts remain with the firm. Although the E.U. proposed a regulatory framework, societal expectations regarding AI governance are currently still directed towards the private sector, and thus, the firm. In addition, while AI development might soon be regulated in the E.U., it is unlikely that this will stop the dynamics companies that find themselves in, since this global phenomenon mainly revolves around the U.S. and China (Cave & ÓhÉigeartaigh, 2019; Geist, 2016; Scharre, 2019; Tomasik, 2013). As for the creation of shared value, these settings favour competitive approaches to dissolving wicked problems—which result in a win-lose-constellation (Roberts, 2000). Winning in this context means the successful dominance of one technology in the market ends the arms race, as it exceeds other technological developments by far and, thereby, ends all competition.

As described in the first chapter, reaching such dominance requires higher amounts of resources than other strategies—a cost that some players in the market, such as China, might be willing to pay (Dafoe, 2018; Girasa, 2020). The race-like character of this endeavour ensures the dispersion of power, as more than one player in the market aims for this advantageous leading position (Roberts, 2000). Hence, referring to Fig. 3.9 depicting polycontextual governance, the market exists in the monolingual form portrayed, driven by companies aiming for market dominance, which in turn results in widening their pricing options—the language of the market (Wieland, 2018, 2020).

3.2.1.2 The Scope of Polycontextual AI Governance

From a theoretical viewpoint, a collaborative approach is favourable, since it aims to include and align the complex stakeholder interests (Holtel, 2016; Rittel & Webber, 1973; Roberts, 2000; Wieland, 2018). In this context, that can include various collaborative multi-stakeholder or interfirm efforts, e.g., the joint development of AI standards, or collective self-regulation among a group of companies (Cihon, 2019; Dafoe, 2018), or norms and treaties, diplomatic agreements, and the initiation of a specialised institution (Dafoe, 2018). Such an approach would lower the risks and costs for all parties involved in the race for dominance through a joint elevation of standards (Dafoe, 2018; Roberts, 2000; Wieland, 2018, 2020). In doing so, the risk involved for the single company is lowered significantly compared to choosing to self-regulate in an otherwise competitive market setting. With this approach, collective progress and mutual advantages are created for all actors involved (Elia & Margherita, 2018; Roberts, 2000; Schoder et al., 2014), or in other words—a shared value (Wieland, 2018, 2020).

However, while a collaborative approach seems most favourable for society, Dafoe (2018) and Roberts (2000) agree that the realisation of collaborative approaches is particularly challenging and only seldom crowned with success. Dafoe presents elemental factors for such a form of cooperation:

> (1) the parties mutually perceive a strong interest in reaching a successful agreement (great risks from non-cooperation or gains from cooperation, low returns on unilateral steps); (2) when the parties otherwise have a trusting relationship; (3) when there is sufficient consensus about what an agreement should look like [...]; (4) when compliance is easily, publicly, and rapidly verifiable; (5) when the risks from being defected on are low [...]; (6) the incentives to defect are otherwise low.
>
> Compared to other domains, AI appears in some ways less amenable to international cooperation conditions (3), (4), (5), (6) – but in other ways could be more amenable, namely (1) if the parties come to perceive existential risks from unrestricted racing and tremendous benefits from cooperating, (2) because China and the West currently have a relatively cooperative relationship compared to other international arms races, and there may be creative technical possibilities for enhancing (4) and (5)." (2018, p. 46)

Particularly in the AI context, various factors seem to oppose the probability of national or global collaboration, such as incomparably higher incentives to defect—namely, the chance of winning the race for a particular use case or technological development—than to collaborate and share the gains of dominance in that specific market (Cihon, 2019; Dafoe, 2018). Based on the many variables influencing and disincentivising the potential interfirm collaboration, the scope of this book is set on collaborative strategies for the single company and on involving its stakeholders. With this, it presents a replicable governance approach for the single company, allowing for a rather bottom-up creation of shared value across industries and nations. Thereby, it fosters and enables the continued existence of a firm in the AI market, its economic success, and its social legitimisation (Wieland, 2018, 2020).

In this way, it covers three out of four dimensions of collaborative governance, as presented by Roberts (2000): shared value creation, stakeholder involvement and self-regulation, resulting in responsible AI adoption. Moreover, it provides a starting point for research and a practicable instrument, which raises the likeliness of its application in practice—and, thereby, of an actual impact on society.

3.2.2 Societal Informal Institutions of the Relational AI Governance

To apply Relational AI Governance to a company setting, the four governance parameters and their interplay need to be analysed.

Generally, economically driven innovation often requires a re-balancing of stakeholders' demands, since new relational transactions emerge. Hence, the governance of such new transactions demands the interaction of individual and collective actors with the relevant formal and informal societal institutions. It is only by stabilising the relations among these parameters, by creating a temporarily stable equilibrium, that the creation of shared value is possible (Wieland, 2020). Hence, effective governance requires an interplay of formal and informal governance measures, such as hard law and soft law, with standards or values (Cao & Lumineau, 2015; Wieland, 2018, 2020).

As presented, such relations between formal and informal measures within the firm can be constituted in four ways: interaction, substitution, complementation, and combination (Wieland, 2018, 2020). An ideal relational governance approach aims at including all four governance parameters but requires the interplay of at least one formal and one informal parameter to be effective. To achieve this objective, the minimum relation of either 'SII' and 'O' or 'SFI' and 'I' needs to be given.

For the case of AI, the conceptual focus is on 'SII'. This is because the role of the individual and the organisation remains the same compared to Wieland's original theory. Hence, their characteristics can be applied to the AI context without much adaptation. As for 'SFI', I will address both the situation of an entirely unregulated market, as is the case at present, and of a partially regulated market, which will arise once the E.U. regulation is passed.

In conclusion, the parameter 'SII' is naturally the most situationally adaptive, since it displays society's perception of the particular phenomenon requiring governance. Especially when lacking the fourth governance parameter, 'SFI', the role of 'SII' becomes crucial in the governance process. Hence, 'SII' is conceptualised in detail in this section.

3.2.2.1 Conceptualising 'Societal Informal Institutions' for Relational AI Governance

Generally, societal informal institutions are part of informal governance measures, as is the Individual's role. Moreover, 'SII' are constituted as a structural element in the model, which promotes the non-normative nature of the Relational Governance approach (Wieland, 2020). Thus, they can be understood as a placeholder for societal values within the model, rather than a specific ethical position the theory promotes. This allows for its application across nations and makes it possible to address the urgent need of global importance (Balfanz, 2017; Cave & ÓhÉigeartaigh, 2019; Feldstein, 2019; Hagerty & Rubinov, 2019).

'SII' "*evaluate every economic act using the guiding difference 'conformity – non-conformity'*" (Wieland, 2020, p. 23). If an economic action and, consequently, a firm, violates these social norms, an explicit event can arise, such as costs in the form of reputational losses (Wieland, 2018, 2020). However, it is important to note that Wieland (2020) indicates the ex-post enforcement mechanism of 'SII' by stating that, even though "*the costs involved in adhering to this guiding difference for individuals and organisations are certainly not meaningless, yet they do not determine the decision made at t1*" (2020, p. 23). Still, Wieland continues: "*no one can, based on cost considerations, systematically choose not to comply with legal and moral norms without facing any costly consequences*" (2020, p. 23). Thus, he ascribes an enforcing power to 'SII'—however, not necessarily for the initial transaction of an individual or collective actor, since 'SII' often serves as an enforcement mechanism for formal measures and contracts among parties involved (Wieland, 2020) and as the normative ground based on which formal measures are developed, such as guidelines.

The conceptualisation of 'SII' is based on existing research in the field of AI ethics. The following section structures and clusters the content of numerous publications and reviews them with the aim of deriving governance strategies for the firm. To ensure the objectivity of the categories and clusters identified, I applied the following methodological approach.

Methodological Approach to Conceptualise the Parameter 'SII'

Mayring's (2000, 2008, 2010, 2015) approach to qualitative content analysis was applied due to its similarity to verified international methods. Qualitative content analysis can be utilised for both deductive and inductive research (Elo & Kyngäs, 2008; Elo et al., 2014; Graneheim et al., 2017; Mayring, 2015). Despite often being interpretative and subjective, qualitative research is suitable for developing new theories or concepts and identifying essential themes in raw data (Mayring, 2000, 2008, 2010, 2015). Further, the strength of qualitative inductive research is in identifying and describing categories and patterns, while structuring larger data sets for the first time (Mayring, 2015; Spöhring, 1989; Thomas, 2006). By applying Mayring's (2010, 2015) systematic and scientific approach to inductive research, the results and categories developed by the book are valid and replicable (Thomas, 2006).

Each category can exist with or without connections to other categories. Connections among categories—if they exist—can be of causal, hierarchical, or network-like nature (Mayring, 2015). Usually, as is the case for this book, the categories identified are subsequently integrated or used as the foundation for developing a model or framework (Mayring, 2008, 2010, 2015; Thomas, 2006).

This methodological approach involves a comparatively high level of researcher's subjectivity (Krippendorff, 1980, 2013; Mayring, 2002, 2010, 2015; Steinke, 2000). Despite this limitation, this approach offers relevant options for this conceptual book, as it allows for the accurate depiction of requirements for AI governance and the consequential need-based development of the model. Further, its findings will be contextualised within the original Relational Governance Theory and complemented by the findings from the systematic literature review of private-sector AI governance. Given the multifaceted approach used to develop the model, I applied no additional verification methods.

3.2.2.2 Defining the Scope and Objectives of Reviewing AI Ethics for 'SII'

To begin with, a delimitation of the term AI ethics is required. Siau and Wang (2020) state that

> to address AI ethics, one needs to consider the ethics of AI and how to build ethical AI. Ethics of AI studies the ethical principles, rules, guidelines, policies, and regulations that are related to AI. Ethical AI is an AI that performs and behaves ethically. One must recognize and understand the potential ethical and moral issues that may be caused by AI to formulate the necessary ethical principles, rules, guidelines, policies, and regulations for AI. (2020, p. 74)

Mittelstadt adds that AI ethics focuses on identifying "*universal high-level values or principles to guide ethical development and deployment of AI*" (2019a, p. 1). The European Commission's High-Level Expert Group on Artificial Intelligence (AIHLEG) further specifies its purpose as being concerned with "*the good life of individuals, whether in terms of quality of life, or human autonomy and freedom necessary for a democratic society*" (2019, p. 5).

Apart from the stream of AI ethics, related research streams focus on ethical dealing with machines or machines' ethical behaviour. Computer ethics examines the developer's behaviour when interacting with and designing computers or machines and their use by humans (Boyles, 2018; Bynum, 2000; Johnson, 1985). Machine ethics, on the other hand, focuses on the ethical conduct of the machines themselves (Boyles, 2018; Cervantes et al., 2016; Mayer et al., 2021; Yu et al., 2018). Finally, robot ethics explores the ethical topics arising from the development and implementation of robots and societal interaction with them (Asaro, 2006; Lin et al., 2012; Wallach & Asaro, 2020).

Thus, current research evolves around AI and the ethical implications of the interaction between humans and machines, particularly machines adopting AI. Further, it addresses decisive factors for ethical behaviour of and between humans and machines. While these research streams appear to be highly interlinked, due to their limited scope, this book will solely focus on AI ethics, since the parameter 'SII' allows for the later integration of numerous additional content-based categories.

However, this book combines the definitions presented for AI ethics by combining two prevalent views: it will differentiate between the ethics of AI, such as philosophical concepts, and ethical AI, which includes technological or social considerations serving as a base to integrate ethics into AI development. Moreover, it clusters existing research on specific values in AI ethics, examining the potential outcome scenarios for AI implementation and its role in society. Consequently, the book adapts and complements existing review structures (Hagendorff, 2020; Kazim & Koshiyama, 2020a) with additional thematic patterns identified in AI ethics literature, using inductive categories. In doing so, it not only clusters existing research but derives dependencies and connections between the streams. This further reduces complexity levels for practice, while promoting the development of a solution-based approach in AI governance. Regarding Relational Economics, it contributes to understanding relevant topics of social normativity and its formalisation in the form of'SII' in AI.

3.2.2.3 Underlying Philosophical Patterns in AI Ethics

Social normativity displays the desirable behaviour of individual and collective actors within a given society (Wieland, 2018, 2020), and it is the discipline of ethics that examines how and based on which considerations actors should act (Burton et al., 2017). From a philosophical perspective, AI ethics and resulting recommendations on solving ethical dilemmas mostly refer to an actor's character or conduct (Bilal et al., 2020). Further, ethical dilemmas are defined as situations requiring new behavioural decisions since predefined behavioural choices lead to infringement of ethical principles (Kirkpatrick, 2015; Yu et al., 2018).

In AI ethics, the phenomenon of dealing with such emerging dilemmas is commonly viewed from three different philosophical perspectives (Bilal et al., 2020; Burton et al., 2017; Yu et al., 2018) as the inductive analysis of this book revealed: they either examine an individual's personal traits and integrity, his desirable actions to solve a dilemma, or his specific behavioural rules to solve such a situation. In philosophy, the first perspective is known as virtue ethics; the second portrays a deontological and the third a utilitarian or consequentialist view (Burton et al., 2017). Thus, these three perspectives present research streams and resulting instruments with which ethical dilemmas in AI can be examined:

1. Stemming from Greek philosophy, specifically Aristotle's ethics, in virtue ethics the actor is understood to act ethically if his actions are in line with particular values, such as, e.g., justice, honesty, and integrity (Wieland, 2018, 2020; Yu et al., 2018). This ethical approach is goal- and character-oriented, as it focuses on sets of abilities leading the actor to reach his goals and flourish (Burton et al., 2017). Apart from an ethical motivation, this kind of behaviour can be driven by a desire to be perceived positively by other members of society (Boddington, 2017; Wieland, 2018, 2020; Yu et al., 2018).
2. In deontological ethics, an actor needs to comply with a specific set of obligatory duties or moral laws (Burton et al., 2017) for his actions to be considered ethical (Boddington, 2017; Yu et al., 2018). Hence, an actor must act according to existing social norms (Yu et al., 2018). This perspective is based on the fundamental idea that universally true regulations can be applied. Thus, much like AI itself, it is a rule-based approach (Burton et al., 2017).
3. Consequentialist ethics require the actor to weigh up the consequences of his actions and choose the option that offers the highest moral output. This school of thought is also referred to as utilitarian ethics, since the actor must identify the option with the best set of aggregated consequences, resulting in welfare for the largest number of individuals (Boddington, 2017; Burton et al., 2017; Yu et al., 2018). In academia, utilitarian ethics are known for being the theoretical foundation of game theory, which is an approach for modelling different decision scenarios for an actor to maximise his preferences (Burton et al., 2017).

Applied to the AI context, deontology resembles a rule-based approach, whereas consequentialism leads to a cost- and outcome-oriented decision frame (Thornton et al., 2016). Due to their routine-based logic, it is particularly the deontological stream that is in line with AI's rule-based nature (Burton et al., 2017). However, the highly adaptable nature of AI poses challenges to the identification of universally applicable rules, e.g., regarding the value 'justice', as its interpretation depends heavily on the objectives and ethical views of the use case it is applied to or the particular society reviewing it (Burton et al., 2017). Current research shows that scholars in AI ethics tend to combine these philosophical approaches since one philosophical view is often not enough to guide systems working entirely autonomously, as does AI.

Hence, a combined framework can address both constraints for AI and its costs (Thornton et al., 2016), while Bilal et al.'s (2020) research suggests that virtue ethics is an underrepresented approach in AI ethics—and a stream that scholars consider highly relevant for AI governance. This is because scholars claim that "*Utilitarianism and Kantianism pay more attention to conscious decision-making while virtue ethics pays more attention to unconscious decision-making*" (Bilal et al., 2020, p. 226). To exemplify their claim, they present evidence that AI requires particularly high levels of self-awareness to remain conscious of the changes AI induces in society (Bilal et al., 2020). I agree with the need for combined approaches, and, thus, integrated advances in AI ethics from all three philosophical perspectives to allow for a holistic development of AI measures.

3.2.2.4 Academic and Public-Sector Value Formulations Relevant for the Parameter 'SII'

Researchers are already critically observing the influence of the private sector on AI ethics, highlighting its influence on both topics and ongoing academic debates (Hagendorff, 2020, 2022). Expecting more objectivity from publications and formulations stemming from academia, I will abstain in this book from integrating practical advancements initiated by the private sector into this section. In this way, it avoids private sector bias in its depiction of social normativity.

Refraining from commenting on private-sector initiatives, the book will focus on advancements made in the public sector and academia. Stemming from the public sector, it presents advancements made by the European Commission (AIHLEG, 2019) and the OECD (2019), as their intergovernmental structure is expected to give an insight into transnationally valid ethical positions on AI ethics and governance. As for academia, it covers AI ethics research from all schools of thought identified, so as to ensure a neutral representation of academic progress in the field.

In this section, the depiction of AI ethics in the form of public guidelines, by public-sector institutions, for example, is understood to be a procedural step towards the formalisation and aggregation of societal values. Moreover, it serves as the process of defining and creating an agreement on social norms (Wieland, 2018, 2020). At a later stage, I address private-sector, company-internal guidelines as an instrument for the firm's relational AI governance management program. While these company-internal guidelines can be inspired by public-sector advancements or academic publications on guidelines, they can entail further elements. Generally, company-internal guidelines can consist of a combination of various elements, such as corporate culture, official compliance restrictions, and societal values—depending on the relational transaction they aim to address (Wieland, 2020). When focusing on the operationalisation of AI governance within the firm, company-internal guidelines serve as a governance instrument within the governance structure. Therefore, the company-internal guidelines suggested for Relational AI Governance will include the demands of a complex set of stakeholders—parts of them being represented by the public-sector guidelines examined in this following section.

3.2.2.5 Contextualising the Public-Sector and Academic Formalisation of AI Ethics

In 2019, both the E.U., or more specifically the AIHLEG, and the OECD presented their non-binding approach to AI ethics in the form of guidelines:

The main focus of the E.U. guidelines is to establish trust among producers, developers, and consumers of AI applications. Therefore, it presents three components, each consisting of four ethical principles that are operationalised in seven requirement steps. The expert group further adds that the components for trustworthy AI shall be implemented throughout the AI lifecycle and, thereby, include the processes and staff involved, instead of only focusing on the AI system itself (AIHLEG, 2019; Gasparotti, 2019; OECD, 2019).

The approach consists of three components—lawful, ethical, and robust AI – which are connected to the four ethical principles of 'respect for human autonomy', 'prevention of harm', 'fairness', and 'explicability' (AIHLEG, 2019). Since these broad terms are harder to implement, the AIHLEG (2019) suggests the following seven operational steps to achieve trustworthy AI systems:

- Human Agency and Oversight
- Technical Robustness and Safety
- Privacy and Data Governance
- Transparency
- Diversity, Non-Discrimination and Fairness
- Societal and Environmental Well-Being
- Accountability

The OECD adopted the vast majority of these seven principles, e.g., the demand for AI to be robust, safe, transparent, and accountable. However, the OECD added two specifications; namely, the objective that AI shall not only aim for fairness but human-centred values and that it shall support inclusive growth and sustainable development (Gasparotti, 2019; OECD, 2019).

In academia, researchers oftentimes analyse existing guidelines from practice to derive common principles (Hagendorff, 2020, 2022; Jobin et al., 2019). While other scholars also reviewed advances in AI ethics, Jobin et al. (2019) presented the most extensive study to date. Hence, their review will serve as an exemplary overview of the field. In particular, Jobin et al. (2019) analysed more than 80 guidelines to examine the most prominent topics in AI research. They identified the following 11 clustered principles:

- Transparency
- Justice and Fairness
- Non-Maleficence
- Responsibility
- Privacy
- Beneficence
- Freedom and Autonomy
- Trust
- Sustainability
- Dignity
- Solidarity

The complementarity and interconnectedness of the value sets stemming from the public sector and academia will be exemplified for the value explicability: the explicability of AI is understood to foster trust in AI technologies (Pieters, 2011; Shin, 2021; Thiebes et al., 2020). This is because the explainability of an AI system's actions leads to a higher acceptance by all parties involved in its adoption (Hagras, 2018; Rai, 2020). Further, researchers link transparency closely to raised levels of accountability and trust, as technological transparency gives a better understanding of machine-made decisions. Thereby, it fosters the ability to explain machine actions and the willingness to trust in AI (Boddington, 2017; Ehsan et al., 2021; Hois et al., 2019). Again, once the steps an AI system takes are explainable, the accountability of its actions, which is highly significant in the ethical context, can be addressed responsibly by the organisation or actor dealing with the AI solution. Thereby, research on accountability helps to ensure the desired justice and fairness (Floridi & Cowls, 2019; Kazim & Koshiyama, 2020a, 2020b; Thiebes et al., 2020). By being able to ensure justice and fairness, the demand for human well-being and safety (Dafoe, 2018; Kazim & Koshiyama, 2020a) can be fulfilled.

Another important standard was published in 2021, namely by the Institute of Electrical and Electronics Engineers, or IEEE. This association is one of the largest professional organisations, with almost 500,000 members across the globe. According to its mission statement, the IEEE is dedicated to ensuring that technologies benefit society. To do so, it particularly focuses on the development of standards and raising awareness among its professional group. To date, the IEEE has successfully published over 1000 standards (IEEE, 2021).

The standard relevant to AI ethics is named "IEEE 7000™-2021 Standard Model Process for Addressing Ethical Concerns during System Design" and aims to integrate ethical requirements into the AI engineering and product design process to lower risks associated with its deployment. To this end, it presents its value-based engineering approach, which will help to conceptualise, prioritise and respect consumer values in the AI design and development process (IEEE, 2021). This process enables developers to translate and integrate stakeholder values and ethical considerations into their design practices, allowing for transparent and traceable outcomes. With the standard in place, companies are able to include ethical criteria based on an elaborate set of processes for the exploration and development stages of AI innovation cycles. However, the standard does not provide guidance regarding a particular design approach that supports the application of ethical values to the algorithm. Instead, it integrates ethical risk-based design and, thereby, lowers risks in the phase of building AI-based products, as well as allowing a stakeholder-oriented value proposition. In this way, the standard aims to foster trust on the side of end-users and stakeholders, as well as raising the overall acceptance of AI in society. As for its relation to the presented approaches by the OECD and academia, the IEEE again chooses principled AI ethics, particularly values such as, among others, transparency, privacy, fairness, and accountability. In addition, it complements these values with the technological values it aims for, such as effectiveness.

Hence, the interdependency of values identified by both sectors solidifies the proceedings of this book, which will allocate the three presented value sets to the previously presented philosophical schools of thought. This step is taken for two reasons: First, all three value sets are combined to ensure coverage of the most prevalent ethical demand companies are currently confronted with. Second, by allocating them to the philosophical perspectives, which determine the form of a given relational governance measure, the book offers a two-dimensional foundation for the subsequent operationalisation of 'SII': Specifically, it combines content-related and form-related insights. While the value sets offer content-related understanding, the form of the suggested 'SII'-based governance measures will stem from the specific philosophical perspective on AI. Consequently, it restructures the presented existing research inductively to present a more manageable decision frame for companies and, thereby, promote the integration of 'SII' into the firm's governance structure.

3.2.2.6 New Inductive 'SII'-Categories for AI Ethics in Relational Governance

The new, self-developed categories stem from a combination of thematic codes and philosophical characteristics and provide an integration of prevalent values from AI ethics guidelines and philosophy-based categories.

Research on Individual Values and Virtues in AI

Prevalent research in this stream includes some scholars' direct demand for virtue ethics in AI, as well as research on correlating values, such as justice or honesty. Further, it subsumes research addressing the individual's character and the development of virtues, often referred to as a change in an individual's mindset.

Yu et al. (2018) and Hagendorff (2020, 2022), especially, expressed the strong need for more virtue ethics-based measures in AI ethics and AI governance. They base their claim on the lack of success of the principle-based guidelines that are primarily in current use, since, according to Yu et al. and Hagendorff, these fail to sufficiently address the individual's character. According to scholars, by focusing on virtue ethics, the psychological component of AI-ethically compliant behaviour is brought to the centre of attention, instead of merely focusing on the identification of dilemma situations—as is the primary goal of principle-based AI ethics.

Thereby, virtue ethics serve as a value-based orientation for behaviour (Yu et al., 2018) but also sheds light on psychological limitations of the mind, such as unconscious biases of the individual, which require consciously chosen countermeasures (Hagendorff, 2022). Table 3.1 presents an overview of the three subcategories identified in virtue ethics research.

The first subcategory of research on virtue ethics focuses on the specific values promoted by this research stream, which include, among others, honesty, justice, courage and empathy (Hagendorff, 2020; Neubert & Montañez, 2020; Vallor, 2016). In his contribution from 2022, Hagendorff specifically added honesty, responsibility, and care to the list of virtues. It should be noted that he derived these values from an

Table 3.1 Own depiction, inductive analysis of AI virtue ethics literature

Category: Virtue Ethics for AI	1st Subcategory: Virtuous Values e.g., honesty, justice, courage, empathy, responsibility, care (Hagendorff, 2021, Neubert & Montañez, 2020; Vallor, 2016)
	2nd Subcategory: Operationalisation e.g., changing mindset and norms through situational training, raising intrinsic motivation (Floridi, 2016; Hagendorff, 2020, 2021; Yu et al., 2018)
	3rd Subcategory: Challenges e.g., little exposure to practice, need for awareness and psychological measures (Hagendorff, 2020, 2021; Yu et al., 2018)

extensive meta-level analysis of existing AI ethics guidelines from various sectors of society, e.g., the public sector and academia. Hence, the identification of virtues in this case can be deemed as demand-driven, whereas traditional virtue ethics stem from Greek philosophy and consist of moral and intellectual elements (Wieland, 2018, 2020). This is significant since virtues imply universal truth and "*represent the ability to implement values in practice*" (Wieland, 2020, p. 141). Nonetheless, the moral virtues identified by Hagendorff (2022) are deemed relevant to relational AI governance. This remark merely highlights the nature of the analysis, to differentiate between virtues stemming from philosophy and the virtues presented in AI ethics, stemming from society's current need. Furthermore, due to the analysis process chosen, so-called 'modern' AI virtue ethics are in line with values promoted by all three, the E.U., the IEEE, and the OECD; namely, with justice, honesty, and fairness (AIHLEG, 2019; OECD, 2019), which allows for interrelated governance measures in 'SII'.

The second subcategory of virtue ethics research deals with the operationalisation of virtue ethics and focuses on changing the mindset, norms and attitudes of stakeholders in the AI context (Floridi, 2016; Yu et al., 2018). Apart from developers, who represent the main target group, researchers state that it is also an organisation's management and society as a whole, who need to be educated regarding AI (Floridi, 2016; Hagendorff, 2020, 2022; Kazim & Koshiyama, 2020a). By training the individual's intrinsic motivation to follow virtuous values, this approach represents personalised, situational ethics measures. Further, it aims to raise levels of self-identification with AI ethics values—a challenge other approaches in the field are currently facing (Hagendorff, 2022; Mittelstadt, 2019a).

The third thematical subcategory of virtue ethics addresses the challenges of implementing virtue ethics in the AI context. To date, this topic only covers a niche in AI ethics research and has little to no support from or exposure to practice (Hagendorff, 2020, 2022; Yu et al., 2018). Much research is still needed on the psychological part of virtue ethics, more specifically on what is consciously accessible by the human mind (Hagendorff, 2022). Therefore, this book suggests that a virtue ethics approach requires the extensive use of awareness-building measures that will allow the individual to identify their subconscious biases. Only by integrating measures of that kind will the individual be able to fully apply virtue ethics approaches in the AI context. Additionally, virtue ethics deal with a certain apprehension from practice, as they are perceived as focusing merely on the character-building of the individual rather than on their actual actions (Hagendorff, 2022). Since companies might apprehend a lack of measurable positive actions after implementing virtue ethics measures, there is currently little exposure to practice. Nonetheless, virtue ethics come with numerous advantages, such as the promotion of trust among stakeholders, both within the company and from external parties. This is because intrinsically motivated ethics approaches are generally perceived as more trustworthy efforts to act responsibly than the mere adoption of ethical checklists, aiming to ensure minimum compliant behaviour (Hagendorff, 2022; Yu et al., 2018).

Research on Principle-Based AI Ethics

For this category, research and public sector documents promoting the application of ethical guiding principles were analysed so as to form thematic subcategories.

Generally speaking, principled guidelines follow a rather action-oriented approach, as they present the addressee of the guidelines with generalised forms of behaviour considered desirable in the AI context. Currently, most AI ethics initiatives and researchers apply a principled approach (Hagendorff, 2020, 2022; Jobin et al., 2019; Mittelstadt, 2019a; Morley et al., 2020; Yu et al., 2018), providing a particular set of rules or values an actor should follow to act responsibly in the context of AI adoption (AIHLEG, 2019; OECD, 2019). Hence, the majority of the values identified in the previous section stem from or represent a deontological, principle-based form of AI ethics. This is because principled ethics come with numerous advantages (Hagendorff, 2022), such as drastically lowering the complexity of AI governance, as established by this book. Thereby, they offer the much-needed broad frame for decision-making in this otherwise unregulated context, as the principles cover, for example, moral issues and organisational specifications of responsible AI adoption.

The following values portray a principled AI ethics approach, as they aim to provide overarching guiding principles, which frame corporate and individual decision-making from a meta-level. To structure the inductive analysis findings, Table 3.2 presents a brief overview of the subcategories identified in principle-based AI ethics literature, before presenting each subcategory in detail.

To ensure the neutrality of the process, they are grouped based on inductively examined similarities:

The first subcategory presents value sets dealing with the nature of the AI system itself, demanding its beneficence (or non-maleficence) and transparency towards users regarding the decisions it makes (AIHLEG, 2019; Gasparotti, 2019; Jobin et al., 2019; OECD, 2019). The second group focuses on the behaviour of the AI system, asking for non-discrimination and diversity, justice, and fairness (AIHLEG, 2019; Gasparotti, 2019; IEEE, 2021; Jobin et al., 2019; OECD, 2019). The third

Table 3.2 Own depiction, inductive analysis of principle-based AI ethics literature

Category: Principle-Based AI Ethics	1st Subcategory: Guiding Principles e.g., transparency, fairness, justice, privacy, dignity, freedom (AIHLEG, 2019; Gasparotti, 2019; Jobin et al., 2019; OECD, 2019)
	2nd Subcategory: Criticism e.g., lacking reinforcement, too broad and generalised, challenging application to practice (Mittelstadt, 2019a; Morley et al., 2019; Yu et al., 2018)
	3rd Subcategory: Operational Research e.g., ethics by design, ethics for design, ethics in design (Floridi et al., 2018; Hagendorff, 2020; Jobin et al., 2019; Morley et al. 2020)

group aims to ensure the general rights of the actors using AI or being affected by AI, namely protecting rights to privacy, dignity, freedom, and continued autonomy, as well as accountability on the side of the organisation deploying AI, for when the users' rights are being harmed (AIHLEG, 2019; Gasparotti, 2019; IEEE, 2021; Jobin et al., 2019; OECD, 2019). Finally, the last group represents principles aiming to ensure society's welfare by emphasising the importance of solidarity (Jobin et al., 2019; OECD, 2019) and the AI deployer's contribution to sustainability (AIHLEG, 2019; IEEE, 2021; Jobin et al., 2019; OECD, 2019).

However, this research stream has faced extensive criticism. Hence, the second subcategory subsumes research criticising principle-based AI ethics. For one, scholars have claimed that the principles are too broad and generalised (Mittelstadt, 2019a, 2019b). Another point of criticism addresses the lack of reinforcement mechanisms principled ethics are associated with. In addition, currently existing ethical principles are not considered to be easily adoptable in either different social or cultural contexts (Boddington, 2017; Wieland, 2018, 2020; Yu et al., 2018). This is due to so-called moral relativism (Boddington, 2017), raising the issue that only very few values are considered to be of universal truth, and even if they are agreed upon on a global scale, they are likely to be interpreted differently across the globe (Boddington, 2017; Wieland, 2018, 2020; Yu et al., 2018). Guidelines and recommendations developed in, for example, Europe, in accordance with European value sets, might not be applicable as such in, for example, the United States. Consequently, one of the greatest criticisms principled ethics faces, at the same time, is perceived by other scholars to be its greatest advantage: While their abstractedness helps lower complexity, it also complicates their applicability to different levels of technical development, making them impractical (Hagendorff, 2020; Morley et al., 2020; Yu et al., 2018).

The third subcategory aggregates more recent research, which has put a stronger focus on the operationalisation of deontological principles (Morley et al., 2020) to address the lack of applicability of this research. Hagendorff (2020) still criticises even the operationalisation of principles on the grounds that it still mostly resembles codes of ethics detailing these principles, instead of presenting actual governance measures helping with the process of implementing ethics-fostering measures. Nonetheless, the transitioning of this research stream led to further differentiation in the forms of application for the development of AI systems. Hagendorff (2022) identifies three main categories of operationalised principles:

1. Ethics by design, which addresses the integration of ethicality into the decision-making of the AI system itself (Hagendorff, 2020; Jobin et al., 2019)
2. Ethics in design, which presents research that helps evaluate the implications stemming from the usage of AI systems (Floridi et al., 2018; Jobin et al., 2019)
3. Ethics for design, which aims to raise behavioural integrity within the stakeholder group of developers, and, for example, human oversight (AIHLEG, 2019; Johnson, 2017)

An additional, more recent, research stream deals with the differentiation of principles for the specific stages of algorithmic development (Morley et al., 2020). Hence, scholars focusing on principled ethics addressed the criticism of challenges regarding the adoptability of principles in the actual development process. By doing so, the transition of research is already closing gaps and addressing criticism. Some critical aspects remain since they are rooted in the philosophical nature underlying this approach:

Moral relativism will continue to challenge principled ethics, as will the tension field between abstraction and operationalisation of principles. This book further suggests a new research focus for principled ethics; namely, addressing desirable futures instead of merely focusing on desirable living conditions for present societies. For instance, the research could focus on capabilities[2] or commons[3] that are worthy of protection, in addition to individual human rights. In doing so, it could ensure safe spaces for future generations, such as protecting autonomy in decision-making and personal freedom in surveillance-guided societies (Dafoe, 2018; WEF & Deloitte, 2020). Pursuing this path, the notion of how to protect future commons[4] could help develop tangible scenarios, whereas future visions might lead to scenarios too abstract to serve as guidance for today's corporate decision-making.

---

[2] Capabilities describe an individual's ability to achieve his own well-being, instead of having it granted in the form of rights. Further, human rights and individual capabilities are particularly empowering when combined (Sen, 2005).

[3] Commons are defined as commonly shared resources or common land belonging to society as a whole, exploited by a few; often discussed in the context of over-exploitation of shared resources (Hardin, 2009).

[4] The notion of commons could serve as a vessel to plan and achieve self-determined futures—future commons (Helfrich, 2014), such as Cyber Commons were thought to help design the future of democracy (Gunitsky, 2015).

Table 3.3 Own depiction, inductive analysis of consequentialist AI ethics literature

Category: Consequentialist AI Ethics	1st Subcategory: Time-Oriented Risk Patterns short-term, such as data protection, jobs; long-term, such as societal security and autonomy, (Dafoe, 2018; Jobin et al., 2019; WEF, 2020)
	2nd Subcategory: Geopolitical Risk Patterns e.g., regional, national, & supranational risks, such as the arms race, or cyber-warfare (Cave & ÓhÉigeartaigh 2018; Dafoe, 2018; Scharre, 2019; WEF, 2020)
	3rd Subcategory: Criticism e.g., little values-based guidance, room for interpretation and misguidance (Hagendorff, 2020; Yu et al. 2018)

Research on Consequentialist AI Ethics

The last philosophical concept and correlating research area focus on the consequences of AI adoption; hence, called consequentialist ethics. This approach, alongside principled ethics, is the most commonly applied form of AI ethics today (Hagendorff, 2020, 2022). Guidelines based on this philosophical perspective are often used when a dilemma situation requires the weighing up of advantages and disadvantages of an action or the decision between two or more guiding principles (Whittlestone et al., 2019). In practice, guidelines focusing on possible consequences of AI adoption are much needed, since cases of misuse of AI technologies are increasing (Dafoe, 2018; Kazim & Koshiyama, 2020a; Yu et al., 2018). Again, Table 3.3, provides an overview of identified themes in this subcategory.

To apply a consequentialist approach, a prior risk assessment is needed to gain insight into the decision context and to be able to weigh up the possible advantages and disadvantages coming with the decision. Consequences can range from short-term to long-term, and from low- to high-level risks (Dafoe, 2018; Jobin et al., 2019). The previously presented, clustered value sets identified by Jobin et al. (2019) and by the AIHLEG (2019), OECD (2019), and IEEE (2021) correlate with the assessment of risks and consequences.

The first subcategory in consequentialist AI ethics summarises time-oriented risk patterns. Short-term consequences in this context can include diminishing jobs, as well as matters of data privacy (Dafoe, 2018). Here, research from data governance can give helpful insight into ways to address data-related challenges (Aaronson, 2019; Abraham et al., 2019; Alhassan et al., 2018). According to the WEF and Deloitte (2020), short-term governance-related risks include bias, fairness, transparency, and lack of explicability. In the long run, risk patterns include, among others, the security of society and the protection of its continued autonomy (Dafoe, 2018). Hence, some of the presented value sets identified by scholars, as well as the E.U. (AIHLEG, 2019) and OECD (2019), are already of great significance in the present and require immediate action on the part of companies. To adhere to the risks associated with a certain timeframe, the WEF and Deloitte (2020) sorted consequences based on the expected timeframe of their urgency. This timeline allocates to the near future the use of autonomous lethal weapons, potentially escalating capabilities coming with such weapons, cyberattacks, and geopolitical technological competition. Both the WEF and Deloitte (2020) urge both the private and public sector to address these risk patterns.

However, risks do not only occur in a certain timeframe. Since they can also be analysed regionally, nationally, or on the supranational level, e.g., regarding the pace of geopolitical competition in AI, also referred to as the AI arms race (Cave & ÓhÉigeartaigh, 2019; Dafoe, 2018; Scharre, 2019; UNICRI, 2021), the second subcategory for consequential AI ethics deals with geopolitical risks. The WEF and Deloitte (2020) rank the level of risk and impact of such geopolitically driven competitive structures as high to very high, which confirms the relevance of this book and its approach to addressing AI governance from a wicked problem perspective—a view that enables collaborative approaches to solve dilemma situations (Roberts, 2000). Further, it highlights the importance of interlinking research fields, such as AI governance and algorithmic governance by the public sector, since the case of geopolitical competition and governmental interests have significant influence on both fields (König, 2019; Mittelstadt & Floridi, 2016; Pentland, 2013; Wachter et al., 2017).

Despite its accurate depiction of risks, this philosophical approach faces criticism, as subsumed in the third subcategory of consequentialist AI ethics. While the approach offers valuable decision frames for the balancing of consequences and for responsible behaviour, it does not include ethical guidance in the form of context-specific principles or values. Since they leave much room for interpretation, consequentialist ethics can be prone to misguidance: for one thing, by guiding according to the maxim of reaching the best possible outcome for the biggest possible group of recipients, it allows collateral damage (Yu et al., 2018). Further, consequentialist ethics do not offer guidance as to evaluating the so-called best possible outcome. Thus, the outcome can be measured by economic, social, or technological indicators, as well as by different ethical value sets; for example, when interpreting according to different cultural backgrounds. While this makes consequential ethics tools globally applicable, it comes with risks inherent to the nature of the approach, as its outcome is often highly arguable.

Therefore, I suggest the use of a consequentialist approach only in combination with measures from either virtue ethics or deontological perspective (Hagendorff, 2020, 2022; Yu et al., 2018). By doing so, the main deficiency of the approach, namely its lack of ethical guidance, is diminished, which helps secure societally desirable decision outcomes. Additionally, it counterbalances the criticism associated with deontological approaches; namely, their lack of transcultural applicability. Finally, this also complements the missing action orientation of virtue ethics'.

Conclusion on AI Ethics Categories as 'SII'

Many scholars highlight the lack of success of operationalised AI ethics through the currently existing AI governance measures (Hagendorff, 2020, 2022; Jobin et al., 2019; Mittelstadt, 2019a; Yu et al., 2018). As for the characteristics of the existing measures, Yu et al. (2018) found that most of them only applied rule-based and example-based instruments to help solve dilemma situations. This again points to the dominance of deontological, generalised ethical positions, and consequentialist approaches.

Regarding non-compliant behaviour despite applying these guidelines, Yu et al. (2018) highlight that AI developers and researchers are trained in a consequence-oriented way, making them less aware of other views. This view seems reasonable since common AI development approaches train AI systems based on consequential "if… then" situations (Funke, 2003), making developers more familiar with consequentialist approaches than deontological or virtue ethics measures.

To overcome such behavioural gaps, several scholars (Floridi, 2016; Hagendorff, 2020, 2022; Mittelstadt, 2019a; Yu et al., 2018) demand a more holistic integration of AI ethics into practice. Consequently, they ask for the inclusion of at least two, if not all three philosophical approaches. With this, the scholars expect all stakeholders involved, especially developers, to get a broader understanding of AI ethics and the impact of their actions on society. This, in turn, will raise their motivation to comply with AI governance measures—an objective equally perceived and promoted through a governance approach that includes all three approaches.

3.3 AI-Specific Adaptivity of the Governance Parameters

This section presents an in-depth analysis of the parameters and their adaptivity for two AI Governance scenarios: an unregulated and a partially regulated market. To develop these two scenarios, Relational Governance is realised in two steps:

In the first step, a company's options to implement AI governance measures are evaluated and the adaptivity of the governance parameters analysed. Thereafter, the results of this theoretical evaluation are complemented with context-related information from AI ethics. In this way, the book aims to identify strategies to implement AI governance measures in the firm from a theoretical perspective. Finally, strategies for combining the parameters and choosing an adequate content-related orientation are turned into a practical model for corporate management programs.

3.3.1 Governance Adaptivity in an Unregulated AI Market

The first scenario is developed based on the assumption of an unregulated market: while recognising the advances made in the E.U. regarding the regulation of AI, its actual realisation within the member states will still take time. Further, the currently existing proposal might change drastically before being passed and, even when passed for the E.U., the regulatory body will not apply to companies outside the E.U. Hence, this book proceeds to develop governance measures on the basic assumption of an unregulated market as the first scenario. Thereby, the results of the first scenario are applicable on a global scale and offer new insights into the adaptivity of an incomplete governance structure for a global market.

3.3.1.1 Existing Governance Parameters in Relational AI Governance

The current lack of formal institutions of society (SFI) changes the dynamic among the four governance parameters in AI.

Still, various countries have passed national AI strategies, such as Canada, the U.S., Mexico, China, Japan, Russia, the U.K., Germany, France, Spain, Portugal, and Italy (OECD, 2021). These strategies, as identified by the OECD (2021), focus on varying yet related topics, such as responsibility (e.g., Belgium, Canada, Czech Republic) and safety (e.g., Colombia, U.K.). Moreover, they aim at future objectives, such as providing an ecosystem for AI development (e.g., Finland, U.K.), specifically securing talent (e.g., Korea) and further training and skill development for their workforce (e.g., Brazil, Italy, UAE, U.K., U.S.) (OECD, 2019, 2021). Again, these strategies are not legally binding (OECD, 2021) and do not directly influence the governance adaptivity among the governance parameters. The World Economic Forum (WEF) addresses this regulatory gap in its Global Technology Governance Report 2021, when stating that "*we should begin to move beyond frameworks and guidelines and into more formal practice and policy*" (WEF & Deloitte, 2020, p. 22). In a second report on AI regulation, the WEF examined challenges and opportunities in AI, stating that

> approaches to regulating AI diverge sharply across regions. In some jurisdictions, a lack of consensus on a path forward and the risk of stifling innovation may deter any action. Emerging controversies surrounding AI can also force governments to implement hastily constructed and suboptimal regulatory policies. (2020, p. 3)

Since, at this moment, the AI market can only be defined as unregulated (OECD, 2019, 2021), this book proceeds under the hypothesis of non-existent 'SFI's and the statements made by the WEF do not indicate the implementation of regulation on a global scale in the near future (WEF, 2020; WEF & Deloitte, 2020). However, especially guidelines presented by institutions, such as, for example, the OECD (2019), contribute to forming socially accepted norms and provide a base for the emergence of formal governance institutions. Therefore, such supranational, overarching guidelines and recommendations will have an influence on the depiction of the parameter 'SII'.

A common threat identified in these strategies is the competitive nature of the national approaches, with many countries specifically aiming to put themselves ahead of global competition (OECD, 2021). This became apparent for Finland, aiming to "*make Finland a front runner in the age of AI*" (Ministry of Economic Affairs & Employment Helsinki, 2019), or the U.S.' aim of "*protecting our technological advantage in AI*" (The White House Office of Science and Technology Policy, 2020, p. iv, para. 5). This observation is in line with the observation made beforehand, that in a wicked problem structure, competitive behaviour prevails (Roberts, 2000). Global governance cooperation becomes rather unlikely in such a competitive dynamic, making the governance structure of the individual company all the more important to ensure its responsible, yet economically compatible, behaviour (Wieland, 2018, 2020).

To conclude, the following figure, Fig. 3.10, and formula summarise the existing governance parameters in an unregulated market; namely the individual, the organisation, and societal informal institutions. Thereby, the scenario portrays an actual depiction of the current global regulatory gap regarding AI development and AI adoption.

Coming back to Wieland's (2018, 2020) original depiction, 'SFI's can either interact with the parameter Individual 'I' or be substituted by it in the form of a functional equivalence. This fact has significant consequences for the development of an AI governance structure within the firm, as the 'SFI's cannot serve as an enforcement mechanism or formal measure in this case. To confirm this claim, I present an example from traditional compliance management:

> One can switch from a criminal law approach (SFI) to appealing to individual virtue (I) or compensate for the weaknesses of formal compliance management (O) through the corporate culture (SII). Or one could also consider the interplay of the crowding out of individual virtue (I) by legal compliance (SFI); lastly, combining compliance management (O) and the corporate culture (SII) can open new avenues. (Wieland, 2020, p. 45)

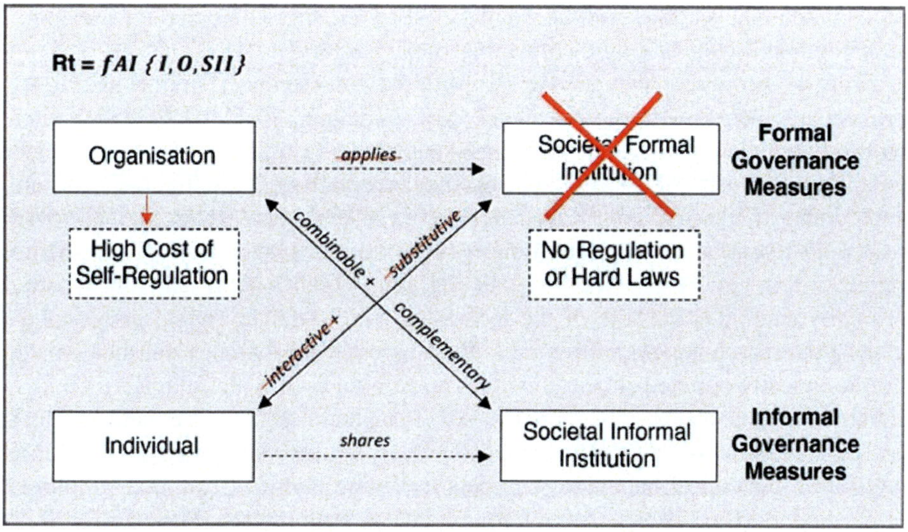

Fig. 3.10 Own depiction of AI governance parameters, according to Wieland (2020)

Since the formal parameter 'SFI' does not currently exist in the context of AI, the role of the individual as its correlating parameter in the model diminishes, too. This is because the two parameters are closely linked, and, consequently, the individual cannot substitute the second informal parameter, 'SII', in the model.

Applied to practice, this means that, while individuals might be concerned about the consequences of AI implementation and about consumers voicing their concerns, without official regulation, they cannot change the dynamics of global AI development (Cave & ÓhÉigeartaigh, 2019; Geist, 2016; Scharre, 2019; Tomasik, 2013). Furthermore, consumers and users often lack information about AI activities, since interactions with AI systems are not always marked as such (Ehsan et al., 2021; Hois et al., 2019; Mozafari et al., 2020; Skjuve et al., 2019). Therefore, given the missing transparency in direct interactions and the strong market-driven dynamics putting pressure on companies, the individual cannot serve as a functional equivalent or substitute for 'SFI' in this case.

According to Wieland (2018, 2020), developing an effective governance approach requires the combination of formal and informal measures, which, in the case of AI, only seems possible through a combination of the parameters 'O' and 'SII'. Hence, the following in-depth examination focuses on the relation between the Organisation (O) and Societal Informal Institutions (SII) and the dilemma situations that must be addressed in AI governance via the interplay of the two selected governance parameters.

3.3.1.2 Conceptualising the Role of the 'Individual' in an Unregulated Market

While the original conceptualisation in Relational Economics suggests that the role of the individual is rather diminished in the AI governance context, there are options to strengthen its role among the governance parameters.

From a theoretical perspective, 'I's limited role stems from the individual's primary interaction with the parameter 'SFI' (Wieland, 2018, 2020), for example, with individual virtue, which potentially substitutes a legal approach or interacts with it. Hagendorff (2020) also confirms the perception of the individual's currently subordinate role in AI governance. However, several scholars present distinctive reasoning to explain that circumstance: According to Hagendorff (2020), Mittelstadt (2019a), and Yu et al. (2018), existing, rather traditional research in AI ethics primarily examines the role of the individual from a deontological perspective—leaving a research gap regarding individualistic ethics approaches. Further, existing deontologically oriented ethics guidelines resemble a list of set principles, rather than situation-specific evaluations (Ananny, 2016; Hagendorff, 2020; Leonelli, 2016; Yu et al., 2018). However, a virtue-oriented approach would focus on the moral intuition, motivation for ethical behaviour and personality traits of, for example, employees or developers (Hagendorff, 2020; Leonelli, 2016; Vallor, 2016; Wieland, 2020; Yu et al., 2018), which, according to academia, makes it a desirable option for practice.

In this way, a virtue ethics approach does not focus on the technology itself but on the role and responsibility of the individuals entrusted with its development, adoption, and management (Ananny, 2016; Hagendorff, 2020; Neubert & Montañez, 2020). Ideally, this should involve every individual in society for educational purposes (Hagendorff, 2020), or at least each person responsible for AI-related impact or consequences for society (Floridi, 2016). Further, a virtue ethics approach supports working against the diffusion of responsibility and helps raise levels of accountability (Floridi, 2016; Hagendorff, 2020; Leonelli, 2016).

As established, the virtue ethics approach serves as an individual ethics decision framework (Yu et al., 2018) and focuses on developing an understanding of values such as honesty, justice, courage, or empathy (Neubert & Montañez, 2020; Vallor, 2016; Wieland, 2020) to raise an individual's ethical decision-making.

The Relational Governance approach supports this demand raised by Hagendorff (2020), since Wieland (2020) also focuses on the individual's intrinsic motivation to act and characterises the individual's virtue as an

> actors' readiness (motivation) and ability to understand the ideals of a given social group and, through suitable actions on the part of individual and collective actors, to grasp said ideals in their proportionality. (2020, p. 33)

Hence, this definition is in line with Vallor's (2016) and Neubert and Montañez's (2020) definition, as well as Hagendorff's (2020) demand for virtue-based governance. Like Vallor (2016) and Neubert and Montañez (2020), Wieland specifies the individual's motivation to act virtuously to be ethical, based, for example, on striving for justice or honesty. Alternatively, it can be led by the reasoning of the individual, stemming from Aristotle's definition of virtues and the individual's wish to be useful or strive in competition (Wieland, 2020).

Given this theoretical overlap, the need for higher individual accountability in AI (Floridi, 2016; Hagendorff, 2020; Vallor, 2016), and Wieland's recommendation to ideally involve all parameters in a governance structure, so as to ensure its effectiveness, promoting the individual's role in AI governance seems a promising path to follow when applying Relational AI Governance to an unregulated market. This is especially significant regarding the weakened structure of the governance parameters in this context, as Wieland (2018, 2020) highlights that the self-enforcement of an effective governance structure might be best supported by focusing on individual virtues.

Another advantage of focusing on virtue-based governance measures to complement existing measures stems from its broader, more innovation-friendly approach, which addresses the common perception that ethical guidelines hinder change and innovation (Boddington, 2017; Hagendorff, 2020). Instead, ethical guidelines should promote self-responsibility and the employee's or developer's freedom in their decision-making (Hagendorff, 2020). Hence, this book supports the demand that existing AI ethics guidelines should be complemented with a more virtues-oriented stream of ethical research and resulting guidelines. In particular, it agrees with Hagendorff's demand to move from

> a more deontologically oriented, action-restricting ethic based on universal abidance of principles and rules, to a situation-sensitive ethical approach based on virtues and personality dispositions, knowledge expansions, responsible autonomy and freedom of action. (2020, p. 114)

Hence, given the highly adaptable general-purpose nature of AI solutions, this book supports virtue-based approaches, which will complement the breadth of the prevailing principle-based ethics guidelines and strengthen the role of the individual in this endeavour. Further, such a combination is expected both to raise awareness of AI ethics within all stakeholder groups and to help raise the company-internal level of accountability.

3.3.1.3 Conceptualising the Role of the 'Organisation' in an Unregulated Market

Since, in the unregulated AI market, neither the parameter 'SFI' nor 'I' play a dominant role, it is primarily the interaction of 'O' and 'SII' that can help realise the relational AI transaction. This is because both parameters can be combined or complement each other within a governance structure (Wieland, 2018, 2020). Given the challenges 'SII' face in the AI context, such as the lack of reinforcement in the formulation and use of guidelines (Hagendorff, 2020; Mayer et al., 2021), the implementation of the parameter 'SII' requires extensive complementary measures on the part of the organisation ('O'). Its operationalisation can best be achieved by precisely building measures based on the philosophical schools of thought discussed previously and their complementary functions within the company.

Generally, the execution of a relational transaction is facilitated by 'O's interaction with the other three governance parameters. This interaction aims to form a new equilibrium, balancing the system-specific needs allocated in the particular relational transaction (Wieland, 2020). The definition of a collective actor is essential in this context in so far as Wieland states that "*the chief effective parameters of a governance form consist in the interests, perceptions, rationales and convictions of individuals as persons or agents (I) and their resulting actions and behaviour*" (2020, p. 50). This statement hints at the strong interrelation of 'SII' and 'O', as both the individual, as well as the collective actor, are understood to be driven primarily by their 'convictions'—the belief systems and the norms they ascribe to themselves. In this context, organisations offer the necessary mechanisms for coordination and cooperation. This is because it is the individual and collective actors that assess economic transactions and manage them according to the expected value-creation potential, which can be gained through their specific guiding difference (Wieland, 2020).

In the unregulated AI market, various stakeholder groups in society engage in developing non-legislative advances, also referred to as soft law (Jobin et al., 2019). This includes, for example, academia, standard-setting agents and especially companies (Whittlestone et al., 2019). However, it is primarily the organisation as a governance structure that is able to and needs to realise the actual alignment of stakeholder interests, their potential for successful cooperation, and especially the demands of civil society (Wieland, 2018, 2020). This view is shared by Hagendorff (2020), stating that it is companies that need to implement AI responsibly and in accordance with society's views (Hagendorff, 2020). Particularly when confronted with the lack of hard law regulation in AI, the demand to integrate stakeholder interests and control possible risks of AI adoption is mainly directed towards the firm (Hagendorff, 2020; Jobin et al., 2019; Morley et al., 2020). Therefore, the company requires a collective decision-making framework, helping to adopt and manage AI responsibly (Yu et al., 2018).

So far, companies mostly do this by implementing company-internal, formal governance measures, which can best be subsumed under the term corporate self-regulation (Benkler, 2019; Jobin et al., 2019; Whittlestone et al., 2019; Wieland, 2018, 2020). Currently, these measures are mostly realised in the form of 'AI ethics guidelines' or 'AI ethics principles' (Hagendorff, 2020; Jobin et al., 2019; Whittlestone et al., 2019). This trend continued to grow exponentially, with the number of AI ethics guidelines doubling from 2019 to the middle of 2020 (AlgorithmWatch, 2020; Mayer et al., 2021).

However, the mere formulation and implementation of guidelines do not have the necessary power to enforce AI ethics in companies (Hagendorff, 2020), confirming Wieland's (2018, 2020) demand that formal and informal governance parameters should be combined to develop effective governance structure. Much like the challenges that formal regulation and AI ethics face, AI ethics guidelines need to deal with the ever-changing progress made in AI research, its sophistication, and the sheer endless and constantly increasing a number of possible applications for AI (Mayer et al., 2021; Mittelstadt, 2019a; Wallach & Marchand, 2019; Yu et al., 2018). Therefore, the guidelines can often only be developed in a very generalised manner, which on the downside, makes them too theoretical, generalised, and abstract to guide corporate actions effectively (Hagendorff, 2020; Mittelstadt, 2019a, 2019b; Whittlestone et al., 2019). Moreover, these guidelines per se are not always effective (McNamara et al., 2018) and can be interpreted as raising transaction costs for companies without reaping any benefits from their implementation (Wieland, 2020).

3.3.1.4 Strengthening the Governance Parameters Through a Threefold 'SII' Approach

Hence, further formal governance measures within the firm are required. To do so, a meta-level examination of suitable measures based on 'SII', specifically the AI ethics research streams, is conducted from a formal governance perspective. Based on the three main ethical categories covering the value sets presented by both public-sector AI initiatives and research, this book presents aggregated superordinate strategies to combine 'SII' with formal measures of the organisation ('O'). In theory, the firm can develop formal measures based on each of the approaches separately (Hagendorff, 2020, 2022; Yu et al., 2018).

To begin with, the company can choose to apply only one philosophical school of thought as a theoretical foundation to develop its AI governance measures; for example, it can select the principled ethics approach and introduce guiding principles of AI ethics to the firm. The same logic applies to both consequentialist ethics and virtue ethics, which can also serve as singular ethical foundations for the development of measures.

The following scenarios provide strategies on how to integrate all three approaches. Initially, the company can focus on, for example, operationalised deontological ethics. As established, companies can decide to implement an 'ethics in design' (Floridi et al., 2018; Hagendorff, 2020; Jobin et al., 2019) or an 'ethics by design' approach (Hagendorff, 2020; Jobin et al., 2019). The first aims to facilitate the evaluation of results stemming from AI usage, whereas the latter focuses on building ethicality into the AI system itself.

As a part of the firm's formal governance structure, the 'ethics by design' approach can be defined as an input-oriented strategy. This is because the company's focus primarily lies on the values it aims to integrate into its AI system. Regarding the operationalisation of this approach, I suggest the integration of ethics alongside the development process of AI, ranging from its design phase to its deployment (Cath et al., 2018; Mayer et al., 2021; Morley et al., 2020; Wu et al., 2020). By doing so, the company provides an ex-ante governance frame for the potential outcomes of its actions. Such an approach is likely to provide good coverage of ethical dilemmas since, for one, it addresses possible challenges before they materialise as consequences for society. Second, since it stems from deontological ethics and provides substantial ethical guidance, it answers societal concerns with more than merely technical adaptations (Jobin et al., 2019). This is of great significance since these newer developments in deontological ethics to operationalise AI ethics are still very recent (Wu et al., 2020) and require oversight and the participation of stakeholders in the process (Jobin et al., 2019).

The 'ethics in design' approach, on the other hand, provides an outcome-oriented strategy, which, nonetheless, provides ex-ante governance. In this case, the company puts a stronger focus on evaluating possible outcomes of its AI adoption, combining the traditional deontological 'ethics by design' approach and subsequent consequentialist decision-making measures.

This approach is quite common, as research reveals that most organisations tend to combine two approaches, usually principled and consequentialist ethics (Thornton et al., 2016). In this scenario, the organisation can develop a code of ethics based on the principles it decides to apply and complement these with consequentialist measures to support decision-making processes in dilemma situations. This is particularly useful for dilemmas that suggest the adoption of more than one principle. In such cases, consequentialist measures can help examine the impact of each decision scenario to identify the best possible outcome (Boddington, 2017; Burton et al., 2017; Yu et al., 2018). Moreover, a company can also decide to combine deontological and virtue ethics, e.g., in the form of an 'ethics for design' strategy (Johnson, 2017), which aims at raising the integrity of behaviour among developers and deployers of AI. Hence, virtue ethics can be operationalised as individualised psychological and moral character-building (Hagendorff, 2022), whereas deontological ethics can serve to derive the resulting guidelines.

Finally, a company can opt to apply a combination of all three ethics approaches—a strategy that rather resembles traditional integrity management programs (Kaptein, 1999; Wieland, 2005, 2014). In this scenario, principled and consequentialist ethics can be applied in the same way as described for the previous case. However, they are complemented by virtue ethics, which close the gap between awareness-building and individual ethical training measures (Hagendorff, 2022). By applying all three approaches, the company educates the individual regarding the ethical consequences of AI development and adoption, according to his specific role within the company (Floridi, 2016; Hagendorff, 2020, 2022; Kazim & Koshiyama, 2020a). Moreover, it provides guiding principles as the general decision frame which guides its corporate decision-making. It can round off its AI ethics strategy by supplying its employees with consequentialist ethics, which, in dilemma situations, help solidify and support the decisions the ethically trained individual takes. Thereby, the individual enters a situation with already higher awareness of his actions' consequences (Hagendorff, 2022). With this, there is no need to raise the questions of whether to act ethically and to what degree, since such debates have already been discussed in the individual training formats. Thus, in the acute dilemma situation, consequentialist ethics measures instead support the individual's decision-making process insofar as they offer procedural instruments to evaluate and further examine their decisions (Thornton et al., 2016).

To apply a threefold approach, traditional integrity management programs (Wieland, 2005, 2014) suggest that the company begins with conducting an extensive risk assessment, as recommended by the WEF for AI governance (Madzou & MacDonald, 2020). The results from such a risk analysis help in choosing company-relevant principles for AI governance, each addressing the previously identified risks. This selection is needed since no company will be able to address the entirety of all value sets presented in the previous section. Hence, a selection based on the company's AI-related risk patterns and risk-management preferences is required, so that the company can introduce a formal code of ethics based on applied principled ethics and the chosen value sets. In the next step, the principle-based measures can be combined with consequentialist ones. This can include scenario-building techniques, as well as analysis tools to identify various degrees of direct and indirect consequences of corporate decision-making. Finally, case-study-based training and psychological awareness-building measures stemming from virtue ethics are introduced. Among other effects, they allow unconscious biases to be addressed (Hagendorff, 2022), their avoidance being of great significance in the AI context. This is because AI systems can only be as good in quality as the ability of the developer team that created them. Thus, these measures might also help avoid the so-called designer bias of an AI system (Brundage & Bryson, 2016; Caliskan et al., 2017; König, 2019). Hence, the better trained the human mind is to identify and address subconscious biases, the higher the quality of the AI system (Brundage & Bryson, 2016; Caliskan et al., 2017; Hagendorff, 2022; König, 2019).

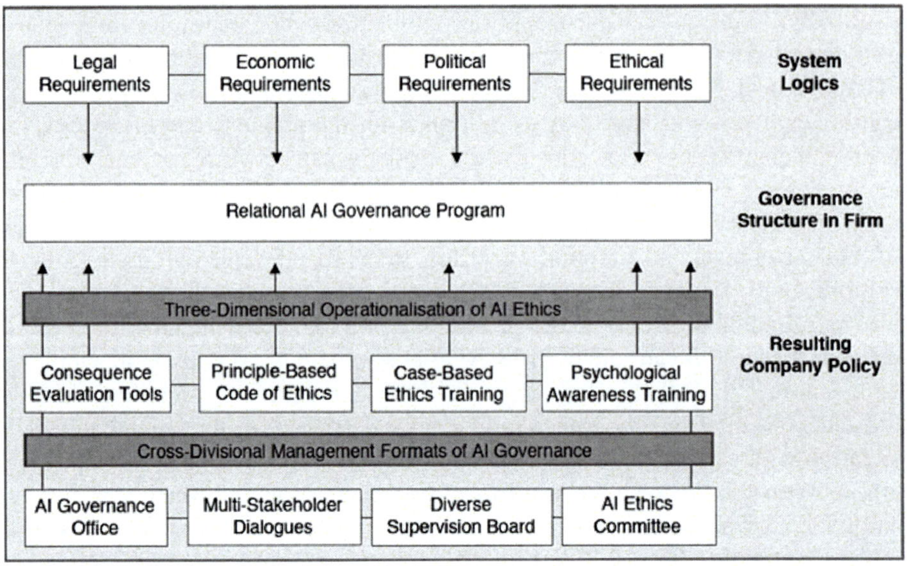

Fig. 3.11 Own depiction of operationalised Relational AI Governance, based on Wieland (2020)

3.3.1.5 The Relational AI Governance Program for Unregulated Environments

In an unregulated market, 'SII' and 'O' can only be supported by integrating the individual actor, 'I', into the governance structure of the firm. Therefore, the mere introduction of 'SII' in the form of guidelines requires additional measures to change corporate decision-making (Hagendorff, 2020; McNamara et al., 2018). Based on the presented elaboration and in line with Wieland (2018, 2020), this book advocates the operationalisation of 'SII', 'I', and 'O' based on all three AI ethics streams through formal and informal governance measures.

Such an approach enables a company to innovate more freely, while at the same time strengthening AI ethical considerations and ethical values within the firm. By applying an operational governance approach, which resembles integrity management[5] measures, I opt for a stronger values orientation. Thereby, it allows for more situationally adaptable measures on the formal side, which, in consequence, gives the company a stronger value set and more freedom in its operational processes. Figure 3.11 presents the operationalisation of the formal parameter 'O' and further integration of both 'SII' and 'I' on the informal side of the structure.

Figure 3.11 consists of various levels:

[5] Integrity Management is a values-oriented approach, which can be combined with formal compliance measures. It allows the individual to reflect on their own value sets and the moral demand they are confronted with (Wieland, 2014).

In accordance with Wieland (2018, 2020), on the top level, the figure portrays examples of system-specific requirements a company is confronted with when developing a Relational AI Governance program. On the middle and lower level, it presents examples of formal and informal management measures suitable for the operationalisation of 'SII' and 'O' via the AI Governance management program.

The middle level focuses on the three philosophical streams in AI ethics and suggests the integration of measures stemming from each ethical stream; thus, it is a three-dimensional operationalisation. The operationalised suggestions are based on contextualised information stemming from both Hagendorff (2020, 2022) and Wieland (2014, 2018, 2020). Case-based ethics training and psychological awareness training are viewed as necessary forms of operationalising virtue ethics (Hagendorff, 2020, 2022). Further, case-based training represents a useful tool in compliance management, as do the additionally suggested consequence evaluation tools (Wieland, 2014; Wieland et al., 2020). The fourth measure, principle-based guidelines, integrates deontological ethics into the structure and suggests their use, as is common practice, in the form of guidelines (Hagendorff, 2020; Jobin et al., 2019).

The lowest level of Fig. 3.11 focuses on the structural requirements of implementing an effective governance structure. Again, the development of these measures stems from Wieland's (2020) original depiction and insights from AI ethics (AIHLEG, 2019; Brundage & Bryson, 2016; Caliskan et al., 2017; Hagendorff, 2020, 2022; Jobin et al., 2019; König, 2019; Mayer et al., 2021). Structurally, the implementation of multi-stakeholder dialogues will, first of all, help to further formalise 'SII' in AI, since so far, there is still no consensus on the presented value sets (Hagendorff, 2020; Jobin et al., 2019; Mittelstadt, 2019a)—especially among society and developers (Mayer et al., 2021). Moreover, their implementation contributes to the fundamental need for collaborative governance forms addressing the underlying wicked problem of AI governance. Hence, an essential role is attributed in this book to multi-stakeholder dialogues in transculturally developing a shared understanding of the company's AI governance strategy and its AI ethical position.

Further, Wieland (2020) advises introducing new departments and boards within the organisation in accordance with the relational transaction the company seeks to realise. This means, for example, that the structural coupling of AI and ethics cannot be enforced by a CSR office or by supervision boards established to oversee compliance measures regarding the company's value chain.

Rather, the introduction of a new structural entity at the intersection of 'Artificial Intelligence' and 'Ethics' is required. Hence, for the structural operationalisation of Relational AI Governance in a company, I suggest implementing various new entities. These can consist of an AI ethics office and, to ensure its compliant decision-making, a supervisory board, and an AI ethics committee. In detail, the positions in the supervisory board, as well as the AI ethics committee recommended here, should be filled diversely to counterbalance potential biases in both the AI strategy and system of the company (Brundage & Bryson, 2016; Caliskan et al., 2017; Hagendorff, 2020, 2022; König, 2019). Integrating an AI ethics committee is advised due to the extensively discussed priorities that companies need to set when dealing with the consequences and risks of their actions: first, to avoid diffusion of responsibility (Floridi, 2016;

Hagendorff, 2020; Leonelli, 2016), and second, to ensure the proportionality and neutrality of decisions, my approach strongly advises companies to implement an AI ethics committee.

Further, the enforcement of such deontological, principle-based guidelines requires the implementation of additional formal elements, such as an AI ethics office and its official positioning in the organisational structure of the firm. Additionally, the authority of the office should be backed by assigning a supervisory board to ensure its effectiveness. Thereby, the guidelines representing 'SII' receive structural, formal support via the parameter 'O'.

In addition, I suggest publicly held multi-stakeholder dialogues (Wieland, 2020) to further strengthen the 'SII's for AI (Hagendorff, 2020; Jobin et al., 2019; Mittelstadt, 2019a), which are not yet sharply defined and do not yet have full acceptance in society as a whole, particularly among all internal stakeholders of the company, e.g., developers (Hagendorff, 2020; Mayer et al., 2021). By allowing for dialogue formats, the participation of all stakeholders is promoted—a measure aiming to raise acceptance of newly developed guidelines and foster the employee's identification with the guidelines (Wieland, 2018, 2020).

The virtue ethics-based instrument can support moral character-building among employees. This provides the parameter 'I' with a strengthened position, since the employees act with an inner compass, allowing them to manoeuvrer the constantly evolving dilemma situations that come with technologies developed at such a high pace, particularly since guidelines are restricted to already existing situations (Hagendorff, 2020; Mittelstadt, 2019a), and can easily be adapted to newly occurring dilemma situations on the technical level (Hagendorff, 2020; Morley et al., 2020; Yu et al., 2018).

In this way, Relational AI Governance covers both the formal side of providing guidelines as well as the situational expertise needed to responsibly adopt AI in practice. Like traditional integrity management approaches, the developed approach offers principle-based guidance and ethical character-building. Moreover, development and agreement on 'SII' is still comparatively weak, which weakens their overall power to enforce the governance measures built upon them (Mayer et al., 2021; Mittelstadt, 2019a, 2019b; Whittlestone et al., 2019). Strengthening the role of the individual with a virtue ethics approach will result in more informed decisions. Additionally, value-based training leads to a higher motivation to act with integrity in critical situations (Hagendorff, 2020, 2022; Leonelli, 2016; Vallor, 2016; Yu et al., 2018).

3.3.1.6 Interpretation of Combining AI's 'SII' and 'O' on the Organisational Level

Both the AIHLEG and academia promote the opportunity for companies to create shared value (Wieland, 2018, 2020) by responsibly adopting AI (AIHLEG, 2019; Floridi et al., 2018; Mayer et al., 2021), as it allows companies to generate more income while, at the same time, managing the societal risks associated with AI implementation. However, the discipline of AI ethics is still developing and faces criticism, for example, as most AI conferences are financed by the private sector, which again shows the strong influence companies have on AI development and its ethical evaluation (Hagendorff, 2020). Furthermore, AI ethics mainly serve to raise awareness and highlight potential risks associated with AI adoption in a structured manner (Morley et al., 2020) and research indicates that there are specific reasons for AI ethics' limited effectiveness.

First, ethical evaluations regarding AI are not yet fully negotiated among societal stakeholders, and not all stakeholders share the same view or understanding (Hagendorff, 2020; Mayer et al., 2021). Whereas in CSR management, for example, society has a clear understanding of the operationalisation of human rights through CSR measures (Wieland, 2018, 2020), in the AI context, the formulation of desirable values and their ideal operationalisation remains vague (Hagendorff, 2020; Mittelstadt, 2019a). This especially holds true since AI governance is a topic of global relevance, with views on what are ethically desirable options in AI development diverging significantly around the globe (Hagerty & Rubinov, 2019; Jobin et al., 2019; Schiff et al., 2020; Wu et al., 2020). This circumstance affects the firm, not only because vague value sets do not have high enforcement power, but also since companies engaging in global markets have stakeholders from more than one nation or continent and, hence, need to align divergent views (Cave & ÓhÉigeartaigh, 2019; Geist, 2016; Scharre, 2019; Tomasik, 2013; UNICRI, 2021).

Second, a virtue ethics approach might be able to counterbalance this challenge, since its promoted values are understood to be inherently universal and foster the actor's own efforts when applied (Neubert & Montañez, 2020). Further, research indicates that measures from this philosophical school of thought led to higher attraction and retention of employees and raised the company's reputation among AI users due to its individualistic and sustainable in-depth approach to AI ethics (Neubert & Montañez, 2020). However, this approach is rarely applied in practice.

Third, the current vagueness of 'SII' leads to an additional challenge: Apart from their general broadness, currently existing guidelines also lack technically applicable recommendations and explanations. Therefore, Hagendorff (2020) and Morley et al. (2020) demand further operationalisation of AI ethics, as they deem current research too abstract and remote from practical needs. Yu et al. (2018) particularly highlight the need to offer technological solutions to implement ethics into AI systems. Hagendorff (2020) expands his claim, stating that developers, in practice, often perceive AI ethics guidelines as an externally imposed instrument, leading him to elaborate on the importance of more practical ethics approaches to avoid diffusion of responsibility in an organisation and allow developers to adopt ethical guidelines for their actual work routine. While my approach supports these demands, I approve of Mittelstadt's (2019a, 2019b) warning that AI governance is a very complex endeavour, and organisations must not oversimplify solutions by restricting their measures merely to technological changes.

The fourth challenge 'SII's face regarding AI, lies in their lack of reinforcement mechanisms, as, thus far, "*deviations from the various codes of ethics have no consequences*" (Hagendorff, 2020, p. 113). This quote is in line with Wieland's (2020) observation that social norms require "*punitive mechanisms like social criticism and loss of status or reputation*" (2020, p. 43). This challenge might be linked to the previously presented concern over the lack of access to information and transparency on the part of the user, making it difficult for end-consumers to make informed decisions about corporate behaviour in AI and formulate substantial criticism (Ehsan et al., 2021; Hois et al., 2019; Mozafari et al., 2020; Skjuve et al., 2019).

Consequently, the fact that 'SII's are not fully formulated and lack reinforcement makes high levels of defection from collaborative behaviour or attempts at ethical greenwashing likely (Dafoe, 2018; Roberts, 2000; Wieland, 2020). This is in line with the behaviour of actors involved in wicked problems, having a higher likelihood of defecting and falling into competitive structures. Hagendorff confirms this assumption when stating that "*especially economic incentives are easily overriding commitment to ethical principles and values*" (2020, p. 114), hinting at organisations disregarding social values, such as the demand for benevolent AI (Hagendorff, 2020; Taddeo & Floridi, 2018a). Thus, this diffusion of responsibility might lead to a lacking sense of accountability (Hagendorff, 2020), requiring significant complementation and extensive substantiation of 'SII' in the form of additional informal and formal measures.

3.3.1.7 Challenges and Opportunities for Corporate AI Governance in an Unregulated Market

The decision to self-regulate by applying AI ethics to its processes comes with various challenges but also opportunities for the company and its environment. Apart from the growing pressure from society on companies to adopt responsible practices, competitive pressure in the field is higher than in other markets (Cave & ÓhÉigeartaigh, 2019; Scharre, 2019; Schiff et al., 2020). Hence, a combined approach can help companies self-regulate by granting more freedom to innovate (Hagendorff, 2020; Yu et al., 2018), instead of imposing extensive, generalised principles. Rather, a company should choose to develop deontological guidelines for previously identified red flags[6] and combine these principles with virtue ethics-based training for the remaining dilemma situations encountered in AI adoption. In consequence, this freedom can give the company the decision space to move ahead of competition responsibly, as it is not as restricted in its decisions in a standardised manner. Hence, when a company is willing to self-regulate, aiming to gain competitive advantages over its competitors, it needs to ensure the effectiveness of its measures—especially since the likelihood of defection is estimated as very high in the AI market (Dafoe, 2018). If a company cannot ensure the lasting success of its AI governance structure and, thereby, loses credibility with its clients, its self-regulation becomes a liability, since self-regulation raises transaction costs to new levels—unmatched by

[6] The term 'Red Flags' is commonly used in compliance management to describe high-risk indicators for potential fraud (Braithwaite et al., 2003; Grabosky & Duffield, 2001).

its competitors—without providing financial benefits in return (Schiff et al., 2020; Wieland, 2020).

Apart from potential financial gains resulting from holistic AI governance, a good reputation for ethical behaviour could lead to another competitive advantage: For one, according to research on public trust (Pirson et al., 2019), consumers validate a company's effort to act responsibly. Further, scholars highlight that investment in public trust is especially needed in times of social and technological disruption to ensure a company's continued existence (Paine, 2003; Pirson, 2007; Pirson et al., 2019). Given the long-standing tradition of the research streams, their findings are expected to hold for the AI context, too (Zhu et al., 2021)—especially since existing research in AI ethics supports this view (Hagendorff, 2020; Neubert & Montañez, 2020; Schiff et al., 2020). Moreover, given the war for talent in the tech industry (Miller & Coldicott, 2019), further research indicates that reputational gains could attract new employees and stop current employees from potentially leaving the company if they consider the impact of their projects to hurt society (Miller & Coldicott, 2019; Neubert & Montañez, 2020). However, developers, especially in the private sector are not always in line with societal concerns regarding AI (Mittelstadt, 2019a). Consequently, again with respect to recruitment benefits, companies need to engage in multi-stakeholder dialogues to ensure the effectiveness of their governance measures and balance out potentially differing ethical value sets among their stakeholders (Wieland, 2018, 2020).

However, society has questioned the motivation of companies to self-regulate (Benkler, 2019). Thus, if stakeholders do not believe in a company's efforts to act responsibly, the expected reputational gains will not show. Therefore, an effective AI governance approach in an unregulated market requires more holistic measures than the mere implementation of AI ethics guidelines (Hagendorff, 2020; Wieland, 2018, 2020). While, so far, there is no legal foundation for these measures, for the company to reap the benefits of its efforts to act responsibly, consumers—hence, society—need to be convinced of the seriousness of the measures. Only then will the reputational gains have a positive effect on a company, since the mere implementation of guidelines is not a unique selling point anymore (AlgorithmWatch, 2020; Hagendorff, 2020; Jobin et al., 2019; Whittlestone et al., 2019).

Given the competitive pressure in an unregulated AI market (Cave & ÓhÉigeartaigh, 2019; Geist, 2016; Scharre, 2019; Tomasik, 2013; Wieland, 2020), companies can only afford to raise their transaction costs compared to their competitors if they can ensure benefits as a result. Otherwise, the likelihood of defection from responsible behaviour, which is high in any case, is further intensified (Dafoe, 2018; Hagendorff, 2020; Mittelstadt, 2019a; Roberts, 2000). Hence, reaping the benefits requires a multi-level approach within the firm, ranging from leadership integrity to introducing new departments, processes, and procedures to complement and substantiate the release of AI ethics measures aligning with its corporate culture (Wieland, 2018, 2020).

3.3.2 *Governance Adaptivity in a Partially Regulated AI Market*

This section examines possible implications resulting from the currently pending regulation for AI research and AI adoption in the E.U. This is because the global AI market can no longer be defined as being entirely unregulated once the regulation proposal passes. Instead, it will shift to being partially regulated, as regulating one region will result in companies having to meet new competitive conditions. While this might not affect economic actors around the globe directly, it will change the dynamic of the market and have indirect effects on the competitors' market positioning strategies.

Thus, this section analyses the European regulatory proposal from a Relational Governance perspective and discusses the possibility of its current adoption by practice. This is because, as soon as the regulation passes, Wieland's (2018, 2020) original governance, including all four governance parameters, applies to European companies and gives guidance for the roll-out of tailored measures within the governance structure of the firm. Therefore, in the case of AI governance, an examination of the advantages and disadvantages a company faces is at the centre of attention (Wieland, 2018, 2020). This section closes with an evaluation of possible consequences for the global AI market and companies in the E.U., as well as a concise contextualisation of Relational AI Governance under these pending circumstances.

3.3.2.1 Regulatory Context in the Global AI Market

The formal regulation of the global AI market, in general, is a complex endeavour. For one thing, the numbers of adopted AI systems rise constantly, and their continuous progression requires high flexibility on the side of the regulatory bodies (Mayer et al., 2021; Mittelstadt, 2019a; Wallach & Marchand, 2019). In particular, it is the uncertainty of consequences coming with AI's adoption (Wallach & Marchand, 2019) and the adaptability of AI solutions (Goldfarb et al., 2019; Klinger et al., 2018; Nepelski & Sobolewski, 2020; Razzkazov, 2020; Trajtenberg, 2018) that further complicate its regulation. Moreover, scholars ascribe an exceptionally high pace of development to AI technologies (Wallach & Marchand, 2019), impeding the traditional processes of ex-post legislation, but especially ex-ante governance and legislation. Additionally, official regulatory institutions still face high information asymmetries regarding new developments in AI (WEF & Deloitte, 2020), partly due to a lack of experts recruited to work in legislation (Calo, 2017).

Nonetheless, in 2021, the E.U. was the first actor worldwide to present a regulation proposal for AI. If the E.U. succeeds in passing this first regional regulation, it will change the status of the currently unregulated market to being partially regulated. Partial regulation is commonly defined as the imposition of different competitive conditions on a specific group of players in the market, which will be the case for

European companies and companies planning to provide for or enter the European market (European Commission, 2021a).

Strategic Positioning of Main Players in the Global Market

Taking this path, the E.U. opts for a contrary position to other actors in the market. While the E.U. chooses a risk-based regulation of AI, which will raise AI's ethicality and trustworthiness, other nations focus on capitalising technological first-mover advantages or seeking dominance in particular fields of technological application.

As of now, the AI market is mainly dominated by the U.S. and China (Cave & ÓhÉigeartaigh, 2019; Dafoe, 2018; Geist, 2016; Rabesandratana, 2018). However, the E.U., Russia, and Israel are making significant efforts to secure their market share (Cyman et al., 2021; Rabesandratana, 2018). Currently, these nations seek to improve their positions in the market with heavy investments into AI research, specific strategic positioning, as well as fast-paced development efforts to gain market power. It is particularly the dynamics of this global competition that has led to the notion of a constantly intensifying race for technological superiority (Cave & ÓhÉigeartaigh, 2019; Geist, 2016).

This is because a first-mover position is associated with, for example, economic, academic, or political advantages. In particular, technological superiority is frequently linked to military superiority, a correlation that could translate to absolute political power for the dominant party. Apart from inherent technological superiority, a dominant position in the market is also believed to lead to a higher attraction rate for talent—which, in turn, would further secure the nation's position in the market. Hence, it is suspected that this dynamic will further intensify over time (Cave & ÓhÉigeartaigh, 2019; Dafoe, 2018; Geist, 2016).

Due to the dominance of the U.S. and China in the market and the consequent influence of their technological applications on consumers around the globe (Dafoe, 2018; Lilkov, 2020), the E.U. focused on a clear differentiation of its approach to AI research from its competitors (European Commission, 2021a).

Over recent years, the U.S.'s AI strategy has been characterised by decentralised regulation and the aim of not hindering innovation—especially in its early stages (Cath et al., 2018). Further, the U.S. publicly promotes its objective of developing AI for the common good and to solve the world's greatest challenges (Cath et al., 2018). As part of this approach, it also engages intensively in research on a superintelligence and entirely autonomous forms of AI (Bostrom, 2014). China's AI strategy, on the other hand, is strongly associated with the term 'digital authoritarianism' (Lilkov, 2020; Polyakova & Meserole, 2019; Sherman, 2021)—a trend also noted by the U.S., which identified it as a possible threat to its democracy and to human rights in general (Sherman, 2021).

Polyakova and Meserole define the term 'digital authoritarianism' as "the use of digital information technology by authoritarian regimes to surveil, repress, and manipulate domestic and foreign populations" (2019, p. 1). Further, apart from associating China with this term (Lilkov, 2020; Polyakova & Meserole, 2019; Sherman,

2021), Polyakova and Meserole (2019) include Russia as an actor contributing to this phenomenon. Lilkov describes this development as a part of China's "techno-nationalism which aims to move the country closer to technological self-sufficiency and to maximise the penetration of its technological giants on the global stage" (ibid., p. 110). Further, in his research, he examines "the unique features of the Chinese model of digital authoritarianism and its international spill-overs" (ibid., p. 110). According to Lilkov, "as a new decade begins, the EU must make sure that its citizens have the necessary institutional and legal protection from abuses of modern technology such as facial-recognition software" (2020, p. 110), since Chinese AI technologies and their applications are exported and introduced to various foreign markets already.

In fact, the European regulation proposal addresses the U.S.'s aim to develop strong AI with little regulatory measures and China's export of AI applications serving surveillance objectives and the related risks stemming from their influence on the European market. For both, the E.U. seeks to regulate by restricting use cases for foreign AI applications and demanding a high standard for transparency and explicability (European Commission, 2021a).

Context in the European Union

For the past few years, the E.U. has been active regarding its regulatory approach towards AI. As early as 2018, it published the European Strategy on AI and a coordinated plan on how to proceed as a result of joint efforts with its member states (European Commission, 2021b). In preparing the field for the recent proposal, in 2019, the European Expert Group AIHLEG published its guidelines for trustworthy AI (AIHLEG, 2019). The proposal for AI regulation was preceded by the General Data Protection Regulation[7] (GDPR) (European Commission, 2018), the Digital Services Act[8] (DSA) (European Commission, 2020c), and the Digital Market Act[9] (DMA) (European Commission, 2020b), which all form part of the European Digital Strategy (Dempsey et al., 2021). Hence, the current proposal for AI regulation neither includes nor addresses market structures or the platform economy, since other regulatory measures within the overall digital strategy cover these topics.

---

[7] The General Data Protection Act (GDPR) "*lays down rules relating to the protection of natural persons with regard to the processing of personal data and rules relating to the free movement of personal data*" (European Commission, 2018, GDPR, Article 1).

[8] The Digital Services Act (DSA) proposed in December 2020, aims at enhancing content moderation and, thereby, avoiding harassment and illegal content on social media platforms (European Commission, 2020c).

[9] The Digital Markets Act (DMA) proposed in December 2020, provides new ex-ante obligations for platform companies. The obligations range in relation to the size of the platform, which is examined based on, e.g., its user numbers or market power (European Commission, 2020b).

3.3.2.2 The European Approach to AI Regulation

In April 2021, the European Commission published the "*Regulation Laying Down Harmonised Rules on Artificial Intelligence*" (European Commission, 2021a). With this proposal, the E.U. suggests a human-centric AI approach, intending to provide safe and trustworthy AI applications for its societies. In particular, the regulation proposal seeks to minimise the risks of AI adoption to ensure that it abides by fundamental human rights (European Commission, 2021a).

With this advance, the E.U. presented the first legal framework around the globe, which was developed specifically for AI, preceded by the DMA (European Commission, 2020b) and the DSA (European Commission, 2020c). However, the proposed AI regulation has significant similarities with the E.U.'s GDPR (European Commission, 2018), passed a few years earlier. This is because both regulations are part of the E.U.'s data strategy, aiming to emphatically position the E.U.'s data and AI approach in global competition (Dempsey et al., 2021). If adopted, the E.U. regulation would apply to all European companies developing, selling or using AI, with sanctions ranging from legal obligations to monitoring and penalties for non-compliant business conduct (European Commission, 2021a)—with penalties, for example, for violations of data requirements suggested to be as high as 30 million Euros. While the European Commission suggests establishing a 'European AI Board', the enforcement of the regulation proposal remains with each member state of the E.U. (European Commission, 2021a).

Risk-Based Framework as Main Part of the Regulation Proposal

In its proposal, the E.U. defines AI as a combination of two elements: a technological dimension, in the form of a list of technologies subsumed under the term AI, and a goal-oriented dimension, in the form of intended outcomes, such as predictions and recommendations influencing decision-making in the environment they are applied to. On this basis, the regulation proposal is structured alongside a risk identification framework addressing both dimensions, which is the core element of the document. Companies can apply the risk framework to their use case to identify whether their AI-based business model or service is considered to be of specific risk, high risk, or if the E.U. won't even allow its deployment or selling in the European Market (European Commission 2021a). Depending on the individual degree of risk, the company is obliged to adopt a set of governance measures to minimise the risks and consequences of its actions. In detail, the regulation introduces a four-step framework, which addresses prohibited AI, high-risk AI, and specific-risk AI (European Commission, 2021a), as subsumed in the following:

1. <u>Prohibited AI of Unacceptable Risk</u>

   The AI regulation bans AI applications belonging to this first group since they are understood to violate existing E.U. legislation and its citizens' fundamental rights directly. This includes techniques of social scoring executed by the public sector; large-scale biometric identification as a part of public surveillance; discriminatory use against vulnerable parts of societies or minorities; and applications manipulating the individual's consciousness and subconsciousness (European Commission, 2021a).

2. High-Risk AI

Applications are considered to be of high risk if they could pose threats to a human being's health, safety, or fundamental rights. Again, this includes surveillance applications, social scoring, such as the ability to obtain credit, and the application of AI for recruitment or promotion processes in the working environment. While the use and application of AI systems assigned to this risk group is allowed in the E.U., it is highly regulated. If deploying a high-risk AI application, organisations need to provide an ex-ante assessment of their application, and they are required to present and implement governance measures, e.g., specific documentation, data governance, transparent user manuals, and human oversight in the deployment of the AI system (European Commission, 2021a). Additionally, companies must commit, among other factors, to submit their applications to an assessment procedure before deployment, to the immediate implementation of corrective measures in the case of non-compliance with the regulation, and to inform national authorities within 15 days in the case of a malfunctioning of their AI system or the emergence of serious incidents linked to it. Finally, the organisation must give access to national authorities, if requested, to confirm the regulation-conforming deployment of its AI systems. Apart from directly addressing organisations deploying AI, most obligations also apply to their distributors, importers, users, and third parties (European Commission, 2021a).

3. Low-Risk or Specific-Risk AI

Adopting limited-risk AI applications mainly requires organisations to mark AI in user interactions, as in the interaction of humans with chatbots. Hence, whenever AI systems recognise human characteristics and interact with users in a non-transparent manner, the organisation is required to bring the interaction with AI to the user's attention. Moreover, this explicitly includes artificially generated or manipulated content, such as deep fakes. According to the proposed regulation, content creators would have to mark its artificiality. (European Commission, 2021a)

In this way, the E.U. aims to implement a flexible, future-oriented framework, a goal it seeks to reach by basing the risk framework on an up-to-date list of AI technologies in the market and possible use cases. These lists are continually adaptable to allow for the inclusion of future technologies. Likewise, the list of high-risk and banned AI use cases can be revised at any point (European Commission, 2021a).

3.3.2.3 Expected Timeline of Adoption

By applying this regulation, the E.U. aims to "*ensure a level playing field*" (European Commission, 2021a, p. 6) for all European organisations in either the public or private sector, engaging in AI development, sale, and use. Further, it offers the first risk-based legal classification of AI systems, which will support the ongoing structured governance of the market and ensure comparability of use cases (European Commission, 2021a). Once passed, it does not require a country-specific adoption process but is of immediate effect in all member states. As for the expected timeframe of its adoption, the E.U. suggests a two-year application phase following the final proposal and its passing (European Commission, 2021a). Thus, as early as 2024, with the end of the current E.U. presidency, the regulation could be implemented—even though in an adjusted form (European Commission, 2021a).

3.3.2.4 Global Implications of the E.U. Regulation

The proposal directly addresses companies deploying or selling AI systems in the E.U.—irrespective of their own location—and users located in the E.U. Further, it includes users and companies analysing data, e.g., about E.U. citizens or based on European data sets, which will be used again in the E.U. after being processed (European Commission, 2021a; MacCarthy & Propp, 2021; Sussmann et al., 2021). Thereby, the proposal is not only directed to European companies and the output or consequences they create when deploying or selling AI, but it controls incoming AI-based products and data-based input the E.U. is provided with from external sources and companies. Hence, it will also impact organisations outside the European Union.

Moreover, by presenting such a centralised approach to AI regulation, the E.U. counterbalances existing decentralised governance approaches delegating duties to various agencies, as currently in place in the U.S. As of now, the U.S. still abide by their mission not to overregulate the market (The White House Office of Science and Technology Policy, 2020; MacCarthy & Propp, 2021; OECD, 2021). However, the Biden administration is expected to be more open than previous administrations to putting additional regulatory measures into place (MacCarthy & Propp, 2021; White House, 2020). While the U.S. will not implement similar regulations, it can be assumed that both the E.U. and the U.S. will work on options to continue their political and economic cooperation, e.g., in the form of U.S.-controlled self-certification of high-risk AI systems (MacCarthy & Propp, 2021). Further, as initiated between the U.S. and the U.K., both regions could form government-led public–private partnerships for AI research and development (MacCarthy & Propp, 2021).

As exemplified by cooperation between the E.U. and the U.S., the proposal presented is likely to have a significant impact, even outside its geographical borders. Nonetheless, based on these first indications, other nations or regions are not expected to adopt this regulation or regulation of similar magnitude. This is because other regions in the AI market follow diverging strategies in dealing with AI, such as the U.S.'s decentralised, innovation-fostering approach, and there is no indication of these nations changing their current approach. Still, they will have to abide by European Law in the future when seeking to continue economic cooperation.

3.3.2.5 Interpretation and Potential Gaps

Overall, the analysis presented in this book suggests the adoption rate and impact of the proposal made by the E.U. will be high.[10] Given the fact that previous, similarly structured E.U. regulations, such as the GDPR, affect other regions and are exported to firms outside the E.U., the same success can be expected for the E.U.'s AI regulation (Peukert et al., 2020). Among other factors, this success stems from the fact that providers save costs by offering the same GDPR-compliant product to all customers, instead of offering different versions for different target groups (Peukert et al., 2020).

Regarding the E.U.'s AI regulation, its adoptability can, for one reason, be expected due to its highly flexible and constantly augmentable nature. Its framework character allows for its adoption by various stakeholder groups, e.g., an organisation from the public or private sector, as well as providers and sellers of AI systems. Moreover, its risk-based assessment can be continuously adapted to advances in research by adding new technologies to the list of AI-defining technologies. Additionally, it can be updated by complementing the list of use cases determining the risk level of a particular AI application (European Commission, 2021a).

As for the governance approach it presents, the proposal offers a non-traditional form of European legislation by introducing various ex-ante regulatory measures. Instead of the traditional European ex-post approaches, especially for high-risk applications, the proposal demands an ex-ante assessment to ensure the lawfulness of an AI system before its introduction to the market (Puddu et al., 2021). It complements this new measure with an additional ex-post monitoring system, aiming to detect possible complications in its usage (European Commission, 2021a; MacCarthy & Propp, 2021). This combination of measures stemming from two complementary governance mechanisms will "*facilitate the respect of fundamental rights by ensuring transparency and traceability of the AI system's functioning throughout its lifecycle*" (Puddu et al., 2021, section 3, para. 8).

Despite its flexible and human-centred perspective, this book's analysis has identified a few gaps and irregularities in the proposal presented by the E.U. To begin with, most demands posed by the regulation only address organisations, without including operating individuals. For example, providers must report violations of personal data rights, but there is no obligation for individuals to abide by this rule (Sussmann et al., 2021). Hence, an adapted version of the regulation should include users in this respect to ensure protection of the individual's data from all operating parties.

Further, American observers criticise the extensive ex-ante regulatory approach for high-risk AI applications (MacCarthy & Propp, 2021), comparing the E.U.'s standards to a so-called 'cradle-to-grave approach' (Tielemans, 2021), hinting at its perceived innovation-constraining nature (Ponce, 2021). This evaluation stems from the E.U.'s complex demand for governance measures addressing the entire AI life

[10] Due to the recentness of the proposal's publication and the resulting lack of academic publications covering it, this section needs to draw from both academic publications and public commentaries made by scholars and professionals to evaluate the quality of the regulation.

cycle, ranging from data security to technical documentation and incident management. In comparison, the efforts to foster innovation in AI and support companies in their endeavour to develop and deploy AI are less elaborate and fall under the member states' responsibility (Tielemans, 2021).

Moreover, the E.U. decided to heavily regulate both live identification and surveillance systems as well as social scoring applications, only allowing for narrowly defined use cases, such as terrorist threats or child safety (European Commission, 2021a). However, evaluating when and under which conditions AI systems are a threat to society will depend on future regulations, since such definitions are not yet finalised (MacCarthy & Propp, 2021). Hence, while this passage protects the fundamental human rights of its citizens in their entirety, it complicates the use of surveillance measures or identification applications in cases of high risk which do not pose an immediate threat—unlike, for example, the case of a terrorist attack. Thereby, the regulation might overrule the possible safety-augmenting potential of AI systems for a more significant number of cases to protect its constitutional rights.

Lastly, the topic of human and algorithmic bias remains vaguely defined by the regulation. While it demands the strict protection of all European citizens' personal data, providers can still access certain categories of personal data, such as health-related information, ethnicity, or political beliefs. They can access this data if used to detect and correct potential bias in the providers' own AI system (European Commission, 2021a; MacCarthy & Propp, 2021; Puddu et al., 2021). However, the providers still must adhere to requirements of privacy protection, which in turn might interfere with the data's intended use for which it was requested in the first place (Puddu et al., 2021). Further, MacCarthy and Propp (2021) highlight that AI providers are not obliged to present documentation on the potential bias to the public and must only disclose their findings to regulators upon request. Thus, this particular aspect of the regulation, the collection, re-use, and anonymisation of data to detect and correct biases in AI, might require adaptation to avoid existing possible legal loopholes. This example depicts a general weakness of the proposal; namely, not addressing questions of actual legal liability (Ponce, 2021).

To conclude, the E.U. offers an opportunity for individuals and organisations alike to benefit from the potential of AI research and adoption, while at the same time carefully addressing the associated risks. Although the platform economy and leading organisations in the field are not the target group of this regulation, the regulation should recognise that they are the ones driving major advances in AI research (Cihon, 2019; Rowsell-Jones & Howard, 2019; Hagendorff, 2020; Makridakis, 2017; PwC, 2019). Hence, a strong interlinkage is required between the DMA, the DSA, and this presented proposal. Nevertheless, the proposal in its current form provides organisations developing, deploying, or using AI with a well-structured risk framework. To be effective and successful on an international level, the E.U. will need to strengthen its role in AI research and form cooperations with other players in the market. By forming additional cooperative partnerships in AI research or regarding AI's commercialisation, it promotes the consequential acceptance of its proposed regulation (European Commission, 2021a, 2021b). If it succeeds in preserving its share in the market, the E.U. will concurrently enforce a rise in worldwide standards for AI and secure for itself a leading role in the development of human-centric, secure, and trustworthy AI—as it did with the GDPR (Peukert et al., 2020).

3.3.2.6 Implications for the Relational AI Governance Approach

The proposed E.U. regulation leads to new competitive conditions for companies in this region or those supplying the European market. The suggested regulation presents a new level playing field for self-regulation and governance regarding competition for these companies in the market.

Having 'SFI' in place, the reinforcement discussed previously challenges that 'SII' face in the AI context are outbalanced. Also, the role of the individual is strengthened, since it is inherently connected to the parameter 'SFI', which is in place in this second scenario. Further, the elaboration of governance measures within the firm combining 'SII' and formal measures on the side of 'O', as presented in the previous subchapter, is still valid. This is because it is merely the interaction among the governance parameters and, thereby, the adaptivity of the governance structure that changes, while the characteristics and findings per parameter remain valid. In particular, this is because the regulation does not interfere with the suggested measures presented in this book but proposes rules, which add the formerly lacking parameter 'SFI'.

Thus, the proposed regulation leads to a partially regulated market, which requires an adaptation of the Relational AI Governance approach, yet not its revision—as presented in Fig. 3.12.

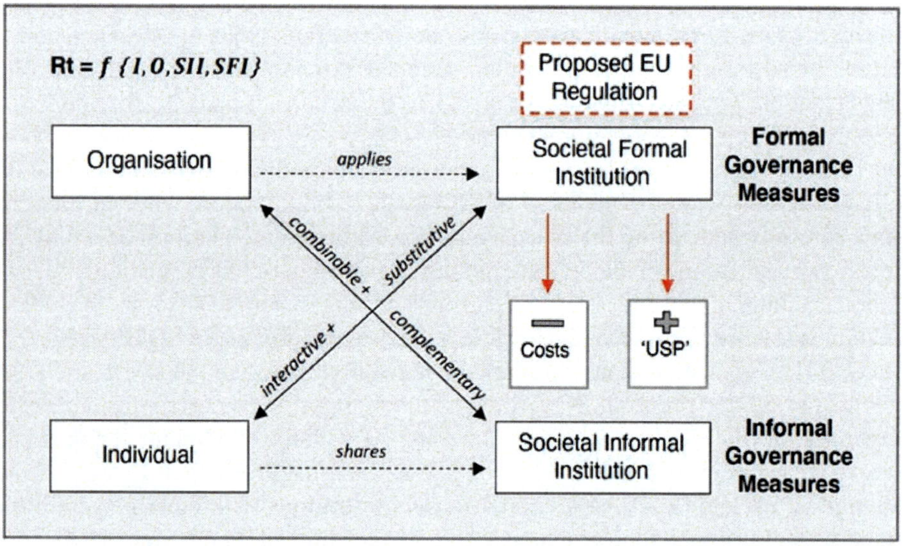

Fig. 3.12 Own depiction of dynamics among AI governance parameters in regulated E.U., according to Wieland (2020)

The initially presented governance parameters, according to Wieland (2018, 2020), can be applied in their original form. Due to the acquired completeness of all four governance parameters, this can serve as the base for developing and adjusting corporate AI governance. With the adoption of the E.U.'s regulation, the relational transaction for AI governance changes, requiring the integration of the system 'law' and its system-specific demand into the governance structure. Hence, once approved, companies affected by the E.U.'s regulation can consult Wieland's (2018, 2020) Relational Governance model for insight into governance parameter adaptivity, since the parameter 'SFI' is required to apply the original model. Still, I advise companies to consult the AI-specific model for recommendations regarding the elaboration of parameters 'SII', 'I', and 'O'.

Altogether, this book's Relational AI Governance approach and the E.U.'s proposal for AI regulation are understood to be complementary in nature. Essentially, the E.U. regulation presents one governance parameter within this book's governance approach. Hence, its passing does not change the overall structure and mechanisms within the Relational Governance of AI but influences the characteristics of the parameters and their interaction with each other. Still, synergies exist, e.g., regarding the principled ethics approach applied in both advances: for one instance, the ethical principles identified in the regulation proposal and the book align, and second, both suggest a risk-based assessment of the consequences of corporate decision-making. Also, further measures presented do not seem to interfere, such as virtue ethics-based training suggested by this book or the post-implementation monitoring of the E.U.'s regulation demands (European Commission, 2021a). Since they address different phases of the AI lifecycle or are implemented as preliminary measures, as virtue-based training could be, they seem complementary in nature. Hence, the core governance measures suggested by the regulation and Relational AI Governance overlap and can easily be integrated.

3.3.2.7 Synthesis on the Relational AI Governance Approach

Based on its conceptual contribution, I provided an in-depth examination of the dynamics a single company faces in both an unregulated and a partially regulated AI market. While exponential levels of disruption in an unregulated market bring about the necessity for new governance processes, many of the risks involved and the competitive pressure on companies to engage in a technological race for market dominion in AI cannot be prised out by a single company (Cave & ÓhÉigeartaigh, 2019; Geist, 2016).

Regarding the competitive dynamics companies face, the E.U. proposal's passing will change these by addressing the competitive conditions for European companies. As stated in the regulation proposal, the E.U. aims at levelling the field for companies to engage in sustainable, trustworthy forms of AI research and deployment. By raising the governance requirements for all E.U. companies, the regulation increases transaction costs for responsible AI adoption equally for all companies. In turn, it lowers the individual company's transaction costs and risks associated with self-regulatory measures.

Nonetheless, due to the complexity of the measures demanded by the E.U., the resulting costs for E.U. companies will be comparatively high. This is because companies can selectively choose the specific measures they seek to implement in an unregulated market, whereas this proposal obliges companies with risk-prone AI applications to adopt a wide range of measures (European Commission, 2021a). Still, due to the extensive nature of the regulation proposal and the resultingly broad levelling effect, this book's analysis estimates the reduction of individual transaction costs for companies to be greater than the costs associated with fulfilling the regulation's requirements.

In addition, the regulation provides all European companies with potential reputational gains for developing and deploying trustworthy and robust AI systems. While, within the E.U., self-regulatory measures are no longer expected to yield reputational gains after the proposal's passing, in the global market, the regulation does indeed lead to a unique selling point[11] (USP) for European companies. This is because other players and nations in the market are applying distinct strategies (Cave & ÓhÉigeartaigh, 2019; Dafoe, 2018; Geist, 2016), instead of also focusing on human-centric AI development (European Commission, 2021a). Due to the significant demand from societies around the globe for companies to develop and deploy responsible AI, European companies seem to have the opportunity to gain significant reputational advantages on the part of consumers. Furthermore, societal perception aligns with the E.U.'s position, as, for example, the critical contestation by Western research against the Chinese approach to AI confirms (Lilkov, 2020; Polyakova & Meserole, 2019; Sherman, 2021).

As for companies outside the E.U., to lower the transaction costs of self-regulation for companies on a larger scale, collective action in the form of interfirm networks, multi-stakeholder-boards, or open innovation platforms are potential options. This is because hybrid, collaborative forms of governance seem to be most suitable for the tech industry (Ferguson et al., 2005a, 2005b; Powell, 1998; Wieland, 2018, 2020; Williamson, 1979).

To conclude, companies located outside the E.U. can apply Relational AI Governance when wanting to develop and implement self-regulatory measures, as this governance model and the governance parameters serve as a foundation for corporate governance and risk-diminishing decision-making in companies that are deploying or selling AI. For European companies, the elaborations on the specific governance parameters provide important contextual information, which can be applied directly to Wieland's (2020) original model once the proposal passes.

[11] According to Forte (2002), the term 'Unique Selling Point' is used to define a specific product or service that can only be offered by that particular provider and his product. Hence, competitors cannot easily replicate this benefit. Thus, it allows the company to secure its position in the market.

References

Aaronson, S. A. (2019). *Data is different, and that's why the world needs a new approach to governing cross-border data flows* (Digital Policy, Regulation and Governance, CIGI Papers, 197). Centre for International Governance Innovation. https://www.cigionline.org/sites/default/files/documents/paper%20no.197_0.pdf

Abraham, R., Schneider, J., & vom Brocke, J. (2019). Data governance: A conceptual framework, structured review, and research agenda. *International Journal of Information Management, 49*, 424–438. https://doi.org/10.1016/j.ijinfomgt.2019.07.008

Algorithm Watch. (2020). *AI ethics guidelines global inventory*. https://inventory.algorithmwatch.org/

Alhassan, I., Sammon, D., & Daly, M. (2018). Data governance activities: A comparison between scientific and practice-oriented literature. *Journal of Enterprise Information Management, 31*(2), 300–316. https://doi.org/10.1108/JEIM-01-2017-0007

Allen, G., & Chan, T. (2017). *Artificial intelligence and national security* (Technical Report). Harvard University. https://www.belfercenter.org/publication/artificial-intelligence-and-national-security

Ananny, M. (2016). Toward an ethics of algorithms: Convening, observation, probability, and timeliness. *Science, Technology, & Human Values, 41*(1), 93–117. https://doi.org/10.1177/0162243915606523

Armstrong, S., Bostrom, N., & Shulman, C. (2016). Racing to the precipice: A model of artificial intelligence development. *AI & Society, 31*, 201–206. https://doi.org/10.1007/s00146-015-0590-y

Asaro, P. M. (2006). What should we want from a robot ethic? *International Review of Information Ethics, 6*, 9–16. https://doi.org/10.29173/irie134

Balfanz, D. (2017). Autonome systeme. Wer dient wem? In W. Schröter (Eds.), *Autonomie des Menschen–Autonomie der Systeme* (pp. 137–150). Talheimer Verlag.

Benítez-Ávila, C., Hartmann, A., & Dewulf, G. (2019). Contractual and relational governance as positioned-practices in ongoing public—Private partnership projects. *Journal of Project Management, 50*, 716–733. https://doi.org/10.1177/8756972819848224

Benkler, Y. (2019). Don't let industry write the rules for AI. *Nature, 569*(7754), 161–162. https://doi.org/10.1038/d41586-019-01413-1

Berendt, B. (2019). AI for the Common Good?! Pitfalls, challenges, and ethics pen-testing. *Paladyn, Journal of Behavioral Robotics, 10*(1), 44–65. https://doi.org/10.1515/pjbr-2019-0004

Bilal, A., Wingreen, S., & Sharma, R. (2020). *Virtue ethics as a solution to the privacy paradox and trust in emerging technologies*. In Proceedings of the 2020 the 3rd international conference on information science and system (pp. 224–228). https://doi.org/10.1145/3388176.3388196

Boddington, P. (2017). Does AI raise any distinctive ethical questions? In P. Boddington (Ed.), *Towards a code of ethics for artificial intelligence* (pp. 27–37). Springer.

Bostrom, N. (2014). *Superintelligence: Paths, dangers, strategies*. Oxford University Press.

Boyles, R. J. M. (2018). A case for machine ethics in modeling human-level intelligent agents. *Kritike, 12*(1), 182–200. https://philpapers.org/archive/BOYACF-2.pdf

Braithwaite, J., Pittelkow, Y., & Williams, R. (2003). Tax compliance by the very wealthy: Red flags of risk. In V. Braithwaite (Ed.), *Taxing democracy: Understanding tax avoidance and evasion* (1st ed., pp. 205–228). Ashgate Publishing Ltd.

Bresnahan, T. F., & Trajtenberg, M. (1995). General purpose technologies 'Engines of growth'? *Journal of Econometrics, 65*(1), 83–108. https://econpapers.repec.org/RePEc:eee:econom:v:65:y:1995:i:1:p:83-108

Brundage, M., & Bryson, J. J. (2016). Smart policies for artificial intelligence. Computing Research Repository. https://arxiv.org/abs/1608.08196

Brynjolfsson, E., & McAfee, A. (2017). The business of artificial intelligence: What it can and cannot do for your organization. *Harvard Business Review*, 1–20. https://hbr.org/2017/07/the-business-of-artificial-intelligence

Bryson, J. J. (2018). Patiency is not a virtue: The design of intelligent systems and systems of ethics. *Ethics and Information Technology, 20*(1), 15–26. https://doi.org/10.1007/s10676-018-9448-6

Bughin, J., & Hazan, E. (2017). The new spring of artificial intelligence: A few early economies. *Voxeu.* https://voxeu.org/article/new-spring-artificial-intelligence-few-early-economics

Bughin, J., Hazan, E., Ramaswamy, S., Chui, M., Allas, T., Dahlstrom, P., Henke, N., & Trench, M. (2017). *Artificial intelligence: The next digital frontier?* McKinsey Research Institute. https://www.calpers.ca.gov/docs/board-agendas/201801/full/day1/06-technology-background.pdf

Burton, E., Goldsmith, J., Koenig, S., Kuipers, B., Mattei, N., & Walsh, T. (2017). Ethical considerations in artificial intelligence courses. *AI Magazine, 38*(2), 22–34. https://doi.org/10.1609/aimag.v38i2.2731

Bynum, T. W. (2000). A very short history of computer ethics. *APA Newsletters on Philosophy and Computers, 99*(2), 163–165. https://aprender.ead.unb.br/pluginfile.php/792554/mod_glossary/attachment/7312/Terrell%20Ward%20Bynum%2C%20A%20Very%20Short%20History%20of%20Computer%20Ethics%2C%202000.pdf

Caliskan, A., Bryson, J. J., & Narayanan, A. (2017). Semantics derived automatically from language corpora contain human-like biases. *Science, 356*(6334), 183–186. https://doi.org/10.1126/science.aal4230

Calo, R. (2017). Artificial intelligence policy: A primer and roadmap. UCDL Review, *51,* 399. https://static1.squarespace.com/static/5b5df2f5fcf7fd7290ff04a4/t/5b8d79a81ae6cf1d7dfb19a4/1535998377033/04+Artificial+Intelligence+Policy+-+A+Primer+and+Roadmap+%28Calo%29.pdf

Cao, Z., & Lumineau, F. (2015). Revisiting the interplay between contractual and relational governance: A qualitative and meta-analytic investigation. *Journal of Operations Management, 33*(34), 15–42. https://doi.org/10.1016/j.jom.2014.09.009

Cath, C. (2018). Governing artificial intelligence: Ethical, legal and technical opportunities and challenges. *Philosophical Transactions of the Royal Society A, 376*(2133), 20180080. https://doi.org/10.1098/rsta.2018.0080

Cath, C., Wachter, S., Mittelstadt, B., Taddeo, M., & Floridi, L. (2018). Artificial intelligence and the 'good society': The US, EU, and UK approach. *Science and Engineering Ethics, 24*(2), 505–528. https://doi.org/10.1007/s11948-017-9901-7

Cave, S., & ÓhÉigeartaigh, S. (2019). An AI Race for strategic advantage: Rhetoric and risks. *Conference Paper for: AI Ethics and Society, 2018*, 1. https://doi.org/10.1145/3278721.3278780

Cervantes, J. A., Rodríguez, L. F., López, S., Ramos, F., & Robles, F. (2016). Autonomous agents and ethical decision-making. *Cognitive Computation, 8*(2), 278–296. https://doi.org/10.1007/s12559-015-9362-8

Chatterji, A. K., Cunningham, C. M., & Joseph, J. E. (2019). The limits of relational governance: Sales force strategies in the US medical device industry. *Strategic Management Journal, 40*, 55–78. https://doi.org/10.1002/smj.2964

Chu, Z., Lai, F., & Wang, L. (2020). Leveraging interfirm relationships in China: Western relational governance or Guanxi? Domestic versus foreign firms. *Journal of International Marketing, 28*(4), 58–74. https://doi.org/10.1177/1069031X20963672

Cihon, P. (2019). *Technical report. Standards for AI governance: International standards to enable global coordination in AI Research & Development*. University of Oxford. https://www.fhi.ox.ac.uk/wp-content/uploads/Standards_-FHI-Technical-Report.pdf

Cihon, P., Maas, M. M., & Kemp, L. (2020). *Should artificial intelligence governance be centralised? Design lessons from history.* In Proceedings of the AAAI/ACM Conference on AI, Ethics, and Society (pp. 228–234). https://doi.org/10.1145/3375627.3375857

Claro, D. P., Hagelaar, G., & Omta, O. (2003). The determinants of relational governance and performance: How to manage business relationships? *Industrial Marketing Management, 32*(8), 703–716. https://doi.org/10.1016/j.indmarman.2003.06.010

Colombelli, A., Paolucci, E., & Ughetto, E. (2017). Hierarchical and relational governance and the life cycle of entrepreneurial ecosystems. *Small Business Economics, 52*(5), 505–521. https://doi.org/10.1007/s11187-017-9957-4

Cyman, D., Gromova, E., & Juchnevicius, E. (2021). Regulation of artificial intelligence in BRICS and the European Union. *BRICS Law Journal, 8*(1), 86–115. https://doi.org/10.21684/2412-2343-2021-8-1-86-115

Dafoe, A. (2018). *AI governance: A research agenda. Governance of AI Program, Future of Humanity Institute*. University of Oxford. https://www.fhi.ox.ac.uk/wp-content/uploads/GovAI-Agenda.pdf

Daly, A., Hagendorff, T., Li, H., Mann, M., Marda, V., Wagner, B., Wang, W., & Witteborn, S. (2019). *Artificial intelligence, governance and ethics: Global perspectives* (The Chinese University of Hong Kong Faculty of Law [Research Paper]). https://doi.org/10.2139/ssrn.3414805

Danaher, J., Hogan, M. J., Noone, C., Kennedy, R., Behan, A., De Paor, A., Felzmann, H., Haklay, M., Khoo, S.-M., Morison, J., Helen Murphy, M., O'Brolchain, N., Schafer, B., & Shankar, K. (2017). Algorithmic governance: Developing a research agenda through the power of collective intelligence. *Big Data & Society, 4*(2). https://doi.org/10.1177/2053951717726554

Dempsey, M., McBride, K., & Bryson, J. J. (2021). The current state of AI Governance—An EU perspective. https://doi.org/10.31235/osf.io/xu3jr

Dunleavy, P. (2016). "Big data" and policy learning. In G. Stoker & M. Evans (Eds.), *Evidence-based policy making in the social sciences: Methods that matter* (pp. 143–157). Policy Press.

Ehsan, U., Liao, Q. V., Muller, M., Riedl, M. O., & Weisz, J. D. (2021). Expanding explainability: Towards social transparency in AI systems. *Proceedings of the 2021 CHI Conference on Human Factors in Computing Systems (1–19)*. https://doi.org/10.1145/3411764.3445188

Elia, G.-L., & Margherita, A. (2018). Can we solve wicked problems? A conceptual framework and a collective intelligence system to support problem analysis and solution design for complex social issues. *Technological Forecasting and Social Change, 133*, 279–286. https://doi.org/10.1016/j.techfore.2018.03.010

Elo, S., & Kyngäs, H. (2008). The qualitative content analysis process. *Journal of Advanced Nursing, 62*(1), 107–115. https://doi.org/10.1111/j.1365-2648.2007.04569.x

Elo, S., Kääriäinen, M., Kanste, O., Pölkki, T., Utriainen, K., & Kyngäs, H. (2014). Qualitative content analysis: A focus on trustworthiness. *SAGE Open, 4*(1), 2158244014522633. https://doi.org/10.1177/2158244014522633

European Commission. (2018). *Statement on artificial intelligence, robotics and "autonomous" systems*. Publications Office of the European Union. European Group on Ethics in Science and New Technologies. https://op.europa.eu/en/publication-detail/-/publication/dfebe62e-4ce9-11e8-be1d-01aa75ed71a1

European Commission. (2020a). *White paper on artificial intelligence: A European approach to excellence and trust*. https://ec.europa.eu/info/publications/white-paper-artificial-intelligence-european-approach-excellence-and-trust_en

European Commission. (2020b). *Proposal for a Regulation on Digital Markets Act*. https://ec.europa.eu/info/strategy/priorities-2019-2024/europe-fit-digital-age/digital-markets-act-ensuring-fair-and-open-digital-markets_en

European Commission. (2020c). *Proposal for a regulation on a single market for digital services (Digital Services Act)*. https://ec.europa.eu/info/strategy/priorities-2019-2024/europe-fit-digital-age/digital-services-act-ensuring-safe-and-accountable-online-environment_en

European Commission. (2021a). *Proposal for a regulation of the European Parliament and of the council laying down harmonised rules on Artificial intelligence (Artificial Intelligence Act) on amending certain union legislative acts*. https://eur-lex.europa.eu/legal-content/EN/TXT/?uri=CELEX%3A52021aPC0206

European Commission. (2021b). *Europe fit for the Digital Age: Commission proposes new rules and actions for excellence and trust in Artificial intelligence*. Press release. https://ec.europa.eu/commission/presscorner/detail/en/IP_21_1682

Feldstein, S. (2019). Artificial intelligence and digital repression: Global challenges to governance. *SSRN Digital*. https://doi.org/10.2139/ssrn.3374575

Ferguson, R. J., Paulin, M., & Bergeron, J. (2005a). Contractual governance, relational governance, and the performance of interfirm service exchanges: The influence of boundary-spanner closeness.

Journal of the Academy of Marketing Science, 33(2), 217–234. https://doi.org/10.1177/0092070304270729

Ferguson, R. J., Paulin, M., Möslein, K., & Müller, C. (2005b). Relational governance, communication and the performance of biotechnology partnerships. *Journal of Small Business and Enterprise Development, 12*(3), 395–408. https://doi.org/10.1108/14626000510612303

Floridi, L. (2016). Faultless responsibility: On the nature and allocation of moral responsibility for distributed moral actions. Philosophical Transactions. *Series A, Mathematical, Physical, and Engineering Sciences, 374*(2083), 1–13. https://doi.org/10.1098/rsta.2016.0112

Floridi, L. (2018). Soft ethics and the governance of the digital. *Philosophy & Technology, 31*(1), 1–8. https://doi.org/10.1007/s13347-018-0303-9

Floridi, L., Cowls, J., Beltrametti, M., Chatila, R., Chazerand, P., Dignum, V., Luetge, C., Madelin, R., Pagallo, U., Rossi, F., Schafer, B., Valcke, P., & Vayena, E. (2018). AI4People—An ethical framework for a good AI Society: Opportunities, risks, principles, and recommendations. *Minds and Machines, 28*(4), 689–707. https://doi.org/10.1007/s11023-018-9482-5

Floridi, L., & Cowls, J. (2019). A unified framework of five principles for AI in society. *Harvard Data Science Review, 1*(1). https://doi.org/10.1162/99608f92.8cd550d1

Forte, A. (2002). *Dare to be different: How to create business advantage through innovation and unique selling proposition*. Forte Financial Group.

Funke, J. (2003). *Problemlösendes Denken*. Kohlhammer Verlag.

Future of Life. (2015). *Autonomous weapons: An open letter from AI & Robotics Researchers*. At: IJCAI conference. https://futureoflife.org/open-letter-autonomous-weapons/

Gamito, M. C., & Ebers, M. (2021). Algorithmic governance and governance of algorithms: An introduction. In M. Ebers & M. C. Gamito (Eds.), *Algorithmic governance and governance of algorithms* (pp. 1–22). Springer.

Gasparotti, A. (2019). EU and OECD ethics guidelines on artificial intelligence a comparison of the two documents. cepInput. https://www.cep.eu/fileadmin/user_upload/cep.eu/Studien/cepInput_Ethische_Richtlinien_fuer_KI/Ethics_Guidelines_on_Artificial_Intelligence_01.pdf

Gasser, U., & Almeida, V. A. (2017). A layered model for AI governance. *IEEE Internet Computing, 21*(6), 58–62. https://doi.org/10.1109/MIC.2017.4180835

Geist, E. M. (2016). It's already too late to stop the AI arms race—We must manage it instead. *Bulletin of the Atomic Scientists, 72*(5), 318–321. https://doi.org/10.1080/00963402.2016.1216672

Gillespie, T. (2014). The relevance of algorithms. In T. Gillespie, P. J. Boczkowski, & K. A. Foot (Eds.), *Media technologies: Essays on communication, materiality, and society* (pp. 167–194). The MIT Press.

Girasa, R. (2020). *Artificial intelligence as a disruptive technology: Economic transformation and government regulation*. Springer Nature.

Goldfarb, A., Taska, B., & Teodoridis, F. (2019). Could machine learning be a general-purpose technology? Evidence from online job postings. *SSRN digital*. https://doi.org/10.2139/ssrn.3468822

Grabosky, P. N., & Duffield, G. M. (2001). *Red flags of fraud*. Australian Institute of Criminology. No. 200. Canberra: Australian Institute of Criminology. https://www.aic.gov.au/publications/tandi/tandi200

Grandori, A. (2006). Innovation, uncertainty and relational governance. *Journal of Industry and Innovation, 13*(2), 127–133. https://doi.org/10.1080/13662710600684290

Graneheim, U. H., Lindgren, B. M., & Lundman, B. (2017). Methodological challenges in qualitative content analysis: A discussion paper. *Nurse Education Today, 56*, 29–34. https://doi.org/10.1016/j.nedt.2017.06.002

Gritsenko, D., & Wood, M. (2020). Algorithmic governance: A modes of governance approach. *Regulation & Governance*. https://doi.org/10.1111/rego.12367

Gunitsky, S. (2015). Corrupting the cyber-commons: Social media as a tool of autocratic stability. *Perspectives on Politics, 13*(1), 42–54. https://doi.org/10.1017/S1537592714003120

Hagerty, A., & Rubinov, I. (2019). Global AI ethics: A review of the social impacts and ethical implications of artificial intelligence. arXiv:1907.07892.

Hagras, H. (2018). Toward human-understandable, explainable AI. *Computer, 51*(9), 28–36. https://doi.org/10.1109/MC.2018.3620965

Harari, Y. N. (2018). *21 Lessons for the 21st century*. Jonathan Cape.

Hardin, G. (2009). The tragedy of the commons. *Journal of Natural Resources Policy Research, 1*(3), 243–253. https://doi.org/10.1080/19390450903037302

Hagendorff, T. (2020). The ethics of AI ethics: An evaluation of guidelines. *Minds and Machines, 30*, 99–120. https://doi.org/10.1007/s11023-020-09517-8

Hagendorff, T. (2022). Blind spots in AI ethics. *AI and Ethics, 2*(4), 851–867.

Hassan, S., & De Filippi, P. (2017). The expansion of algorithmic governance: from code is law to law is code. *Field Actions Science Reports* (Special Issue 17), 88–90. http://journals.openedition.org/factsreports/4518

Helbing, D., Frey, B. S., Gigerenzer, G., Hafen, E., Hagner, M., Hofstetter, Y., van den Hoven, J., Zicari, R. V., & Zwitter, A. (2019). Will democracy survive big data and artificial intelligence? In *Towards digital enlightenment* (pp. 73–98). https://www.scientificamerican.com/article/will-democracy-survive-big-data-and-artificial-intelligence/

Helfrich, S. (2014). Commons: Für eine neue Politik jenseits von Markt und Staat (transcript Verlag). In S. Helfrich & H. B. Stiftung (Eds.). *Commons: Für eine neue Politik jenseits von Markt und Staat* (p. 528). https://www.boell.de/sites/default/files/2012-04-buch-2012-04-buch-commons.pdf

High-Level Expert Group on Artificial Intelligence (AIHLEG). (2019). *Ethics guidelines for trustworthy AI*. https://ec.europa.eu/digital-single-market/en/news/ethics-guidelines-trustworthy-ai

Hois, J., Theofanou-Fuelbier, D., & Junk, A. J. (2019). How to achieve explainability and transparency in human AI interaction. In C. Stephanidis (Ed.), *HCI International 2019—Posters. HCII 2019. Communications in Computer and Information Science*, vol. 1033, Conference on Human-Computer Interaction (pp. 177–183). Springer. https://doi.org/10.1007/978-3-030-23528-4_25

Holtel, S. (2016). Artificial intelligence creates wicked problem for the enterprise. *Procedia Computer Science, 99*, 171–180. https://doi.org/10.1016/j.procs.2016.09.109

Horowitz, M. C. (2018). Artificial intelligence, international competition, and the balance of power. *Texas National Security Review, 1*(3). https://doi.org/10.15781/T2639KP49

IEEE. (2021). IEEE standard model process for addressing ethical concerns during system design. *IEEE Std, 7000–2021*, 1–82. https://doi.org/10.1109/IEEESTD.2021.9536679

Jobin, A., Ienca, M., & Vayena, E. (2019). Artificial intelligence: The global landscape of ethics guidelines. *Nature Machine Intelligence, 1*, 389–399. https://doi.org/10.1038/s42256-019-0088-2

Johnson, D. G. (1985). *Computer ethics*. Prentice-Hall.

Johnson, D. G. (2017). Can engineering ethics be taught? *The Bridge, 47*(1), 59–64. https://www.nae.edu/168649/Can-Engineering-Ethics-Be-Taught

Ju, M., & Gao, G. Y. (2017). Relational governance and control mechanisms of export ventures: An examination across relationship length. *Journal of International Marketing, 25*(2), 72–87. https://doi.org/10.1509/jim.16.0070

Kaplan, A., & Haenlein, M. (2019). Siri, Siri, in my hand: Who's the fairest in the land? On the interpretations, illustrations, and implications of artificial intelligence. *Business Horizons, 62*(1), 15–25. https://doi.org/10.1016/j.bushor.2018.08.004

Kaptein, M. (1999). Integrity management. *European Management Journal, 17*(6), 625–634. https://doi.org/10.1016/S0263-2373(99)00053-5

Kazim, E., & Koshiyama, A. (2020a). A high-level overview of AI ethics. *Centre for Financial Regulation and Economic Development*. https://www.legalanalytics.law.cuhk.edu.hk/post/a-high-level-overview-of-ai-ethics

Kazim, E., & Koshiyama, A. (2020b). No AI regulator: An analysis of artificial intelligence and public standards report (UK Government). *SSRN Digital*. https://doi.org/10.2139/ssrn.3544871

Kirkpatrick, K. (2015). The moral challenges of driverless cars. *Communications of the ACM, 58*(8), 19–20. https://doi.org/10.1145/2788477

Klinger, J., Mateos-Garcia, J. C., & Stathoulopoulos, K. (2018). *Deep learning, deep change? Mapping the development of the artificial intelligence general purpose technology.* Mapping the Development of the Artificial Intelligence General Purpose Technology. https://arxiv.org/abs/1808.06355

König, P. D. (2019). Dissecting the algorithmic leviathan: On the socio-political anatomy of algorithmic governance. *Philosophy & Technology, 1–19*,. https://doi.org/10.1007/s13347-019-00363-w

Krippendorff, K. (1980). *Content analysis. An introduction to its methodology.* Sage.

Krippendorff, K. (2013). *Content analysis. An introduction to its methodology* (3rd ed.). Sage.

Leonelli, S. (2016). Locating ethics in data science: Responsibility and accountability in global and distributed knowledge production systems. *Philosophical Transactions. Series A, Mathematical, Physical, and Engineering Sciences, 374*(2083), 1–12. https://doi.org/10.1098/rsta.2016.0122

Lessig, L. (1999). *Code and other laws of cyberspace.* Basic Books.

Lilkov, D. (2020). Made in China: Tackling digital authoritarianism. *European View, 19*(1), 110–110. https://doi.org/10.1177/1781685820920121

Lin, P., Abney, K., & Bekey, G. A. (Eds.). (2012). *Robot ethics: The ethical and social implications of robotics. Intelligent Robotics and Autonomous Agents series.* MIT Press.

Liu, Y., Li, Y., Shi, L. H., & Liu, T. (2017). Knowledge transfer in buyer-supplier relationships: The role of transactional and relational governance mechanisms. *Journal of Business Research, 78*, 285–293. https://doi.org/10.1016/J.JBUSRES.2016.12.024

Luhmann, N. (1995). *Social systems.* Stanford University Press.

Luhmann, N. (1996). The sociology of the moral and ethics. *International Sociology, 11*(1), 27–36. https://doi.org/10.1177/026858096011001003

Luhmann, N. (1997). *Die Gesellschaft der Gesellschaft.* Suhrkamp Verlag.

MacCarthy, M., & Propp, K. (2021). Machines learn that Brussels writes the rules: The EU's new AI regulation. *Brookings.* https://www.brookings.edu/blog/techtank/2021/05/04/machines-learn-that-brussels-writes-the-rules-the-eus-new-ai-regulation/

Madzou, L., & MacDonald, K. (2020). How to put AI ethics into practice: A 12-step guide. *World Economic Forum.* https://www.weforum.org/agenda/2020/09/how-to-put-ai-ethics-into-practice-in-12-steps/

Makridakis, S. (2017). The forthcoming Artificial Intelligence (AI) revolution: Its impact on society and firms. *Futures, 100*(90), 46–60. https://doi.org/10.1016/j.futures.2017.03.006

Mayer, A. S., Haimerl, A., Strich, F., & Fiedler, M. (2021). *How corporations encourage the implementation of AI ethics* (ECIS 2021 Research Papers). 27. https://aisel.aisnet.org/ecis2021_rp/27

Mayring, P. (2000). Qualitative content analysis. Forum *Qualitative Sozialforschung/Forum: Qualitative Social Research, 1*(2), Art. 20. https://doi.org/10.17169/fqs-1.2.1089

Mayring, P. (2002). *Einfuḧrung in die qualitative Sozialforschung. Eine Anleitung zu qualitativem Denken.* Weinheim: Beltz Verlag.

Mayring, P. (2008). *Qualitative inhaltsanalyse. Grundlagen und Techniken.* Beltz Verlag.

Mayring, P. (2010). *Qualitative Inhaltsanalyse* (11th ed.). Beltz Verlag.

Mayring, P. (2015). *Qualitative Inhaltsanalyse Grundlagen und Techniken* (12th ed.). Beltz Verlag.

McNamara, A., Smith, J., & Murphy-Hill, E. (2018). Does ACM's code of ethics change ethical decision making in software development? *In Proceedings of the 2018 26th ACM joint meeting on European software engineering conference and symposium on the foundations of software engineering* (pp. 729–733). https://doi.org/10.1145/3236024.3264833

Miller, C., & Coldicott, R. (2019). People, power and technology: The tech workers' view. *Dot Everyone.* https://doteveryone.org.uk/report/workersview

Ministry of Economic Affairs and Employment Helsinki. (2019). *Leading the way into the age of artificial intelligence Final report of Finland's Artificial Intelligence Programme 2019.*

Publications of the Ministry of Economic Affairs and Employment. https://julkaisut.valtioneuvosto.fi/bitstream/handle/10024/161688/41_19_Leading%20the%20way%20into%20the%20age%20of%20artificial%20intelligence.pdf

Mittelstadt, B. D., & Floridi, L. (2016). The ethics of big data: Current and foreseeable issues in biomedical contexts. *Science and Engineering Ethics, 22*(2), 303–341. https://doi.org/10.1007/s11948-015-9652-2

Mittelstadt, B. (2019a). Ai ethics–too principled to fail? *arXiv preprint* . arXiv:1906.06668

Mittelstadt, B. (2019b). Principles alone cannot guarantee ethical AI. *Nature Machine Intelligence, 1*(11), 501–507. https://doi.org/10.1038/s42256-019-0114-4

Morley, J., Floridi, L., Kinsey, L., & Elhalal, A. (2020). From what to how: An initial review of publicly available AI ethics tools, methods and research to translate principles into practices. *Science and Engineering Ethics, 26*(4), 2141–2168. https://doi.org/10.1007/s11948-019-00165

Moore, G. (2006). Moore's law at 40. In D. Brock (Ed.), *Understanding Moore's law: Four decades of innovation* (pp. 67–84). Chemical Heritage Foundation.

Mozafari, N., Weiger, W. H., & Hammerschmidt, M. (2020). The Chatbot disclosure dilemma: Desirable and undesirable effects of disclosing the non-human identity of Chatbots. *Proceedings of the 54th Hawaii International Conference on System Sciences | 2021.* https://doi.org/10.24251/HICSS.2021.355

Nakashima, E. (2012). Stuxnet was work of U.S. and Israeli experts, officials say. *The Washington-Post.* https://www.washingtonpost.com/gdprconsent/?next_url=https%3a%2f%2fwww.washingtonpost.com%2fworld%2fnational-security%2fstuxnet-was-work-of-us-and-israeli-experts-officials-say%2f2012%2f06%2f01%2fgJQAlnEy6U_story.html

Ndubisi, N. O., Ehret, M., & Wirtz, J. (2016). Relational governance mechanisms and uncertainties in nonownership services. *Psychology & Marketing, 33*(4), 250–266. https://doi.org/10.1002/mar.20873

Nepelski, D., & Sobolewski, M. (2020). Estimating investments in General Purpose Technologies. The case of AI Investments in Europe. In *Publications Office of the European Union, Luxembourg.* https://doi.org/10.2760/506947

Neubert, M. J., & Montañez, G. D. (2020). Virtue as a framework for the design and use of artificial intelligence. *Business Horizons, 63*(2), 195–204. https://doi.org/10.1016/j.bushor.2019.11.001

Nilsson, N. J. (2009). *The quest for artificial intelligence.* Cambridge University Press.

Organisation for Economic Co-operation and Development (OECD). (2019). *Recommendation of the Council on Artificial Intelligence.* OECD/LEGAL/0449. https://oecd.ai/assets/files/OECD-LEGAL-0449-en.pdf

Organisation for Economic Co-operation and Development. OECD.AI Policy Observatory. (2021). *Database of National AI Policies.* https://oecd.ai

Paine, L. S. (2003). *Value shift.* McGraw-Hill Professional.

Pentland, A. (2013). The data-driven society. *Scientific American, 309*(4), 78–83. https://doi.org/10.1038/scientificamerican1013-78

Perc, M., Ozer, M., & Hojnik, J. (2019). Social and juristic challenges of artificial intelligence. *Palgrave Communication, 5*(61). https://doi.org/10.1057/s41599-019-0278-x

Petralia, S. (2020). Mapping general purpose technologies with patent data. *Research Policy, 49*(7), 104013. https://doi.org/10.1016/j.respol.2020.104013

Peukert, C., Bechtold, S., Batikas, M., & Kretschmer, T. (2020). Regulatory export and Spillovers: How GDPR affects global markets for data. *VoxEU.* https://voxeu.org/article/how-gdpr-affects-global-markets-data

Pieters, W. (2011). Explanation and trust: What to tell the user in security and AI? *Ethics and Information Technology, 13*(1), 53–64. https://doi.org/10.1007/s10676-010-9253-3

Pirson, M. (2007). *Facing the trust gap: How organizations can measure and manage stakeholder trust.* University of St. Gallen.

Pirson, M., Martin, K., & Parmar, B. (2019). Public trust in business and its determinants. *Business & Society, 58*(1), 132–166. https://doi.org/10.1177/0007650316647950

Polyakova, A., & Meserole, C. (2019). Exporting digital authoritarianism: The Russian and Chinese models. *Policy Brief, Democracy and Disorder Series (Washington, DC: Brookings, 2019)*, 1–22. https://www.brookings.edu/wp-content/uploads/2019/08/FP_20190827_digital_authoritarianism_polyakova_meserole.pdf

Polyakova, A., & Boyer, S. P. (2018). *The future of political warfare: Russia, the West and the coming age of global digital competition*. Brookings Institution. https://www.brookings.edu/wp-content/uploads/2018/03/fp_20180316_future_political_warfare.pdf

Ponce, A. (2021). The AI Regulation: entering an AI regulatory winter? Why an ad hoc directive on AI in employment is required. *Why an ad hoc directive on AI in employment is required (June 25, 2021). ETUI Research Paper-Policy Brief*. SSRN digital. https://doi.org/10.2139/ssrn.3873786

Poppo, L., & Zenger, T. (2002). Do formal contracts and relational governance function as substitutes or complements? *Journal of Strategic Management, 23*(8), 707–725. https://doi.org/10.1002/smj.249

Poppo, L., Zhou, K. Z., & Zenger, T.R. (2008). Examining the conditional limits of relational governance: specialized assets, performance ambiguity, and longstanding ties. *Journal of Management Studies, 45*(7), 1195–1216. https://doi.org/10.1111/j.1467-6486.2008.00779.x

Powell, W. W. (1998). Learning from collaboration: Knowledge and networks in the biotechnology and pharmaceutical industries. *California Management Review, 40*(3), 228–40. https://doi.org/10.2307/41165952

PriceWaterhouseCoopers. (2019). *Sizing the prize What's the real value of AI for your business and how can you capitalise*? PriceWaterhouseCoopers. https://www.pwc.com/gx/en/issues/analytics/assets/pwc-ai-analysis-sizing-the-prize-report.pdf

Puddu, S., Rollán Galindo, A. I., & Firth-Butterfield, K. (2021). What the EU is doing to foster human-centric AI. *World Economic Forum*. https://www.weforum.org/agenda/2021/05/ai-and-ethical-concerns-what-the-eu-is-doing-to-mitigate-the-risk-of-discrimination/

Rabesandratana, T. (2018). Europe moves to compete in global AI arms race. *Science, 360*(6388), 474–474. https://doi.org/10.1126/science.360.6388.474-a

Rai, A. (2020). Explainable AI: From black box to glass box. *Journal of the Academy of Marketing Science, 48*(1), 137–141. https://doi.org/10.1007/s11747-019-00710-5

Razzkazov, V. E. (2020). Financial and economic consequences of distribution of artificial intelligence as a general-purpose technology. *Finance: Theory and Practice, Scientific and Practical Journal, 24*(2), 120–132. https://doi.org/10.26794/2587-5671-2020-24-2-120-132

Rittel, H. W. J., & Webber, M. M. (1973). Dilemmas in a general theory of planning. *Policy Sciences, 4*, 155–169. https://doi.org/10.1007/BF01405730

Roberts, N.C. (2000). Wicked Problems and Network Approaches to Resolution. *The International Public Management Review, 1*(1), 1–19. http://www.economy4humanity.org/commons/library/175-349-1-SM.pdf

Rosa, H. (2016). *Resonanz. Eine Soziologie der Weltbeziehung*. Suhrkamp.

Rosenblatt, B., Trippe, B., & Mooney, S. (2002). *Digital rights management business and technology*. M&T Books.

Rothwell, R. (1994). Towards the fifth-generation innovation process. *International Marketing Review, 11*(1), 7–31.

Rowsell-Jones, A., & Howard, C. (2019). *2019 CIO Survey: CIOs Have Awoken to the Importance of AI. Gartner Research*. https://www.gartner.com/en/documents/3897266/2019-cio-survey-cios-have-awoken-to-the-importance-of-ai

Scharre, P. (2019). Killer apps: The Real Dangers of an AI Arms Race. *Foreign Affairs*. https://www.foreignaffairs.com/articles/2019-04-16/killer-apps

Schiff, D., Biddle, J., Borenstein, J., & Laas, K. (2020). What's next for AI ethics, policy, and governance? A global overview. In *Proceedings of the AAAI/ACM Conference on AI, Ethics, and Society* (pp. 153–158).https://doi.org/10.1145/3375627.3375804

Schoder, D., Putzke, J., Metaxas, P. T., Gloor, P., & Fischbach, K. (2014). Information Systems for "Wicked Problems." *Business & Information Systems Engineering, 6*, 3–10. https://doi.org/10.1007/s12599-013-0303-3

Sen, A. (2005). Human rights and capabilities. *Journal of Human Development, 6*(2), 151–166. https://doi.org/10.1080/14649880500120491

Sherman, J. (2021). Digital authoritarianism and implications for US national security. *The Cyber Defense Review, 6*(1), 107–118. https://cyberdefensereview.army.mil/Portals/6/Documents/2021_winter_cdr/06_CDR_V6N1_Sherman.pdf?ver=_8pKxD7hOFkcsIANHQZKDw%3d%3d

Shin, D. (2021). The effects of explainability and causability on perception, trust, and acceptance: Implications for explainable AI. *International Journal of Human-Computer Studies, 146*, 102551. https://doi.org/10.1016/j.ijhcs.2020.102551

Siau, K., & Wang, W. (2020). Artificial Intelligence (AI) ethics: Ethics of AI and ethical AI. *Journal of Database Management, 31*(2), 74–87. https://doi.org/10.4018/JDM.2020040105

Sjödin, D. R., Parida, V., & Kohtamäki, M. (2019). Relational governance strategies for advanced service provision: Multiple paths to superior financial performance in servitization. *Journal of Business Research, 101*, 906–915. https://doi.org/10.1016/j.jbusres.2019.02.042

Skjuve, M., Haugstveit, I. M., Følstad, A., & Brandtzaeg, P. B. (2019). Help! Is my Chatbot falling into the uncanny valley? An empirical study of user experience in human-chatbot interaction. *Human Technology, 15*(1). https://doi.org/10.17011/ht/urn.201902201607

Spöhring, W. (1989). *Qualitative Sozialforschung*. Springer Verlag.

Steinke, I. (2000). Gütekriterien qualitativer Forschung. In U. Flick, E. V. Kardorff, & I. Steinke (Eds.), *Qualitative Forschung. Ein Handbuch* (pp. 319–331). Rowohlt Taschenbuch.

Sussmann, H., Blair, K., Schröder, C., Yavorsky, S., & Hall, J. (2021). *The new EU approach to the regulation of artificial intelligence*. https://www.orrick.com/en/Insights/2021/05/The-New-EU-Approach-to-the-Regulation-of-Artificial-Intelligence

Taddeo, M., & Floridi, L. (2018a). How AI can be a force for good. *Science, 24*, 751–752. https://doi.org/10.1126/science.aat5991

Taddeo, M., & Floridi, L. (2018b). Regulate artificial intelligence to avert cyber arms race. *Nature, 556*(7701), 296–298. https://doi.org/10.1038/d41586-018-04602-6

The White House Office of Science and Technology Policy. (2020). *American intelligence initiative: Year one annual report*. https://www.nitrd.gov/nitrdgroups/images/c/c1/American-AI-Initiative-One-Year-Annual-Report.pdf

Thiebes, S., Lins, S., & Sunyaev, A. (2020). Trustworthy artificial intelligence. *Electronic Markets, 31*, 447–464.https://doi.org/10.1007/s12525-020-00441-4

Thomas, D. R. (2006). A general inductive approach for analyzing qualitative evaluation data. *American Journal of Evaluation, 27*, 237–246. https://doi.org/10.1177/1098214005283748

Thornton, S. M., Pan, S., Erlien, S. M., & Gerdes, J. C. (2016). Incorporating ethical considerations into automated vehicle control. *IEEE Transactions on Intelligent Transportation Systems, 18*(6), 1429–1439. https://doi.org/10.1109/TITS.2016.2609339

Tielemans, J. (2021). *A look at what's in the EU's newly proposed regulation on AI*. https://iapp.org/news/a/a-look-at-whats-in-the-eus-newly-proposed-regulation-on-ai/

Tomasik, B. (2013). International cooperation vs. AI arms race. *Foundational Research Institute, Center on Long-term Risk, 5*. https://longtermrisk.org/files/international-cooperation-ai-arms-race.pdf

Trajtenberg, M. (2018). AI as the next GPT: A Political-Economy Perspective (No. w24245). *National Bureau of Economic Research*. https://doi.org/10.3386/w24245

Uhlaner, L. M., Floren, R. H., & Geerlings, J. R. (2007). Owner commitment and relational governance in the privately held firm: An empirical study. *Small Business Economics, 29*, 275–293. https://doi.org/10.1007/s11187-006-9009-y

United Nations Educational, Scientific and Cultural Organization (UNESCO). (2019). *Elaboration of a Recommendation on the ethics of artificial intelligence*. https://en.unesco.org/artificial-intelligence/ethics

United Nations Interregional Crime and Justice Research Institute (UNICRI). (2021). *Artificial intelligence and robotics*. http://www.unicri.it/topics/ai_robotics

Vallor, S. (2016). *Technology and the virtues: A philosophical guide to a future worth wanting*. Oxford University Press.

Vought, R. T. (2020). Guidance for regulation of artificial intelligence applications. Memorandum for the Heads of Executive Departments and Agencies. *The White House Office*. https://www.whitehouse.gov/wp-content/uploads/2020/01/Draft-OMB-Memo-on-Regulation-of-AI-1-7-19.pdf?utm_source=morning_brew

Wachter, S., Mittelstadt, B., & Floridi, L. (2017). Why a right to explanation of automated decision-making does not exist in the general data protection regulation. *International Data Privacy Law, 7*(2), 76–99. https://doi.org/10.1093/idpl/ipx005

Wacker, J. G., Yang, C., & Sheu, C. (2016). A transaction cost economics model for estimating performance effectiveness of relational and contractual governance: Theory and statistical results. *International Journal of Operations & Production Management, 36*(11), 1551–1575. https://doi.org/10.1108/IJOPM-10-2013-0470

Wallach, W., & Marchant, G. (2019). Toward the agile and comprehensive international governance of AI and robotics. *Proceedings of the IEEE, 107*(3), 505–508. [8662741]. https://doi.org/10.1109/JPROC.2019.2899422

Wallach, W., & Asaro, P. (Eds.). (2020). *Machine ethics and robot ethics*. Routledge.

World Economic Forum (WEF). (2020). *Reimagining regulation for the age of AI: New Zealand pilot project*. http://www3.weforum.org/docs/WEF_Reimagining_Regulation_Age_AI_2020.pdf

World Economic Forum (WEF) & Deloitte. (2020). *Global technology governance report 2021: Harnessing fourth industrial revolution technologies in a COVID-19 world*. https://www.weforum.org/reports/global-technology-governance-report-2021

Weng, Y., & Izumo, T. (2019). Natural law and its implications for AI Governance. *Delphi—Interdisciplinary Review of Emerging Technologies, 2*(3), 122–128. https://doi.org/10.21552/delphi/2019/3/5

Whittlestone, J., Nyrup, R., Alexandrova, A., & Cave, S. (2019). The role and limits of principles in AI ethics: Towards a focus on tensions. *Proceedings of the 2019 AAAI/ACM Conference on AI, Ethics, and Society (195–200)*. https://doi.org/10.1145/3306618.3314289

Wieland, J. (2005). Corporate governance, values management, and standards: A European perspective. *Business & Society, 44*(1), 74–93. https://doi.org/10.1177/0007650305274852

Wieland, J. (2008). Governanceökonomik: Die Firma als Nexus von Stakeholdern Eine Diskussionsanregung. In J. Wieland (Ed.), *Die Stakeholder-Gesellschaft und ihre Governance, Studien zur Governanceethik* (6th ed., pp. 15–38). Metropolis Verlag.

Wieland, J. (2014). *Governance ethics: Global value creation, economic organization and normativity*. Springer International Publishing.

Wieland, J. (2018). *Relational economics. Ökonomische Theorie der Governance wirtschaftlicher Transaktionen*. Metropolis.

Wieland, J. (2020). *Relational economics: A Political economy*. Springer.

Wieland, J., Steinmeyer, R., & Grüninger, S. (2020). *Handbuch compliance-management Konzeptionelle Grundlagen, praktische Erfolgsfaktoren, globale Herausforderungen* (3rd ed.). Berlin: Erich Schmidt Verlag.

Williamson, O. E. (1979). Transaction-cost economics: The governance of contractual relations. *Journal of Law and Economics, 22*(2), 233–261. https://doi.org/10.1086/466942

Williamson, O. E. (2002). The theory of the firm as governance structure: From choice to contract. *Journal of Economic Perspectives, 16*(3), 171–195. https://doi.org/10.1257/089533002760278776

Williamson, B. (2014). Knowing public services: Cross-sector intermediaries and algorithmic governance in public sector reform. *Public Policy and Administration, 29*(4), 292–312. https://doi.org/10.1177/0952076714529139

Wu, W., Huang, T., & Gong, K. (2020). Ethical principles and governance technology development of AI in China. *Engineering, 6*(3), 302–309. https://doi.org/10.1016/j.eng.2019.12.015

Yampolskiy, R. (2015). From seed AI to technological singularity via recursively self-improving software. arXiv:1502.06512v1

Yu, H., Shen, Z., Miao, C., Leung, C., Lesser, V. R., & Yang, Q. (2018). *Building ethics into artificial intelligence*. arXiv preprint arXiv:1812.02953

Zaheer, A., & Venkatraman, N. (1995). Relational Governance as an interorganizational strategy: An empirical test of the role of trust in economic exchange. *Strategic Management Journal, 16*, 373–392. https://doi.org/10.1002/smj.4250160504

Zheng, J., Roehrich, J. K., & Lewis, M. A. (2008). The dynamics of contractual and relational governance: Evidence from long-term public-private procurement arrangements. *Journal of Purchasing and Supply Management, 14*, 43–54. https://doi.org/10.1016/j.pursup.2008.01.004

Zhu, L., Xu, X., Lu, Q., Governatori, G., & Whittle, J. (2021). *AI and ethics—Operationalising responsible AI*. arXiv preprint arXiv:2105.088

Chapter 4
Contextualisation of Relational AI Governance in Existing Research

This chapter reports a systematic literature review on private-sector AI governance to position the conceptual contribution of this book in existing research and highlight its potential connectivity to further advances in the research discipline. Thereafter, Relational AI Governance is discussed according to the literature review's findings. To do so, I proceed to present the methodology applied, describing the research design and the formulation of the review process, as well as keywords used in the review process and selection criteria for the data retrieval. Subsequently, the review findings are analysed descriptively and examined according to the research stream they stem from. Lastly, publications correlating with this book's scope are selected for an in-depth analysis, with its findings being interpreted in the light of its conceptual contribution. With this, I aim to complement my conceptual contribution with empirical findings and, thereby, strengthen the validity of the Relational AI Governance model.

4.1 Research Design: Systematic Literature Review

While reviews do exist on the progress of responsible AI research (Morley et al., 2020; Mueller et al., 2019) and the status quo of the development of AI ethics guidelines (Hagendorff, 2020), a review of AI governance from a private-sector perspective has not yet been at the centre of scholarly attention (Hagendorff, 2020). Thus, this niche is still not sufficiently developed and can be described as under-researched. Since the corporate sector is argued to be the main driver for change and progress in AI research and adoption, it is a vital force in the implementation of AI governance measures and

Supplementary Information The online version contains supplementary material available at https://doi.org/10.1007/978-3-031-25023-1_4.

S. Wiesmüller, *The Relational Governance of Artificial Intelligence*,
Relational Economics and Organization Governance,
https://doi.org/10.1007/978-3-031-25023-1_4

has already been called on to take action (Brundage et al., 2018; Bryson, 2018; Cihon et al., 2020a; Schwab & Davis, 2018). Thus, a comprehensive review of private-sector governance is needed that includes research on AI standards and norms in its research scope. Thereby, a holistic view of the progress can be given, and scholars provided with a solid base for their future contributions. The comprehensive review of such advancements will allow this book to derive implications for both theory and practice.

4.1.1 Description of Selected Methodology

In academia, especially when new research fields are evolving, significant amounts of content are produced in a short amount of time. However, the findings or approaches taken by scholars often differ strongly or are based on conflicting positions (Jesson et al., 2011). Thus, the overall aim of conducting a literature review is to give a comprehensive review that structures and contextualises existing literature, which is important for a particular research question, a specific topic, or phenomenon (Kitchenham & Charters, 2007)—as is the case for the topic at hand.

4.1.1.1 Choice of Method

According to Cooper (1988), the minimal requirement for any literature review is for it to be solely based on publications of primary origin, rather than claiming to be a primary source itself. The publications presented can be of different methodological natures. Both the searching process and the specifications of the data selection and analysis processes need to be well-documented and reproducible, without errors or scholarly bias (Crossan & Apaydin, 2010; Denyer & Tranfield, 2009; Tranfield et al., 2003). Moreover, a systematic review is argued to be "*the heart of 'pragmatic' management research*" (Tranfield et al., 2003, p. 220), as, through its descriptive and accessible format, it provides insights and information for both academia and practitioners (Webster & Watson, 2002). A review not only structures its findings according to other scholars' conceptual work but also demonstrates controversy, accord, and gaps for further research (Crossan & Apaydin, 2010; Ginsberg & Venkatraman, 1985; Knopf, 2006; Webster & Watson, 2002).

4.1.1.2 Standardised Review Process

To ensure the quality of the review, I applied a standardised process based on the work of various renowned authors (Baumeister & Leary, 1997; Bem, 1995; Conn et al., 2003; Crossan & Apaydin, 2010). First, all publications published within the defined time period are included in the study. Second, the review depicts existing relations and commonalities among emerging streams of research, as well as contradictions, inconsistencies, and gaps. Third, the findings are clustered based on the researcher's theoretical background and the publication's conceptual basis. Thereby, rather than merely summarising existing positions, this book's position is integrated (Bem, 1995; Sternberg, 1991). Fourth, I evaluate existing theories, commenting on or extending them, to ensure that the review's findings are transparent. In the fifth step, implications are given for practice (Tranfield et al., 2003).

4.1.1.3 Detailed Review Conduction

To generate a systematic literature review of high quality, the review process follows a strict order. For the data selection, various variables, such as the research interest, a definition of sources, and the identification of keywords must be defined upfront. Moreover, the selection criteria, as well as the process of executing the search and, especially, the filtration of relevant papers must be made transparent (Jesson et al., 2011; Siebels & Knyphausen-Aufseß, 2012; Tranfield et al., 2003). These steps are crucial to ensure the author's neutrality to previously conducted research in the field.

When focusing on an emerging field, as is the case for this book, the review of existing literature can be shorter due to the existence of fewer academic publications. Here, a review can contribute by proposing a newly developed conceptual model or overview advancing the efforts thus far made by other scholars (Webster & Watson, 2002). Hence, the review's findings will be structured by inductively developed categories, either adding to or complementing the Relational AI Governance model. This approach ensures that the presentation of the review results follows a specific, content-related structure, rather than merely listing them chronologically or based on their methodological nature.

4.1.2 Execution of Systematic Literature Review for AI Governance

According to Jesson et al. (2011), a scoping process consists of two steps: first, defining precise research questions, and second, ensuring that either no review has yet been conducted in this field, or if so, that a specific amount of time has passed since its conduction.

As established, no comprehensive review has yet been conducted for AI governance stemming from or related to the private sector. Hence, this review screens all publications found for AI governance, the development of AI (governance) standards, and norms for AI development. Thus, the keywords 'AI governance', 'AI standards', and 'AI norms' provide the fundamental basis for data retrieval. All publications including these keywords in their title are presented descriptively and their content-related focus is analysed. The choice of keywords will ensure an implementation focus for AI governance measures and close the identified gap in research (Hagendorff, 2020).

4.1.2.1 Data Selection Process

To ensure the objectivity of the review sample, strict steps have been applied so that the search process might be replicated by scholars in the future (Crossan & Apaydin, 2010; Jesson et al., 2011; Tranfield et al., 2003). Therefore, before conducting the actual review process, I developed preliminary inclusion and exclusion criteria, and conducted a pilot review (in June 2020). While a full-text search for keywords seemed suitable for this research question, I had to depart from this first approach, as it led to more than 56,000 results (as of June 2020), which went beyond the scope of this book. Hence, the search was limited to keyword mentions in the title only.

Definition of Review Sources

For the search process for academic literature, the review included two databases, considered to be the essential sources for peer-reviewed publications (Asher et al., 2012; Crossan & Apaydin, 2010; Vieira & Gomes, 2009): Business Source Premier (Ebsco) and Scopus, formerly known as ISI Web of Knowledge—Social Sciences Citation Index (SSCI). To ensure the review's quality, the choice of databases was made in accordance with mainstream literature on the selected review design (Asher et al., 2012; Crossan & Apaydin, 2010; Vieira & Gomes, 2009).

Moreover, the review aims to avoid a type of bias called 'publication bias' (Coburn & Vevea, 2015; Sutton, 2009), meaning academic work that is only published if the piece's results are significant (Conn et al., 2003; Lipsey & Wilson, 2001; Vevea & Woods, 2005). This is because, especially in an emerging field, such a bias can lead to a strong misconception of the status quo in research. Although this effect seems more common in quantitative research (Cumming, 2014; Lipsey & Wilson, 2001), it can also occur in the early stages of research, when not much theory or data is available. For those reasons, according to Conn et al. (2003) and Lipsey and Wilson (2001), including both published and unpublished sources in a systematic literature review is an accepted and important method, which is why the review also includes so-called 'grey literature' (Jesson et al., 2011). This term defines publications not controlled by any commercial publisher and can include technical reports, working papers, conference proceedings, or official publications (Jesson et al., 2011). As leading institutions in the field, such as the Future of Humanity Institute in Oxford, publish articles of this exact type, such as Cihon's (2019) technical report on AI Governance, their inclusion seems imperative. Therefore, I decided to use Google Scholar as a third source to access data and, since non-peer-reviewed publications form part of the organic and ongoing professionalisation of research in this emerging field, a natural process in academia. Hence, by using two databases and one search engine, highly validated sources from journals, as well as rather practice-oriented literature, are examined, expanding the scope of the data collection (Jesson et al., 2011).

Table 4.1 Inclusion criteria for initial data sample

Inclusion criteria: Academic Literature	IC01: Articles published between 01 January 2015 and 25 July 2021 IC02: Articles matching the search string mentioned below and within the scope of analysis IC03: Articles must involve the term 'Artificial Intelligence' or 'AI' IC04: Articles must involve the term 'Governance', or 'Standard' or 'Norm' in their title

Identification of Keywords

Given the recency of academic work in the field and the broad positioning of research, the search included the terms 'AI norms' and 'AI standards' in addition to 'AI governance'. In the search process, the keywords were checked for in the title of the publications only. The following Boolean search strings[1] were applied in the research process, as the algorithms are known to improve the effectiveness of a literature retrieval process (Jesson et al., 2011; Kitchenham & Charters, 2007). To build search strings, the keywords are connected by Boolean connectors:

- (artif* AND intel*) AND X OR (AI) AND governance*
- (artif* AND intel*) AND X OR (AI) AND standards*
- (artif* AND intel*) AND X OR (AI) AND norms*

They were also applied in written form, leading the book to retrieve six data sets per database, two for each search term.

Selection Criteria for the Data Sample

Apart from keywords, inclusion and exclusion criteria are needed to ensure the literature sample's quality before accessing the literature databases (Duff, 1996) and to minimise the risk of biases in selecting relevant literature. As a substantial rise of publications in this young research field can be observed, the scope of the review process is set on a six-year period, beginning with 01 January 2015, ending with 25 July 2021. Table 4.1 provides an overview of the inclusion criteria adopted in the review.

Since English was established as the common language for research in the field, the entire sample consists of English publications, to allow the analysis of global proceedings in AI governance. Table 4.2 presents the exclusion criteria applied.

[1] Boolean search string: sophisticated search strings for data retrieval in electronic databases (Kitchenham & Charters, 2007).

Table 4.2 Exclusion criteria for initial data sample

Exclusion criteria: Academic Literature	EC01: Articles not written in English EC02: Articles not belonging to the included categories EC03: Articles purely focusing on the technical advancement of AI without including, e.g., social or economic perspectives

Execution of the Review's Search Process

The execution of the search began on 20 July 2021 and was concluded on 25 July 2021. The search process included the two databases presented above and the use of Google Scholar as a search engine, which resulted in an initial sample of 899 publications. All documents were retrieved in PDF.

4.1.2.2 Filtering of Sample for Relevant Publications

The filtering process is crucial for narrowing down the sample of retrieved literature (Jesson et al., 2011; Tranfield et al., 2003). Due to the size of the sample and its heterogeneity, I narrowed down the findings per database before merging the findings across databases. Figure 4.1 visualises the filtering process in detail and displays the resulting sample sizes for each step. All filtering steps and the correlating sample lists are documented in an aggregated worksheet (cf., Appendix D).

As presented in Fig. 4.1, I screened the subsamples for duplicates per database in the first filtering step. This step reduced the initial sample of 899 publications to 790. The initial sample, as well as the list of 790 remaining publications, are added to the appendix (cf., Appendix D).

In the second phase, the relevancy of the remaining sample was scanned per database in title and abstract. After this filtering step, a total of 481 publications remained. At this stage, I excluded publications incompatible with its research scope, if their focus, for example, merely included AI supporting governance, public governance, IT governance, or medical AI governance topics, or if only the abstract existed in English, whereas the publication itself was written in another language (cf., Appendix D). If obtainable, the publications considered relevant after this screening were saved as PDF for lasting documentation.

In the third filtering phase, I combined the reduced number of publications retrieved across databases according to each keyword, as, in preparation for the thematic analysis, further examination per keyword was required. Thereafter, I filtered the keyword-merged publications for duplicates, leading to a reduced interim sample of 378 relevant publications.

In the fourth phase of the filtering process, I examined the full text of the remaining 378 publications to derive the final sample for the in-depth thematic analysis. While the review did not exclusively refer to peer-reviewed articles or articles published

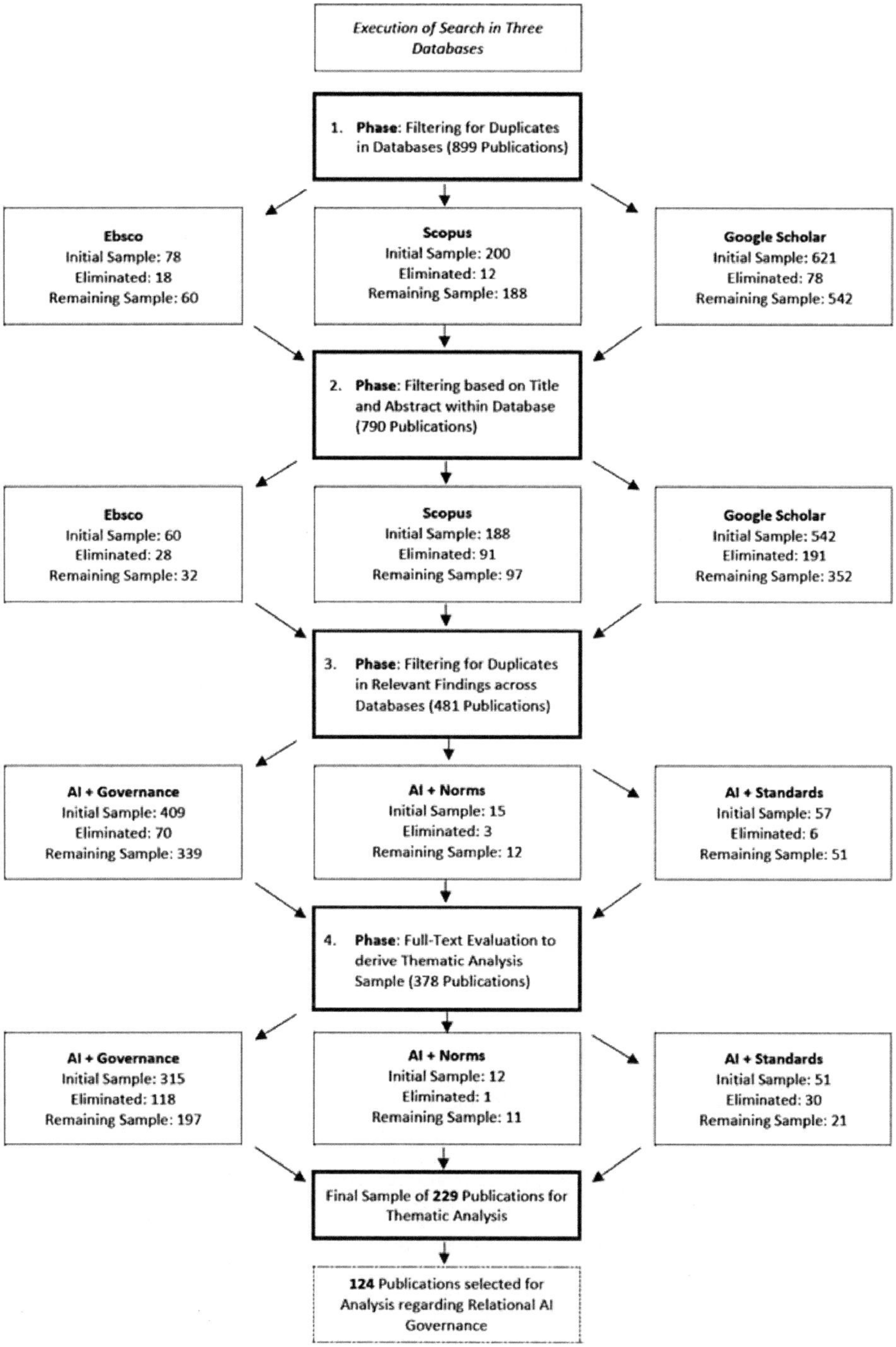

Fig. 4.1 Own depiction of sample filtering process

in an academic journal, a certain academic standard had to be ensured. Thus, only articles that complied with common academic requirements, such as correct referencing of sources and a neutral tone, were further analysed. After having evaluated the full text of these publications, a final sample of 229 publications remained. Here, the documentation includes both lists, listing the sample before and after the full-text evaluation (cf., Appendix D, Appendix A.1).

The fifth and last filtering step focuses on selecting publications of relevance for the Relational AI Governance. In this phase, I screened for publications either confirming or complementing it, leaving a remaining sample of 124 publications (cf., Appendix B.1), which were then analysed thematically, e.g., regarding their focus on 'SII', the role of 'SFI' for AI governance, the implications for the individual, 'I', or interrelations between the governance parameters. Thereafter, the findings were integrated into the Relational AI Governance.

4.2 Results and Interpretation

The review sample was analysed both descriptively and thematically: the descriptive analysis provides an aggregated depiction of the review results, whereas the thematic analysis summarises and interprets the review results according to their content. Both parts of the analysis were conducted separately. The thematic analysis and data synthesis aim to understand which measures work in the specific AI context. Hence, an explanatory and interpretative approach to analysis seems a promising avenue for this endeavour (Denyer et al., 2008; Rousseau et al., 2008). With this, the research design can give implications for and inform political and corporate knowledgeability and decision-making (Cook et al., 1997; Denyer & Tranfield, 2009; Tranfield et al., 2003). Also, it will foster the interconnection of research, economy, and policymaking (Nutley & Davies, 2002) relevant for the dynamic process of AI governance requiring constant dialogue and adaptation.

4.2.1 Descriptive Data Analysis

Since the descriptive analysis aims to present an aggregated depiction of the sample's characteristics, it presents a quantifiable overview, sorting the publications, for example, according to the database, the keyword they address, or their publication date.

4.2.1.1 Descriptive Analysis of Initial Review Sample

As presented in Fig. 4.2, seven percent of the publications were retrieved from the database Ebsco, 24% from Scopus, and 69% stemmed from the keyword search in Google Scholar. In detail, 60 publications were identified using Ebsco, 188 publications using Scopus, and 542 via Google Scholar.

Further analysis allowed an insight into the distribution of publications according to the keyword they addressed. Thus, Fig. 4.3 again depicts the initial sample, sorted according to search terms:

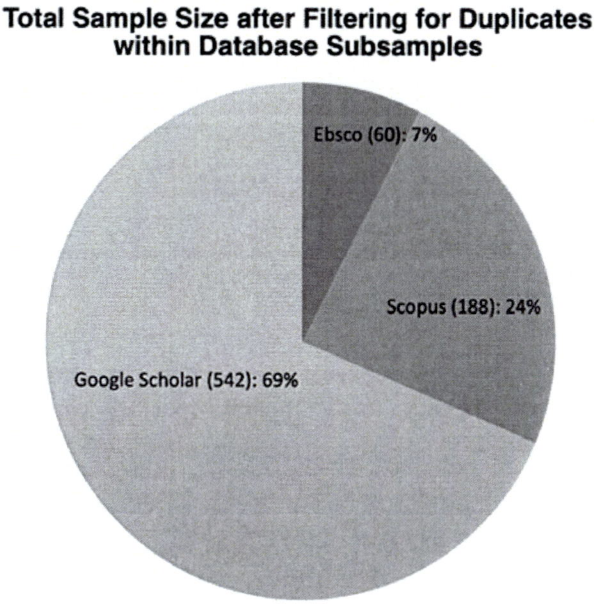

Fig. 4.2 Own depiction of initial sample sorted by database of retrieval

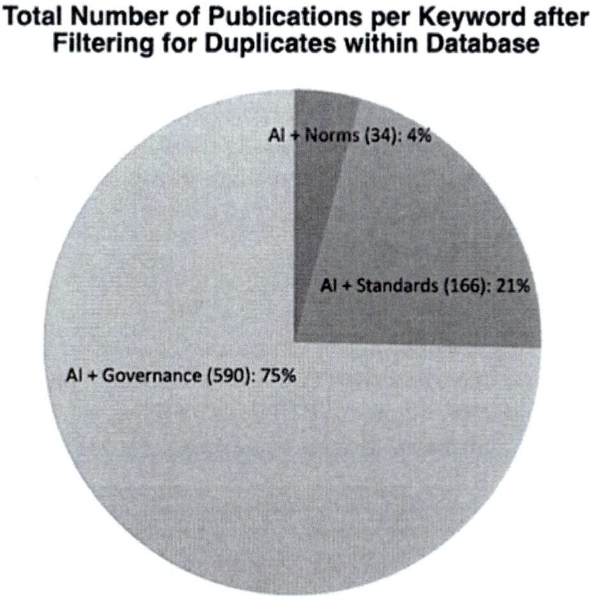

Fig. 4.3 Own depiction of initial sample sorted by keywords

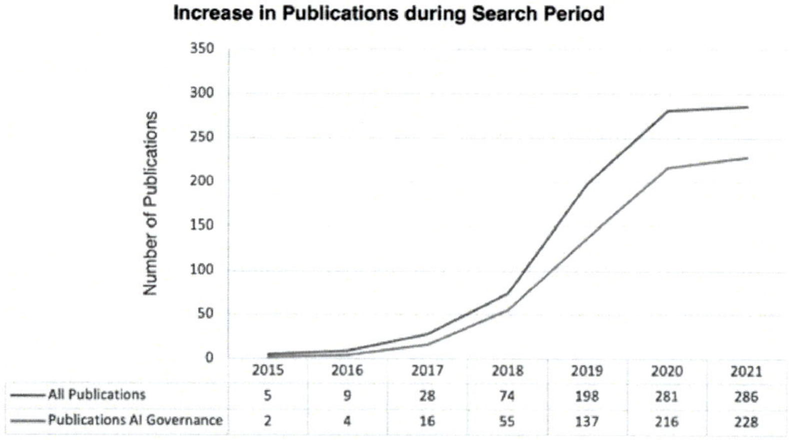

Fig. 4.4 Own depiction of increase in publications over search period

Figure 4.3 shows a significant trend for publications focusing on the specific search term 'AI Governance', with 590 publications identified for the keywords 'AI governance' and 'Artificial Intelligence Governance'. The second-largest number of publications, 166, was retrieved for 'AI standards', resulting from searches including both the terms 'AI Standards' and 'Artificial Intelligence Standards'. Finally, 34 publications from an overall total of 790 publications focus on 'AI Norms'.

As mentioned previously, over recent years, the number of publications for the search term AI governance increased significantly. Since the retrieved publications stem from a wide range of fields, the book can confirm this trend across disciplines, e.g., informatics, AI-aided medical sciences, AI ethics, and management studies. Especially between 2018 and 2021, the number of publications rose noticeably compared to the previous years. Hence, Fig. 4.4 sorts 790 publications by their publication date.

While, in 2015 and 2016, the number of publications was quite low, from 2017 onwards a strong increase can be observed. Particularly between the years 2019 and 2020, the incremental trend of publications addressing all three search terms rose by 40%. The publications retrieved for the first seven months of 2021 confirmed this rising trend.

I completed the findings with an estimated number of publications for 2021, by assuming both the overall number of publications in total and the specific number of publications focusing on AI governance. The estimation is based on a continuation of the average publication numbers published in the first seven months of 2021. Based on this information, the trends hold for the sample of all publications retrieved and, in particular, for the publications focusing 'AI governance'.

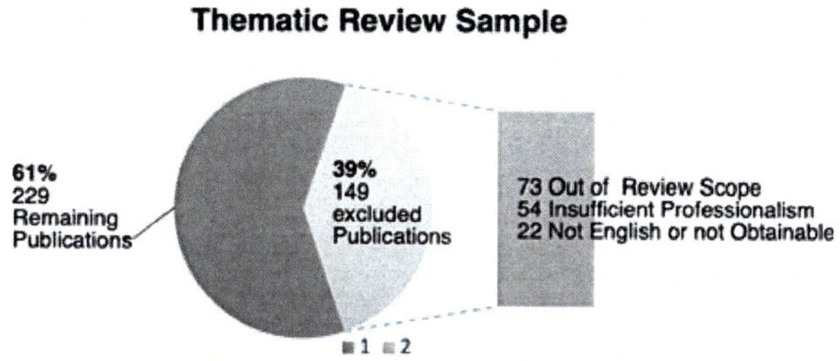

Fig. 4.5 Own depiction of thematic review sample

4.2.1.2 Descriptive Analysis of Thematic Review Sample

The sample of publications was significantly reduced during the full-text filtering phase. This is because I reduced the interim sample of 378 to 149 publications based on the presented exclusion criteria, leaving 229 publications for the thematic analysis.

Figure 4.5 gives an overview of the excluded publications, with 22 publications not being obtainable or not written in English while including an English abstract. 54 publications did not meet the level of professionalism expected in a scientific book, and 73 publications resulted in either having a predominantly public-sector focus, or, for example, addressing the specific national AI governance strategy of a particular country. Since they are not relevant to this book's scope, they were excluded from the sample.

However, the sample shows an increase in peer-reviewed publications over the last three years, hinting at the beginning of formalisation of the research discipline and the entrance of AI governance research into formal academia (cf., Appendix A.1).

4.2.1.3 Descriptive Analysis of Relational AI Governance Review Sample

Finally, I selected publications for the thematic review sample that allowed for the enhancement of Relational AI Governance. This includes publications addressing its governance parameters, e.g., the role of board members in the AI context, or that present new insights into, for example, the global context of AI governance. Further, this sample includes publications focusing on additional measures the AI context requires, which are not explicitly mentioned in the original Relational Governance Model by Wieland (2018, 2020), e.g., inclusivity and agility (cf., Appendix B.1, Appendix B.7), and the selected publications serve as base for the subsequent thematic analysis.

4.2.2 Thematic Data Analysis

The thematic analysis applies both deductive and inductive categories to structure the data retrieved from the review process systematically. 229 publications remained for the thematic analysis of the research field, with 124 publications serving to complement the Relational AI Governance model. At this stage, the theoretical perspectives taken are analysed in depth before contextualising them regarding the scope of this book.

4.2.2.1 Formal Specifications of the Thematic Review

As established, the remaining publications either address the private sector directly or allow for transferable insights. Thus, publications only addressing the public sector, or, for example, the medical field were excluded from this analysis as it is restricted to the scope of this book. All publications of generalisable nature, allowing for knowledge transfer across disciplines, were integrated into the thematic analysis since they are understood to influence developments in the private sector. The publications are referenced only if their content was cited directly or indirectly in the following section.

4.2.2.2 Structure of This Section

The first part of the thematic analysis structures the research about and regarding 'AI Governance Implications for the Private Sector' by sorting the publications according to their research focus. For each research focus, I developed a corresponding category. The categories used can either be deductive in nature or developed inductively. For the deductive sorting, I applied established categories, such as those previously developed to depict research streams in AI ethics. Finally, an overview of all research foci and a synthesis are presented, as well as implications for the research field.

The second part of the thematic analysis aims to revise this book's conceptually developed Relational AI governance. To do so, publications with a complementary research focus or position are selected to enhance the existing model. This subsample includes, for example, publications presenting a theoretical AI governance model, practical tools, or specific insights into or required characteristics of specific governance parameters. Further, contextual insights regarding the importance of the context and societal mechanisms influencing the governance model are highlighted, since the nature of Relational AI governance is inherently embedded in social structures. Thus, mechanisms such as public trust and the inclusion of social normativity are crucial to its success. This section also closes with theoretical implications for the research field and a contextualisation of findings regarding Relational AI governance.

First Level of Thematic Analysis: Structuring the Research Field

The remaining 229 publications were analysed for the thematic analysis according to the categories presented in the previous chapter and their specific research focus. All 229 publications were assigned to at least one category. If addressing an intersection of topics, both research foci were depicted by allocating the publication to two categories.

To this end, I applied the established categories, e.g., AI ethics and its subcategories, and examined the publications to highlight congruences. Further, I inductively developed additional categories—based on a given topic's frequency of occurrence. In total, sixteen categories were identified inductively and sorted according to the number of publications they included. The two publications not depicted in the map addressed, first, the need to avoid publication bias in AI research (Gupta et al., 2020) and second, a basic definition of AI Governance (Lewis, 2018).

4.2.2.3 Visualisation of Review Findings

For the depiction of the review findings, I apply a grouping and clustering approach (Popay et al., 2006). This approach makes the sample more manageable and allows for the highlighting of similar patterns and research foci in and across cluster categories. Thus, Fig. 4.6 presents the self-developed mapping approach summarising all research interests in the field. In this way, I ensure that all publications are part of at least one category and present an aggregated overview of all categories developed.

As for the structure of Fig. 4.6 I adopted a common and fundamental research theme, which summarises one of its core questions in the field—namely, whether to address AI in a centralised or polycentric manner (Cihon, 2019; Cihon et al., 2020a, 2020b; Kemp et al., 2019). A centralised approach is commonly understood as either nationally centralised regulatory strategies guiding AI development and deployment, or a form of transnational governance executed by a central governing institution. I counterbalance the centralistic pole with polycentricity, the opposite approach, defined as a fragmented, individualistic form of AI governance, e.g., in the form of industry- and country-specific standards for AI development and deployment.

Due to the recentness of the establishment of this research field, many publications have not been peer-reviewed or do not present practical instruments, without, however, linking them to a theoretical school of thought. Hence, the second axis of Fig. 4.6 allocates publications according to their level of abstraction—ranging from theoretical to practical. This structuring approach was required due to the heterogeneous nature of the publications and to depict the existing fragmentation of research interests in the field. Having chosen this broad and inclusive structuring form, the overview allows for the allocation of a wide range of research streams and facilitates the positioning of the book's contribution in the field. Moreover, other scholars can apply the overview of research advances made in the field to allocate their own research.

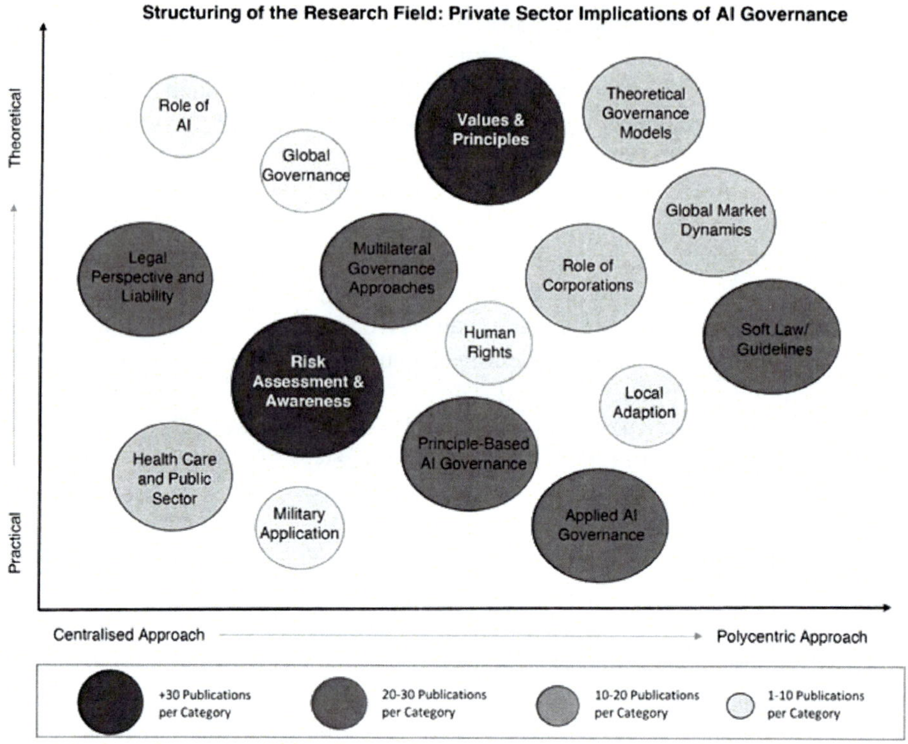

Fig. 4.6 Own depiction of thematically mapped review findings

4.2.2.4 Categorised Research Advances in Private-Sector AI Governance

Hence, the overview presented in Fig. 4.6 includes 16 inductively developed categories. As depicted in the key, the size of the illustrated categories correlates with the number of publications they include. The content analysis of the publications resulted in two categories with more than 30 publications, five categories with 20 to 30 publications per category, four categories including 10 to 20 publications each, and five categories with 1 to 10 publications allocated to them. All categories were sorted according to the level of abstraction the publications represent. Moreover, the category's position in the figure indicates whether the assigned publications serve a further centralisation of AI governance or if they contribute to the polycentric governance of AI.

Categories Consisting of More Than 30 Publications

– *AI Ethics and Principles*

This category, consisting of 36 publications, includes various research interests:

First, I allocated publications further formalising AI ethics and principles to this category. As established, such an aggregated depiction of existing principles contributes to the consolidation of the field (cf., Appendix A.2). Thus, it included publications presenting overviews and contextualising AI ethics in, for example, industries (cf., Béranger, 2021; Dupont et al., 2020; Winfield, 2019), or regarding existing regulation (cf., Ngai, 2020). Second, publications adding to established research on principled AI ethics were also allocated to this category. This encompasses publications on country-specific values (cf., Besaw & Filitz, 2019) or professional norms (Gasser & Schmitt, 2020). Third, the category entails theoretical assessments of the challenges AI ethics faces, the lack of existing reinforcement mechanisms (cf., Bostrom, 2017; Wong, 2020; Zhang et al., 2021), and structural solutions for ethical challenges associated with AI research and adoption (cf., Dencik, 2021).

– *Risk Awareness and Assessment*

33 publications focus on the risks coming with AI development or deployment. For one, this category includes research discussing the overall existence and detection (cf., Cremer & Whittlestone, 2021), of risk types ascribed to AI Governance, such as short- and long-term risks. Thus, these publications contribute to a higher awareness of associated risks accompanying AI adoption. Moreover, this category includes research examining either theoretical or practical approaches to mitigate those risks (cf., Appendix A.3). These mitigation approaches can address, for example, specific risk cases outside the general scope of governance (cf., Maas, 2018a, 2018b), risks coming with autonomous AI systems and weapons (cf., Garcia, 2019), or specific industries, such as finance (cf., Torrie & Payette, 2020).

Categories Consisting of 20–30 Publications

– *Principle-Based AI Governance*

As established in the previous chapter, most of the AI governance approaches that exist so far in practice are based on principled AI ethics. The analysis confirms this trend, since 27 publications, across sectors, applied a principle-based AI governance approach, whereas neither consequentialist ethics measures nor virtue-based measures were explicitly represented (cf., Appendix A.4). This category includes findings from various sectors to present a holistic view of the dominance of this approach in the field. Further, it includes overviews on the operationalisation of ethics in general (cf., Newman, 2020) and specific forms of application (cf., Agbese, 2021; Alqudah & Muradkhanli, 2021).

– *Soft Law and Guidelines*

25 publications are allocated to this category, given that they contribute either to standards or the development and further formalisation of guidelines in AI governance (cf., Appendix A.5). Further, the scope of the publications ranges from national (cf.,

Kazim & Koshiyama, 2020) to international (cf., Gutierrez & Marchant, 2021), and from theoretical contributions (Cihon et al., 2020a, 2020b) to practical instruments (cf., Juntura, 2021; Larsson, 2021).

- *Multilateral AI Governance*

25 publications highlight the importance of a governance approach combining measures from both the public and private sector (cf., Appendix A.6). On the one hand, scholars stress the importance of soft law and hard law to grasp the phenomenon of AI governance successfully and address the correlating risks holistically (cf., Gasser et al., 2018). On the other hand, research demands international cooperation to enhance the effectiveness of the still fragmented and uncoordinated governance endeavour (cf., Cihon et al., 2020a, 2020b; Thelisson, 2019).

- *Applied AI Governance*

23 publications examined frameworks, models, or measures to realise AI governance on an organisational level. In this category, publications stem from all disciplines identified in the review process (cf., Appendix A.7). They were included if their findings allowed for trans-sectoral and transdisciplinary adoption—ranging from the corporate sphere (cf., Lobana, 2021) to the financial industry (cf., Kurshan et al., 2020), and the health sector (cf., Reddy et al., 2020).

- *Legal Perspective and Liability*

21 publications focus on the legal implications of AI development and adoption in organisations. Within this category, the contributions encompass both theoretical and practice-oriented research (cf., Appendix A.8) in the legal sphere. Scholars present legal options to address the impact of AI development (cf., von Ungern-Sternberg, 2021) and evaluate the European regulatory proposal (Dempsey et al., 2021). Further, it includes the specific legal aspect of liability, which, in the case of AI, seems challenging—due, for example, to an undetermined agency of actors (cf., Jackson, 2018).

Categories Consisting of 10–20 Publications

- *Global Market Dynamics*

16 publications in the sample address the dynamics in the global market. This includes the research topic of market dynamics, such as arms races (cf., Dafoe, 2018), and the examination of the role specific countries have in these dynamics. In particular, scholars address China's (cf., Xia, 2020) or the E.U.'s role (cf., Berge, 2021) in the market (cf., Appendix A.9). Finally, it includes publications questioning whether AI governance needs to be centralised or if a polycentric approach is better suited for the endeavour (cf., Cihon et al., 2020a).

- *Theoretical Governance Models*

14 publications presented theoretical models for AI governance, which either provide a theoretical underpinning for the evolution of the field (cf., Fernandes et al., 2020),

or critically examine alternatives (cf., Liu & Maas, 2021) to existing approaches (cf., Appendix A.10). These models are examined in detail in their subsequent comparison to the Relational AI governance approach.

– *Health and Public Sector*

This category includes 11 publications addressing the public or health sector in this in-depth analysis. This is because these publications were found to present insights that are transferable and applicable across sectors. The contributions in this category comprise frameworks, applied models (cf., Appendix A.11), and more theoretical suggestions, for example, for an anticipatory governance approach (cf., Cremer & Whittlestone, 2021; Kolliarakis & Hermann, 2020).

– *Role of Corporations*

11 publications critically assess the role of corporations and the private sector in the governance of AI (cf., Appendix A.12). Research positions in this category range from criticism on the dominant position of corporations in AI governance (cf., Dignam, 2020) to confirming effective enhancements in AI governance through corporations' self-regulation (cf., Roski et al., 2021). Moreover, scholars highlight the importance of successful risk mitigation through the involvement of the private sector (cf., Scheltema, 2019).

Categories Consisting of 1–10 Publications

– *Human Rights*

8 publications assessed human rights in the context of AI (cf., Appendix A.13). These publications either examined the applicability of human rights law to AI governance (cf., Yeung et al., 2019) or focused on protecting them through disruptive times caused by AI adoption. Scholars from various disciplines focus on this topic, leading to a broad range of disciplines being included in this category, such as legal studies (cf., Lane, 2021) and computing (cf., Scheltema, 2019).

– *Global Governance*

The need for and demand to establish a single centralised governance approach, aligning AI governance measures globally, was examined by 8 publications (cf., Appendix A.14). The nature of the publications ranges from policy briefs (cf., Jelinek et al., 2021) to frameworks (cf., Ala-Pietilä & Smuha, 2021) and suggestions for structural solutions, such as the establishment of an international committee (cf., Jelinek et al., 2020).

– *Role of AI*

7 publications examined AI's current and future role in society (cf., Appendix A.15). The topics in this category encompass, for example, the demand for a new rationality (cf., Mhlambi, 2020) or the representation of AI as a C-suite member in an organisation (cf., Tokmakov, 2020).

– *Military Application*

7 publications specifically addressed the risks and governance measures required for the application of AI systems to autonomous weapons (cf., Appendix A.16). The scope of this category is mainly on risk mitigation in an international context—including the implementation of norms, standards, and governance structures (cf., Dafoe, 2018; Falconer, 2020; Maas, 2018a, 2018b). With this, scholars hope to control potential power shifts and scenarios of cyber-warfare.

– *Local Interpretation*

The smallest category, consisting of 5 publications, highlights the importance of culturally contextualising AI ethics principles (cf., Appendix A.17). On the one hand, these publications present cases of culturally specific interpretations of AI ethics principles. Despite using the same terms, the local interpretation of principles differs (cf., Ho, 2020a, 2020b; Wong, 2020). On the other hand, research shows that applying principles requires awareness for the country- and culture-specific values, relevant to both the development of AI systems and the implementation of AI governance (cf., ÓhÉigeartaigh et al., 2020).

Positioning of Relational AI Governance in Existing Research

The Relational AI Governance model conceptualised in the book can be allocated to three different categories depicted in this overview. Figure 4.7 presents the interconnection of Relational AI Governance with the categories presented above and possible allocations of the theoretical model.

First, the Relational AI governance model addresses the phenomenon from a theoretical, socio-economic perspective. As established, the perspective chosen in this book stems from both transaction cost economics and systems theory. Thus, it conceptualises its governance approach based on theoretical considerations and can, consequently, be allocated to the category 'Theoretical Governance Models' (cf., Appendix A.10).

Second, Relational AI Governance is based on four fundamental governance parameters; namely, societal formal and informal institutions, the organisation, and the role of the individual ('SFI', 'SII', 'O', and 'I') (Wieland, 2018, 2020). By integrating social normativity in the form of 'SII' into its governance structure, the Relational AI Governance model inherently draws from ethical principles developed for the responsible adoption of AI. Hence, especially on the operationalised, application-oriented level, the model can be assigned to the category 'Principle-Based AI Governance' (cf., Appendix A.4).

Third, the operationalisation of Relational AI Governance includes various elements inherent to traditional corporate governance, such as introducing new processes, formats, and departments as part of strategic decision-making. Given the apparent focus on measures for strategy adoption on an organisational level,

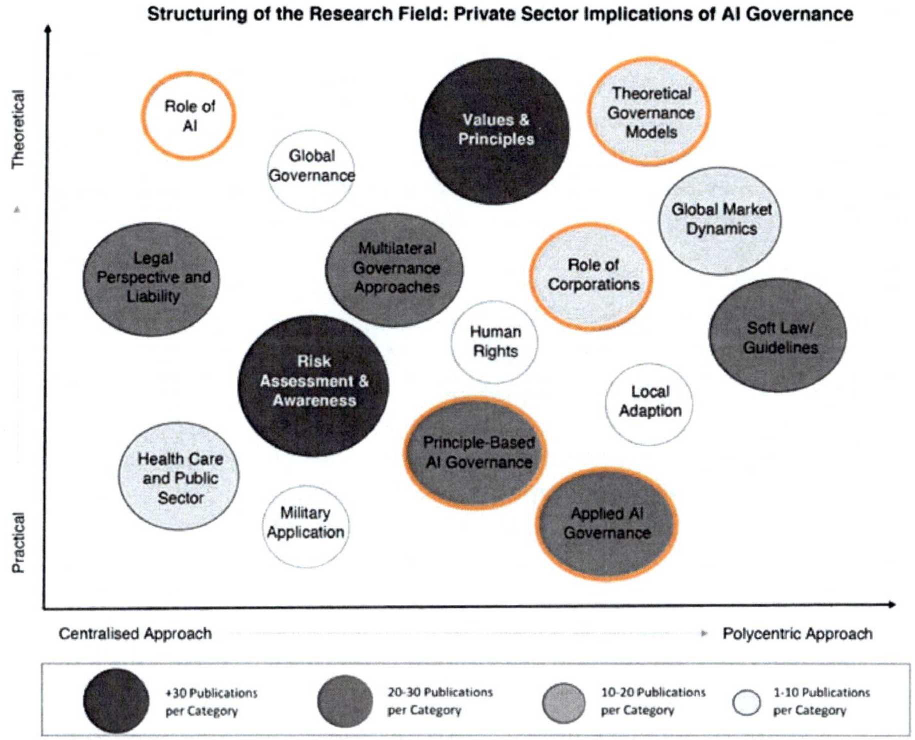

Fig. 4.7 Own positioning of Relational AI Governance in research field

this book's contribution can—in operational form—also be allocated to the category 'Applied AI Governance' (cf., Appendix A.7).

Fourth, the theoretical background of this book allows it to indirectly contribute to two other categories: however, it should not be allocated directly to these categories, since these aspects are not at the centre of this publication. With its conceptualisation of AI as an autopoietic system in society, this book adds to research in the category 'The Role of AI', addressing its effect on societal systems. Moreover, Wieland's Relational Economics (2018, 2020) inherently addresses the role of corporations in societies—an aspect this book contextualises for AI. Thus, it also contributes to the category 'The Role of Corporations', which focuses on the influence of corporations in AI governance and their AI-specific influence on society.

4.2.2.5 Second Level of Thematic Analysis: Revisiting the Relational AI Governance

The second part of the thematic analysis focuses on such publications providing specific conceptional contributions to the centrepiece of this book, the Relational AI Governance model. Thus, it only examines the direct influence of publications on Wieland's (2018, 2020) Relational Governance Model. Indirect findings, such as the confirmation of principle-based AI governance measures being overrepresented in practice, are not subject to this second analysis. Instead, it focuses on factors confirming, negating, or complementing the conceptual approach of this book or the specific elements of the Relational AI Governance model. Thus, publications are examined as to whether they can contribute to the effectiveness and applicability of Relational AI Governance.

In total, 124[2] publications were selected for the second thematic analysis (cf., Appendix B.1). These publications were chosen from the interim sample of 378 relevant findings, independently of the selections made for the first thematic analysis. This is because the objective of the first thematic analysis was to give an aggregated overview of the research field, whereas the second thematic analysis aims to present a theoretically guided, in-depth analysis of a smaller publication sample. Thus, while this section draws from the categories presented in the previous section, it presents additional, more detailed insights into the research sample.

Description of Categories for Relational AI Governance Sample

In total, I clustered the publications according to seven categories. The categories were developed inductively, based on a qualitative content analysis and a subsequent clustering according to a topic's frequency of occurrence. For this examination, all publications were allocated to one category only.

- Conceptual Approaches to AI Governance

Beginning at the most abstract level of analysis, I examined 17 publications belonging to the category 'Conceptual Approaches' (cf., Appendix B.2) in detail. These publications address AI governance by presenting a conceptual, theoretical approach to AI governance, as does this book. Overall, this category can be divided into four subcategories, each focusing on AI governance from a different angle.

In the first subcategory, two publications address AI governance from a meta-level; Fernandes et al. (2020) from an economic perspective, and Pagallo et al. (2019) from a legal perspective.

Fernandes et al. (2020) raise the concern that AI systems are only adopted by a given party if the decision results in an advantageous outcome. However, its adoption might lead to disadvantages for the non-adopting counterpart. Thus, the non-adopters might demand regulation to protect their interests. On an abstract level, the researchers focus on balancing out individual and societal gains stemming from AI adoption by applying an agent-based game-theoretical model. The authors conclude that, by implementing humanly conscious AI systems, there is a balancing point where the gains for one party would not result in costs for the other.

---

[2] Since the book presents the entirety of 124 publications and the content of each publication, the citations for the whole sample are documented in the appendix. Only publications whose content is integrated into the Relational AI Governance model are added to the reference list.

Pagallo et al. (2019) present a conceptual model to address AI governance called the middle-out approach. This approach is located between traditional top-down and bottom-up approaches in governance. Pagallo et al. (2019) define regulatory measures and legal governance as top-down, and, voluntary self-regulation, for example, as bottom-up approaches. The middle-out approach can be realised in the form of co-regulation, coordination mechanisms for good governance, or monitored self-regulation. Thus, it addresses an organisation's balancing of various regulatory systems, the alignment of various legal standards and laws, and the coordination of bottom-up and top-down measures. Having done so, the authors direct scholarly attention towards new forms of governance to address the complexity of current legislation, specifically regarding legal AI governance.

The second subcategory includes nine publications specifically developing approaches addressing organisations and the private sector.

On the one hand, two publications by the Tencent Research Institute (2021) and Scheltema (2019) analyse the environment and dynamics within which companies are adopting AI. The study presented by the Tencent Research Institute (2021) includes an in-depth examination of the challenges AI governance faces from a conceptual, meta-level perspective. This includes the generally slow nature of ex-post regulation, the existence of significant information asymmetries, and of hidden agendas actors in the field pursue. Doing so, the publication presents a comprehensive overview allowing companies to navigate the complex topic of AI governance. Scheltema (2019) agrees that AI, while having the potential to enhance society's prosperity, comes with significant risks and discusses the possible form and realisation of private-sector-led standards in practice.

On the other hand, the following publications examine potential measures companies could adopt in their endeavour to take on responsibility in AI adoption.

O'Keefe et al. (2020) suggest that companies should implement a windfall clause, binding them to donate a given percentage of their earnings if they were to reap exponentially high profits from the development of an AI system. Thus, the authors suggest a model making companies share their profit with society to make up for potential risks. Reed and Ng (2019) present a technological option to protect personal data, protecting the privacy and interests of the individual the data belongs to. By building so-called data trusts, organisations adopting AI could implement a mechanism which would require the data owner's consent if seeking to analyse and use it. Thereby, the fundamental rights of the individual are protected through a technological solution. In 2017, Gasser and Almeida presented their multi-layered model for AI governance, which Gasser et al. (2018) further specified. Gasser and Almeida criticise the existing information asymmetries between developers, society, and the public sector, aiming to bridge this gap by presenting their comprehensive yet intuitive governance framework. The framework divided AI governance into various layers, including a social and legal layer, an ethical layer, and a technological layer (Gasser & Almeida, 2017). The social layer contains regulations, norms, and legislation, the ethical layer represents principles and criteria, and the technological layer addresses topics such as accountability and data governance. Apart from providing organisations with a framework for ethical AI adoption, the authors suggest measures to diminish the existing information asymmetries, such as capacity building and recruiting external expertise (Gasser et al., 2018).

Pagallo et al. (2019) offer, as well as the middle-out approach presented above, an operational framework. However, Pagallo et al. (2019) focus on linking the systems of law and ethics. This includes a bottom-up and top-down approach, as well as the middle-out approach mentioned previously. According to the authors, each approach fulfils a particular purpose, complementary to the other two:

- the top-down approach builds on taking direct AI governance measures;
- the bottom-up approach focuses on actions that engage the stakeholders;
- the middle-out approach represents mechanisms of coordination.

Hence, this second publication of the authors provides an operational guide to applying lawful and ethical AI governance measures in organisations, as well as an elaborate academic background to the model.

Brundage (2019) aims to contribute to advancing AI governance by examining its classification as general-purpose technology to practices of responsible research and innovation. In doing so, the author presents general suggestions for the field, such as the need for coordination and publication norms. Further, to develop anticipatory and flexible AI governance, the author suggests the consultation of experts, scenario planning, and modelling methods.

Four publications aim to strengthen the role and impact of civil society in AI governance approaches. Ulnicane et al. (2021) ask for transparent governance in AI, including the three main stakeholders of the public and private sector, as well as civil society. Further, they suggest the integration of academia. Regarding the responsibilities coming with such a multilateral approach to governance, the authors assign the tasks of risk mitigation, stakeholder management, and the facilitation of public participation to the public sector. Almeida et al. (2020) offer a framework designed to provide civil society with an instrument to evaluate whether and to what degree an AI technology should be regulated. Thereby, the authors aim to support collective decision-making in society and raise trust in policymaking. Aliman and Kester (2019), as well as Luo and Lu (2021), bring civil society to the forefront of actively shaping AI technologies. Aliman and Kester (2019) suggest a consequential framework within which users are responsible for quantifying their ethical conception of AI. This is because implementing quantifiable feedback-loops into the AI development and application process will allow for the dynamic improvement of ethical AI. Luo and Lu (2021) critically assess the interlinkage of AI governance and social governance, intending to address the increasingly diverse demands and risks in society more efficiently. To do so, they present measures to better social governance.

Finally, two publications connect AI governance to the term 'wicked problems'.

Gurumurthy and Chami (2019) characterise AI governance as a wicked endeavour. However, the authors do not present a definition of the concept or a theoretical model to confirm their hypothesis. Instead, they focus on the long-term societal risks coming with AI governance, pointing out how the governance of AI is a significant challenge for societies, especially in a globalised world where new developments transcend national borders and authorities. To address these challenges, the authors call for human-centricity and an alignment of global efforts aiming to protect the (human) rights of individuals around the globe and create one overarching vision. While Liu and Maas (2021) also use the term 'wicked problem' in the context of AI governance, the authors combine the concepts differently: according to Liu and Maas, the emergence of numerous wicked problems is driven by AI adoption and development. However, current AI governance approaches focus on traditional problem-solving, instead of allowing for a broad initial problem-finding approach. This is deemed necessary by the authors, since AI comes with formerly unknown wicked problems requiring an open examination to allow for the subsequent derivation of effective AI governance strategies—solving for 'X', as the authors describe the traditional deductive approach, will not accomplish this task. Despite the causal chain of AI and wicked problems in this publication, the findings are still relatable to this book since both contributions attempt to solve the governance challenge of AI.

– *Market Dynamics and Global Governance*

This category encompasses 26 publications (cf., Appendix B.3), all focusing on the global, meta-level implications stemming from AI development and adoption.

In detail, the sample depicts two research foci—the dynamics and players in the global AI market and the debate about implementing a centralised form of global governance. Regarding the first research focus, scholars particularly examine the role of specific players in the market. The data indicates that especially the role of the E.U. (Berge, 2021; Dempsey et al., 2021; Kozuka, 2019; Kuziemski & Misuraca, 2020; Stix, 2021; Vanberghen & Vanberghen, 2021), the U.S. (Mitchell, 2018), and of China (Cantero Gamito, 2021; Weiguang, 2017; Xia, 2020) are at the centre of scholarly attention. Further, Boesl and Bode (2016) analyse the need for AI governance in this context, whereas Tan and Ding (2019) examine whether AI could be governed through markets. Complementarily, Wagner (2018) focuses on how AI is changing the global economy. Araya and Nieto-Gómez (2020) highlight the potential geopolitical and democratic threats coming with AI adoption, whereas Shackelford et al. (2021) present the other side of the coin, analysing whether AI could have a leading contributor's role in building global peace. This brief depiction goes to show the broad debate and discordance in determining AI's impact on societies around the globe, making global AI governance a complex and challenging endeavour.

The second research stream in this category contains publications discussing adequate or effective forms of governing AI on a global scale: in 2020, Cihon et al. (2020a, 2020b) openly discussed whether AI should be governed in a centralised or polycentric manner. The scholars concluded that a lock-in situation created by implementing an ill-suited global institution should be prevented. However, if soft law advances should continue being developed in such a fragmented manner around the globe, their impact would be significantly lowered—resulting in them also becoming unsuitable to fulfil the demand.

Like Cihon et al. (2020a, 2020b), the research community seems to be divided: on the one hand, in 2019, Cihon still focused on soft law measures, as do Gutierrez and Marchant (2021), allocating them to a rather polycentric perspective. On the other hand, numerous scholars suggest variations of a relatively centralised form of global AI governance. Wallach and Marchant (2018), Jelinek et al. (2020) suggest a global coordinating committee, aligning global advances in AI governance, without, however, having the power of ultimate decision. Ala-Pietilä and Smuha (2021) continue this line of thought by presenting a global cooperation framework, which will ensure humanity is benefitting from AI adoption. Gill and Germann (2021) present a variation of this approach, presenting a human rights-based framework for global stakeholder regulation. Wang et al. (2018) even go as far as demanding the establishment of a global regulatory body. This suggestion is partially supported by Kemp et al. (2019), when laying out the alternative of a high-level UN panel that could provide globally aligned governance while allowing for regional interpretation.

Independently of whether advances in AI governance will proceed on a national or global level, in either centralised or polycentric form, Maas' (2018a) findings regarding global arms races should be considered: While society often assumes arms races to be unstoppable, Maas' research, based on historical evidence, shows that they can indeed be impeded or fended off by applying informed measures.

– *Collaborative and Multilateral AI Governance*

16 publications (cf., Appendix B.4) examine collaborative forms of AI governance and the role of multilateral, public-private governance structures. Given the relative homogeneity of the demand raised by academia, the data indicates a relative trend towards collaborative approaches.

The publications in this category point to the risks involved in AI governance and, consequently, focus on suitable governance forms to address these challenges. The category includes two research foci: publications asking for public- and private-sector cooperation and others focusing on multi-stakeholder forms of cooperation. I begin by presenting ten publications that suggest the collaboration between the public and private sector in AI governance, also called hybrid governance, and multilateral governance.

Miailhe (2018) highlights the complex dynamics that characterise AI governance, demonstrating why multilateral governance approaches are deemed necessary to level out the fragmented field of global ethical safety-related standards and soft law advances. He calls for intergovernmental collaboration and multi-stakeholder dialogues to align and advance the currently fragmented and relatively loose governance structures. Thelisson (2019) aligns himself with this view. Identifying AI governance as a wicked problem, the author states that, to solve this challenge, the cooperation of public and private stakeholders is needed. Al Zadjali (2020) and Taeihagh (2020) confirm the demand for hybrid AI governance, in the form of public- and private-sector cooperation. Beduschi (2020) agrees with their view but adds that AI ethics is not a sufficient base for governance. Instead, he recommends the combination of human rights law and AI ethics, realised through hybrid public-private governance. Csernatoni and Lavallée (2020) examine current AI governance for the field of drones, concluding that the effective governance of technological advances requires a multilateral governance approach—involving both public- and private-sector engagement. Miailhe and Lannquist (2018) agree with the demand raised.

The authors present an overview of the risks of AI adoption, also concluding that its governance requires collaboration among stakeholders and multilateral cooperation.

The following approaches present additional aspects, relevant to the success of cooperative AI governance forms: Abdala et al. (2020) present a policy brief, arguing that cooperation and AI governance should be established with the aim of functioning across borders. Specifically, the authors highlight the role of the G20[3] in this scenario. By developing and enforcing AI governance through such a transnational, multi-stakeholder structure, the authors expect the development of global standards societies have trust in. Crăciunescu (2020) points to another advantage coming with collaboratively developed governance measures: According to the author, a multi-stakeholder approach would allow for the transfer and expansion of knowledge in societies, eventually leading to the advancement of technology and progress. This is in line with Bostrom's (2017) view that collaboration, be it in the development or governance of AI, yields significant potential for the secure development of AI, e.g., in the form of open innovation. However, Sharkey (2017) adds for consideration the tone and language used in the development of AI governance measures on the side of AI safety commissaries. This is because the risk-focused communication in the field, in the author's view, hinders open dialogue and the objective determination of AI governance measures. Thus, to ensure the success of such governance processes, Sharkey asks for adaptation of the language used and the development of a shared understanding among all stakeholders involved.

Additionally, four publications shed light on the role of specific actors in this endeavour: Juntura (2021) focuses on the role of intergovernmental organisations as entities for coordination and collaboration in global AI Governance, while Cihon et al. (2020a) seek to understand whether centralised AI governance is required to counterbalance the power of private tech companies. However, they conclude that, due to the pace of technology development, for example, and high information asymmetries between the public and private sector, a centralised form of governance could be beneficial only if well-designed, while possible negative effects seem to predominate. Thus, they suggest monitoring current multi-stakeholder advances closely. Carpanelli (2020) examines private-sector self-regulation and the corporation's role as a standard-setter, concluding that collective self-regulation requires collaboration, at least among companies, to be impactful and yield its potential. Finally, Chelvachandran et al. (2020) and Ulnicane et al. (2021) demand the combination of multiple approaches, leading to inclusive and participatory governance strategies, including the public and private sector, but, more importantly, civil society.

– *Legal Perspective on AI Governance*

The analysis allocated 17 publications to this category (cf., Appendix B.5). On the one hand, Spiro (2020) describes AI governance on the meta-level as particularly challenging due to the pace, complexity, and ever-changing nature of the technologies, before proceeding to present suggestions for the U.S. market. Renda (2019), on

[3] The 'Group of Twenty' is an intergovernmental platform and forum made up of the 20 countries which constitute the 20 largest economies in the world (Cooper & Thakur, 2013).

the other hand, focuses on the role of the E.U. in advancing the legal frame for AI governance—presenting the state before the announcement of the E.U.'s regulatory proposal. This advance answers Dignam's (2020) demand: highlighting the problematic nature of governance approaches in AI being driven by the private sector, the scholar calls for more substantial public-sector involvement.

Eight publications examine the relation between hard law and soft law from different angles. First, Chatila et al. (2017) focus on advancing soft law to cover for the current lack of regulation and to ensure human well-being. Marchant and Lucille (2019) share this view, highlighting soft law's crucial role in managing AI. However, the authors do recognise the importance of combining both soft and hard law. Weng and Izumo (2019) further examine the existing gap between hard and soft law to allow both fields to advance effectively. Moreover, researchers understand soft law, in the form of standards and guidelines, to be the necessary foundation for subsequently following hard law measures (Kwan & Spohrer, 2021; Langlois & Régis, 2021; Schiff et al., 2020). Nevertheless, Hill (2020) points to an additional challenge regulation faces: the necessity to coordinate various stakeholders in regulation, but also stakeholders affected by regulation. Walz and Firth-Butterfield (2018) claim that alternative regulatory measures, such as technical standardisation, may even be more effective in ensuring responsible AI adoption, since they address the technological root that many ethical concerns and actual AI-related risks stem from.

On an organisational level, Baig et al. (2020) call for the combination of governance frameworks and regulatory measures—pointing out the importance of their claim with the example of the needs of the health sector. Zekos (2021) even presents a comprehensive handbook including all thus far existing managerial and legal aspects an organisation needs to address when adopting AI.

Out of 17 publications, four address questions of liability in the AI context. As early as 2016, Nurus et al. stressed the importance of addressing liability, examining the topic for the case of autonomous driving. Jackson (2018) attributes troubles in defining legal liability to the undetermined agency in AI adoption—an issue Jackson finds particularly challenging to solve for general-purpose technology, such as AI. Both Mazzini (2019) and Béranger (2021) endorse the significance of liability in the AI context, with Béranger indicating that liability in AI includes both designers and owners.

– *Risks and Social Normativity*

This category includes 13 publications (cf., Appendix B.6), addressing the interplay between AI-related risks and potential socially desirable measures to delimit them.

Buenfil et al. (2019) demonstrate the challenges of applying principle-based AI governance measures to the AI development process without obstructing and setting back advances in AI development. Additionally, scholars critically examine the effect of organisation-driven AI adoption in general (Dignam, 2019), regarding rising inequality in society (Karpenko et al., 2020), and in the context of low trust levels in tech companies (Zhang et al., 2021). Further risks are presented for managerial decision-making in the public sector (Filgueiras, 2021), privacy issues (Dilmaghani et al., 2019), again stemming from the insufficient interplay of hard and soft law in the medical field (Guan, 2019).

Addressing the risks involved in AI adoption involves various measures: Kerr et al. (2020) provide a guide for linking governance structures and principles in practice, whereas Ngai (2020) suggests the constant adaptation of principles due to the constantly changing nature of the technologies. Gasser and Schmitt (2020) suggest the integration and translation of professional norms into governance measures.

Overall, Kolliarakis and Hermann (2020) demand the combination of principles, regulation, and the additional support of innovation for successful AI governance—with academia and civil society acting as counterparts to ensure the inclusion of social normativity. Subirana (2020) follows this line of thought, stating that AI has the potential to protect society. However, it can only do so if society proactively defines desirable scenarios of AI adoption and clearly defines the role AI should take on. Corrêa (2020) points out that the role of AI ethics in this endeavour must not be mistaken—the role of ethics should remain to criticise the status quo and highlight better options, rather than serving as a soft law substitute due to a lack of regulation.

- *Local Interpretation, Diversity, and Inclusion*

Out of the 15 publications in this category (cf., Appendix B.7), 10 address the local adoption and interpretation of AI principles.

Overall, this category confirms the need for local adaptation of AI ethics principles and measures. Further, it highlights the need to allow for participation and inclusion, to ensure that there is no regional bias in developing principles, guidelines, measures, or standards. This holds true for cultural backgrounds, as well as across professions and different societal sectors. Generally, the lack of universal definitions complicates this process even further (Biswas, 2020).

Ten publications focus on AI governance from a cross-cultural perspective, while some of the publications compare the cultural differences in the adoption of principles and regarding the particular AI governance strategy a country implements (Bode, 2020; Daly et al., 2019; Ho, 2020a, 2020b; Laskai & Webster, 2019; Roski et al., 2021; Wong, 2020). Others directly refer to the need for local adaptation of values.

It is, in particular, the latter that is relevant to this section: Wong (2020) highlights the importance of an AI governance approach remaining responsive to cultural values, since specific normative standards might differ from region to region; a claim which Liu and Lin (2020) support. ÓhÉigeartaigh et al. (2020) specifically state that the "*full benefits of AI cannot be realized across global societies without a deep level of cooperation — across domains, disciplines, nations, and cultures*" (2020, p. 589). According to the authors, cultural misunderstandings might lead to further differences between nations and regions, particularly in a highly competitive environment.

Following the line of thought that integrating diverse backgrounds is essential for responsible AI adoption, the topic of inclusion is inherently connected to its success. Within this sample, three publications focus on this specific topic from different perspectives: Corrêa (n.d.) argues that the global ethical debate in AI governance is significantly biased by the dominance of the E.U. and the U.S. and their interests. To ensure the development of a just, ethical AI governance approach that addresses the interests of all globally affected stakeholders, the scholar demands a more inclusive debate. De Gasperis (2020) focuses on the inclusion of trans-sectoral insights and sector- as well as stakeholder-specific needs. Larsson (2021) confirms this view by highlighting the importance of developing a multidisciplinary AI governance understanding. Continuing this line of argument, Todolí-Signes (2019) and Macrae (2021) demand that this insight should be put into action by implementing participatory measures in the development process of AI governance.

– *Applied AI Governance*

In total, 20 publications (cf., Appendix B.8) present insights into applied forms of AI governance and corporate AI governance.

Benbouzid (2021) begins to state that organisations theoretically have three main options when engaging in AI governance: self-regulation based on principles and guidelines; applying soft regulation; or following hard law. However, due to the currently fragmented nature of AI governance, the author suggests knowledge mapping to operationalise and deduce measures for AI governance on the organisational level. As for the operationalisation of principles and guidelines, Smuha (2020) warns that these guidelines show Western biases, since it was mostly Western countries that dominated their development and establishment. Thus, according to Smuha, a human rights-based approach seems a more promising path for operational AI governance.

Within the firm, Thuraisingham (2020) points to the importance of reassessing roles and responsibilities, particularly on the board level, to ensure the successful and sustainable realisation of AI governance in companies. Torré et al. (2019) address the same niche, stating that research on corporate boards' reactions to AI governance and recommendations on how to do so is limited. Thus, they suggest two competencies that boards need to hold, namely the capabilities to guide AI operationally and to supervise it. Cihon et al. (2021) confirm the need to put an in-depth focus on company-internal stakeholders to improve the way companies govern their adoption of AI.

Mannes (2020) accentuates the significance of risk assessment in organisational AI governance, not least to present comprehensive communication of risk to society and, thereby, ensure ongoing public trust for the company. Ozlati and Yampolskiy (2017) confirm this demand, presenting risk assessment approaches for practice. Cremer and Whittlestone (2021) even present an innovative approach to risk management, having developed a model for warning signs, allowing for anticipatory governance within organisations. By applying such a proactive, ex-ante governance measure, organisations can avoid the potential realisation of irreversible AI-related damage.

As well as reporting specific advances achieved, 11 publications present general AI governance instruments and approaches on an operational level: Generally, Mika et al. (2019) suggest the development of a shared understanding, as well as the combination of hard and soft law measures. Tubella et al. (2019) demand the explicit operationalisation of the rather broad AI ethics principles to ensure the trust of the organisation's stakeholders. Further, they highlight the need for a common understanding in the market regarding the application and meaning of these principles.

Wallach and Marchant (2018) even offer a comparison of organisational governance models and measures. However, Winfield and Jirotka (2018) developed the most comprehensive AI governance model on the operational level, including various layers and extensive elaboration of potential measures.

Papagiannidis et al. (2021) examine dimensions of AI governance within the firm and present resulting measures to realise it. Gulenko et al. (2020) add a technical perspective to AI governance, portraying AI governance at the intersection with IT governance, whereas Schneider et al. (2020) focus on data and IT governance in the AI context. Kurshan et al. (2020) further specify the relation between AI governance and technical aspects by stressing the importance of technical robustness and complementary compliance measures, such as monitoring and mitigation capabilities within the firm. Wu et al. (2020) confirm the need for technical robustness and showcase Chinese approaches to ensure this aspect of AI governance. As presented above, risk assessment is just as necessary on the operational level: Huck et al. (2020) stress its importance in AI governance to derive individualised and valid governance measures.

Finally, two publications originally addressing the public sector present transferable frameworks for organisational-level AI governance (Personal Data Protection Commission Singapore, 2019; Wirtz et al., 2020), which shows that on the operational level the requirements for AI governance measures are similar across sectors.

Overview of Findings Relevant for the Relational AI Governance Approach

Stemming from the in-depth analysis of publications presented above, I derived three types of insights gained from the systematic literature review: insights either confirming, complementing, or criticising the argumentation and approach presented in the form of the Relational AI Governance. For one, this serves to delimit this book from existing concepts in the field. Second, it gives insight into potentially required adaptations, contributing to both the quality of this book and Wieland's original theory. However, it is not within its scope to structurally adapt Wieland's original model. In consequence, the review findings merely highlight optional adjustments to Wieland's Relational Governance approach and its applied Relational AI Governance.

Moreover, due to the recentness of the research field's emergence and the insecurities regarding future developments in AI, the recommendation of this book is that advances in the research fields of both AI governance and AI research should be closely observed. This is because the complexity of the phenomenon does not allow for categorical claims as to whether certain elements do or do not need to be covered by a theoretical approach. Hence, all observations made stem from qualitative content analysis, rather than being imperative for change. Table 4.3 summarises the findings gained from analysing this sample that either confirm or complement the current scope of Relational AI Governance, or present critical arguments contrasting with its chosen perspective.

Table 4.3 Own depiction of review findings relevant for Relational AI Governance[4]

Overview of Review Findings for Relational AI Governance Approach					
	Conceptual Level	SFI	SII	O	I
Confirming	Complexity (Miailhe, 2018; Spiro, 2020; Zhang et al., 2020) Defined as wicked problem (Gurumurthy & Chami, 2019; Liu & Maas, 2021; Thelisson, 2019) Arms race shape global dynamics (Maas, 2018) AI as General-Purpose Technology (Brundage, 2019) Importance of including civil society (Aliman & Kester, 2019; Ulnicane et al., 202)	Combination of soft and hard law on meta-level (Marchant & Lucille, 2019) and organisational level (Mika et al., 2019) Collective self-regulation and polycentric governance currently dominant form of AI governance (Cihon et al., 2019; Schiff et al., 2020b)	Developing a shared understanding (ÓhÉigeartaigh et al., 2020) Calling for cross-cultural examination and Local Adaptivity (Liu & Lin, 2020; Wong, 2020) Supporting transcultural management (De Gasperis, 2019; Larsson, 2021)	Significance of risk assessment (Huck et al., 2020; Mannes, 2020; Ozlati & Yampolskiy, 2017) Combination of different governance elements (Winfield & Jirotka, 2018)	General confirmation of individual's integration into governance structure (Gasser & Schmitt, 2020; Macrae, 2021; Todolí-Signes, 2019)
Complementing	Integration of tech-layer (Gasser & Almeida, 2017) Balancing individual and societal gains (Fernandes et al., 2020) Reactive, feed-back-based AI governance (Aliman & Kester, 2019)	Liability (Béranger, 2019; Jackson, 2018) Middle-Out approach (Pagallo et al., 2019a) Anticipatory governance (Brundage, 2019; Cremer & Whittlestone, 2021)	Inclusion (Correa, n.d.; De Gasperis, 2020; Larsson, 2021) Diversity (Liu & Lin, 2020; ÓhÉigeartaigh et al., 2020; Wong, 2020) Participation (Macrae, 2021; Todolí-Signes, 2019)	Tech dimension (Reed & Ng, 2019; Wu et al., 2020) Compliance warning signs (Cremer & Whittlestone, 2021) C-Level responsibilities (Thuraisingham, 2019)	Address particular stakeholder groups: internal stakeholders (Cihon et al., 2021) Role of board (Torré et al., 2019) Integration of professional norms (Gasser & Schmitt, 2020)
Criticism or Negating	Unsuitability of private sector to lead AI governance (Dignam, 2019), Engagement in Standards (Scheltema, 2019)	Need for collaborative and multilateral governance (cf., AI Zadjali, 2020; Csernatoni & Lavallée, 2020; Taeihagh, 2020)	Inclusion of more countries to avoid biased principles (Smuha, 2020) Soft law is not AI ethics' purpose (Corrêa, 2020)	Including a tech-layer in operational governance (Gasser & Almeida, 2017) Open search for wicked problems (Liu & Maas, 2021)	Participation in development of AI ethics principles and governance structure (Macrae, 2021; Todolí-Signes, 2019)

[4] The publications cited in the overview are directly relevant to this book, and thus, cited in its reference list.

4.2.2.6 Evaluation of Findings on Conceptual Level

The assessment of publications confirms and supports the underlying argument this book presented as its base for conceptualising AI Governance. The central hypotheses were confirmed, with scholars linking AI to particularly high levels of complexity and wicked problem structures. Further, the data supports AI's characterisation as a general-purpose technology, and the fact that companies find themselves in global arms race dynamics. Additionally, Wieland's (2018, 2020) definition of the firm as a nexus of stakeholders proved itself in the light of publications demanding a more substantial involvement of civil society in AI governance.

Nevertheless, the review revealed aspects of AI governance which neither Wieland's Relational Economics nor this book had considered. One such issue is that Relational Governance aims to create shared value to collaboratively solve the wicked problem nature of AI governance. However, it does not explicitly aim to find the perfect equilibrium between individual and societal gains. This aspect could be integrated to advance the approach further in the future. Additionally, Relational AI Governance does not yet include a technological parameter or layer. To fully address and operationalise AI governance, this aspect seems of great importance and should also be integrated into the model. Doing this would allow for the development of technological solutions for governance challenges and help address risks stemming from technological characteristics of AI, e.g., through iterative feedback loops. Yet, the integration of this layer or governance parameter would require structural changes in Wieland's Relational Governance.

Little criticism of the chosen approach was identified on a conceptual level. However, the general suitability of companies to engage in AI governance was questioned, and scholars demand that companies' engagement in developing standards should create governance instruments of lasting, trans-sectoral effect. This demand is in line with this book's initial remarks on the importance of collaboration in solving wicked problems. Thus, based on the fundamental findings of AI governance for the single corporation, companies should additionally engage in interfirm networks to collectively raise industry standards—as suggested in this book. Thereby, they can further promote the responsible adoption of AI governance outside their companies' boundaries and, at the same time, also contribute to solving the wicked problem structure of AI governance, as does this book.

4.2.2.7 Evaluation of Findings for Governance Parameter 'SFI'

Regarding societal formal institutions, most publications suggest a combined AI governance approach—including soft and hard law measures on both the organisational and meta-level. Additionally, the data confirms that the E.U.'s proposal for AI regulation is, indeed, the first global advance in this regard. Thus, the hypothesis of an unregulated AI market primarily being regulated in a polycentric manner holds true.

Again, the review uncovered three relevant aspects that Relational AI governance does not yet cover within the parameter 'SFI': to further specify its governance measures, the approach could adopt the structure of top-down, bottom-up, and middle-out measures. Besides, it should be required to address the aspect of liability in the AI context, due to the technology's significant action- and outcome-orientation. This characteristic and the associated potential risk pattern could additionally be covered by applying anticipatory governance measures, preventing harm from happening. Again, governance mechanisms are a structural element in Relational Economics (Wieland, 2018, 2020). Therefore, adaptations would need to be made to Wieland's original theory.

Due to the substantial trend in data pointing to the importance of collaborative and multilateral governance forms in AI, this book's lack of focus on the public sector could be considered a point of criticism. Nevertheless, I recognise the importance of addressing AI governance in a multilateral form.

4.2.2.8 Evaluation of Findings for Governance Parameter 'SII'

As for societal information institutions, the publications support the presented need to develop a shared understanding among all stakeholders involved in the governance process and allow for local adaptations of predefined AI ethics principles. By asking for trans-sector-applicable principles, measures, and strategies, the data indirectly confirms the additional need for transcultural management measures.

Following this line of thought, many publications identify the relevance of including stakeholders from all parts of society, diversity, and explicit enablement of participation as success factors for responsible AI governance. I consider these three aspects as complementary to its conceptual contribution. Despite inherently supporting all three aspects, Relational AI Governance does not explicitly make them a priority in developing its strategies and measures. While it suggests controlling for biases and inclusion of stakeholders, it does not particularly integrate, for example, minorities or groups that are disadvantaged or potentially discriminated against. Thus, the development of inclusion- and participation-fostering measures should be considered.

Lastly, the analysis highlights two general points of criticism directed to the research field of AI governance, which could consequently also be considered a point of criticism for this book. First, scholars criticise the dominance of Western countries in the development of AI ethics principles, stating that the currently existing guidelines do not represent a global perspective. Second, the scholars refute AI ethics' instrumentalisation of developing soft law measures, since this leads to a failure of the discipline, since its overall objective should be cautiously observing and criticising the status quo, rather than actively contributing to it. Hence, scholars and organisations should consciously examine the ethical guidelines they apply and seek the revitalisation of the discipline as a critical observer of the status quo. As for Relational AI Governance, by applying its inherent multi-stakeholder perspective to the development process of the principles, it defies this criticism. With this, it can counteract the observed Western bias—at least within a company's boundaries and without requiring structural adaptations of the Relational AI Governance model.

4.2.2.9 Evaluation of Findings for Governance Parameter 'O'

As for the parameter 'O', the data confirmed both the significance of deploying an extensive risk assessment and the need to combine both formal and informal measures in the development of governance programs.

Interestingly, the complementary aspects identified for this governance parameter match the findings for the parameter 'SFI': Regarding possible risk aversion and governance of risks, the publications suggest the implementation of warning signs and the consideration of developing technological solutions as a part of risk avoidance. Further, an explicit assignment of responsibilities to individuals on board level can help ensure the governance program's positive impact and effect.

Thus, the missing tech layer in the Relational AI Governance approach can, indeed, be considered a point of criticism, since it excludes technological solutions from being part of the governance process. While AI remains the subject of the governance strategy, covering risks in the form of the adoption and process of AI through technological revision, can play an important role in adopting AI responsibly. This is because the constantly changing nature of the technologies makes deductive, predefined risk assessments insufficient. Hence, to bring the argument full circle, the risk assessment phase requires a leading role in the governance process of AI—a requirement which can be realised by applying Relational AI governance. However, the effect would be augmented significantly by integrating technological governance measures into Relational AI Governance, e.g., by focusing on measures stemming from the research stream 'ethics in design'.

4.2.2.10 Evaluation of Findings for Governance Parameter 'I'

For the last governance parameter, 'I', the data supports strengthening the role of the individual within the governance structure. The publications specifically examine and give recommendations regarding the involvement of particular stakeholders, e.g., the board of a given company. Further, the data suggests adopting and integrating target group-specific professional norms into the governance program to allow for synergies and raise the individual's personal motivation and levels of personal integrity.

A general criticism in the research field concerns the individual's lacking participation in developing the currently existing AI ethics guidelines, indicating missing identification with these principles as a result. This Relational AI Governance addresses this point of criticism by applying a bottom-up approach to identify AI ethics principles for its self-regulation measures and by realising transcultural management measures to create a shared understanding of predefined AI ethics principles and integrate local values. Thereby, it can raise the individual's level of identification with the AI ethics principles deployed in the organisation. Given that this book has already established the need for holistic AI ethics-based governance measures, these insights do not require structural changes in the model and must merely be added as a measure when operationalising an AI governance program.

4.2.2.11 Synthesis and Discussion of Review Findings for Relational AI Governance

Having analysed the review sample regarding the conceptualisation of Relational AI Governance, the data indicates that the approach presented by this book is among the most comprehensive and theoretically substantiated approaches in the field, while at the same time being operationalisable for adoption on the organisational level. This is because most publications do not present theoretical concepts as a foundation for their hypothesis but derive their findings from practical observations and immediate needs identified in practice. Thus, the review validated Relational AI Governance, both on a conceptual level and in operationalised form.

However, the analysis has uncovered potential gaps: primarily, the findings point to the need to include an additional variable into Wieland's original model of Relational Governance. To be precise, the integration of a technological layer or AI layer seems to be required, either in the form of an additional governance parameter or as a fixed element within the parameter 'O'. This is because the technology itself can contribute to closing governance gaps by providing technological solutions to ethical challenges, and governance measures should be integrated into the AI solution itself, e.g., via an ethics-in-design approach.

Since the inclusion of this element requires structural changes within the Relational Governance approach by Wieland (2018, 2020), it is not within the scope of this book. Nevertheless, I support the demand identified in this review sample, suggesting structurally allowing for a higher governance adaptivity in technological governance application cases, such as AI governance. Relational Economics could address this demand by integrating an additional, neutral variable into its governance structure. Thereby, publications basing their work on Wieland's theory could adapt the structure to their particular field of application; in this case, AI governance.

Moreover, I identified one other pressing aspect in the research sample, which has not yet been covered sufficiently in Relational AI Governance; the assumption of liability in the AI context. Given that AI is characterised by its partially autonomous action and strong outcome orientation, it seems imperative for responsible AI governance to determine questions of agency and liability for unforeseeable or undesirable consequences of AI adoption. Consequently, the Relational AI Governance approach should eventually be complemented by a focus on corporate assumption of liability, even though the review summarised publications stating that procedures and precedent cases regarding liability and agency in AI governance currently remain unsolved. Thus, for the case of liability assumption, I again suggest monitoring advances made in theory and practice before implementing measures, even though corporate assumption of liability is regarded as imperative when adopting AI.

On a voluntary basis, additional findings, as presented in Table 4.3, can be included in Relational AI Governance without requiring structural changes. This is because they mostly concern the operational level and are covered by the governance parameters and governance structure, which allow for individual adaptation by the organisation applying them.

4.2.3 Discussion and Conclusion of Review Findings

This section presents an interpretation and discussion of the review's main findings and the degree to which the review answers this book's research questions. I proceed to illustrate identified limitations and potential methodological weaknesses (Piper, 2013). The section closes with suggested directions for further research in the field.

4.2.3.1 Discussion of Research Gaps

Research regarding AI Governance and responsible AI is primarily driven by the high risk-perception associated with AI adoption. This observation was confirmed by theoretical and practice-oriented research and seems to hold true on the organisational, national, and global levels. In contrast to the prevalent problem-solving orientation, only a small number of publications choose a proactive approach so as to shape a desirable future with AI in it. The few publications that do present such a proactive approach include, for example, Fernandes et al. (2020), who discuss a game-theoretical model suitable for helping to help create an ex-ante balance between individual and societal gains from AI adoption. While Aliman and Kester (2019) present a reactive AI governance framework, they ask civil society to actively evaluate their perception of AI use cases to allow for iterative feedback loops and the constant improvement of the technologies. Thereby, they move from a merely reactive to a participative and iterative approach to AI governance.

Notwithstanding, most publications apply a deductive and, thus, reactive governance approach: the review confirmed the identified main research streams in AI ethics, as established in the previous chapter, when presenting a review of AI ethics research. As expected, deontological, principle-based AI governance approaches and measures were presented in most publications. Based on already existing, known risk patterns, they develop or apply deontological AI ethics measures. This pattern was identified across sectors and industries.

Despite the relevance of principled AI ethics, as Liu and Maas (2021) rightfully state, AI governance requires an open, future-oriented problem examination, since the risks and consequences associated with AI adoption change as quickly as the technologies themselves. Particularly on a global level, principles are open to local interpretation and do not ensure ethical behaviour. While most scholars focus on the operationalisation of standards or the critical examination of their role or expected success, there are some innovative advances:

Among others, Reed and Ng (2019) present a technological solution to one of the main risk patterns underlying AI adoption, i.e., data privacy. By suggesting the implementation of data trusts, the authors present an innovative and proactive approach to AI governance, complementing the adoption of guidelines, standards, and regulations. With this, they aim to prevent harm, instead of reacting to negative consequences of AI adoption ex-post.

While the formalisation of subtopics in the field advances, such as principled AI ethics and the evaluation of soft law, it is of great significance to professionalise research regarding the implementation of AI governance. In particular, research in the field lacks innovative and critical voices. As proclaimed by various scholars (cf., Kolliarakis & Hermann, 2020; Ulnicane et al., 2021), critically examining the status quo and providing society with innovative, proactive approaches should be precisely the role of academia. Hence, I strongly suggest putting a stronger focus on theoretical contributions explaining the need and the dynamics behind operational AI governance measures, as well as the examination of new approaches for risk and liability assessment (Liu & Maas, 2021).

4.2.3.2 Discussion of Findings

The review findings confirm the fragmentation of advances made in AI governance for theory and practice alike. Furthermore, only 14 out of the initial 790 publications—less than two per cent of the overall sample—examine AI governance from an abstract, theoretical perspective. Thus, while many publications offer insights into operational governance measures, they lack a plausible analysis of the dynamics driving the need for AI governance. Content-wise, the review demonstrated the current research foci on principled AI ethics and risk assessment. Hence, the findings support the initially established demand for both the systematic review literature conducted and the scope, argumentation, and objective of this book.

Thereby, the relevance of this book's addressing the conditions under which companies can successfully engage in self-regulatory measures was confirmed. The categories of *Soft Law* and *Multilateral AI Governance* particularly validate the necessity for collaboration to achieve the adoption of an effective governance approach. However, most publications do not present suggestions on the theoretical level regarding how to assess this challenge. Merely Fernandes et al. (2020) findings allow for game-theoretical implications for AI governance and can be connected to this book's research question from an economics perspective on a conceptual level. Still, given that the book conceptualises its governance approach mainly from a systems-theoretical and economics perspective, an economics-based examination of the patterns underlying the wicked problem this book addresses remains outside its scope.

Instead, the findings from the review contribute to the Relational AI Governance approach primarily on an operational level. While existing literature does not allow for extensive controversy on the theoretical level, it supports the critical reassessment and complementation of the hypotheses per governance parameter. Further, it highlights the importance of combining formal and informal governance measures on the international, national, and organisational levels—as does this book. Thus, the review findings confirm the urgency of the matter at hand and contribute somewhat to its self-developed Relational AI Governance model.

From a methodological view, there are limitations to this review since it only included two academic databases and combined them with Google Scholar. The inclusion of further databases might have allowed for the retrieval of additional theoretical publications—especially of additional peer-reviewed publications. For the work at hand, its conceptual argumentation and the complementary role of this review were at the centre of attention. Therefore, the inclusion of additional databases was outside its scope. Consequently, a minor form of publication bias cannot be avoided, as the review can only retrieve and depict publications published beforehand. Albeit it deliberately included non-peer-reviewed publications, research findings hindered from publication do not show. Hence, not even the broad review scope this book applied can counteract such a form of publication bias.

Moreover, the generalisability of findings might be limited due to the lack of intercoder reliability. While I transparently described each step of the review's retrieval and filtering process, the screening of publications to determine their inclusion or exclusion in the final sample was conducted only by me. Thus, despite following a transparently established set of exclusion criteria, the selection of publications might be regarded as subjectively biased by the author.

4.2.3.3 Conclusion

Overall, the systematic literature review presented in this book contributes to a clearer understanding of research advances in the field of AI governance—with a particular focus on the private sector. It rehashed the findings in an aggregated manner to allow for a meta-level perspective on the research field, enabling scholars to identify gaps more easily and position their contributions.

Based on the review findings presented, I identified existing thematic gaps and further research requirements. First, stemming from the review's limitations, the book suggests that a review with an even broader scope should be conducted—including all major academic databases and with a greater variety of keywords. Additionally, a review across sectors to identify all existing research across disciplines and directed to all target groups seems advisable. This is because I am convinced that an effective AI governance approach requires the integration of all stakeholders and sectors affected. Therefore, an extensive literature review should build on the presented preliminary findings and expand the scope of the review to advance the formalisation of the research field further. In doing so, it can highlight existing overlaps, synergies, and complementary measures.

The structuring of the field revealed significant directions for further research. As established, the theoretical analysis of the phenomenon of AI governance is still not at the centre of scholarly attention. To dissolve the primarily reactive focus of current research and practical AI governance, the book stresses the importance of developing further theoretical models for AI governance. By doing so, academia could contribute significantly to the advances of AI governance approaches on the international, national, and organisational levels.

As for the operationalisation of AI governance strategies in organisations, I continue to support the development of holistic approaches, including consequentialist and virtue-based measures, as established in the course of this chapter. Thus, I recommend research detailing potential measures according to their ethical perspective, as well as research presenting combinatory management programs on the organisational level, including instruments from all perspectives.

Moreover, research could contribute to establishing strategies for coordinating the roles of soft law and regulatory proposals in AI governance. Particularly in an international context, analysing the conditions for an effective interplay of these two elements is essential, as highlighted by Cihon (2019) and Cihon et al. (2020a, 2020b). Academia's ability to assess complex structures objectively, as did Fernandes et al. (2020), could lower the complexity of current discourse on the topic while at the same time ensuring the neutrality and objectivity of the recommendations presented. In this way, suggestions might be accepted across the globe—despite diverging views, interests, and political agendas.

Finally, I suggest the continuous monitoring of research advances in the form of systematic literature reviews for each research stream. This close monitoring could contribute to significant formalisation and the specialisation of research in the field, which I deem necessary since current research has not yet applied specific research terms or definitions. The review confirms this observation, given that most findings were retrieved for the term 'AI governance'. Only a few of those publications assigned their contributions to specialised categories, such as applied AI governance or principle-based AI governance, which would allow direct allocation of the contribution to a research stream.

References

Abdala, M. B., Ortega, A., & Pomares, J. (2020). *Managing the transition to a multi-stakeholder artificial intelligence governance.* http://www.realinstitutoelcano.org/wps/wcm/connect/349f7c90-d812-4d1b-92cc-aaf0e34389f5/T20_TF5_PB6.pdf?MOD=AJPERES&CACHEID=349f7c90-d812-4d1b-92cc-aaf0e34389f5

Agbese, M. (2021). *Implementing artificial intelligence ethics in trustworthy systems development: Extending ECCOLA to cover information governance principles.* http://urn.fi/URN:NBN:fi:jyu-202105283279

Ala-Pietilä, P., Smuha, N. A. (2021). A framework for global cooperation on artificial intelligence and its governance. In B. Braunschweig & M. Ghallab (Eds.), *Reflections on Artificial Intelligence for Humanity. Lecture Notes in Computer Science* (Vol. 12600, pp. 237–265). Springer. https://doi.org/10.1007/978-3-030-69128-8_15

Aliman, N. M., & Kester, L. (2019). Transformative AI governance and AI-empowered ethical enhancement through preemptive simulations. *Delphi—Interdisciplinary Review of Emerging Technologies, 2*(1), 23–29. https://doi.org/10.21552/delphi/2019/1/6

Almeida, V., Filgueiras, F., & Gaetani, F. (2020). Digital governance and the tragedy of the commons. *IEEE Internet Computing, 24*(4), 41–46. https://doi.org/10.1109/MIC.2020.2979639

Alqudah, M. A., & Muradkhanli, L. (2021). Artificial intelligence in electric government; ethical challenges and governance in Jordan. *Electronic Research Journal of Social Sciences and Humanities, 3*, 65–74. https://www.researchgate.net/publication/350558134_Artificial_Intelligence_in_Electric_Government_Ethical_Challenges_and_Governance_in_Jordan

Al Zadjali, H. (2020). Building the right AI governance model in Oman. In *Proceedings of the 13th International Conference on Theory and Practice of Electronic Governance* (pp. 116–119). https://doi.org/10.1145/3428502.342851

Araya, D., & Nieto-Gómez, R. (2020). Renewing multilateral governance in the age of AI. *Modern conflict and artificial intelligence, A CIGI essay series.* https://www.cigionline.org/articles/renewing-multilateral-governance-age-ai/

Asher, A. D., Duke, L. M., & Wilson, S. (2012). Paths of discovery: Comparing the search effectiveness of EBSCO Discovery Service, Summon, Google Scholar, and conventional library resources. *College & Research Libraries, 74*(5), 464–488. https://doi.org/10.5860/crl-374

Baig, M. A., Almuhaizea, M. A., Alshehri, J., Bazarbashi, M. S., & Al-Shagathrh, F. (2020). Urgent need for developing a framework for the governance of AI in healthcare. *Studies in Health Technology and Informatics, 272*, 253–256. https://doi.org/10.3233/SHTI200542

Baumeister, R. F., & Leary, M. R. (1997). Writing narrative literature reviews. *Review of General Psychology, 1*, 311–320. https://doi.org/10.1037%2F1089-2680.1.3.311

Beduschi, A. (2020). *Human rights and the governance of artificial intelligence.* The Geneva Academy. https://www.geneva-academy.ch/joomlatools-files/docman-files/Human%20Rights%20and%20the%20Governance%20of%20Artificial%20Intelligence.pdf

Bem, D. J. (1995). Writing a review article for Psychological Bulletin. *Psychological Bulletin, 118*(2), 172–177. https://psycnet.apa.org/doi/10.1037/0033-2909.118.2.172

Benbouzid, B. (2021). Tentative governance of artificial intelligence regulation. Representing governance as a virtual network of documents. *Eu-SPRI Annual Conference Oslo, Virtual, Session 8.* https://www.euspri2021.no/wp-content/uploads/2021/06/Session-8.3.pdf

Béranger, J. (2021). Ethical governance and responsibility in digital medicine: The case of artificial intelligence. *The Digital Revolution in Health, 2*, 169–190. https://doi.org/10.1002/9781119842446.ch8

Berge, M. V. (2021). *The EU as a Normative Power in the field of artificial intelligence?: Challenges and concepts in the governance and regulation of digital technologies using the example of the EU and its human-centred approach to AI* [Master's thesis]. University of Twente.

Besaw, C., & Filitz, J. (2019). *AI & Global Governance: AI in Africa is a double-edged sword.* United Nations University Centre for Policy Research. https://cpr.unu.edu/publications/articles/ai-in-africa-is-a-double-edged-sword.html

Biswas, D. (2020). *Ethical AI: Its implications for enterprise AI use-cases and governance.* Towards Data Science. https://towardsdatascience.com/ethical-ai-its-implications-for-enterprise-ai-use-cases-and-governance-81602078f5db

Bode, I. (2020, July). Weaponised artificial intelligence and use of force norms. *The Project Repository Journal, 6*, 140–143. https://findresearcher.sdu.dk:8443/ws/portalfiles/portal/173957438/Open_Access_Version.pdf

Boesl, D. B., & Bode, B. M. (2016). Technology governance. *2016 IEEE International Conference on Emerging Technologies and Innovative Business Practices for the Transformation of Societies (EmergiTech)*, 421–425. https://doi.org/10.1109/EmergiTech.2016.7737378

Bostrom, N. (2017). Interactions between the AI Control Problem and the Governance Problem. *Future of Life. Talk at the 2017 Asilomar Conference.* https://www.youtube.com/watch?v=_H-uxRq2w-c

Brundage, M. (2019). *Responsible governance of artificial intelligence: An assessment, theoretical framework, and exploration* [Doctoral dissertation]. Arizona State University.

Brundage, M., Avin, S., Clark, J., Toner, H., Eckersley, P., Garfinkel, B., Dafoe, A., Scharre, P., Zeitzoff, T., Filar, B., Anderson, H., Roff, H., Allen, G. C., Steinhardt, J., Flynn, C., Ó hÉigeartaigh,

S., Beard, S., Belfield, H., Farquhar, S., ... Amodei, D. (2018). The malicious use of artificial intelligence: Forecasting, prevention, and mitigation. *arXiv preprint* arXiv:1802.07228

Bryson, J. J. (2018). Patiency is not a virtue: The design of intelligent systems and systems of ethics. *Ethics and Information Technology, 20*(1), 15–26. https://doi.org/10.1007/s10676-018-9448-6

Buenfil, J., Arnold, R., Abruzzo, B., & Korpela, C. (2019). Artificial Intelligence ethics: Governance through social media. In *2019 IEEE International Symposium on Technologies for Homeland Security (HST)* (pp. 1–6). https://doi.org/10.1109/HST47167.2019.9032907

Cantero Gamito, M. (2021). *From private regulation to power politics: The rise of China in AI private governance through standardisation*. SSRN Digital. https://doi.org/10.2139/ssrn.3794761

Carpanelli, E. (2020). The role of corporations as standards setters: The case of business actors involved in the development and deployment of artificial intelligence tools. In M. Buscemi, N. Lazzerini, L. Magi, & D. Russo (Eds.), *Legal sources in business and human rights* (pp. 171–195). https://doi.org/10.1163/9789004401181_010

Chatila, R., Firth-Butterflied, K., Havens, J. C., & Karachalios, K. (2017). The IEEE global initiative for ethical considerations in artificial intelligence and autonomous systems [standards]. *IEEE Robotics & Automation Magazine, 24*(1), 110–110. https://doi.org/10.1109/MRA.2017.2670225

Chelvachandran, N., Trifuljesko, S., Drobotowicz, K., Kendzierskyj, S., Jahankhani, H., & Shah, Y. (2020). Considerations for the governance of ai and government legislative frameworks. In H. Jahankhani, S. Kendzierskyj, N. Chelvachandran, & J. Ibarra (Eds.), *Cyber defence in the age of AI, smart societies and augmented humanity* (pp. 57–69). Springer Publishing.

Cihon, P. (2019). *Technical report. Standards for AI Governance: International standards to enable global coordination in AI research & development*. University of Oxford. https://www.fhi.ox.ac.uk/wp-content/uploads/Standards_-FHI-Technical-Report.pdf

Cihon, P., Maas, M. M., & Kemp, L. (2020a). Should artificial intelligence governance be centralised? Design lessons from history. In *Proceedings of the AAAI/ACM Conference on AI, Ethics, and Society* (pp. 228–234). https://doi.org/10.1145/3375627.3375857

Cihon, P., Maas, M. M., & Kemp, L. (2020b). Fragmentation and the future: Investigating architectures for international AI governance. *Global Policy, 11*(5), 545–556. https://doi.org/10.1111/1758-5899.12890

Cihon, P., Schuett, J., & Baum, S. D. (2021). Corporate governance of artificial intelligence in the public interest. *Information, 12*(7), 275. https://doi.org/10.3390/info12070275

Coburn, K. M., & Vevea, J. L. (2015). Publication bias as a function of study characteristics. *Psychological Methods, 20*(3), 310–330. https://psycnet.apa.org/doi/10.1037/met0000046

Cook, D. J., Mulrow, C. D., & Haynes, R. B. (1997). Systematic reviews: Synthesis of best evidence for clinical decisions. *Annals of Internal Medicine, 126*(5), 376–380. https://doi.org/10.7326/0003-4819-126-5-199703010-00006

Cooper, A. F., & Thakur, R. (2013). *The group of twenty (G20)*. Routledge.

Cooper, H. M. (1988). Organizing knowledge syntheses: A taxonomy of literature reviews. *Knowledge in Society, 1*(1), 104–126. https://doi.org/10.1007/BF03177550

Conn, V. S., Valentine, J. C., Cooper, H. M., & Rantz, M. J. (2003). Grey literature in meta-analyses. *Nursing Research, 52*(4), 256–261. https://psycnet.apa.org/doi/10.1097/00006199-200307000-00008

Corrêa, N. K. (2020). *Blind spots in AI ethics and biases in AI governance*. https://philarchive.org/archive/CORASv3

Crăciunescu, C. (2020). The role of artificial intelligence in collaborative governance, trust building and community development analysis. *Collaborative Governance, Trust Building and Community Development*, 99. http://real.mtak.hu/112630/1/TICPA_Proceedings_2019.pdf#page=100

Cremer, Z., & Whittlestone, J. (2021). Artificial Canaries: Early warning signs for anticipatory and democratic governance of AI. *International Journal of Interactive Multimedia and Artificial Intelligence, 6*(5), 100–109. https://doi.org/10.9781/ijimai.2021.02.011

Crossan, M. M., & Apaydin, M. (2010). A multidimensional framework of organizational innovation: A systematic review of literature. *Journal of Management Studies, 47*(6), 1154–1191. https://doi.org/10.1111/j.1467-6486.2009.00880.x

Csernatoni, R., & Lavallée, C. (2020). Drones and artificial intelligence: The EU's smart governance in emerging technologies. In A. Clacara, R. Csernatoni, & C. Lavallé (Eds.), *Emerging security technologies and EU governance* (pp. 206–223). Routledge.

Cumming, G. (2014). The new statistics: Why and how. *Psychological Science, 25*(1), 7–29. https://doi.org/10.1177%2F0956797613504966

Dafoe, A. (2018). *AI governance: A research agenda.* Governance of AI Program, Future of Humanity Institute, University of Oxford. https://www.fhi.ox.ac.uk/wp-content/uploads/GovAI-Agenda.pdf

Daly, A., Hagendorff, T., Li, H., Mann, M., Marda, V., Wagner, B., Wang, W., & Witteborn, S. (2019). *Artificial intelligence, governance and ethics: Global perspectives.* The Chinese University of Hong Kong Faculty of Law [Research Paper]. https://dx.doi.org/10.2139/ssrn.3414805

De Gasperis, T. (2020). *Futures of responsible and inclusive AI: How might we foster an inclusive, responsible and foresight-informed AI governance approach?* [Graduate Studies]. http://openresearch.ocadu.ca/id/eprint/2998

Dempsey, M., McBride, K., & Bryson, J. J. (2021). *The current state of AI governance—An EU perspective.* https://doi.org/10.31235/osf.io/xu3jr

Dencik, L. (2021). Towards data justice unionism? A labour perspective on AI governance. In P. Verdegem (Ed.), *AI for everyone? Critical perspectives* (pp. 267–284). Westminster University Press.

Denyer, D., & Tranfield, D. (2009). Producing a systematic review. In D. A. Buchanan & A. Bryman (Eds.), *The Sage handbook of organizational research methods* (pp. 671–689). Sage Publications Ltd.

Denyer, D., Tranfield, D., & Van Aken, J. (2008). Developing design propositions through research synthesis. *Organization Studies, 29*, 393–413. https://doi.org/10.1177%2F0170840607088020

Dignam, A. J. (2019). *Artificial intelligence: The very human dangers of dysfunctional design and autocratic corporate governance* (Queen Mary School of Law Legal Studies Research Paper 314). https://www.law.ox.ac.uk/business-law-blog/blog/2019/06/dysfunctional-design-and-autocratic-corporate-governance-ai

Dignam, A. J. (2020). Artificial intelligence, tech corporate governance and the public interest regulatory response. *Cambridge Journal of Regions, Economy and Society, 13*(1), 37–54. https://doi.org/10.1093/cjres/rsaa002

Dilmaghani, S., Brust, M. R., Danoy, G., Cassagnes, N., Pecero, J., & Bouvry, P. (2019). Privacy and security of big data in AI systems: A research and standards perspective. In *2019 IEEE International Conference on Big Data (Big Data)* (pp. 5737–5743). IEEE. https://doi.org/10.1109/BigData47090.2019.9006283

Duff, A. (1996). The literature search: A library-based model for information skills instruction. *Library Review, 45*(4), 14–18. https://doi.org/10.1108/00242539610115263

Dupont, L., Fliche, O., & Yang, S. (2020). *Governance of artificial intelligence in finance.* Banque De France. https://acpr.banque-france.fr/sites/default/files/medias/documents/20200612_ai_governance_finance.pdf

Falconer, S. A. (2020). *Artificial intelligence and Article 36: Implementing minimum standards for reviewing artificially intelligent military systems* [Master Thesis]. http://hdl.handle.net/11343/243067

Fernandes, P. M., Santos, F. C., & Lopes, M. (2020). Norms for beneficial AI: A computational analysis of the societal value alignment problem. *AI Communications* (Preprint), 1–17. https://doi.org/10.3233/AIC-201502

Filgueiras, F. (2021). New Pythias of Public Administration: Ambiguity and choice in AI systems as challenges for governance. *AI & Society*, 1–14. https://doi.org/10.1007/s00146-021-01201-4

Garcia, E. V. (2019). *AI & global governance: When autonomous weapons meet diplomacy.* United Nations University, Centre for Policy Research. https://cpr.unu.edu/publications/articles/ai-global-governance-when-autonomous-weapons-meet-diplomacy.html

Gasser, U., & Almeida, V. A. (2017). A layered model for AI governance. *IEEE Internet Computing, 21*(6), 58–62. https://doi.org/10.1109/MIC.2017.4180835

Gasser, U., Budish, R., & Ashar, A. (2018). *Module on setting the stage for AI governance. Interfaces, infrastructures, and institutions for policymakers and regulators.* Artificial Intelligence (AI) for Development Series. https://www.itu.int/en/ITU-D/Conferences/GSR/Documents/GSR2018/documents/AISeries_GovernanceModule_GSR18.pdf

Gasser, U., & Schmitt, C. (2020). The role of professional norms in the governance of artificial intelligence. In *The Oxford handbook of ethics of AI* (p. 141). Oxford University Press.

Gill, A. S., & Germann, S. (2021). Conceptual and normative approaches to AI governance for a global digital ecosystem supportive of the UN Sustainable Development Goals (SDGs). *AI and Ethics*, 1–9. https://doi.org/10.1007/s43681-021-00058-z

Ginsberg, A., & Venkatraman, N. (1985). Contingency perspectives of organizational strategy: A critical review of the empirical research. *The Academy of Management Review VO, 10*(3), 421. https://doi.org/10.5465/amr.1985.4278950

Guan, J. (2019). Artificial intelligence in healthcare and medicine: Promises, ethical challenges and governance. *Chinese Medical Sciences Journal, 34*(2), 76–83. http://dx.doi.org/10.24920/003611

Gulenko, A., Acker, A., Kao, O., & Liu, F. (2020). AI-Governance and levels of automation for AIOps-supported system administration. In *2020 29th International Conference on Computer Communications and Networks (ICCCN)* (pp. 1–6). IEEE. https://doi.org/10.1109/ICCCN49398.2020.9209606

Gupta, A., Lanteigne, C., & Heath, V. (2020). Report prepared by the Montreal AI Ethics Institute (MAIEI) for Publication Norms for Responsible AI by Partnership on AI. *arXiv e-prints* arXiv-2009

Gurumurthy, A., & Chami, N. (2019). The wicked problem of AI governance. In *Friedrich-Ebert-Stiftung India, Artificial intelligence in India* (Vol. 2). Electronic Edition. http://library.fes.de/pdf-files/bueros/indien/15763.pdf

Gutierrez, C. I., & Marchant, G. E. (2021). *A global perspective of soft law programs for the governance of artificial intelligence.* SSRN Digital. https://doi.org/10.2139/ssrn.3855171

Hagendorff, T. (2020). The ethics of AI ethics: An evaluation of guidelines. *Minds and Machines, 30*, 99–120. https://doi.org/10.1007/s11023-020-09517-8

Hill, A. D. (2020). *Regulatory accountability for AI governance mechanisms: Coordinating multiple regulators.* SSRN Digital. https://doi.org/10.2139/ssrn.3735203

Ho, M. T. (2020a). *Understanding AI governance in Confucian contexts.* https://doi.org/10.31219/osf.io/wsjny

Ho, M. T. (2020b). *Three relevant bodies of the literature to understand the ethics, design, and governance of emotional AI in Confucian contexts.* https://doi.org/10.31219/osf.io/vxjeg

Huck, P., Johnson, A., Kiritz, N., Larsom, C. E. (2020). Why AI governance matters. *The RMA Journal.* https://www.promontory.com:3000/static/pdf/1588624225_title.pdf

Jackson, B. W. (2018). Artificial intelligence and the fog of innovation: A deep-dive on governance and the liability of autonomous systems. *Santa Clara High Technology Law Journal, 35*(4). https://digitalcommons.law.scu.edu/chtlj/vol35/iss4/1

Jelinek, T., Wallach, W., & Kerimi, D. (2020). *Coordinating committee for the governance of artificial intelligence.* G20 Insights, Global Solutions Initiative Foundation. https://www.g20-insights.org/policy_briefs/coordinating-committee-for-the-governance-of-artificial-intelligence-2/

Jelinek, T., Wallach, W., & Kerimi, D. (2021). Policy brief: The creation of a G20 coordinating committee for the governance of artificial intelligence. *AI and Ethics, 1*(2), 141–150. https://doi.org/10.1007/s43681-020-00019-y

Jesson, J. K., Matheson, L., & Lacey, F. M. (2011). *Doing your literature review: Traditional and systematic techniques.* Sage.

Juntura, P. (2021). *Multilateral approach to ethics of AI: Intergovernmental organizations (as an instrument of global governance) shaping the global landscape of ethical frameworks of AI* [Thesis]. http://urn.fi/URN:NBN:fi:aalto-202105096542

Karpenko, O., Osmak, A., & Karpenko, Y. (2020). Mechanisms of the overcoming the digital inequality of the population in Ukraine: Interoperable governance, educational technologies of artificial intelligence and geoinformational startups. *Prace Komisji Geografii Komunikacji PTG, 23*(3), 84–90. https://doi.org/10.4467/2543859XPKG.20.022.12790

Kazim, E., & Koshiyama, A. (2020). *No AI regulator: An analysis of artificial intelligence and public standards report (UK Government).* SSRN Digital. https://doi.org/10.2139/ssrn.3544871

Kemp, L., Cihon, P., Maas, M. M., Belfield, H., Cremer, Z., Leung, J., & ÓhÉigeartaigh, S. (2019). *UN high-level panel on digital cooperation: A proposal for international AI governance.* Centre for Existential Risk, Cambridge University. https://www.cser.ac.uk/news/advice-un-high-level-panel-digital-cooperation/

Kerr, A., Barry, M., & Kelleher, J. D. (2020). Expectations of artificial intelligence and the performativity of ethics: Implications for communication governance. *Big Data & Society, 7*(1), 2053951720915939.

Kitchenham, B., & Charters, S. (2007). *Guidelines for performing systematic literature reviews in software engineering* (Technical Report EBSE-2007–01, School of Computer Science and Mathematics). Keele University. https://www.elsevier.com/__data/promis_misc/525444systematicreviewsguide.pdf

Knopf, J. W. (2006). Doing a literature review. *Political Science and Politics, 39*(1), 127–132. http://hdl.handle.net/10945/50674

Kolliarakis, G., & Hermann, I. (2020). *Towards European anticipatory governance for artificial intelligence.* German Council on Foreign Relations. https://dgap.org/sites/default/files/article_pdfs/dgap_report_no._9_april_29_2020_60_pp.pdf

Kozuka, S. (2019). A governance framework for the development and use of artificial intelligence: Lessons from the comparison of Japanese and European initiatives. *Uniform Law Review, 24*(2), 315–329. https://doi.org/10.1093/ulr/unz014

Kurshan, E., Shen, H., & Chen, J. (2020). Towards selfregulating AI: Challenges and opportunities of ai model governance in financial services. *arXiv preprint* arXiv:2010.04827

Kuziemski, M., & Misuraca, G. (2020). AI governance in the public sector: Three tales from the frontiers of automated decision-making in democratic settings. *Telecommunications Policy, 44*(6), 101976. https://doi.org/10.1016/j.telpol.2020.101976

Kwan, S. K., & Spohrer, J. (2021). Reducing industry complexity with international standards: Current efforts for services, e-commerce, artificial intelligence. In C. Leitner, W. Ganz, D. Satterfield, & C. Bassano (Eds.), *Advances in the Human Side of Service Engineering. AHFE 2021. Lecture Notes in Networks and Systems* (Vol. 266, pp. 67–76). Springer.

Lane, L. (2021). *Protecting human rights through artificial intelligence law and governance initiatives: A multi-level comparative analysis.* SSRN Digital. https://ssrn.com/abstract=3848526

Langlois, L., & Régis, C. (2021). Analyzing the contribution of ethical charters to building the future of artificial intelligence governance. In B. Braunschweig & M. Ghallab (Eds.), *Reflections on Artificial Intelligence for Humanity. Lecture Notes in Computer Science* (Vol. 12600, pp. 150–170). Springer.

Larsson, S. (2021). AI in the EU: Ethical guidelines as a governance tool. In K. Engelbrekt, A. M. Leijon, & L. Oxelheim (Eds.), *The European Union and the technology shift* (pp. 85–111). Springer International.

Laskai, L., & Webster, G. (2019). *Translation: Chinese expert group offers' governance principles' for 'responsible AI'.* New America Foundation. https://www.newamerica.org/cybersecurity-initiative/digichina/blog/translation-chinese-expert-group-offers-governance-principles-responsible-ai/

Lewis, S. (2018). *What is AI governance.* Tech Target. https://searchenterpriseai.techtarget.com/definition/AI-governance

Lipsey, M. W., & Wilson, D. B. (2001). *Practical meta-analysis.* Sage.

Liu, H. W., & Lin, C. F. (2020). Artificial intelligence and global trade governance: A pluralist agenda. *Harvard International Law Journal, 61*, 407. https://harvardilj.org/2020/04/artificial-intelligence-and-global-trade-governance-a-pluralist-agenda/

Liu, H. Y., & Maas, M. M. (2021). 'Solving for X?' Towards a problem-finding framework to ground long-term governance strategies for artificial intelligence. *Futures, 126*, 102672. https://doi.org/10.1016/j.futures.2020.102672

Lobana, J. (2021). *The governance of AI-based information technologies within corporate environments* [Doctoral dissertation]. McMaster University. http://hdl.handle.net/11375/26685

Luo, S., & Lu, Y. (2021). The "Artificial Intelligence + Social Governance" mode: Risk Ppevention and governance ability improvement. In Z. Xu, R. M. Parizi, O. Loyola-González, & X. Zhang (Eds.), *Cyber security intelligence and analytics. CSIA 2021. Advances in Intelligent Systems and Computing* (Vol. 1343). Springer. https://doi.org/10.1007/978-3-030-69999-4_37

Maas, M. M. (2018a). Two lessons from nuclear arms control for the responsible governance of military artificial intelligence. In *Robophilosophy/TRANSOR* (pp. 347–356). https://doi.org/10.3233/978-1-61499-931-7-347

Maas, M. M. (2018b). *Regulating for 'normal AI accidents' operational lessons for the Responsible Governance of Artificial Intelligence deployment*. https://doi.org/10.1145/3278721.3278766

Macrae, C. (2021). From Blade Runners to Tin Kickers: What the governance of artificial intelligence safety needs to learn from air crash investigators. *AI & Society*. https://doi.org/10.1007/s00146-021-01246-5

Mannes, A. (2020). Governance, risk, and artificial intelligence. *AI Magazine, 41*(1), 61–69. https://doi.org/10.1609/aimag.v41i1.5200

Marchant, G., & Lucille, T. (2019). *Indirect enforcement of "soft law" governance of artificial intelligence* (Working Paper). SSRN Digital.

Mazzini, G. (2019). A system of governance for artificial intelligence through the lens of emerging intersections between AI and EU Law. In A. F ranceschi, R. Schulze, M. Graziadei, O. Pollicino, F. Riente, S. Sica, & S. Pietro (Eds.), *Digital revolution—New challenges for law* (pp. 245–298). Beck International. https://doi.org/10.17104/9783406759048-245

Mhlambi, S. (2020). *From rationality to relationality: Ubuntu as an ethical and human rights framework for artificial intelligence governance* (Carr Center for Human Rights Policy Discussion Paper Series, 9). https://carrcenter.hks.harvard.edu/files/cchr/files/ccdp_2020-009_sabelo_b.pdf

Miailhe, N. (2018). AI & global governance: Why we need an intergovernmental panel for artificial intelligence. *Centre for Policy Research, United Nations University, 20*. https://cpr.unu.edu/publications/articles/ai-global-governance-why-we-need-an-intergovernmental-panel-for-artificial-intelligence.html

Miailhe, N., & Lannquist, Y. (2018). A challenge to global governance. In "Plant Algorithm: Artificial Intelligence for a predictive and inclusive form of integration in Latin America"; INTAL-IDB. *Integration and Trade Journal, 22*(44), 207–217. http://dx.doi.org/10.18235/0001287

Mika, N., Nadezhda, G., Jaana, L., & Raija, K. (2019). Ethical AI for the governance of the society: Challenges and opportunities. In *CEUR Workshop Proceedings* (Vol. 2505, pp. 20–26). http://ceur-ws.org/Vol-2505/paper03.pdf

Mitchell, S. (2018). *Political norms and their impact on the security and value of alignment of artificial intelligence* [Thesis]. http://dx.doi.org/10.13140/RG.2.2.19273.60008

Morley, J., Floridi, L., Kinsey, L., & Elhalal, A. (2020). From what to how: An initial review of publicly available AI ethics tools, methods and research to translate principles into practices. *Science and Engineering Ethics, 26*(4), 2141–2168. https://doi.org/10.1007/s11948-019-00165-5

Mueller, S. T., Hoffman, R. R., Clancey, W., Emrey, A., & Klein, G. (2019). *Explanation in human-AI systems: A literature meta-review*. Synopsis of Key Ideas and Publications, and Bibliography for Explainable AI. https://arxiv.org/abs/1902.01876

Newman, J. C. (2020). *Decision points in AI governance: Three case studies explore efforts to operationalize AI principles*. CLTC [White Paper]. https://cltc.berkeley.edu/ai-decision-points/

Ngai, M. C. (2020). *AI ethics through the lens of GDPR: Understanding ethics' interaction with law, its impact on GDPR and subsequently governance of AI ethics* [Master's thesis]. https://www.duo.uio.no/bitstream/handle/10852/74845/Master-Thesis-140120.pdf?sequence=1&isAllowed=y

Nurus, S. F. M. S. P., Hartini, S., & Sheela, J. K. (2016). Artificial intelligence governance: A heads up from driverless cars. *World Applied Science Journal, 34*(3), 376–382. https://elmnet.ir/vslg?url=https%3A%2F%2Fwww.magiran.com%2Fpaper%2F1548201&type=0&id=1502141

Nutley, S. M., & Davies, H. T. (2002). *Evidence-based policy & practice: Moving from rhetoric to reality* (Discussion Paper 2). Research Unit for Research Untilization. https://www.researchgate.net/profile/Huw-Davies-3/publication/242419804-_Discussion_Paper_2_Evidencebased_policy_and_practice_moving_from_rhetoric_to_reality/links/56013a2b08ae07629e52bd4c/Discussion-Paper-2-Evidence-based-policy-and-practice-moving-from-rhetoric-to-reality.pdf

ÓhÉigeartaigh, S. S., Whittlestone, J., Liu, Y., Zeng, Y., & Liu, Z. (2020). Overcoming barriers to cross-cultural cooperation in AI ethics and governance. *Philosophy & Technology, 33*(4), 571–593. https://doi.org/10.1007/s13347-020-00402-x

O'Keefe, C., Cihon, P., Flynn, C., Garfinkel, B., Leung, J., & Dafoe, A. (2020). *The windfall clause: Distributing the benefits of AI, Centre for the governance of AI research report*. Future of Humanity Institute, University of Oxford. http://dx.doi.org/10.1145/3375627.3375842

Ozlati, S., & Yampolskiy, R. (2017). The formalization of ai risk management and safety standards. In *Workshops at the Thirty-First AAAI Conference on Artificial Intelligence*. https://www.aaai.org/ocs/index.php/WS/AAAIW17/paper/viewFile/15175/14655

Pagallo, U., Casanovas, P., & Madelin, R. (2019). The middle-out approach: Assessing models of legal governance in data protection, artificial intelligence, and the Web of Data. *The Theory and Practice of Legislation, 7*(1), 1–25. https://doi.org/10.1080/20508840.2019.1664543

Papagiannidis, E., Enholm, I. M., Dremel, C., Mikalef, P., & Krogstie, J. (2021). Deploying AI Governance practices: A revelatory case study. In D. Dennehy, A. Griva, N. Pouloudi, Y. K. Dwivedi, I. Pappas, & M. Mäntymäki (Eds.), *Responsible AI and analytics for an ethical and inclusive digitized society. I3E 2021. Lecture Notes in Computer Science* (Vol. 12896). Springer. https://doi.org/10.1007/978-3-030-85447-8_19

Personal Data Protection Commission Singapore. (2019). *A proposed model artificial intelligence governance framework*. Personal Data Protection Commission Singapore.

Piper, R. J. (2013). How to write a systematic literature review: a guide for medical students. *National AMR, Fostering Medical Research, 1*.

Popay, J., Roberts, H., Sowden, A., Petticrew, M., Arai, L., Rodgers, M., Britten, N., Roen, K., & Duffy, S. (2006). *Guidance on the conduct of narrative synthesis in systematic reviews. A product from the ESRC methods programme*. http://dx.doi.org/10.13140/2.1.1018.4643

Reddy, S., Allan, S., Coghlan, S., & Cooper, P. (2020). A governance model for the application of AI in health care. *Journal of the American Medical Informatics Association, 27*(3), 491–497. https://doi.org/10.1093/jamia/ocz192

Reed, C., & Ng, I. (2019). *Data trusts as an AI governance mechanism*. SSRN Digital. https://doi.org/10.2139/ssrn.3334527

Renda, A. (2019). *Artificial Intelligence. Ethics, governance and policy challenges*. CEPS Centre for European Policy Studies.

Roski, J., Maier, E. J., Vigilante, K., Kane, E. A., & Matheny, M. E. (2021). Enhancing trust in AI through industry selfgovernance. *Journal of the American Medical Informatics Association, 28*(7), 1582–1590. https://doi.org/10.1093/jamia/ocab065

Rousseau, D. M., Manning, J., & Denyer, D. (2008). Evidence in management and organizational science: Assembling the field's full weight of scientific knowledge through syntheses. In A. Brief & J. Walsh (Eds.), *Annals of the academy of management* (Vol. 2(1), pp. 19–32). https://doi.org/10.1080/19416520802211651

Scheltema, M. (2019). Embedding private standards in AI and mitigating artificial intelligence risks. In *IEEE SmartWorld, Ubiquitous Intelligence & Computing, Advanced & Trusted Computing, Scalable Computing & Communications, Cloud & Big Data Computing, Internet of People and Smart City Innovation (SmartWorld/SCALCOM/UIC/ATC/CBDCom/IOP/SCI)* (pp. 305–310). https://doi.org/10.1109/SmartWorld-UIC-ATC-SCALCOM-IOP-SCI.2019.00096

Schiff, D., Ayesh, A., Musikanski, L., & Havens, J. C. (2020). IEEE 7010: A new standard for assessing the well-being implications of artificial intelligence. In *2020 IEEE international conference on systems, man, and cybernetics (SMC)* (pp. 2746–2753). IEEE.

Schneider, J., Abraham, R., & Meske, C. (2020). AI governance for businesses. *arXiv preprint* arXiv:2011.10672.

Schwab, K., & Davis, N. (2018). *Shaping the fourth industrial revolution.* World Economic Forum.

Shackelford, S., Asare, I. N., Dockery, R., Raymond, A., & Sergueeva, A. (2021). Should we trust a black box to safeguard human rights? A comparative analysis of AI governance. *UCLA Journal of International Law and Foreign Affairs.* http://dx.doi.org/10.2139/ssrn.3773198

Sharkey, L. (2017). *An intervention to shape policy dialogue, communication, and AI research norms for AI safety.* https://forum.effectivealtruism.org/posts/4kRPYuogoSKnHNBhY/an-intervention-to-shape-policy-dialogue-communication-and

Siebels, J., & Knyphausen-Aufseß, D. (2012). A review of theory in family business research: The implications for corporate governance. *International Journal of Management Reviews, 14*, 280–304. https://doi.org/10.1111/j.1468-2370.2011.00317.x

Smuha, N. A. (2020). Beyond a human rights-based approach to AI governance: Promise, pitfalls, plea. *Philosophy & Technology*, 1–14. https://doi.org/10.1007/s13347-020-00403-w

Spiro, M. (2020). The FTC and AI governance: A regulatory proposal. *Seattle Journal of Technology, Environmental & Innovation Law, 10*(1), 2. https://digitalcommons.law.seattleu.edu/sjteil/vol10/iss1/2

Sternberg, R. J. (1991). Editorial. *Psychological Bulletin, 109*, 3–4. https://doi.org/10.1037/h0092473

Stix, C. (2021). *The ghost of AI governance past, present and future: AI governance in the European Union.* https://arxiv.org/abs/2107.14099

Subirana, B. (2020). Call for a wake standard for artificial intelligence. *Communications of the ACM, 63*(7), 32–35. https://doi.org/10.1145/3402193

Sutton, A. J. (2009). Publication bias. In H. Cooper, L. V. Hedges, & J. C. Valentine (Eds.), *The handbook of research synthesis and meta-analysis* (2nd ed., pp. 435–452). Russel Sage Foundation.

Taeihagh, A. (2020). The governance of artificial intelligence and robotics. *Policy & Society, 40*(1), 1–21. https://doi.org/10.1080/14494035.2021.1928377

Tan, J. Z., & Ding, J. (2019). *AI governance through AI markets.* University of Oxford. http://www.joshuatan.com/wpcontent/uploads/2019/08/AI_governance_through_AI_markets.pdf

Tencent Research Institute, CAICT, Tencent AI Lab, Tencent open platform. (2021). Challenges of AI governance. In Tencent Research Institute, CAICT, Tencent AI Lab, Tencent open platform (Eds.), *Artificial Intelligence* (pp. 281–284). Palgrave Macmillan. https://doi.org/10.1007/978-981-15-6548-9_27

Thelisson, E. (2019). The central role of states for building a balanced AI governance. *Delphi—Interdisciplinary Review of Emerging Technologies, 2*(4),155–157. https://doi.org/10.21552/delphi/2019/4/3

Thuraisingham, B. (2020). Artificial intelligence and data science governance: Roles and responsibilities at the C-level and the board. In *2020 IEEE 21st International Conference on Information Reuse and Integration for Data Science (IRI)* (pp. 314–318). IEEE. https://doi.org/10.1109/IRI49571.2020.00052

Todolí-Signes, A. (2019). Algorithms, artificial intelligence and automated decisions concerning workers and the risks of discrimination: The necessary collective governance of data protection. *Transfer: European Review of Labour and Research, 25*(4), 465–481. https://doi.org/10.1177%2F1024258919876416

Tokmakov, M. A. (2020). Artificial intelligence in corporate governance. In S. I. Ashmarina & V. V. Mantulenko (Eds.), *Digital economy and the new labor market: Jobs, competences and innovative HR technologies. IPM 2020. Lecture Notes in networks and systems* (Vol. 161, pp. 667–674). Springer. https://doi.org/10.1007/978-3-030-60926-9_83

Torré, F., Teigland, R., & Engstam, L. (2019). AI leadership and the future of corporate governance: Changing demands for board competence. In F. Torré, R. Teigland, & L. Engstam (Eds.), *The digital transformation of labor* (pp. 116–146). Routledge.

Torrie, V., & Payette, D. (2020). AI governance in Canadian banking: Fairness, credit models, and equality rights. *Banking & Finance Law Review 5, 36*(1). https://doi.org/10.2139/ssrn.3736926

Tranfield, D., Denyer, D., & Smart, P. (2003). Towards a methodology for developing evidence-informed management knowledge by means of systematic review. *British Journal of Management, 14*(3), 207. https://doi.org/10.1111/1467-8551.00375

Tubella, A. A., Theodorou, A., Dignum, V., & Dignum, F. (2019). Governance by glass-box: Implementing transparent moral bounds for AI behaviour. *arXiv preprint* arXiv:1905.04994

Ulnicane, I., Eke, D. O., Knight, W., Ogoh, G., & Stahl, B. C. (2021). Good governance as a response to discontents? Déjà vu, or lessons for AI from other emerging technologies. *Interdisciplinary Science Reviews, 46*(1–2), 71–93. https://doi.org/10.1080/03080188.2020.1840220

Vanberghen, C., & Vanberghen, A. (2021). AI governance as a patchwork: The regulatory and geopolitical approach of AI at international and European level. In T. E. Synodinou, P. Jougleux, C. Markou, & T. Prastitou-Merdi (Eds.), *EU internet law in the digital single market* (pp. 233–246). Springer.

Vevea, J. L., & Woods, C. M. (2005). Publication bias in research synthesis: Sensitivity analysis using a priori weight functions. *Psychological Methods, 10*(4), 428–443. https://doi.org/10.1037/1082-989X.10.4.428

Vieira, E. S., & Gomes, J. A. N. F. (2009). A comparison of Scopus and Web of Science for a typical university. *Scientometrics, 81*(2), 587–600. https://doi.org/10.1007/s11192-009-2178-0

von Ungern-Sternberg, A. (2021). Discriminatory AI and the Law–Legal standards for algorithmic profiling. Draft Chapter. In S. Vöneky, P. Kellmeyer, O. Müller, & W. Burgard (Eds.), *Responsible AI*. Cambridge University Press.

Wagner, D. (2018). *AI & Global Governance: How AI is changing the global economy*. United Nations University Centre for Policy Research. https://cpr.unu.edu/publications/articles/ai-global-governance-how-ai-is-changing-the-global-economy.html

Wallach, W., & Marchant, G. E. (2018). *An agile ethical/legal model for the international and national governance of AI and robotics*. Association for the Advancement of Artificial Intelligence. https://www.aies-conference.com/2018/-contents/papers/main/AIES_2018_paper_77.pdf

Walz, A., & Firth-Butterfield, K. (2018). Implementing ethics into artificial intelligence: A contribution, from a legal perspective, to the development of an AI governance regime. *Duke Law & Technology Review, 17*, i.

Wang, J., Yu, X., Li, J., & Jin, X. (2018). Artificial intelligence and international norms. In J. Donghan (Ed.), *Reconstructing our orders* (pp. 195–229). Springer. https://doi.org/10.1007/978-981-13-2209-9

Webster, J., & Watson, R. T. (2002). Analyzing the past to prepare for the future: Writing a literature review. *MIS Quarterly, 26*(2), xiii–xxiii. https://web.njit.edu/~egan/Writing_A_Literature_Review.pdf

Weiguang, C. (2017). *Some thoughts on the issue of artificial intelligence governance*. Frontiers. http://www.en.cnki.com.cn/Article_en/CJFDTotal-RMXS201720007.htm

Weng, Y., & Izumo, T. (2019). Natural law and its implications for AI governance. *Delphi—Interdisciplinary Review of Emerging Technologies, 2*(3), 122–128. https://doi.org/10.21552/delphi/2019/3/5

Wieland, J. (2018). *Relational Economics. Ökonomische Theorie der Governance wirtschaftlicher Transaktionen*. Metropolis.

Wieland, J. (2020). *Relational economics: A political economy*. Springer.

Winfield, A. (2019). Ethical standards in robotics and AI. *Nature Electronics, 2*(2), 46–48. https://doi.org/10.1038/s41928-019-0213-6

Winfield, A. F., & Jirotka, M. (2018). Ethical governance is essential to building trust in robotics and artificial intelligence systems. *Philosophical Transactions of the Royal Society A: Mathematical, Physical and Engineering Sciences, 376*(2133), 20180085. https://doi.org/10.1098/rsta.2018.0085

Wirtz, B. W., Weyerer, J. C., & Sturm, B. J. (2020). The dark sides of artificial intelligence: An integrated AI governance framework for public administration. *International Journal of Public Administration, 43*(9), 818–829. https://doi.org/10.1080/01900692.2020.1749851

Wong, P. H. (2020). Cultural differences as excuses? Human rights and cultural values in global ethics and governance of AI. *Philosophy & Technology, 33*(4), 705–715. https://doi.org/10.1007/s13347-020-00413-8

Wu, W., Huang, T., & Gong, K. (2020). Ethical principles and governance technology development of AI in China. *Engineering, 6*(3), 302–309. https://doi.org/10.1016/j.eng.2019.12.015

Xia, L. (2020). Research on the development of China's concept of international order under the global governance of artificial intelligence. *Frontiers in Educational Research, 3*(5). https://doi.org/10.25236/FER.2020.030520

Yeung, K., Howes, A., & Pogrebna, G. (2019). AI governance by human rights-centred design, deliberation and oversight: An end to ethics washing. In M. D. Dubber, F. Pasquale, & S. Das (Eds.), *The Oxford handbook of AI ethics*. Oxford University Press. https://doi.org/10.1093/oxfordhb/9780190067397.013.5

Zekos, G. I. (2021). Artificial intelligence governance. In *Economics and law of artificial intelligence*. Springer.

Zhang, B., Anderljung, M., Kahn, L., Dreksler, N., Horowitz, M. C., & Dafoe, A. (2021). Ethics and governance of artificial intelligence: Evidence from a survey of machine learning researchers. *arXiv preprint* arXiv:2105.02117

Chapter 5
Discussion and Conclusion

The purpose of this book was to present a theoretical conceptualisation of private-sector-driven AI governance, addressing the complex, uncertainty-driven, and wicked nature of the phenomenon. Ideally, this type of problem structure should be dealt with by high levels of collaboration—among the different stakeholders involved and, for example, within stakeholder groups as well as by shared value creation. Due to the exceptionally high interrelatedness of interests and actors, as well as having little existing research to draw from, I restricted the book's scope to conceptualising AI and focusing on how companies can engage in self-regulatory measures without facing competitive disadvantages, especially through shared value creation. Thereby, I set the foundation for further research on collaborative AI governance and can enable companies to include the interests of their societal stakeholders for their own benefit, instead of merely attending to the competitive pressure exerted by the market.

Wieland's (2018, 2020) Relational Economics and inherent Relational Governance approach proved to be a suitable theoretical foundation to develop a holistic AI governance approach for the private sector. Thus, I proceeded to apply the theory to the context of AI. Since Wieland's original theory has been empirically tested and stems from the long-standing disciplines of systems theory and transaction cost economics, at least partial generalisability can be assumed of this book's conceptual contribution to theory and practice, despite presenting one of the first conceptualisations for Relational AI Governance.

Additionally, the findings of the systematic literature review conducted to present an overview of advances in private-sector AI governance confirmed the need for theoretical examinations and contributions to the field. This is because most research in the field analyses and contributes to AI governance from a rather practical perspective. Only very few scholars present approaches that stem from a theoretical analysis of the phenomenon. Despite this restriction, the review supported the book's problem definition and the decision to build its governance approach based on the identified

S. Wiesmüller, *The Relational Governance of Artificial Intelligence*,
Relational Economics and Organization Governance,
https://doi.org/10.1007/978-3-031-25023-1_5

characteristics of AI governance's wicked problem structure, its exceptionally high levels of complexity, and the inherent need for cooperation among actors.

5.1 General Discussion

In the light of previous research and regarding the concepts this book draws from, each of the following paragraphs is dedicated to examining the meaning of this book's findings for the particular research stream.

First, few scholars have yet linked the notion of wicked problems to AI. However, previous research had not attempted to address this intersection from a theoretical point of view and, thereby, present a theoretical examination of the field of AI governance. In its attempt to examine possible options for the wicked problem of AI governance, the book mainly drew from Roberts's (2000) well-established paper on general governance strategies to address wicked problems. Having excluded authoritative strategies as not providing the private sector and, in consequence, society with the requirements for responsible AI adoption, the book presented in detail the conditions for and effects of competitive and collaborative approaches. With competitive strategies being prevalent in private-sector AI development and adoption, I sought to elaborate on the conditions allowing companies to move from competitive to collaborative forms of AI governance. Thereby, it provides a conceptual contribution to Roberts's research applied to the AI context.

Throughout the book, the aspects of multi-stakeholder governance, self-regulation, raising the standards for all stakeholders, and collective action, e.g., in raising industry standards, were identified. I support and confirm Roberts's (2000) evaluation that collaborative forms of governance, while being the most promising form of addressing wicked problems, are also the most challenging strategies to realise. Particularly when contextualising collaborative governance in practical evaluations, I presented various arguments (Dafoe, 2018) indicating the challenges for such strategies in AI governance. This includes the arms race dynamics (Dafoe, 2018; Geist, 2016; Maas, 2018), related hidden agendas (Dafoe, 2018; Lilkov, 2020; Polyakova & Meserole, 2019), and significant involvement of the public sector and governments (Lilkov, 2020).

However, according to my findings, the prevalent dynamics mainly affect forms of collective governance involving various companies, whereas collaborative forms of governance performed by the single company, in collaboration with its stakeholders, do not seem to be as restricted by the identified dynamics. As presented, multi-stakeholder-formats, corporate self-regulation as well as the creation of shared value can be realised in the scenarios of both a partially regulated and an unregulated market. Thus, the book successfully focused on developing measures allowing the single company to integrate social normativity into its decision-making, despite being caught in a highly competitive environment. With that, I still addressed responsible AI adoption in practice, albeit for the single organisation instead of a network of actors.

Moreover, the observations made in this book suggest that it is particularly the creation of shared value which should be understood as the starting point and necessary foundation for all other forms of collaborative governance. Especially due to the high complexity, the interrelatedness of dimensions, and the concurrency of developments in the global AI market, I recommend an approach that is, indeed, decentralised—focusing on the redirection of corporate realisation of profits in a company towards creating shared value. By aligning its corporate processes towards this objective, the single company is able to navigate potential negative consequences. Further, it can integrate social normativity and is empowered to proactively reassess its reputation in society—all of which, in turn, secure its continued existence. This fundamental shift in strategy builds the foundation for a company to then engage in other, more operational forms of collaborative governance, such as multi-stakeholder formats. This is because operationalised governance forms either result from a company's shared value creation strategy, such as multi-stakeholder formats, or are enabled by it, based on the company's secured position in the market. Having already secured its continued existence through shared value creation, a company might be less likely to defect when engaging in collective action with other companies—as is particularly likely in the AI context (Dafoe, 2018). Hence, by focusing on the single company and the fundamentals of its responsible decision-making, the book contributes and is connected to research on collaborative strategies for solving wicked problems, specifically regarding the wicked problem of AI governance.

Second, while applying a theory that combines transaction cost economics and systems theory, the AI conceptualisation this book presents is relatable to existing research originating from Luhmann's (1996, 1998) theory. Whether the findings of this book are applicable to this research stream rather depends on the chosen form of conceptualisation than on the shared theoretical origin.

While Baecker (2015), Esposito (2017a, 2017b), and Harth and Lorenz (2017) have already contextualised or conceptualised AI in Luhmann's tradition of systems theory, they are in conflict as to how to define the technologies subsumed under this umbrella term. While the scholars conceptualise AI as a form of communication (Esposito, 2017a, 2017b), a communicating agent (Baecker, 2015), or machine agent (Harth & Lorenz, 2017), I argue for the introduction of AI as an autopoietic system in Luhmann's tradition. Apart from Reichel (2011), whose conceptualisation of technology is in line with this book's approach, the presented contribution contradicts existing research. This is because this book's definition of AI as an autopoietic system rejects the above-mentioned concepts. This results in AI becoming realised in the form of a transaction, attracting transactions from other systems and, thereby, creating a relational transaction.

In my view, conceptualising AI as a system in society corroborates and interprets Luhmann's original theory in a more realistic form. This is because research indicates that AI's achievement of autonomy, human-like consciousness, or agency is a condition that is not yet within reach—if ever (Balfanz, 2017; Fuchs, 2020; Soto & Sonnenschein, 2019). In this, it departs from discussions revolving around an AI's potential consciousness or agency—aspects that need to be addressed in depth and with urgency when defining AI as a potential agent in society, as does Baecker (2011,

2015). Thus, according to this book's findings, portraying AI as an agent does not depict the impact AI currently has in practice. Further, this decision would require the definition of AI in a similar form to the individual, interacting with system logics, but being outside the direct scope of a systems-theoretical approach.

However, mainly due to its status as a general-purpose technology (cf., Klinger et al., 2018; Nepelski & Sobolewski, 2020), AI will eventually interact and create interactions with all systems in society. Thus, its influence and impact exist on a grander scale and are instead comparable to a system-wide disruption on the meta-level. Therefore, in their entirety, this book's findings support the claim that portraying AI as a form of communication (Esposito, 2017a, 2017b) or as an agent (Baecker, 2011, 2015) does not seem sufficient to cover the entirety of its structural impact. Consequently, based on my findings and contribution, I aim to promote further debate in the field.

Third, with the structural integration of social normativity in the form of societal concerns and AI ethics, this book enables a company's continued existence and social legitimacy (Wieland, 2020). Thus, Relational AI Governance offers a structural solution to translating the perspective of company-external stakeholders into corporate processes (Wieland, 2020) and supports the company in bridging varying views on AI governance within its organisational boundaries (Hagendorff, 2020; Mayer et al., 2021). Research in the field suggests that company-internal stakeholders do not always agree upon the guidelines implemented in companies (Cihon et al., 2021; Hagendorff, 2020; Jobin et al., 2019; Mittelstadt, 2019a), as developers, especially, are not always in favour of principled AI governance (Mayer et al., 2021). Through management measures supporting the development of a shared understanding, the Relational AI Governance model supports the involvement of all stakeholder groups to develop commonly agreed-upon values and solutions. Thereby, it ensures their applicability to the actual technological development phases of the AI lifecycle, which is often criticised (Hagendorff, 2020; Morley et al., 2020; Yu et al., 2018). In the case of global value chains, the model can also be applied to integrate and give room to culturally specific views (ÓhÉigeartaigh et al., 2020). This is because it allows for local adoption and pursues a non-normative approach. As a result, it promotes a combinatory approach for AI ethics, including principled, consequential, and virtue-based AI ethics. With this, it advocates for philosophical perspectives as an element of comprehensive AI governance instead of pursuing a single normative approach, which would not be applicable across cultures. As for the realisation of the program, I recommend a transcultural approach, allowing for a particular level of cultural adaptation (Wieland, 2020). Thereby, it aims to create higher levels of acceptance among all stakeholders of a given company.

Applying the combinatory, modular nature inherent to Wieland's (2018, 2020) Relational Governance concept, I support the interlinkage of the elements of social normativity with complementary governance elements, such as formal governance measures, as presented above. In this, my findings corroborate the required combination of formal and informal measures in AI governance on the meta-level of AI regulation (Jelinek et al., 2020; Mialhe, 2018; Miailhe & Lannquist, 2018), as well as on the organisational level (Gasser & Almeida, 2017; Liu & Maas, 2021; Winfield & Jirotka, 2018).

5.2 Theoretical Contribution and Practical Implications

Since the field of AI governance only emerged a few years ago, it has not yet been researched extensively. Therefore, related disciplines, such as AI ethics (Hagendorff, 2020, 2022; Mittelstadt, 2019), and stakeholder groups from society (Brundage et al., 2018; Bryson, 2018; Cihon, 2019) have demanded governance for AI and urged scholars to contribute to establishing the field by developing such approaches.

By presenting a conceptual AI governance approach, this book provides both a theoretical model and a practical contribution, supporting companies wanting to engage in self-regulation regarding AI or successfully implementing a governance approach in a partially regulated AI market. With this, it helps to advance and professionalise further the field of AI governance.

5.2.1 Theoretical Contribution

From a theoretical perspective, the book contributes to four streams of research: Relational Economics (Wieland, 2018, 2020), systems theory in Luhmann's (1996, 1998) tradition, the research stream of relational governance (cf., Cao & Lumineau, 2015; Poppo et al., 2008), and the recently emerged field of AI governance.

First, having chosen Relational Economics as the theoretical foundation for the AI governance approach presented, the book advances the theory and links it to one of the most pressing topics for governance: the general-purpose technology of AI (Klinger et al., 2018; Nepelski & Sobolewski, 2020; Razzkazov, 2020; Trajtenberg, 2018). Thereby, the book confirms the applicability and adaptability of Wieland's Relational Economics to yet another practical governance phenomenon. While the theory has already been successfully applied to the field of CSR in global value chains (Wieland, 2018, 2020), this book is the first to connect it to the context of digital technologies, more specifically to AI. Moreover, it confirms the theory's potential to be adapted to constantly new contexts and governance challenges. This is because the theory's modular structure allows the constant adaptation of existing parameters and the integration of new variables and parameters, as presented by this book. With this, I hope to have presented a precedent case for the further development and an extension of Relational Economics by new variables and parameters. While outside the scope of this book, future research could apply the theory to other digital technologies, such as the blockchain, which could be conceptualised within Relational Economics in a similar form.

Second, it offers a new definition of AI in Luhmann's systems-theoretical research tradition. In this, it builds on the contribution of Reichel (2011), who suggests the definition of technology as an autopoietic system and presents an opposing position to mainstream research in the field. However, Reichel did not include AI in his contribution and instead examined the case of the super-category, technology. Hence, the book closes the gap between existing research in the field and Reichel's first advance, introducing technology as equivalent to other autopoietic systems in society. Thereby, it presents a new perspective for critical debate in this research stream and a conceptual starting point for other scholars to develop further. In contrast to existing research, it concedes that AI has a dominant role in society, mainly due to its general-purpose nature and the resulting impact, influence, and role it already has and is expected to extend in the future. Hence, the book's advances contribute to further connection of the disciplines of systems theory and AI governance.

Third, the findings of this book and the review of AI governance confirm the importance of applying relational governance to the AI context, specifically via the complementary use of formal and informal parameters. Again, to the best of my knowledge, it is the first publication to link this particular research stream of relational governance to AI. So far, relational governance has been linked to cultural studies or corporate relation-building (Chu et al., 2020; Ju & Gao, 2017; Sjödin et al., 2019; Zheng et al., 2008), or the general examination of dynamics between formal and informal governance measures (cf., Cao & Lumineau, 2015; Poppo et al., 2008). Connecting Wieland's (2018, 2020) relational governance concept allows for linking an empirically tested and theoretically established approach with the topic of AI governance, which provides the book with an adequate foundation for developing a comprehensive governance model, including formal and informal measures. With this, it complements and enhances literature in relational governance, while at the same time formalising the young field of AI governance with a traditional model. Given that the applied approach presented in the book is among the most substantial and comprehensive in the field, it confirms the suitability and applicability of Relational Economics and its Relational Governance model to practice. Thus, by connecting these two schools of thought, the book contributes to closing the gap for AI governance, moving from the demand for other scholars to address the lack of implementation of AI ethics to actually providing an option for how AI ethics-based AI governance can be accomplished.

Fourth, I presented a theoretical contribution to the field of AI governance. This is because the book realises an elaboration of its underlying problem structure, conceptualises AI as a new variable within an existing socio-economic theory and analyses the demand for AI governance through the lens of Relational Economics. Thereby, it allows for the further theoretical abstraction of the dynamics of AI governance and the characteristics of AI technologies. Based on this conceptualisation, scholars can address AI in the light of sociological and economic lenses alike. Having identified the situation governance needs to address, more specifically, the relational transaction underlying the governance structure, the book proceeds to develop the relational governance model for the AI context. In addition, the operationalised Relational AI Governance model represents a contribution to the field of applied AI governance—a research stream the book identifies through its review analysis.

Further, it contributes to the research field of AI governance by having conducted a systematic literature review regarding its advances. I conducted a meta-level analysis, which included the structuring of the field and clustering of the research streams according to the topic they address. With this, the book presents an overview of the current state of research in the field, while at the same time positioning its own contribution. Again, since no review has yet been conducted to the best of the author's knowledge, it closes another current gap. By having developed an applied AI governance model, which entails theoretical explanations, the book closes a current gap in the research field. This is because, to the best of my knowledge and based on the review findings, only very few publications present applied models originating from theory. While most publications derive their suggestions from practical needs (cf., Huck et al., 2020; Lobana, 2021; Torré et al., 2019), only this book and Gasser and Almeida (2017) seem to examine and address applied AI governance with a solid structural model. Thus, by operationalising its theoretical insights on AI, the book offers a practical governance model which advances the research stream by formalising applied forms of AI governance.

As the review findings indicate, there are still very few theoretical examinations of the topic, since most publications address the currently prevalent challenges based on an immediate practical need and with reactive practical suggestions. Only a few traditional disciplines have been linked to this research field so far, with only one publication applying a traditional economic model (cf., Fernandes et al., 2020) and one other linking it to social governance (cf., Luo & Lu, 2021). Thus, from a theoretical viewpoint, it is primarily the field of AI ethics—also still young—that advances and formalises AI governance research.

Fifth, Relational AI Governance serves scholars stemming from other disciplines and targeting other societal sectors and systems with a theoretical foundation for further research. This is because Relational Economics is applicable for deriving insights for the public sector, legislation, as well as civil society. Thus, already having conceptualised AI within Relational Economics, I provide scholars with the theoretical foundation to examine system-specific governance strategies and the role, for example, of the public sector and legislation, based on this book's findings. Hence, it not only contributes to the disciplines and research streams it includes and addresses but is of intersectoral relevance and applicability.

5.2.2 *Practical Implications*

In addition to the theoretical contributions, the book provides relevant insights for decision-makers in practice across sectors, but especially for the private sector. Apart from providing a combinatory, comprehensive AI governance instrument, I identified various relevant aspects of the successful implementation of a governance structure in practice.

First, this book offers companies a structural, comprehensive approach to implementing AI governance in a private-sector organisation. To ensure the effectiveness and acceptance of an AI governance program within the firm, it is essential for organisations to apply a combinatory approach. This book's Relational AI Governance provides practice with a theoretically funded governance instrument that—stemming from Wieland's (2018, 2020) relational governance approach—combines both formal and informal governance parameters. With this, it integrates hard and soft law advances, as well as the individual's role in the successful adoption of AI governance and society's concerns. Thereafter, it examines the interaction between formal and informal measures on a meta-level, such as hard and soft law, a topic of significant practical interest, as the review revealed. By covering this aspect, it allows companies to navigate the currently highly fragmented regulatory environment. These insights are redirected into the governance approach by including specified suggestions as per governance parameters to promote the model's applicability to various use cases in practice. Lastly, the book established the relevance of conducting an extensive risk assessment and answering questions of corporate liability with great urgency. In this way, it provides companies with strategic recommendations to ensure the advantageous realisation of an AI governance structure.

Second, the findings support the strategic development and subsequent implementation of an AI governance program on an organisational level. This is because it provides insights for both formal and informal operational measures based on its theoretical governance model. The suggestions include the introduction of new departments, processes, and measures. By presenting such strategic guidelines, the book provides companies with the necessary instruments to implement an effective AI governance program. Furthermore, it gives insights into the conditions of effective self-regulation for the companies. This includes evaluating the conditions for reputational gains, instead of facing competitive disadvantages due to the introduction of self-regulatory measures. Thus, in its operationalised form, it includes, for example, the formal implementation of a multidimensional integrity management program and informal measures, such as AI ethics-based training measures, and dialogues to develop and promote a shared understanding among all stakeholders.

Third, I established the significance of including and addressing the individual in an organisational context, giving decision-makers insights into various aspects influencing the personal integrity of employees. From the perspective of the governance structure, the role of the individual is relevant on an individual, operational, and strategic level. On the strategic level, research indicates that the board level needs to reconsider its roles and responsibilities (Thuraisingham, 2020), as well as a specific skill set, to manage and govern AI successfully (Torré et al., 2019). Still, a comprehensive AI governance structure should include competence training. Further, since the acceptance of the governance program on the part of the internal stakeholders is of great significance to its success (Mayer et al., 2021), I suggest virtues-based training (Hagendorff, 2020, 2022), the inclusion of professional norms (Gasser & Schmitt, 2020), and measures to create a shared understanding. While these measures support the realisation of the governance program, they further aim to motivate and involve employees (Wieland, 2020) and might attract new talent due to reputational gains (Miller & Coldicott, 2019; Neubert & Montañez, 2020). The latter should not be underestimated in times of extensive war for talents in the field (Mayer et al., 2021; Miller & Coldicott, 2019; Neubert & Montañez, 2020).

Second, in the light of the pending E.U. regulation for AI, the book provides decision-makers with an evaluation of both scenarios; the unregulated and partially regulated AI market. Consequently, it develops two versions of the Relational AI Governance model, each addressing one of the scenarios. It presents a holistic governance instrument for companies inside and outside the E.U., applicable in the present and following the eventual passing of the regulation.

Fourth, having conceptualised the relational transaction underlying the AI governance structure, the book offers policymakers and the legislation alike with the necessary foundation to further analyse the underlying dynamics in AI governance. Since the insights stemming from Relational Economics are applicable across disciplines and sectors, actors from the public sector, legislation, and civil society can build on the findings of this book and develop system-specific solutions complementing its scope. Further, while the operationalisation of Relational AI Governance primarily addresses companies, its core structure and mechanisms are applicable to organisations from all sectors. Due to its modular nature, it can be adapted to organisation-specific needs.

To conclude, the book contributes to promoting self-regulation by private-sector organisations in the AI context—presenting them with a holistic approach that supports companies in advantageously engaging in self-regulatory AI governance.

5.3 Limitations and Future Research

To view the findings of this book in a contextualised manner, a few limitations need to be mentioned. For one, the generalisability of the review findings is limited by a potential bias. Generally, qualitative content analysis is more prone to bias, albeit I incorporated measures to counterbalance this risk, such as using transparent selection criteria. Nevertheless, given that the selection and analysis of the data were realised by one researcher only, these steps can be perceived as being subjectively biased and, as they were not tested by another scholar, lacking intercoder reliability. Further, the development of inductive categories was, again, conducted by one researcher. Since I applied transparent criteria to the selection process, the limitation was mitigated but should still be considered. Due to the scope of the review, the book cannot make assumptions or present generalisable findings for the entire research field. This is because it excluded publications which only present findings of niche relevance, with this exclusion covering publications focusing specifically, for example, on the medical field or the public sector only. While the exclusion only affected a small group of publications, it limited the scope of the review. As the conduct of the review did not serve as the centrepiece of this book but to position and complement its theoretical approach, this does not affect the quality of this book or its conceptual contribution. However, I suggest that future research closely monitors advances in the field and repeats this review at a larger scale, including more keywords, more databases, and findings from all disciplines. Furthermore, I recommend that future reviews should involve a group of researchers to avoid subjective bias.

Moreover, due to a lack of research studies on the topic of AI governance, especially theoretical approaches, this book had to develop an entirely new research typology. In particular, the theory chosen has neither dealt with AI before nor the governance approach it entails, and research in the emerging field of AI governance does not yet include publications of similar magnitude. While the decision to conceptualise AI based on Luhmann's (1996, 1998) systems theory resulted from its initial presentation of the problem structure underlying AI governance, the chosen form of an autopoietic system within Relational Economics is a contribution of this book. This is because it presents an unprecedented advance, based on a self-developed conceptual argumentation, rather than a long-standing research tradition.

As Relational Economics integrates both systems theory and transaction cost economics, this book's contribution could have benefitted from a detailed examination of AI from an economics perspective. For one, such an economic examination would have complemented the findings of this book; moreover, the review confirms the general need for contributions from the economics discipline: so far, only Fernandes et al. (2020) examined AI governance from this perspective, applying game theory to balance individual and societal gains from AI adoption. Despite the significant economic relevance of AI, stemming from its classification as a general-purpose technology by this very discipline (Dafoe, 2018; Goldfarb et al., 2019; Klinger et al., 2018; Nepelski & Sobolewski, 2020; Razzkazov, 2020), there is a clear lack of scholarly attention, and in this book I urge scholars to integrate the variable AI into traditional economic models. Hence, being the first conceptualisation of AI governance from a socio-economic perspective, the findings of this book require formalisation and empirical testing.

While the book initially set out to contribute to collective forms of collaborative governance, this aim could only partially be fulfilled: among other things, the theory chosen to conceptualise AI governance focuses on the single firm as a governance structure, instead of putting network governance at its centre. Thus, this book naturally applied its scope. Furthermore, conceptualising AI governance requires its contextualisation in the dynamically changing environment the private sector is faced with. Therefore, the extensive examination of collective forms of AI governance exceeded its scope. Nonetheless, this book gives valuable insights for collaborative AI governance by depicting prevalent dynamics in the market and pointing to research gaps. By linking AI governance to wicked problems and collaborative strategies to solve it, it allows AI governance to be addressed structurally and in operationalised form. Again, while collective governance faces high complexity and is complicated by the hidden agendas related, for example, to public actors in the field (Dafoe, 2018; Lilkov, 2020; Polyakova & Meserole, 2019), I urge future research to address and examine the topic.

My review findings confirm this necessity, since 'collaborative governance' was one of the most prominent research categories in the field, despite being mainly examined from a practical viewpoint and with a focus on soft law advances so far. Therefore, future studies should consider the complexity of collective forms of

AI governance, such as interfirm networks, regarding the perspectives of both the unregulated and partially regulated global market.

5.4 Conclusion

This book set out to present a theoretical answer to the challenges facing AI governance. Many of them point to the need for collaboration among actors, be it multilateral collaboration or cooperation in the private sector, since the challenges seem to overarch industries, countries, and regions around the globe.

My fundamental research question led me to proceed to conceptualise AI within Relational Economics, more specifically in systems-theoretical research, according to Luhmann. Having established the theoretical foundation for AI governance, I went on to build the Relational AI governance model allowing for the application of my theoretical contribution to practice. Mapped in a comprehensive framework, the book entails relevant research from related research fields, such as AI ethics, to complement its own contribution and further enhance it. Additionally, Relational AI Governance was positioned in the research field of AI governance via the systematic literature review.

Particularly by classifying existing research in AI ethics, this book allows for a structured overview of advances made in the field. I critically compared my own contribution with existing research in the field, allowing for additional insights to complement and compare my contribution to other publications in AI governance. In conclusion, the insights gained throughout this book and the review findings indicate that, first, self-regulation can lead to various advantages for companies—if implemented holistically and in a comprehensive manner. Second, due to the rising societal demand for regulatory measures and the pending E.U. regulation, I emphasise the significance of proactively applying a well-structured AI governance program, including both formal and informal measures. By doing so, a company can ensure the effectiveness of its governance program and its acceptance on the part of its employees. In turn, this can lower the risk of legal consequences due to unwanted incidents caused by AI adoption, which is of particular importance since questions of liability are not yet fully answered in the AI context (Béranger, 2021; Jackson, 2018; Nurus et al., 2016). In turn, this could put organisations in the position of being subjected to lengthy and costly trials, as well as harmful public exposure, and lead to reputational losses.

Further, the research question was examined with a particular focus on the single firm and its fundamental decision to create a shared value. While collaborative approaches of governance are the most comprehensive way of addressing wicked problem structures, I established the exceptional challenges such strategies face. The book presented various arguments when applying the chosen theoretical approach to practice (Dafoe, 2018), indicating the difficulties particularly for collective forms of collaborative AI governance—such as interfirm networks. Furthermore, the wicked problem structure in the AI context proved to be linked closely to public-sector interests and agendas—particularly to the interest of states around the globe in dominating the market (Dafoe, 2018; Lilkov, 2020; Polyakova & Meserole, 2019). Due to this book's focus on the single company, an additional, extensive elaboration of the dynamics of interfirm networks engaging in the development of standards, exceeded the scope of this book. Thus, I focused on developing measures allowing the single company to integrate social normativity into its decision-making, despite being caught in a highly competitive environment.

Mainly due to Relational Economics' inherent aim of creating shared value through the structural alignment of system-specific interests and demands, I was still able to develop the theoretical foundation for further collaborative AI governance approaches. By providing a solution for the fundamental objective of collaborative strategies regarding wicked problems, namely through the concurrent improvement of the situation of each involved stakeholder, this book contributes to collaboration's core challenge. Having presented a theoretical approach able to tackle this challenge, this contribution supports future research on each operational form of collaborative governance—be it interfirm networks, multi-stakeholder governance, multilateral governance, or further aspects of private-sector self-regulation.

In conclusion, my findings have confirmed the importance of examining the challenges AI governance faces from a theoretical perspective. In doing so, I uncovered the high interrelatedness of sectors, players, and interests involved and reduced the phenomenon's complexity by applying systems-theoretical concepts. Presenting a solution-oriented, adaptive AI governance approach, my contribution provides a theoretical foundation, able to depict such levels of complexity and to address this topic of great urgency and relevance for societies around the globe. Thereby, I hope, through this book, to provide a substantial foundation for further research and an applicable instrument for decision-makers in practice.

References

Baecker, D. (2011). Who Qualifies for Communication? A Systems Perspective on Human and Other Possibly Intelligent Beings Taking Part in the Next Society. *Technikfolgenabschätzung—Theorie und Praxis, 20*(1), 17–26. https://doi.org/10.14512/tatup.20.1.17

Baecker, D. (2015). Ausgangspunkte einer Theorie der Digitalisierung. In B. Leukert, R. Gläß, & R. Schütte (Eds.), *Digitale Transformation des Handels* (pp. 1–26). Springer Verlag.

Balfanz, D. (2017). Autonome systeme. Wer dient wem?. In W. Schröter (Eds.). *Autonomie des Menschen–Autonomie Der Systeme* (pp. 137–150). Mössingen-Talheim: Talheimer Verlag.

Béranger, J. (2021). Ethical governance and responsibility in digital medicine: The case of artificial intelligence. *The Digital Revolution in Health, 2*, 169–190. https://doi.org/10.1002/9781119842446.ch8

Brundage, M., Avin, S., Clark, J., Toner, H., Eckersley, P., Garfinkel, B., ... & Amodei, D. (2018). The malicious use of artificial intelligence: Forecasting, prevention, and mitigation.*arXiv preprint* arXiv:1802.07228.

Bryson, J. J. (2018). Patiency is not a virtue: The design of intelligent systems and systems of ethics. *Ethics and Information Technology, 20*(1), 15–26. https://doi.org/10.1007/s10676-018-9448-6

Cao, Z., & Lumineau, F. (2015). Revisiting the interplay between contractual and relational governance: A qualitative and meta-analytic investigation. *Journal of Operations Management, 33*(34), 15–42. https://doi.org/10.1016/j.jom.2014.09.009
Chu, Z., Lai, F. & Wang, L. (2020). Leveraging interfirm relationships in China: Western relational governance or Guanxi? Domestic versus foreign firms. *Journal of International Marketing, 28*(4), 58–74. https://doi.org/10.1177/1069031X20963672
Cihon, P. (2019). Technical report. Standards for AI governance: International standards to enable global coordination in AI research & development. University of Oxford. https://www.fhi.ox.ac.uk/wp-content/uploads/Standards_-FHI-Technical-Report.pdf
Cihon, P., Schuett, J., & Baum, S. D. (2021). Corporate governance of artificial intelligence in the public interest. *Information, 12*(7), 275. https://doi.org/10.3390/info12070275
Dafoe, A. (2018). AI governance: A research agenda. Governance of AI program, future of humanity institute, University of Oxford. https://www.fhi.ox.ac.uk/wp-content/uploads/GovAI-Agenda.pdf
Esposito, E. (2017a). Artificial communication? The production of contingency by algorithms. *Zeitschrift Für Soziologie, 46*(4), 249–265. https://doi.org/10.1515/zfsoz-2017-1014
Esposito, E. (2017b). Algorithmic memory and the right to be forgotten on the web. *Big Data & Society, 4*(1), 2053951717703996. https://doi.org/10.1177/2053951717703996
Fernandes, P. M., Santos, F. C., & Lopes, M. (2020). Norms for beneficial AI: A computational analysis of the societal value alignment problem. *AI Communications*, (Preprint), 1–17. https://doi.org/10.3233/AIC-201502
Fuchs, P. (2020). *Redebeitrag* in Vogt, W. (2020). Verschränkung in der soziologischen Systemtheorie. In W. Vogt (Ed.). *Quantenphysik und Soziologie im Dialog* (pp. 199–1244). Springer Spektrum.
Gasser, U., & Almeida, V. A. (2017). A layered model for AI governance. *IEEE Internet Computing, 21*(6), 58–62. https://doi.org/10.1109/MIC.2017.4180835
Gasser, U., & Schmitt, C. (2020). The role of professional norms in the governance of artificial intelligence. In *The Oxford handbook of ethics of AI* (p. 141). Oxford University Press.
Geist, E. M. (2016). It's already too late to stop the AI arms race—We must manage it instead. *Bulletin of the Atomic Scientists, 72*(5), 318–321. https://doi.org/10.1080/00963402.2016.1216672
Goldfarb, A., Taska, B., & Teodoridis, F. (2019). Could machine learning be a general-purpose technology? Evidence from online job postings. *SSRN digital.* https://doi.org/10.2139/ssrn.3468822
Hagendorff, T. (2020). The ethics of AI ethics: An Evaluation of guidelines. *Minds and Machines, 30*, 99–120. https://doi.org/10.1007/s11023-020-09517-8
Hagendorff, T. (2022). Blind spots in AI ethics. *AI and Ethics, 2*(4), 851–867.
Harth, J., & Lorenz, C.-F. (2017). "Hello World"—Systemtheoretische Überlegungen zu einer Soziologie des Algorithmus. *kommunikation @ gesellschaft, 18*, 1–18. https://nbn-resolving.org/urn:nbn:de:0168-ssoar-51502-9
Huck, P., Johnson, A., Kiritz, N., Larsom, C. E. (2020). Why AI governance matters. *The RMA Journal.* https://www.promontory.com:3000/static/pdf/1588624225_title.pdf
Jackson, B. W. (2018). Artificial intelligence and the fog of innovation: A deep-dive on governance and the liability of autonomous systems. *Santa Clara High Tech. LJ*, 35. https://digitalcommons.law.scu.edu/chtlj/vol35/iss4/1
Jelinek, T., Wallach, W., & Kerimi, D. (2020). Coordinating committee for the governance of artificial intelligence. *Berlin, G20 Insights, Global Solutions Initiative Foundation.* https://www.g20-insights.org/policy_briefs/coordinating-committee-for-the-governance-of-artificial-intelligence-2/
Jobin, A., Ienca, M., & Vayena, E. (2019). Artificial intelligence: The global landscape of ethics guidelines. *Nature Machine Intelligence, 1*, 389–399. https://doi.org/10.1038/s42256-019-0088-2

Ju, M. & Gao, G.Y. (2017). relational governance and control mechanisms of export ventures: An examination across relationship length. *Journal of International Marketing, 25*(2), 72–87. https://doi.org/10.1509/jim.16.0070

Klinger, J., Mateos-Garcia, J. C., & Stathoulopoulos, K. (2018). Deep learning, deep change? Mapping the development of the Artificial intelligence general purpose technology. Mapping the Development of the Artificial Intelligence General Purpose Technology. https://arxiv.org/abs/1808.06355

Lilkov, D. (2020). Made in China: tackling digital authoritarianism. *European View, 19*(1), 110–110. https://doi.org/10.1177/1781685820920121

Liu, H. Y., & Maas, M. M. (2021). 'Solving for X?'Towards a problem-finding framework to ground long-term governance strategies for artificial intelligence. *Futures, 126*, 102672. https://doi.org/10.1016/j.futures.2020.102672

Lobana, J. (2021). The governance of AI-based information technologies within corporate environments [doctoral dissertation]. McMaster University. http://hdl.handle.net/11375/26685

Luhmann, N. (1996). the sociology of the moral and ethics. *International Sociology, 11*(1), 27–36. https://doi.org/10.1177/026858096011001003

Luhmann, N. (1998). *Die Gesellschaft der Gesellschaft*. (2nd ed.). Frankfurt a. M.: Suhrkamp Verlag.

Luo S., & Lu Y. (2021). The "Artificial intelligence + social governance" mode: Risk prevention and governance ability improvement. In Z. Xu, R. M. Parizi, O. Loyola-González & X. Zhang (Eds.). *Cyber security intelligence and analytics: CSIA 2021. Advances in intelligent systems and computing,* vol 1343. Springer. https://doi.org/10.1007/978-3-030-69999-4_37

Maas, M. M. (2018). Two lessons from nuclear arms control for the responsible governance of military artificial intelligence. In *Robophilosophy/TRANSOR* (pp. 347–356). https://doi.org/10.3233/978-1-61499-931-7-347

Mayer, A. S., Haimerl, A., Strich, F., & Fiedler, M. (2021). How corporations encourage the implementation of AI ethics. *ECIS 2021 Research Papers*. 27.https://aisel.aisnet.org/ecis2021_rp/27

Miailhe, N. (2018). AI & global governance: Why we need an intergovernmental panel for artificial intelligence. *Centre for policy research, united nations university, 20.* https://cpr.unu.edu/publications/articles/ai-global-governance-why-we-need-an-intergovernmental-panel-for-artificial-intelligence.html

Miailhe, N., & Lannquist, Y. (2018). A challenge to global governance. In Plant Algorithm: Artificial Intelligence for a predictive and inclusive form of integration in Latin America; INTAL-IDB. *Integration and Trade Journal, 22*(44), 207–217. https://doi.org/10.18235/0001287

Miller, C., & Coldicott, R. (2019). People, power and technology: The tech workers' view. *Dot Everyone.* https://doteveryone.org.uk/report/workersview

Mittelstadt, B. (2019). Ai ethics–too principled to fail?. *arXiv preprint* arXiv:1906.06668.

Morley, J., Floridi, L., Kinsey, L., & Elhalal, A. (2020). From what to how: An initial review of publicly available AI ethics tools, methods and research to translate principles into practices. *Science and Engineering Ethics, 26*(4), 2141–2168. https://doi.org/10.1007/s11948-019-00165-5

Nepelski, D. & Sobolewski, M. (2020). Estimating investments in General Purpose Technologies. *The case Of AI investments in Europe.* Publications Office of the European Union, Luxembourg. https://doi.org/10.2760/506947

Neubert, M. J., & Montañez, G. D. (2020). Virtue as a framework for the design and use of artificial intelligence. *Business Horizons, 63*(2), 195–204. https://doi.org/10.1016/j.bushor.2019.11.001

Nurus, S. F. M. S. P., Hartini, S., & Sheela, J. K. (2016). Artificial intelligence governance: A heads up from driverless cars. *World Applied Science Journal, 34*(3), 376–382. https://elmnet.ir/vslg?url=https%3A%2F%2Fwww.magiran.com%2Fpaper%2F1548201&type=0&id=1502141

ÓhÉigeartaigh, S. S., Whittlestone, J., Liu, Y., Zeng, Y., & Liu, Z. (2020). Overcoming barriers to cross-cultural cooperation in AI ethics and governance. *Philosophy & Technology, 33*(4), 571–593. https://doi.org/10.1007/s13347-020-00402-x

Polyakova, A., & Meserole, C. (2019). Exporting digital authoritarianism: The Russian and Chinese models. *Policy Brief, Democracy and Disorder Series (Washington, DC: Brookings, 2019)*, 1–22. https://www.brookings.edu/wp-content/uploads/2019/08/FP_20190827_digital_authoritarianism_polyakova_meserole.pdf

Poppo, L., Zhou, K. Z. & Zenger, T. R. (2008). Examining the conditional limits of relational governance: Specialized assets, performance ambiguity, and longstanding ties. *Journal of Management Studies, 45*(7), 1195–1216. https://doi.org/10.1111/j.1467-6486.2008.00779.x

Razzkazov, V. E. (2020). Financial and economic consequences of distribution of artificial intelligence as a general-purpose technology. *Finance: Theory and Practice, Scientific and Practical Journal, 24*(2), 120–132. https://doi.org/10.26794/2587-5671-2020-24-2-120-132

Reichel, A. (2011). Technology as system: Towards an autopoietic theory of technology. *International Journal of Innovation and Sustainable Development, 5*(2–3), 105–118. https://doi.org/10.1504/IJISD.2011.043070

Roberts, N. C. (2000). Wicked problems and network approaches to resolution. *The International Public Management Review, 1*(1), 1–19. http://www.economy4humanity.org/commons/library/175-349-1-SM.pdf

Sjödin, D. R., Parida, V., & Kohtamäki, M. (2019). Relational governance strategies for advanced service provision: Multiple paths to superior financial performance in servitization. *Journal of Business Research, 101*, 906–915. https://doi.org/10.1016/j.jbusres.2019.02.042

Soto, A. M. & Sonnenschein, C. (2019). Could machines develop autonomous agency?. In E. De Angelis, A. Hossaini, R. Noble, D. Noble, A. M. Soto, C. Sonnenschein, & K. Payne (Eds.). *Forum: Artificial Intelligence, Artificial Agency and Artificial Life, The RUSI Journal, 164*(5–6), 120–144.https://doi.org/10.1080/03071847.2019.1694264

Thuraisingham, B. (2020). Artificial intelligence and data science governance: Roles and responsibilities at the c-level and the board. In *2020 IEEE 21st international conference on information reuse and integration for data science (IRI)* (pp. 314–318). IEEE. https://doi.org/10.1109/IRI49571.2020.00052

Torré, F., Teigland, R., & Engstam, L. (2019). AI leadership and the future of corporate governance: Changing demands for board competence. In F. Torré, R. Teigland, & L. Engstam (Eds.), *The Digital Transformation of Labor* (pp. 116–146). Routledge.

Trajtenberg, M. (2018). *AI as the next GPT: A political-economy perspective* (No. w24245). National Bureau of Economic Research. https://doi.org/10.3386/w24245

Wieland, J. (2018). *Relational economics. Ökonomische Theorie der Governance wirtschaftlicher Transaktionen*. Metropolis.

Wieland, J. (2020). *Relational economics: A political economy*. Springer.

Winfield, A. F., & Jirotka, M. (2018). Ethical governance is essential to building trust in robotics and artificial intelligence systems. *Philosophical Transactions of the Royal Society a: Mathematical, Physical and Engineering Sciences, 376*(2133), 20180085. https://doi.org/10.1098/rsta.2018.0085

Yu, H., Shen, Z., Miao, C., Leung, C., Lesser, V. R., & Yang, Q. (2018). Building ethics into artificial intelligence. arXiv preprint arXiv:1812.02953

Zheng, J., Roehrich, J. K., & Lewis, M. A. (2008). The dynamics of contractual and relational governance: Evidence from long-term public-private procurement arrangements. *Journal of Purchasing and Supply Management, 14*, 43–54. https://doi.org/10.1016/j.pursup.2008.01.004